MEMORIES BEYOND BLOOMERS

Author in 1924.

MEMORIES BEYOND BLOOMERS

(1924–1954)

Mabel Lee

Professor Emeritus, University of Nebraska—Lincoln

Sequel to
MEMORIES OF A BLOOMER GIRL
(1894–1924)

AMERICAN ALLIANCE FOR HEALTH, PHYSICAL EDUCATION, AND RECREATION

Dedicated
With Fond Memories
To all those eager young girls
who in the years 1924–1952
majored in physical education
at the University of Nebraska
under my direction
and
To the many fine young women
who were members of my departmental
staff during those years

Illustrations

Foreword

"Mabel Lee has been enamoured with physical education for most of her life, and physical education has reciprocated." So wrote Celeste Ulrich, 1976-77 Alliance president, in the foreword to the first volume of these memoirs, published in 1977. She went on to write: "The Alliance has been grateful to Mabel Lee for many things—for her presidency, for her committee work, for her writings, for her archival organization, for her example.... Now we accept, with gratitude, one more gift, *Memories of a Bloomer Girl*. We will continue to draw upon her wisdom, her insights, her knowledge and hope that she will continue to be a part of the great physical education adventure for a long time."

With publication of this book, *Memories Beyond Bloomers*, the Alliance again expresses its gratitude, its appreciation, and its respect for the First Lady of AAHPER. Mabel Lee has had an impact on the organized profession of physical education that is unequaled. For over half a century she has been in the forefront of the movements that have advanced this area of education. Her personal philosophy, her abilities to adapt to change and to cope with new problems, her positive approach to solutions, her reactions to the people and events of the educational world—all have significance for us today and for those who will follow us. Her feelings and experiences, as charmingly and candidly expressed in these memoirs, constitute a history of physical education in microcosm.

The first sentence of the first volume refers to the "women of vision and intuitive drive" who had tried to improve conditions for the education of women over the years. Mabel Lee herself is one of these women whose vision of physical education for girls and women has come about because of her drive, her enthusiasm, her courage and perseverance. Always the lady, she led the way to expanded opportunities in physical activities for girls through her example, her teaching, her administrative decisions and accomplishments.

Learning about Mabel Lee, from reading her own story of a dedicated career, is a prerequisite for professional understanding. The Alliance is proud to add to its AAHPER Leaders Speak Series this book by and about Mabel Lee.

George Anderson
Executive Vice President
American Alliance for Health,
Physical Education, and Recreation

Prologue

As with my earlier book, *Memories Of A Bloomer Girl*, this book is written with workers in the field of physical education particularly in mind and deals primarily with my personal experiences. A continuation of that earlier story, this book covers from the mid-twenties to my retirement at mid-twentieth century.

I regret that I have been so long producing these two books since Wellesley College granted me the Amy Morris Homans Award to write my professional memoirs. By now practically all of my professional contemporaries, as well as practically all my school friends with whom I shared the experiences of the earlier years of these two books, are deceased.

Memories Of A Bloomer Girl covered experiences of my years of schooling and early teaching years at Coe College, Oregon Agriculture College and Beloit College. It also covered the last years of bloomers as a gymnastic and sports costume. This book picks up the story with the year 1924 when I went to the University of Nebraska which marked a great change in my professional experiences as I then entered teacher-training work.

Although much of this story deals with experiences at a national level, the home base for all of it is Lincoln and the University of Nebraska. From there I journeyed forth and had most interesting experiences in spreading my wings.

Many other topics are treated but briefly since I am enlarging upon them in a later book for lay readers. It may seem that I have given undue space to a few of the topics discussed herein such as the creation of the Women's Athletics Section of AAHPER, which has grown into today's National Association for Girls and Women in Sport (NAGWS); the Women's Division of National Amateur Athletic Federation; and the Division of Physical Fitness of the World War II period. All these stories

1

I am able to tell from first-hand experience, which results in "behind-the-scenes" stories for the record.

Again I wish to acknowledge the help of Ruth Diamond Levinson and Marie Hermanek Cripe, both former pupils and former staff members of mine—both ever my friends—whose interest and concern over this manuscript made the task of preparing much easier than it would have been without their good services. My continuing thanks also go to Wellesley College for the Amy Morris Homans Award which opened the door to the possibility of my writing these books. To Joseph Svoboda, archivist of the University of Nebraska, my thanks for his generous aid in searching out records of University concerns, and to the reference departments of the Lincoln Public Library and the University of Nebraska-Lincoln Library for their helpful services.

My continuing thanks to George Anderson, executive secretary of AAHPER and his staff, including Constance Lacey and Louise Sindler, editors, for their concerned interest in and editing of this book.

As with *Memories Of A Bloomer Girl*, it would have been impossible to write this story in such detail had I not had at hand my diaries to fall back on to set the memories straight, as well as many boxes of records and correspondence of the years 1924-1952, which still clutter my home. For all these several years in which I have been at work on these books, my sister and two nieces, all that remain of my immediate family, as well as close friends and neighbors have been most patient with my shutting myself away alone in my study for long periods of time. My thanks to all for their kind understanding.

This book is very different from the earlier book. But then the temper of the times through the turbulent late twenties, the Depression and World War II years was far different from that of the Gay Nineties, the turn of the century, and the Great War era. Also I was a far different person in the late twenties on from the shy, slow-blooming young girl of the early twentieth century. I had grown up! The world, even I, was changed. The changed world, the changed type of position, brought totally different experiences. Deeper responsibilities took over.

The gift of this second book I gladly make to the American Alliance for Health, Physical Education and Recreation as further expression of gratitude for all the opportunities it has given me throughout my professional career for service to my profession, also for the several honors it has so generously bestowed upon me. May the Alliance ever prosper and serve well our beloved country!

Mabel Lee
Lincoln, Nebraska
September 1977

2

Chapter I

An Insistent Offer— A New Challenge

New professional adventures—a new challenge awaited me! It had been 14 years since I had completed my two years of professional training work at the Boston Normal School of Gymnastics and the Department of Hygiene and Physical Education at Wellesley College, after four years of undergraduate work at Coe College. I had eight years back at my alma mater as director of physical education for women, then a year in the same position at Oregon Agricultural College where the flu epidemic of the Great War had forced my resignation for a year, followed by four years in the same position at Beloit College.

When Chancellor Samuel Avery of the University of Nebraska invited me to come to Lincoln, he followed up the invitation with a letter explaining the physical education setup—one department for both men and women, with the head football coach overall director of physical education and athletics. Under him there were the director of physical education for men, who was also head of all teacher training in physical education for both men and women, and the director of physical education for women, who was head of all physical education and athletics for the general run of women students exclusive of professional preparation. Knowing the frustrations of several women acquaintances in trying to give women students a good physical education program where they were under men coaches, I was at once skeptical about the position at Nebraska. The very fact that the professional training work for women

3

in physical education was under the director of physical education for men seemed ominous to me in light of the fact that I had been affiliated with both the Middle West Society of Directors of Physical Education for College Women and the Middle West Society of Physical Education for six years and not once had I met or heard of a living soul at meetings of either group who was from the University of Nebraska. This was only the second time I had ever heard of the university offering professional training in my field.

Although I had been teaching in the Middle West for 12 years, I had never encountered a graduate of this professional training department other than Vera Barger (whom I had met in Oregon in 1919 when she was in Portland on national YWCA work) or even a person who was teaching or had ever taught at Nebraska. Also I felt that if I were going to make a move, I would want to advance professionally and the thought of getting into professional training work intrigued me. But Chancellor Avery's letter threw cold water on thoughts of an opportunity in that direction.

Although unaccustomed to using the telephone for long distance except for real emergencies, I called the chancellor and told him that in view of the fact that the director of physical education for women was subservient to both the football coach and the director of physical education for men for important parts of the physical education work, I would not be interested in the opening there. But he begged me to come and talk it over anyway. Having warned him of my doubts, my conscience was clear, so I accepted the invitation. What an eye-opening experience awaited me!

Immediately upon my arrival on the morning train from Chicago, I was taken to meet the chancellor. I was instantly attracted to his down-to-earth, homespun personality. He was warmly friendly, a person one could feel at ease with at once. We chatted for almost an hour and he told me that the women students were quite unhappy with the present situation. I was soon to learn that the women's athletics received no help or encouragement from anyone on the staff, man or woman, and that what little they had, they put on entirely on their own, even raising their own money to finance the Women's Athletic Association. The general women students were offered nothing but gymnastics all nine months of the school year for two years—no classes outdoors in the spring or fall, no sports, no dance except a class in esthetic dancing to majors and upperclass fine arts students. Worst of all, the professional training courses for physical education majors were taught by only two persons, and one of these taught from lecture notes that were at least 15 years old, according to a woman major whose class lecture notes had been handed down to her niece.

It seems that the women students were deeply aroused and had demanded a complete reorganization of physical education for women. They had even gotten a hearing with the regents who, in turn, had asked the chancellor to start a search for a woman from "the outside" world to head an independent department for women. This had been a special request of the students for, as they put it, the women's department was at a standstill, with all its staff graduates of the department and they in turn children of graduates—a long history of inbreeding.

It was a sorry story, quite an indictment, and I admired the chancellor for having the courage to display at once the skeleton in the family closet to me, a stranger. To ease his embarrassment, for he quite humbly confessed that he was afraid he had been guilty of neglecting the women through allowing himself to be so ignorant of the predicament they were in, I hastened to assure him that this was somewhat the situation of women in other universities where the head of physical education for women, well prepared professionally, was all too frequently under a man coach who didn't even realize that he didn't know the physical education profession or under a man physical director who was assumed to be professionally prepared in the field but was after all only a coach, not an educator, with no professional training in the field. Then I timidly inquired about the educational backgrounds of Nebraska's director of physical education and athletics and of the director of physical education for men. Seemingly a bit reluctantly, the chancellor informed me that he was afraid Nebraska was one more such school. And later information proved his fears well-grounded.

He wished me first of all to meet the women students who were demanding changes and said he had asked that a private meeting be arranged with them and that I would be escorted there at once by Dr. Raymond Gustavus Clapp, a medical doctor and the director of physical education for men. The chancellor asked me to beg the women students to talk freely of their criticism of the present setup and of their hopes. To my surprise the meeting was a regularly scheduled meeting of a teacher-training course with both men and women physical education majors there, the class teacher (the acting director of physical education for women who with no professional training beyond the bachelor's degree had not been given the directorship), and all the women staff, all of whom turned out to be graduates of the department and none of whom had as far as I could learn studied elsewhere.

Dr. Clapp introduced me to the class and asked those with complaints please to speak out since I was being considered for the position of director of physical education for women. Needless to say, no one had anything to say since this meeting was anything but private. But the looks of disappointment and dismay on the faces of many women students told me much. However the period was not a dead loss, for one of the women teachers had just received a sample pair of girls' shorts which she brought to the meeting. Thus I saw this new garment for the first time, as apparently did all others present, from the "ohs" and "ahs."

When the class bell rang, a few of the girls ran up to me, exclaiming that the chancellor had promised them an opportunity to talk with me privately. I assured them I would report the situation to him and that I would insist on the private meeting. These girls interested me very much and I wanted to hear what they had to say.

At noon Dr. Clapp took me to the University Club (a town club), then located on N Street, where a group of six or eight faculty women had been invited to meet me. I was drawn at once to the head of the home economics department, Margaret Fedde, but sensed immediately that I was being looked over most critically by the dean of women, Amanda Heppner, a history professor, Laura Pfeiffer, and the head of the drama department, Alice Howell. I was glad I had worn my prettiest hat—the lavender braid one lined in sky blue silk and trimmed by a large pink rose which broke the austerity of my pearl gray tailored suit and my premature gray hair. I had worn the hat and suit which I had worn the year before when I made my maiden speech on intercollegiate athletics at the University of Chicago before a mixed audience.

These women were very critical of an upcoming university track meet for women which was being ballyhooed all over town with a parade planned down O Street (the city's main street) to open the meet, with the track women displaying the latest style, shorts. At least, this was the talk. What did I think of it? Were I director of physical education for women at the University of Nebraska, would the women students be parading down O Street and in shorts? At my instant and strong "no" to both the parade and the shorts in public, I apparently satisfied these ladies because from then on they relaxed.

The afternoon was filled with looking over the facilities and with brief conferences with the women physical education staff members, each of whom sought me out for a private conference with but one main problem—the hope that if I came to Nebraska I would see that she would get a raise in salary. Although I was shocked that none expressed concern about upgrading department work, I tried to keep a poker face.

The next morning the chancellor informed me that "everyone" wanted me to come to the university and he was prepared to make me an offer of $2,500, which I rejected at once since Beloit College was raising my salary there to $2,600 for next year. At this, he raised the offer to $3,000 but I demurred, saying that I had as yet had no opportunity to talk privately with the women students who had demanded changes. This surprised him and he called Dr. Clapp by telephone and informed him that I was to have the day free to roam about unescorted and to arrange for myself whatever conferences I desired with faculty and students.

Conferences with two or three of the women staff members left me shaken. There was one thing all the women were agreed upon, staff as well as students—the professional training work for the women must be removed from under the control of the men's physical education director, who, they said, may have been a famous track star at Yale but was unqualified to handle their professional courses. Also there were other things all the staff agreed about. Each complained about her heavy schedule. When I inquired into this, I was stunned at their ideas of what a heavy schedule was. It also soon became apparent that when it came to principles and philosophy of physical education, we did not talk the same professional language.

As I roamed about the gymnasium, a few students cornered me (I was unable to arrange a group conference hour with the protesting leaders) and, seizing upon what little opportunity presented itself, they individually poured out tales of woe about the lack of proper professional training of their teachers, their own lack of respect for the department, and their insistence that it must be divorced from the men's department.

When I returned to the chancellor late in the afternoon I frankly told him that the department was in such a sorry condition that nothing could induce me to accept his offer. He told me that if I would only come and straighten things out I would receive a warm welcome, for a group of women students had been in earlier in the day and begged him to offer me the position and that the dean of women and the head of the home economics department had both urged him to put through my appointment and even his wife was campaigning for me.

"I've been thinking it over and since you say it involves teacher-training work beyond what you have at Beloit and since the men's physical education director is loathe to give up this work I still offer the $3,000 and you need have no responsibility for that part of the work."

"But that is the very thing the women majors are complaining about the most. They want to bring the teacher-training work up-to-date to hold its own with professional work in other universities."

"Then why won't you come?"

"Do you want the truth?" I countered.

"Yes, the truth—all of it as you see it."

7

So I enumerated the difficulties as I saw them, such as outmoded professional courses, lack of control by a woman recognized as actual head of women's work, subservience of women to men incompetent to be heads over women's work, too many part-time teachers instead of a few full-time on the women's staff, lack of cooperation within the women's staff plus lack of loyalty to each other or to the department, staff members inadequately prepared for their positions, all professional courses taught by only two persons neither of whom demanded the respect of the students as teachers, for the regular college woman an outmoded and inadequate program, and facilities which were entirely too limited. I also reminded him that women students unhappy with their second-class treatment in the one gymnasium were begging for a building of their own, and for good measure I stressed what I saw as a serious case of provincialism that was a detriment to the professional training—the failure of the staff to keep abreast of the times within the profession. I pointed out that just a few weeks before I had been present at the birth of a very important national organization, the National Association of Physical Education for College Women, when Nebraska's neighboring states were represented but not a soul from Nebraska.

It was quite an indictment, all of which Chancellor Avery took calmly, no doubt since the students had already poured out all of this to the regents from their own point of view. My findings verified their complaints. I added one item—that since no woman on the staff cared to be bothered with extracurricular activities, the Women's Athletic Association was completely under the control of a sportswoman on the faculty from another department. This I could not countenance were I head of the department.

The chancellor contemplated for some time my many reasons why I felt the position would be "nothing but a headache," and finally rising from his swivel chair, he paced his office floor for a round or two, hands clasped behind his back and head bowed. Then he suddenly dropped back into his big chair and leaning towards me, said:

"We all want you to come. How about a full professorship and $3,500?"

"Oh, no, Chancellor Avery, I am not playing a game with you to get a still better offer. I do not want this position at any price!"

He was dumbfounded, yet adamant. "Not if I tell you I am in sympathy with all of your criticisms and will give you my 100 percent backing and support in clea_ing up this department and reorganizing it!"

"Does that mean I would be absolute head of my own department

8

for all work, in absolute control of both required work and professional training for women and all women's out-of-class physical activities, such as WAA?"

"Yes, but—we can't make all these changes without going through necessary red tape and the regent's approval. It may take a year to accomplish all these changes, but you can count on my backing to get them made as fast as possible. The staff has already been rehired for next year but they do not have tenure and the year after that you can bring in a staff of your own choosing. And as to the women having a building of their own—we hope to have a women's gymnasium soon now and we will want you to plan it. That will be one of the first things we will expect of you."

All this put a different light on things—there was hope now that maybe the department could be rescued from its present decay. But then the chancellor quickly added:

"We'll have to take it easy—particularly go slow on the teacher-training part. The present head of that work will not let go of his authority readily and he has been in charge of this work for 22 years now. Couldn't you take my word for it that you will be, as far as I am concerned, head of the women's work in all aspects but for next year accept the two men as the heads until the regents can make a change officially? You can have your own way ultimately and maybe can get many things changed even next year by being tactful—and patient."

This odd way of working didn't sound too hopeful to me, so I said I couldn't accept the offer. Then Chancellor Avery begged me to stay over another day.

"You haven't seen our lovely city. I'll arrange for someone to drive you around this evening, sleep over my offer tonight. After a good night's sleep you'll wake up in the morning ready to accept my offer, I'm sure."

So I agreed to stay over. In the night I awakened from a bad dream calling for help. In my dream I was standing with my back against a wall fighting off attackers and I cried out, "Isn't there one person who will help me?" That was it! Awakened from my bad dream, I knew where the weak spot was in the chancellor's offer. So when I arrived at his office the next morning he asked if I could now say "yes" and let him report my acceptance to the women students and faculty pestering him for my reply.

"No, I still can't accept and wage this battle all by myself."

"But you won't be waging it alone. I will be standing back of you!"

9

"Yes, I know and appreciate that but there will be no one on my staff whose loyalty I can depend on. I just couldn't stand up to all that I will surely encounter without the support of at least one loyal staff member."

"Oh! Is that all that stands between us?" he exclaimed with a gleam of an idea in his eyes. "Would you come if you could have one full-time staff member of your own choosing?"

"Well," I said in surprise, not expecting that favor, "that does put a different light on it."

"How about $1,800 for another full-time staff member, an instructor? Go out and find her yourself. Just send me her name and I'll put through the necessary papers. Now will you say 'yes'?" he added laughing. Then he quickly added as an afterthought:

"But wait before you answer. I'll go even further. You can have one trip out of the state each year to attend one professional meeting of your own choosing, all expenses paid. We'll want you to keep up with your professional organizations."

"Yes! I can say yes now," I replied, laughing at his insistence. "I guess it was fear of having no loyal co-worker on my staff that was really standing in the way of acceptance."

"Good, I'll have my secretary call the newspapers and announce your appointment."

"Oh, please, not yet," I begged. "I can't formally accept until I have told President Mauer at Beloit. I can't let him learn of it through the newspapers."

It was agreed that I would see President Mauer as quickly as possible on my return, tender my resignation and then wire Chancellor Avery my formal acceptance. He escorted me to the train and as I mounted the parlor car steps, he called, "I'll be waiting for that telegram of acceptance." So it came about that I was to leave Beloit College and pursue my professional career in Nebraska, Mother's girlhood home state, which was completely strange to me.

As to my salary, as I learned later, there were four women on the faculty whose salaries were above mine—all graduates of the university, all on the faculty from 10 to 30 years and getting salaries from $3,600 to $4,500. So Chancellor Avery had done very well for me at a starting salary of $3,500. Only two faculty members, the chancellor and the dean of the Medical College, received salaries that topped the $6,416 salary of Coach Fred Dawson, head of physical education and athletics. Football seemed to be the tail that wagged the dog at Nebraska.

* * * *

And that full professorship was a victory for women, although I little appreciated it at the time. For some reason which I cannot explain satisfactorily, the change in my academic situation for the second time in my life from no academic rank to full professorship gave me no special thrill as it also had not six years previously when I went from a position at Coe College to Oregon Agricultural College. Perhaps the reason it meant so little was because at that time it was the title of "director" that meant much to us women, even more than academic rank, and fortunately that title had been granted to us readily.

The full professorship of 1918 at Oregon Agricultural College I had inherited from my predecessor, but the one offered me at Nebraska in 1924 was a first for the position there. The few other women who held professorships at Nebraska were all graduates of the university. I was the one outsider. I little realized then how favored I was, considering the many years of service of the other women professors there before they achieved full professorial rank.

When we women working in college physical education in the early years of the twentieth century got together, we never talked of academic rank. If any of my women acquaintances held professorships I had no knowledge of it, and it never entered my head to tell my professional friends, not even my family, that I had been granted such rank. I knew that Amy Morris Homans had held a professorship at Wellesley College since 1915, but that was the extent of my knowledge concerning women in my profession. I wasn't even curious about who else might hold such rank.

The title "director" I had held from my very first year of teaching. (Of my 41 years of teaching, all were in the college field, all as a director of a department; 12 of the 41 years were with no academic rank whatsoever, 29 as a full professor.) I never knew the joys or woes of advancing step by step from an instructorship to a full professorship. Circumstances handed this last rank to me too easily, perhaps the directorships, too.

As I came off the professional assembly line in 1910 there was such a scarcity of professionally trained women in my field that we who were prepared were a favored few, and the few of us who had a college degree besides were the exceptions. Good salaries, the choicest titles and academic recognition came to those few of us easily. In later years when we finally did become academic-rank conscious, I was amazed to realize that I was one of only a few women in my profession holding a full professorship.

* * * *

The facilities of the departments of physical education and athletics consisted of Grant Memorial Hall (a building whose east wing, Grant Hall, was then 33 years old, and the west wing, Memorial Hall, 25 years old, a new stadium, which was a memorial to the soldiers of the Great War, and the coliseum, then under construction, which when completed would house the departments of athletics and physical education for men.

My concern was Grant Memorial Hall which the women shared on what was most probably a 20 to 80 percent basis with the men. In a couple of years it was to become a 100 percent facility for women's physical education until the women could have a new gymnasium built for them alone, a building which would truly be a woman's gymnasium.

Grant Memorial Hall, a very large building, was the third oldest on campus. It was in fact two buildings back to back. The larger east wing, built in the late 1880s, had been named for General Grant since

Grant Memorial Hall, University of Nebraska. Window at left on second floor marks the office of Lt. John J. Pershing, commandant of ROTC, 1891-1895. (Courtesy of University of Nebraska).

it was primarily an armory for the Military Department as well as a gymnasium. The west wing, Memorial Hall, was built in 1899–1900 as a memorial to the university soldiers of the Spanish-American War. It housed a pipe organ and had balconies along the north and south walls. The wall separating the two wings on the main floor level had been torn out recently and replaced by great folding doors which when opened, threw the two gymnasium floors into one huge room for intercollegiate basketball games, large assemblies and university dances. The men's athletic and physical education and military departments claimed the entire east wing as their special domain, leaving the entire new but smaller west wing for the women's physical education department except for certain choice hours which the men demanded for wrestling and the music department for band practice. Because of the pipe organ and two balconies, the Music School demanded the wing at frequent intervals for musical programs and the university demanded it now and then for convocations.

The balcony of the east wing, Grant Hall, had been converted into a sort of mezzanine floor with a level floor laid over the original slanting floor with a runway at the front leading to a series of offices, one used as headquarters for the Military Department, one for the college band, one for the student newspaper staff, and one for the Student Council. In fact, the building was an armory, gymnasium, sports area, auditorium, dance hall, chapel, student union, college mess hall, and music hall all in one. In this situation, I soon became adept at crawling over wrestlers, band instruments and music racks, to say nothing of musicians themselves whenever I ventured out of my office anytime of late afternoons, which was practically every day.

For our athletic field we were allowed to use a large vacant stretch between the Social Science Building on the west and the Teachers College and Ellen Smith Hall on the east where now stand Love Library and the Administration Building. Most of that space (much of it today a stretch of lawn south of Love Library) was vacated by a string of residences facing on R Street with their basements recently filled in and levelled off. At every big rain, all sorts of broken crockery, dishes and glassware worked their way to the surface and the players had to clear the field before starting. At times, old basements and wells caved in unexpectedly and play had to be stopped until the holes were filled and levelled. One day when too many girls converged on the hockey ball at one spot, their combined weight was too much for a fill-in and the place caved in tumbling all the players to the ground. On another occasion when caretakers were dragging the hockey field, another basement fill-in gave way so deeply under the weight of the horse and drag that it took several men to extricate the frightened horse.

13

Since this area had long been a sort of public passageway from north 13th Street to O Street, the town's main throughway, the university refused to fence it off for a women's athletic field so that at the sight of every pedestrian approaching, especially with small children, baby carriages, a child's wagon or what not, the teacher was to halt all play until the passersby were out of the way.

It was quite frustrating to conduct outdoor classes or after-school-hour sports under such a situation. But it was better than nothing.

The town campus in 1924 stretched from 10th to 14th streets and from R to W Streets—a four-block square domain, with one building, the Temple (where the YMCA, YWCA, drama department, and the university cafeteria were located) across the campus at 12th and R, in the direction of Q Street and the downtown shopping district.

The 6,500 students of that day lived all over town in their own homes, in rooming houses or in fraternity and sorority houses which were usually large nineteenth century residences abandoned by their owners for modern homes in new residential sections. There were no dormitories for either men or women students. The faculty also lived scattered all over the city.

Lincoln, a city of around 85,000 population, was large enough not to be dominated by the university. It was a lovely city with wide streets and lots of shade trees—all planted by the earlier settlers when the area was a treeless prairie.

Here I cast my lot in 1924 and from that day to this, Lincoln has been home for me. For my first year I rented an apartment in the first apartment house ever erected in Lincoln—the Ingleside, south of the southeast corner of the State Capital grounds—today a parking lot. In my second year at the university Mother came to Lincoln to make a home for me. Father had passed away, my two younger sisters were married, one living in Norman, Oklahoma and one in Guthrie Center, Iowa, and my older sister had become a buyer at Marshall Fields in Chicago. I had been living for the past 21 years, ever since my first year in college, in college dormitories for 12 years and in apartments for 9 years. Now I was to have the joy of home life once more and Mother's good cooking and green-thumb gardening. And Mother was returning to the state of her girlhood years of the 1870s—to be exact, returning on the 45th anniversary of the very day she left Nebraska as a bride to make her home in Iowa. She had longed to attend the University of Nebraska but fate had other plans for her. Now one of her daughters was a professor there.

We lived happily in a small Cape Cod house at 2248 Ryons Street in what was then spoken of as South Lincoln. Since Mother's death in 1947, I have lived in this little cottage alone. The "old settler" of this neighborhood, I have lived in this house for 53 years as this book goes to press. As far as I know, no member of my family on either my mother's or father's side ever lived in the same house for so many years—and that predates the War of the Revolution. The over 200-year-old migration westward from Europe to America stopped with my mother's Aikman family in south central Nebraska.

Chapter II
The Torch Is Handed On

As I took up my work at Nebraska and began meeting early women graduates of the physical education department who still lived in Lincoln, I soon realized that the department I had inherited was indeed a pioneering one, especially in the Missouri Valley. But the more I learned of the beginnings of the academic major, other than from uncertain, random hearsay, the more I became bewildered over conflicting tales.

It took several years of my own research delving into old catalogs, college yearbooks, student and local newspapers and registrar office records to help me set straight the many conflicting stories of enthusiastic raconteurs. From these forays into history, I learned that of the public universities west of the Alleghenies, the University of California (Berkeley) offered the first bona fide department of physical education for women—1889. As early as 1877, the University of Illinois had offered some classes in calisthenics to women taught part-time by a teacher in another field, but this could not be considered the beginning of a real department any more than the military drill offered before the 1890s in many land grant schools.

At the University of Nebraska I belatedly learned that in a letter dated December 18, 1883, 74 "young ladies" petitioned the board of regents to give the "lady students" three hours a week of gymnastics training "equivalent to the military drill provided for gentlemen."[1] The petition was granted in that a room was furnished but no teacher was employed. Two years later (no doubt at more petitioning from the young ladies), a teacher from the local Conservatory of Music was hired to teach calisthenics. Another three years later, Lt. Griffith, commandant of the ROTC, organized a Ladies Cadet Corps to give the "young ladies" physical exercise.

In 1890, with the completion of Grant Memorial Hall as an armory-gymnasium, a physical education department was born but without a special teacher, and Lt. Griffith continued to teach both the men and women. In 1891 Wilbur Bowen came to Nebraska from the faculty of the Normal School of Ypsilanti, Michigan to organize a physical education department. At the same time Lt. John J. Pershing, a recent graduate of West Point, replaced Lt. Griffith. Disapproving of women being taught physical activities by a man, Lt. Pershing begged the chancellor, then James H. Canfield, to employ a woman to take over these courses, offering to carry on with the military marching and fencing for the ladies until the chancellor could find a woman teacher and stipulating that the marching he taught to women was to be carried on strictly indoors away from public view. [2]

By the fall of 1892 Mr. Bowen had located in Lincoln a young woman, Anne Barr, who had learned to swing Indian clubs at the town YMCA, to teach this activity on an hour-pay basis. With Mr. Bowen teaching calisthenics and barbell and dumbbell drills, the young women had their requested physical education program.

The following summer (1893), Miss Barr attended the Chautauqua Summer School of Physical Education in New York State, which Mr. Bowen had attended earlier, [3] and there she had a first experience with professional training in physical education. She received training in Swedish gymnastics under Jacob Bolin, a leader in that field, and had her first experience in esthetic dancing under Rebecca Larsen, a pupil of Melvin Ballou Gilbert, [4] famous dance master of Boston. It was three years later, however, before she introduced any form of dance to the girls at Nebraska.

Throughout Miss Barr's second year of teaching, both Mr. Bowen and Lt. Pershing urged Chancellor Canfield to hire her on a salary basis, recognizing her work on a faculty appointment. In the fall of 1894 she did join the faculty as "Class Leader of Physical Education for Women," a first recognition at Nebraska of physical education for women. With the close of the school year 1893-1894, Mr. Bowen resigned to return to the faculty of the Ypsilanti Normal School where he remained all the rest of his professional career, becoming an outstanding leader in the profession. A year later, Lt. Pershing returned to West Point as a faculty member.

* * * *

*Anne Barr, first woman physical education teacher,
University of Nebraska, 1894-1908. (Courtesy of University of Nebraska).*

Succeeding Mr. Bowen was Robert Clark, M.D., a graduate of Williams College and the Medical College of the University of Vermont. He came to Nebraska in the fall of 1894 from the faculty of the International YMCA Training School of Springfield, Massachusetts, where he had been teaching for the past three years under Luther Halsey Gulick.[5] Dr. Clark, a great camera enthusiast, introduced the use of the camera at Nebraska as a part of posture examinations with a female nurse conducting the examinations of women students. In the following year (1895-1896), Dr. Clark started anthropometric studies of students' physiques, as announced in the catalog of 1895-1896:

Every student in the University is entitled to a physical examination each year, and members of gymnastic classes are expected to take the examination. A plotted chart of measurements is furnished to each student desiring it, at the cost of the price of the chart. Instructions for special practice will be given when necessary, and photographs will be taken of spinal cases.

The last part of the announcement, "photographs will be taken of spinal cases," is intriguing.

This is probably one of the earliest records of the use of the camera for such work in the Midwest. However, Dr. Dudley Sargent had been using the camera as early as 1888 for his posture work with Harvard students, and Dr. Paul Phillips had been using it since 1892 at the New York City YMCA[5a] before joining the Amherst faculty. Now Dr. Clark was using it at the University of Nebraska by 1895 with the work later carried on by his successor, Dr. W. W. Hastings. Since there are no other reports of such work at Nebraska, I assume it died out with the departure from Nebraska of these two men.

When I arrived at Nebraska, 30 years later, and attempted to use a schematograph for such work with women (a later development which was a far cry from an actual camera), there was such an uproar on campus and in the community that it threatened to land me in jail. Shaken from that experience, imagine my amazement years later when I stumbled upon the catalog announcement quoted above.

In the summer of 1896 Anne Barr attended the Harvard Summer School of Physical Education and came under Dr. Sargent's influence. (When she studied at the Chautauqua Summer School of Gymnastics in 1893, she met Jay Seaver, M.D., of Yale University who was a recognized leader in work in anthropometry. But as yet Miss Barr, whose earlier interest in courses as a special student at Nebraska seemed to be in the line of music, in all probabilities had not as yet studied anatomy.) Following Miss Barr's summer study of 1896, the next year's catalog of 1896-97 announced that all women students "requiring special attention, and whose health will not permit taking the general class work, will be given special work under the direction of the instructor." One wonders where Miss Barr got the idea of such work since she did not have professional training other than a few weeks course in the summer of 1893 at the Chautauqua Summer School and this second summer course at Harvard in 1896. Dr. Clark must have passed on his enthusiasm to her and set her to studying on her own, inspiring her summer study at Harvard.

* * * *

19

In the spring of 1898, Miss Barr had a leave of absence (according to the board of regents' minutes, from April 18, 1898 to September 1, 1898) to travel in Europe to visit and observe work in physical education. These dates contradict the memories of both Dr. Clapp and Mrs. Adelloyd Williams (an early graduate of the department and an early assistant to Anne Barr). In October 1941 the National Association of Physical Education for College Women published, as a Supplement to the APEA's *Research Quarterly,* its *Pioneer Women in Physical Education.* At my insistence it carried a biography of Anne Barr (since 1903 Mrs. R. G. Clapp) written by Miss Barr's former assistant, Adelloyd Williams, in which Mrs. Williams stated:

> ... she attended the Anderson Summer School of Gymnastics at Chautauqua, New York, in the summer of 1894 [other records give 1893]. In 1896 she entered the Sargent School of Gymnastics at Cambridge, Massachusetts, attending a part of the winter term and continued through the following summer ....
>
> In the fall of 1897 she went to Sweden and spent the following year in the Royal Central Gymnastic Institute in Stockholm .... Here she did intensive work in corrective and Swedish gymnastics ..... She observed work in the Normal School in Copenhagen. She spent several weeks in Berlin where ... she was permitted to observe work there ....
>
> During her year in Stockholm .... [6]

Mrs. Clapp had approved Mrs. Williams' biography in all details. So imagine my surprise in 1945 shortly after Mrs. Clapp's death and four years after the material was off press, to have Dr. Clapp inform me that Mrs. Williams was wrong in writing that Anne Barr had been in Europe during 1897–1898 instead of 1898–1899. He said she had returned in the early summer of 1899 and had gone directly to the Chautauqua Summer School of Gymnastics as a member of the staff as a folk dance specialist. There Dr. Clapp first met Anne Barr. Although he disagreed with Mrs. Williams on the year Anne Barr travelled in Europe, he, too, claimed that she had spent a full school year there chiefly studying at the Royal Central Gymnastics Institute in Stockholm.

My August 1972 research into the university archives indicated that Mrs. Williams and Dr. Clapp were in error not only as to dates but also as to the length of time Anne Barr was absent for European travel and study. The full year turns into a 20-week trip (according to the regents' minutes) which included travel in the United States to and from ports, two ocean voyages and time spent in Copenhagen and Berlin, leaving little time for study in Stockholm.

20

Dr. Clapp told me, shortly after Mrs. Clapp's death, that his wife had travelled in Europe under the guidance of Dr. and Mrs. Jay Seaver. Whether she was the only person travelling with the Seavers or was a member of a party of physical educators is pure conjecture; if the latter, this trip may have been one of the earliest study-travel groups.

My research indicates that the Royal Central Gymnastics Institute had no tuition charges for foreigners who were admitted to courses only as auditors or observers, and that the school operated only from September 15 to May 25.[7] Therefore, at the most, Anne Barr could have observed work for less than a month since she didn't leave Lincoln until April 18.

Later, other discrepancies in Anne Barr's biography came to light but not until after she, Dr. Clapp and Mrs. Williams were all deceased. Wishing to check on the exact dates of Anne Barr's attendance at the Sargent School of Gymnastics, mentioned in her biography, and the courses she took there, I was astonished to learn from today's Sargent College of Boston University (successor of the old Sargent School) that no such person had ever matriculated there. However, the registrar had checked with the archivist of Harvard College and learned that Anne Barr of Lincoln, Nebraska was registered at the Harvard Summer School of Gymnastics in 1896. Since the University of Nebraska catalog recorded Anne Barr as also having studied at the Anderson School of Gymnastics, I checked with Arnold College (today's successor of the Anderson School) to be informed that no one by her name had ever registered there but that she may have attended the Chautauqua Summer School directed by Anderson. So the university catalogs that for several years listed Anne Barr as having studied at both of these schools had been in error. But in her biography, Mrs. Williams had named the Chautauqua School for 1893, not the Anderson School in New Haven.

In regard to Anne Barr's appointment on the staff of the Chautauqua School for the summer of 1899, Dr. Clapp claimed that she came there that summer directly from Europe. The fact is she returned home late August 1898 and reported directly to the University of Nebraska where she taught the year 1898–1899 before going to teach at Chautauqua. (Many local newspaper records and registrar's reports attest to her presence at the university throughout most of the school year 1897–1898 and the full year 1898-1899.)

The errors indicated here in Mrs. Williams' biography of Mrs. Clapp cannot be blamed on the author; they occurred because of the unavailability of 1890 records at that time and Mrs. Clapp's seeming reluctance to discuss the beginnings of the department.

* * * *

In September 1898 a "Special Course in Physical Education" was inaugurated at the University of Nebraska. This was an academic major leading to the bachelor's degree and a certificate in physical education. Nebraska was the first state university to establish such a major, although not the first school of collegiate rating to do so.

It was George Wells Fitz, a physiologist, who started the ball rolling for academic status for professional training in physical education when in 1891 he established a department of anatomy, physiology, and physical training at Harvard College offering the first academic major in physical education leading to the bachelor's degree. Two years later, James F. Jones was the first graduate of this course. He went from Harvard to Marietta College in Ohio as director of its gymnasium.[8]

In 1892 Thomas D. Wood, M:D., at Leland Stanford Jr. University, established the second such academic major (the first in a coeducational private college) and in 1897 graduated its first student, Walter Wells Davis of Maynard, Iowa, who went to Iowa College in Grinnell as director of physical training and later served from 1916 to 1942 as supervisor of health and physical education for the Seattle, Washington schools.[8a]

In September 1899, the first woman in America to take an academic major in physical education, Stella Rose, graduated at Leland Stanford Jr. University. A year later she returned to her alma mater as a member of the staff of physical education for women.[9]

In June 1900, Alberta Spurck became the University of Nebraska's first graduate with an academic major in physical education. After graduation she studied at the Chautauqua Summer School before going to a private girls' school in Seattle for her first year of teaching, followed by an assistant professorship at the University of Washington where she helped establish the department of physical education for women. A year later she married and, as was the custom in those years, was immediately lost to the profession.[10]

The story of the development of this branch of collegiate professional training—the first at a private eastern men's college in 1891, the second at a private western coed college in 1893, and the third at a midwest state university in 1898 in a span of seven years—is an interesting story of educational doors opening for women as well as for men. The Nebraska story is a strange tale of many years of search for the truth, sorting out from actual records fact from fiction and false memories

22

Alberta Spurck, Nebraska 1900, first student to graduate from a state university with an academic major in physical education. (Courtesy of University of Nebraska).

once the University of Nebraska established its archives and made records available as it did in the late 1960s.[11]

Early graduates of the physical education department at the University of Nebraska and Dr. Clapp (in a letter to the board of regents of February 21, 1905) both claimed that Anne Barr originated the normal training course. The records, however, point quite definitely to Dr. Clark and Dr. Hastings as the prime movers in this educational venture.

Immediately on coming to Nebraska in 1894, Dr. Clark set up a certificate short course in teacher-training in physical education, and in 1896 he offered a special summer teacher-training course in physical education for public school teachers. Many years of experience with college faculties and their red tape attest to the fact that new major courses are usually quite some time in the making before they are listed in school catalogs so that Dr. Clark, with his concern for offering teacher-training courses, must have done all of the spadework for this major in physical education leading to the bachelor's degree before he left the university at the close of the 1896-1897 school year. His graduate work and several years' teaching experience in professional training in physical education at the Springfield YMCA Training School strongly point to him as the creator of the physical education major rather than Miss Barr with her lack of a bachelor's degree and of physical education professional training except for a few weeks for a couple of summers. Dr. Clark was recognized as an innovator and was a member of Phi Beta Kappa of Williams College,[12] Nebraska Chancellor Canfield's alma mater, which doubtless opened doors at Nebraska for the acceptance of Dr. Clark's ideas. Dr. Hastings, who most certainly put the new major into action, held four degrees in addition to being a graduate of the International YMCA Training School of Springfield.

Although public announcement was made of the establishment of the new academic major in the *University Calendar* of 1897-1898, the major was not actually offered until September 1898. The June 1898 *University Calendar* reported that a new Special Collegiate Course in Physical Education was to be offered by the university, the fourth such course of specialization leading to a college degree. (The other three were a teachers course, a law and journalism course, and a medical course.) The catalog and class schedules listed Dr. Hastings as the teacher of all the theory courses and Miss Barr as "assistant to Dr. Hastings, the instructor." Miss Barr also was listed to teach pelvic anatomy for women, Swedish gymnastics for women and the activity classes for all women. The Special Physical Education Course called for 77 credit hours of specialization in related sciences which included for theory: 10 credit hours each of chemistry, physics and zoology, 4 of physiology, 2 each in hygiene and pedagogy, 33 in specialization in physical education including 27 hours of theory—(3 each in anthropometry, history and philosophy of physical education, kinesiology, and physiology of exercise; 2 each in educational gymnastics, equipment in physical education, methods, physical diagnosis, physical measurements, practice teaching, and prescription of exercises; 1 hour of emergencies), and 6 credit hours of practical work, which meant training in physical activities.

Although the professional course at Nebraska was designed for both men and women, no positive records have come to light of men registering for the course in the earliest days other than Elmer Berry who, when Dr. Hastings resigned in December 1900, dropped the physical education major at Nebraska but completed the work for the bachelor's degree the following June. He then followed Dr. Hastings to Springfield to complete his professional training. Elmer Berry later became recognized as a distinguished graduate of that school.

Alberta Spurck's graduation from the University of Nebraska as the first person in a state university to earn a bachelor's degree with a major in physical education passed unnoticed within the profession for 40 years until I learned of it most belatedly and brought the fact to public notice.[13] (However, because of my too ready acceptance of memories of early graduates, I erroneously claimed her to be the first person to earn a bachelor's degree with an academic major in physical education instead of merely the first in a state university. It was 1969 before researchers brought to light the earlier graduates at Harvard and Stanford, as mentioned earlier, and it was 1973 before Stanford's first woman graduate of 1899 was publicly proclaimed to the profession in one of my articles.[14]

* * * *

The year 1898-1899 was momentous for physical education for women at Nebraska in that Soldiers Memorial Hall (the west wing of Grant Memorial Hall) was completed, greatly expanding facilities and specifically offering the women facilities of their own. Now Anne Barr was given the official title "Director of Women's Gymnasium."

After three and a half years at Nebraska, Dr. Hastings resigned unexpectedly, December 31, 1900, to return to the Springfield YMCA Training School on an emergency appointment, this time as a member of the faculty there.[15] When the university was unable to find a replacement for Dr. Hastings, Anne Barr carried on alone as acting head of physical education for both men and women, being thereby promoted from instructor to adjunct professor. Surely this must mark an American first in physical education in the college world—a woman head of both men's and women's physical education at the turn of the century (all of the calendar year 1901 and first half of 1902).

Dr. Hastings was still teaching at the Springfield school in 1909 and 1910, where he was publishing the magazine *Hygiene* to which we students at the Boston Normal School of Gymnastics were ordered to subscribe, so that his name was familiar to us students. The magazine died shortly thereafter when he left Springfield to enter the ministry, thus becoming lost to the profession.

* * * *

When in 1899 Anne Barr became a member of the staff of the Chautauqua Summer School of Physical Education, specializing in the teaching of Swedish folk dancing, she met another new staffer, Raymond Gustavus Clapp, who was the track and field coach. A recent Yale graduate and star pole vaulter, Dr. Clapp had become a well-known track record holder for some athletic club in the East and had started medical studies at the Keokuk (Iowa) Medical School.[16] Elected to succeed Dr. Hastings at Nebraska when he completed his medical studies, Dr. Clapp came to Nebraska in September 1902 with the rank of full professor, a recognition not granted to his predecessors.

The following summer, Dr. Clapp and Anne Barr were married and as the early graduates of the professional course at Nebraska put it, he also married the department of physical education for women because from then on a unique liaison developed between the men's and women's physical education departments that was to persist until I arrived there 21 years later. In 1902 he took over completely the major in physical education and Anne Barr, now Mrs. R. G. Clapp, continued as "head of women's gymnasium" under his directorship until 1908. Evidently controversy soon arose among some of the state's taxpayers over the university's employing two persons from the same family, enough controversy that apparently the subject was broached to Dr. Clapp, who replied in a letter of February 21, 1905, to the board of regents:

> I believe the question arising as it does in the Physical Education Department should be considered differently from the general policy, because in this department questions of a delicate nature regarding the health of young men and women in the University are constantly arising and therefore make it very desirable for the directors of these two departments to be man and wife. At the University of California this arrangement has been in vogue for some time and is considered the ideal system. Ohio University quite recently engaged a man and wife to direct the joint work for this reason.[17]

The regents' reply is not on record but it was shortly determined that Mrs. Clapp would give up her position and that it would be offered to another woman.

The salary budget was finally determined by June with Mrs. Clapp listed at $600 compared to $1,000 she had been receiving for the year 1904-1905. So apparently she had been retained but, presumably to appease some of the critics, only for part-time.

*   *   *   *

In 1908 Mrs. Clapp resigned, succeeded as "Director of the Women's Gymnasium" by Alice Towne, a 1905 Nebraska graduate who had stayed on for two years as an instructor under Mrs. Clapp and for the third year travelled in Europe, visiting physical education schools and auditing some work at Stockholm's Royal Central Gymnastic Institute. Under the overall directorship of Dr. Clapp, she gave promise of leading the department to a wider program by bringing in fresh ideas from the outside world but after only one year in the position she resigned to be married.

From 1909 until 1924, according to reports from several graduates, the department remained at a standstill for 10 or 11 years and then for the next 4 years sadly deteriorated because of too much inbreeding (practically all the staff were Nebraska trained) and domination by Dr. Clapp.

The years following Anne Barr Clapp's resignation were turbulent with a succession of women directors all under the doctor's thumb and unable to advance any new ideas. In 16 years, 1908 to 1924, there were six different women as "Head of the Women's Gymnasium." The second was Ina Gittings, a Nebraska graduate of 1906, who after five stormy years (1909-1914) went on leave of absence for one year, to step back into the head position for two more years, serving in such a troubled atmosphere that she finally resigned in 1917.

The third Head of Women's Gymnasium was Bessie Park, a graduate of the New York State Teachers College, Cortland and the New Haven Normal School of Gymnastics. She brought to the program German gymnastics and esthetic dancing, both taught for many years elsewhere in the country. Having been Miss Gittings' assistant for one year, she served as head of women's work while Miss Gittings was on leave of absence, 1914-1915. Miss Park, at the close of that year, returned to her alma mater in Cortland where she taught until her retirement.

The fourth head, Marion Young, was also a graduate of the New Haven Normal School of Gymnastics. She remained less than a school year, having angered Dr. Clapp, who fired her in April 1918, supposedly for backing a young teacher (Jessie Beghtol Lee, a Nebraska graduate and sister of a prominent attorney in Lincoln) who was fired for trying to organize a Women's Athletic Association against Dr. Clapp's wishes. The board of regents ignored the firings, accepting instead the resignations of the two, the young instructor's to take effect "at once," the head of the department's in May, the latter presumably to permit time to find someone to take over in the emergency.

To fill the position, Mrs. Clapp was prevailed upon to return to her old position on a part-time basis. She stayed for two years while the authorities searched for a new director.

By the end of World War I the professional training work in physical education at Nebraska had deteriorated so seriously that the profession did not even recognize its existence. When in the late 1910s the American Physical Education Association made a survey of schools offering such training, the University of Nebraska was not included.[18]

In 1920, the year the survey results were announced, the position was finally given to one of the department graduates who had previously served on the staff in a lesser position. But she was granted only the title of acting director. She meekly got along with Dr. Clapp as best she could and the search for a director now bogged down for the next four years until the women students declared war on the drifting situation.

All these years Dr. Clapp (so the stories from graduates go) kept a firm grip on the women's department, brooking no suggestions from women teachers and sternly disciplining any of them who questioned his decisions or procedures.[19] And for the last four years in particular the department deteriorated with 100 percent inbreeding within the staff. Apparently there was much uncertainty as to just what Dr. Clapp's authority covered. His title was under constant change, no doubt each change representing some fresh argument and yet another effort to define more clearly just how far his authority over the women stretched.[20]

In 1920, Frederick Luehring accepted the position at Nebraska as director of physical education and athletics, but apparently only reluctantly, for after a visit to the campus he wrote the chancellor and regents a long letter enumerating the many things wrong with the department and advising changes and additions. He urged that the work for both men and women be updated and that the needs of the men and women be provided impartially. He pointed out the need for improvement in the physical and medical examinations as paramount and

28

called for the establishment of a university infirmary. He called for a course in fundamentals of physical education for all students as quickly as possible and, stated that since 70 colleges and universities and hundreds of high schools had swimming pools, Nebraska could no longer neglect the need for such a facility. He called for an intramural program for all students, requiring at once at least 10 baseball diamonds, 4 soccer fields, 50 tennis courts, and 10 volleyball courts. In regard to professional training, he wrote:

> Nebraska, I understand, has developed the first Normal Course in Physical Education and Athletics in a state university. This is a fact to be proud of . . . . The work should (now) be greatly expanded.[21]

He also called for a full-time physician to be head of physical and medical examinations with Dr. Clapp to serve as the assistant rather than head of that work. He pointed out the need to hire a head of men's intramurals at once. To this lengthy epistle the chancellor replied, in part:

> You will come to Nebraska with united support and backing from everyone . . . . In so far as we can cause the donors and taxpayers of the state of Nebraska to catch our visions, these visions will become a reality.[22]

In light of this exchange of letters, the events of the next four years take on new meaning.

Mr. Leuhring stayed in Nebraska from 1920 to 1922, stirring things up and awakening the department. Dr. Clapp, however, protected his domain as head of professional training in physical education for both men and women. When Mr. Leuhring left, things apparently reverted to the old status quo routine.

Succeeding Mr. Luehring was Fred Dawson who came from Princeton University as head football coach and director of all physical education and athletics.

Twenty-four years after the graduation of its first major in physical education, in June 1900, 111 young women and a few young men had received their college degrees at Nebraska with the major in physical education.

Whatever prestige the department of physical education had acquired, by the 1920s it had drifted into professional anonymity to the despair particularly of its women students. Finally in the class of 1925 there were many women students who, joined by a group of juniors, actually waged battle to force the administration to bring in a new head of physical education for women, one from the outside world who had received professional training at a school of prestige and who would be given authority to break the ties that for so many years had bound the women's professional training work in physical education to a man director who, according to the women students, was unqualified and inadequate. The chancellor and regents listened to their demands. I had been chosen for the position and now it was up to me to carry on. Knowing nothing of this department's history, since it had successfully "hidden its light under a bushel," I had accepted the challenge, well aware, however, that there were going to be many tough thorns in this rose garden.

* * * *

Mary Wheeler, my very efficient assistant at Beloit College,[23] had happily accepted the instructorship I was able to offer her at Nebraska. Well that she did, for the staff I inherited was entirely too small for the work to be done, with most of them (five out of seven) being on part-time duty only, and the total time of the five scarcely equalling one full-time assignment as I interpreted full-time. Even with Mary Wheeler and myself both full-time, the staff was still too small for the university enrollment, but I was determined that we would nevertheless do as good a job as possible, and in the meantime I would work toward a larger and better trained staff, and most certainly for none but full-time teachers insofar as possible.

For the past several years the physical education classes for women at Nebraska had been about 90 to 120 pupils per section, thus reducing the number of teaching hours. All work in the department ran from 9 a.m. to 3 p.m. on Monday, Wednesday and Friday only. At all other times everything was locked up and all teachers unavailable. Not one stayed to help with late after-school sports which the WAA girls ran on their own, furnishing their own sports equipment since, for service classes, the department was teaching nothing but gymnastics and therefore owned no sports equipment.

The teachers offered no scheduled conference hours for students, held no staff meetings, and apparently made no efforts to get together to coordinate department work. In fact, when I discovered that Mary and I were the only ones to report for work on Tuesdays and Thursdays (not to mention Saturdays), I immediately called for staff meetings on those two days and was informed by the other staff members that I need not expect them to attend since they had been hired solely to teach the classes scheduled on Monday, Wednesday and Friday. However I posted notice that the staff would meet every Tuesday and Thursday morning in my office to plan the reorganization of the departmental work and whoever desired to participate in these plans should make every effort to come. This brought out some of them now and then but usually with much grumbling. As a rule, Mary and I held the staff meetings alone, and when it came time to make out class schedules for second semester we rejoiced to be alone for without hindrance we put in classes for all five days of the week, filling all five days with class sections and limiting enrollment in all sections drastically. This of course meant more teaching hours for the entire staff, and I all but had a riot on my hands.

The only courses that had been offered for the past several years by the department to the credit classes required of all university underclassmen were two—Swedish gymnastics, all nine months for the freshmen, and German gymnastics, all nine months for the sophomores—no sports, no rhythms, no outdoor classes. There was elective classwork in esthetic dancing offered to upperclass women, mostly fine arts students and P.E. majors, taught by a faculty member's wife who had a private dance studio in town and came to campus for this one class. Since she had been taught dancing by excellent teachers in the United States and in England she was well prepared, but she knew nothing of physical education. However she was deeply interested in her classwork and thoroughly competent.

Gradually I was able to build a staff of full-time teachers and of persons trained in the finest schools in the country, opening the doors to some fresh breezes from other parts of the educational world. These new teachers gave the department vigor and life, new perspectives. By the end of the 1920s I had a staff of nine full-time teachers and was able to reduce the service classes to around 30 pupils per section compared to as many as 120 in 1924.

Gradually, too, I managed to get control of the majors' theory courses, but for the first two years at the expense of a terrific teaching load for myself and Mary Wheeler. In addition to administrative work and WAA after-school sports, Mary and I worked five days a week, 8 a.m. to 6 p.m. and on Saturdays from 8 a.m. to 2 and 3 p.m. and were frequently back on Sundays to clear out office work and keep things moving properly until I could have a full staff of competent and willing workers, including an office girl.

Once I got things completely in my own hands and had a good staff, the physical examinations (that before my coming had taken up all class hours all fall even at times almost up to Thanksgiving vacation) were completed in two weeks and we quickly had the girls out for field hockey or tennis all the rest of the wonderful weeks of autumn.

The costumes the students at Nebraska were wearing for physical education work in the early 1920s were unbelievably old-fashioned—the sort that had already been old-fashioned when I started my teaching career 15 years earlier. Apparently no one had cared enough to order a new style. Many suits were so worn out that it was obvious they had been handed down for years. Some were so old that they were faded and greenish black with age. At best, the suits more recently manufactured were also hopelessly out of style and the students intensely disliked them. No wonder the girls hated gym classes as in large numbers they claimed they did. This had to be remedied quickly. As soon as possible I contacted the firm that made these odd costumes, asking that their representative come with up-to-date samples. When he arrived I learned that no other school used the old-fashioned suit still worn at Nebraska. This firm served schools nationwide and the Nebraska order had to be made up as a special lone item much to the amusement and annoyance of the entire firm, but since they had been unable to interest earlier directors to take the time to decide on a new style they quietly filled the old order, year by year, and were careful not to let any other firms know they were still making this old style suit for this one school. They were happy about discarding the old style. (It was the delighted salesman who jokingly started the saying among other salesmen of professional books, equipment and costumes, "I am going to Lincoln to see Lee in Grant." This quip persisted throughout my directorship at Nebraska.)

Bloomers with middy blouses had been the preferred style for the past 15 years everywhere else, but at Nebraska only the girls who came out for after–school WAA sports had adopted this style on their own. The new suits (odd looking today but selected by students as well as staff) consisted of a pair of soft black flannel (not stiff serge) skimp bloomers with practically no knee hangover, worn with a white cotton shirt-style blouse, and black ribbed cotton hose and white canvas sneakers. Silk hose had by now become common for street wear by the affluent and greatly desired even by many who could not afford them. We ruled that silk hose were not to be worn with gymnasium suits, since they were expensive. Silk hose never did become an acceptable feature of a gymnastics costume, for by the time the social scene had changed to accepting them for all-round everyday wear, gymnastic costumes called for bare legs and ankle socks!

* * * *

Through the years students had built up a great dislike for the old-time Swedish and German gymnastics, so we eliminated these activities. However old-fashioned the physical education program for women was in the early 1920s at the University of Nebraska, Indian Club swinging and dumbbell exercises had at least been discarded even though some programs elsewhere still clung to them. As late as 1913, according to a program for the Ninth Annual Gymnastic Exhibition at the University Armory, the men were still having barbell and dumbbell drills and the women wand drills.

In keeping with a search for change, the college women of America were taking a great fancy to the Danish gymnastics of Nils Bukh who had toured the country in the mid-twenties with a group of his students, exhibiting the gymnastics he taught at his school in Ollerup. Several American college women physical directors who had taken his summer course in Denmark had introduced his gymnastics into their programs. In my third year at Nebraska I hired on my staff a young Swedish teacher who had come to America with Bukh on his first tour and had remained here to teach. After a season or two at the University of Illinois, she came to Nebraska and introduced Bukh's work. As this form of gymnastics stressed flexibility and was of a marked swinging, rhythmical nature, the girls took to it at once. Gymnastics now became so popular that one of my new staff members, Miriam Wagner, a graduate of Beloit and Wellesley, went to Ollerup to study under Bukh, so that shortly we had two staff members trained to offer this work. But we could not drop the old forms of gymnastics completely until the old staff members were weeded out, for apparently these were the only activities they were prepared to teach.

My immediate personal concern was for corrective gymnastics for students with unusually poor postures and/or with need for restriction in their exercise programs. All my teaching years I had been offering such work. At Nebraska I soon discovered that correctives, at least by name, were nothing new. (As I learned later they had been available off and on in some form from the days of Anne Barr's and Alice Towne's visitations in the late 1890s and early 1900s of work at the Royal Central Gymnastics Institute in Stockholm, where medical gymnastics were in high favor. But with both of them gone it had been mostly "off" from what I could learn.) What I found going on in the mid-twenties in the name of correctives was a sad imitation of what such work should be. Fortunately, very few students were registered for the course since it soon became evident that a large percentage of underclass women, supposedly physically unfit, had been granted "reprieves" from the departmental requirement by the acting director of physical education "to cut down on enrollment" as one staff member informed me. Evidently the few enrolled in correctives really desired such work or they, too, would have been given reprieves.

To get correctives offered to a college woman needing special attention for her own particular physical developmental needs I had to educate the University Health Service as to my own definition, aims and objectives of correctives and to explain to those skeptics what we were prepared to do for special cases of varying disabilities if only they would support us and get these students to us instead of demanding that because they were not physically fit they should be excused from work in physical education. This concern for the physically inadequate caused a great uproar in certain parts of the campus, with most disapproving of my philosophy of what physical education was for. However, there were a few who applauded our stand.

* * * *

Dancing (heretofore offered in the form of interpretive dance to the majors and fine arts students and a few upperclass girls who wished to take it as an elective beyond the first two years' requirement in physical education) we now offered to all students, in the form of folk, tap (as clogging was now being called), and interpretive dancing. For the last we leaned decidedly upon pupils of Margaret H'Doubler of the University of Wisconsin. Shortly I was able to bring one of her finest students, Dorothy Simpson, to the staff who introduced this form of dance to the university and in 1926 established the dance group, Orchesis, a chapter of the original Orchesis born earlier at the University of Wisconsin. Although there had been a dance club in the department at the university in the late 1910s and early 1920s, this was not a modern dance club as one graduate thesis asserts, since the term *modern dance* did not come into use until the late 1920s and early 1930s. It had died out so completely that it was unknown to both students and staff by 1926, so that this venture of Miss Simpson's was in no way a revival of the earlier efforts. The girls loved this new form of dance, thus ringing the death knell for the old esthetic dance which had its heyday in the 1890s and early 1900s and had hung on too long at Nebraska.

The evening before Ivy Day, 1929, Orchesis presented on campus a three-part recital of *Miscellany*, *Lake Spirits* (a tribute to Lorado Taft's monument *The Great Lakes* then but recently unveiled in Chicago), and the *Nibelungen Ring*. Wilbur Chenowith, a rising young musician of Lincoln, had arranged the music for the last two parts, using a small orchestra of piano, violin, cello, cornet and tympani. It was an ambitious program for amateurs and for our young, new dance instructor, Beatrice Richardson, who was a pupil of Miss

H'Doubler. She had succeeded Dorothy Simpson as head of dance. In just five years our department had made a definite and recognized contribution to culture on the campus.

With great enthusiasm, the women responded to our early announcement that sports were to have a big place in the physical education classwork. We offered a variety of both team and individual sports for the girls to choose from and they were so intrigued with field hockey, a novelty to the campus in 1924, that we made it a fall requirement for all freshmen taking regular work.

When I first arrived, students and staff both insisted that this game had never been played at Nebraska. I was most unbelieving for as a college freshman I had played field hockey in Iowa 20 years earlier and it had been popular there all the years since. How could Nebraska have missed this fascinating game? After 50 years of "off and on" research into department history I have unearthed the facts as best I can! According to Margaret Kiefer, a 1914 graduate of the department (who as Mrs. Joel McLafferty of Lincoln became Nebraska's Mother of the Year in 1959), as early as the fall of 1910 Ina Gittings, then head of women's physical education, introduced the game to Nebraska which lasted through 1913. Then it died out for a couple of years until Dorothy Baldwin came to the staff from the outside world in 1915 and revived it. With her departure two years later it died again, not to be revived until I came in 1924.

The Women's Athletic Association, established in 1917, had a membership in 1924 of mostly physical education majors. This group was crying for help and Mary Wheeler took over the sponsorship. She attended all their practices and games, and her office and all facilities were open to them. For the more strenuous team sports, Mary interested the girls in a regime of healthful living. With much enthusiasm they entered upon a schedule of three regular meals a day, not eating between meals, no coffee, and in bed by 11 p.m. on weeknights. "No smoking" would certainly have been on the schedule had it not been that as yet it was unthinkable for any college girl other than a rare "far outer" to do such a socially unacceptable thing.

One of our first moves was to open the organization to all women students and to offer a varied sports program to interest a great variety of students. We also urged giving up the custom of spending money on awards to individuals, such as medals, bracelets, loving cups, and expensive college N blankets and N sweaters, and urged stopping payment for meals at downtown hotels for executive committee and board meetings, as attested to in WAA minutes of earlier years. Instead we suggested that money be spent on sports supplies and equipment for all to use and on continuing to send delegates to the Athletic Conference of American College Women athletic conferences.

There was one big fly in the ointment. Mary Wheeler and I had become a bitter disappointment to the English teacher on the faculty who, at the turn of the century, had put on an ambitious women's intercollegiate basketball program at Nebraska and had assumed that we would revive her program and lead the university into another so-called golden era of women's athletics. When she learned that we would not be following in her footsteps but instead would promote sports for all women, she roundly denounced us on campus.

But the girls were delighted with this new form of organization and in the spring, under Mary Wheeler's tutelage, they printed a booklet in blue and gold containing the story of the Nebraska WAA reorganization, copies of the Athletic Conference constitutions of both the ACACW and the new Nebraska WAA, and the local program for the coming year. As a surprise, they dedicated the booklet to me:

To Mabel Lee

Director of Physical Education for Women of the University of Nebraska, who stands as our living ideal of a sportswoman, do we lovingly dedicate this Constitution of the Women's Athletic Association

Their pleasure over the booklet touched me deeply. In fact they were so pleased with the venture that they printed an extra supply and when their delegate went to the spring convention of ACACW at the University of Illinois, she took along enough copies to present one to each delegate.

The minute the booklet was off press, the officers ran to my office to present me the first copy and then dashed to the English professor's office to give her the second one, evidently unaware of her displeasure with Mary Wheeler and me.

She took the booklet, read the dedication to me out loud with much sarcasm, and to the amazement of the girls, threw the booklet down on her desk in disgust exclaiming, "Sissy! Just a sissy!" For a split second there was dead silence. Then she picked up the booklet again and turned to the next page on which the officers of WAA had recorded their beliefs about sports for women which ended with "We play for the fun of the game." Reading that entire statement too, out loud, with a second burst of disgust she threw the booklet down once more, exclaiming: "Sissies! All sissies! Bah!"

With deep dismay, also deeply hurt, the girls ran back to my office to report this incident. I calmed them down as best I could but was secretly delighted to sense their unshaken loyalty to Mary and me and our philosophy of sports. The English professor, recognized locally as the great sports woman of the day, never forgave me.

Not to be deterred in our dream of helping the high school girls of Nebraska find an opportunity to engage in wholesome sports open to all, Mary and I set about in 1925 to organize a Nebraska State League of High School Girls Athletic Associations. At first we encountered much resistance from the state high schools superintendents in their false suppositions that we were trying to get interscholastic sports for girls underway in imitation of a Girls Athletic Union in Iowa which was receiving considerable attention from the press. We calmed the superintendents and they gave us their support and the plans finally did go through. After several years, the organization, like so many others, fell victim to the exigencies of the Depression.

* * * *

Of all parts of the departmental program, the professional training of women majoring in physical education presented the greatest challenge to me, and the greatest difficulty was that Dr. Clapp was unwilling to relinquish his over 20-year direction although this was the very thing the women were protesting most. I have never been able to understand why, in face of the uprising of the women students demanding a change, the chancellor and board of regents hesitated to relieve him officially of his control although they gave me a mandate to reorganize and rebuild the program from the ground up and to have complete control albeit as quietly and patiently as possible, while they would maneuver to edge him out. As I understood it, he was to be gently yet determinedly crowded out in such a way that he would ask to be relieved from this work, but they evidently misjudged his determination to keep everything in the old mold.

There never was any question about the work for the few men taking the physical education major. Apparently they, too, were satisfied with the status quo, and it was only the women who were to be freed from Dr. Clapp's direction.

Since the turn of the century there had been a steady growth in the number of collegiate institutions offering professional training in physical education. Now in the late twenties, according to a report from the U.S. Bureau of Education,[24] there were 20 state universities and 93 other colleges and universities offering four-year curricula in physical education leading to a degree and 29 private non-collegiate schools and 44 state teachers colleges offering such specialization but without degree. At last I was becoming part of that teacher-training world. I was to find in it the greatest satisfactions of all my teaching career.

If I had found midwest girls quite different from eastern girls, Iowa girls quite different from Oregon girls, the general run of Coe girls quite different from Beloit girls, here in my new home I found Nebraskans a new sort of people with whom to deal. Never before had I encountered so many snobs, so many people with chips on their shoulders, or so many special-privilege seekers; yet on the other hand never had I encountered a more wonderful group of dedicated earnest young women seeking an education than the group of girls at the University of Nebraska who, against great odds, were trying to earn a college degree with a major in physical education, and as things were going in the 1920s on the Nebraska campus, finding it rough going. The physical education majors of the classes of 1925, 1926 and 1927 welcomed me wholeheartedly and were ever after my loyal supporters. To them I was their redeemer. To me they were my one big reason for sticking it out in my first years at Nebraska, standing for the many unpleasantnesses handed to me from many different directions just because I couldn't bear even to consider deserting these fine young women until I had straightened things out for them.

It was my task now to bring this major for the women up-to-date, which meant building anew from the ground up. It was a challenge that appealed to the great-great-granddaughter of a circuit-riding preacher, but little did she dream of the difficulties awaiting her.

The curriculum itself needed immediate overhauling and updating and the enrollment of those women majoring in the department needed drastic housecleaning. This major course had become a dumping ground for other departments to get rid of undesirables and for girls who liked physical activity but hated to study and thought that by donning a gym suit and romping about for four years they could easily pick up a degree. Fortunately many serious and studious young women were preparing to enter the profession, but were handicapped by an inadequate curriculum, poor teaching, and by being held back by irresponsible students who cluttered up the classes.

One thing working in our favor was that the athletic department was only too glad to help us separate the men's and women's professional training courses. For many years it had been the easy way out for the football coaches to have their star players who chanced (as some did at times) to be backward in their studies register as physical education majors—with the assurance that these poor or lazy students would at least come out of their physical education courses with good grades. Apparently there had been no worries about their flunking courses and thus being ineligible to play football now and then. The easygoing man director of the professional training course let them "pull the wool" over his eyes for it was generally known that anyone, as long as he was still breathing, whether he did the classwork or not, could expect at least an average grade in any subject in the department for which he was registered.

This pretense at being a bona fide student and keeping up in studies was promptly challenged by me and my new staff. After issuing a series of flunks to the football "greats" who were not doing passing classwork, a great hue and cry went up from the coaches, resulting in their insistence that separate sections be set up for all courses in our department taken by both men and women, so that the men would take all their theory physical education class work from the doctor, leaving the women students to us serious-minded women teachers. This suited us fine.

Having a group of men begging to be separated from us women helped our cause. Once separated, it was not difficult to get chemistry, physics and a foreign language added to the four-year physical education course for women, and to revamp the old courses, add several new ones, and drop a few antiquated courses.

As I looked over the records of courses taken by each major, I was filled with dismay over the large number who had taken junior and senior courses in their earlier years without the prerequisites, and at the many juniors and seniors taking sophomore work. It was slipshod advising all along the four-year course and I was shocked. Apparently there had been no supervision of the registrations of these students for the past several years, also no weeding out of undesirables and the inadequate. These things I tackled as rapidly as possible. And I must have had success for within three years, students elsewhere, hearing of our improved course, were transferring from colleges in neighboring states to take work under my direction.

The professional-training students who were left after a rigorous screening process (which turned out to be difficult to apply in a state school where the children of all citizens were to be given a chance regardless of scholastic aptitude) were a fine group of young women. The seniors of my first year were the ones who had, for the most part, borne the brunt of the demands for a new director and a complete departmental reorganization, and looking upon me as their chosen one, I was accepted wholeheartedly, given a royal welcome and their constant, devoted backing. Never have I forgotten them although I was on campus but one year with them and never had any of them in a class. But in reality I had them in several courses—informal, unofficial, unregistered classes—when they would ask me to go for a picnic supper to one of the few picnic spots available (Lincoln did not have the several parks it now has). There, seated about the sorry little bonfire we could stir up from a meager supply of wood, the girls asked me what I would have covered and what books I would have had them study if I had taught them this and that course. They knew their courses had been inadequate and being eager students, drank in all the help I could give them in this strange way. My helping them in their groping for knowledge bound us together, and we have been close all these years. A few of the seniors of that first year still keep in touch.

From the very first day at Nebraska I quickly came to see that these major students were going to be my joy. And so it was! On many an occasion when the going was rough, when other faculty members, at times even some of my own staff, became almost impossible to work with, it was these students' loyalty and faith that kept me on an even keel and would not let me desert them despite tempting offers of positions elsewhere. They became my pride, my joy in my work. Now I came to appreciate the statement of the essayist Benson from his own college teaching experiences:

> . . . it is better to stimulate than to correct, to fortify rather than to punish, to help rather than to blame.[25]

Yes, I saw that my task with majors in particular was indeed one of stimulating, fortifying and helping. And it started with these seniors with whom I was to have so little time to work, so little opportunity to come in contact. Eager for help, they made opportunities for brief conferences and long chats wherever possible. In fact they about walked me to death. Never have I forgotten how my all too-weak flesh would moan on those days of my first year at Nebraska when I had been sorely tried by the foot-dragging staff and these girls would turn up at the end of the day armed with picnic supplies and dressed in knickers, blithely announcing they were taking me "out for supper and some talking" and I, so weary, couldn't see how I could walk the long distance I knew such an invitation meant, and yet I hadn't the heart to disappoint them. So I would set aside my worries and reluctance and make myself go.

It was unthinkable for a student to have a car in those days and streetcars didn't run to picnic spots, so we walked. Evening after evening I walked with those girls, from the downtown campus out south to Pen Woods (the woods by the penitentiary) and back, the round trip at least 8 to 10 miles, or out east O street to the edge of town, about the same distance. I always returned renewed in spirit, the walk doing me much physical good, and the companionship with those eager girls renewing my courage to tackle the next day's many unpleasantries that were sure to be awaiting me in this strange new position full of controversy at every turn. These were the "walkingest" and "talkingest" students I ever encountered—full as they were of challenges about everything. And the nicest thing about them was that they all clung together in a group, some sorority girls, some not, but no crushes with two here and two there shutting others out of friendship.

With the help of these girls and the equally loyal juniors I got a Physical Education Club organized to fill the many gaps in their education. I tackled first of all with this club the many complaints that trickled into my office about some of the majors which put our profession in a bad light on campus. For instance, many professors objected to our girls reporting to their classes in gymnasium suits, as some had been doing for the past several years. I disapproved of this heartily as did many other faculty members, so I enlisted these seniors to help me stop this practice of those girls who were too lazy to change into street dress if they were going to another building. There was much grumbling at first from some, but with senior student opinion backing up my own views, such bad manners soon became a thing of the past. But through the years I have smiled at the memory of how outraged an old bachelor professor was to have a girl come to his class in bloomers. He informed me that he would hold me personally responsible for such unladylike behavior if the practice continued. I got it stopped quickly, however not without unhappy glares from a few students.

*　*　*　*

Chancellor Avery, true to his promise when I finally accepted the position, did give me his 100 percent backing but the board of regents kept dragging its feet on giving me official recognition free of Dr. Clapp's dictatorship. With the coliseum to be completed in early summer of 1926, staff members of all departments and groups formerly housed in Grant Memorial, except those of the department of physical education for women, were informed that they were to be moved out as quickly as possible to prepare that building for a woman's gymnasium. Each had been given orders to pack all personal, departmental and group belongings ready for moving before leaving town for the summer. All obeyed these orders meticulously except Dr. Clapp who, the day after commencement, merely walked out his office door, dropping the key in his pocket and leaving at once for Estes Park, Colorado. His old office was to be my new office, and when the cleanup, painting, and moving crews got to that room, they found that Dr. Clapp had packed nothing, had not even emptied his desk, but had left a note that he and the department of physical education for men were not moving into the coliseum along with all the other men's groups and the athletic department and to "leave his office alone."

A call to the chancellor by the head of buildings and grounds resulted in orders from the chancellor to get the university trucks over to Grant Memorial Hall at once and to pack all of Dr. Clapp's office things and the men's equipment and supplies as best they could and take them to the coliseum. Having packed all of my things to be moved to Dr. Clapp's old office as soon as it was done over, I had left town so that I knew nothing of Dr. Clapp's actions and announcement. Imagine my surprise on the opening day in the fall when Dr. Clapp returned to his old office only to find that his keys no longer worked and to find me enthroned in his freshly done over office. He angrily demanded to know where his things were and how dared I take over his office in his absence. Amazed at his amazement to find things changed, all I could do was meekly insist that I knew nothing of how his things got moved and suggested that he see the chancellor, at which he stormily headed for the administration building. This was one thing of which I was innocent. He did not return to Grant Hall. The old building had been entirely done over for the women's exclusive use. From then on things began to calm down a bit. However, in the end I did not achieve freedom from his constant efforts to block my plans on practically every move until after Chancellor Avery had given up the chancellorship after over 20 years in that position to return to his chemistry teaching.

When Dr. Edgar Burnett, dean of the Agriculture College, succeeded Dr. Avery in the chancellorship in 1927, and the board of regents was still dragging its feet as to my official standing, my heart sank for I feared I might not have the loyal backing of the new chancellor.

On several occasions in my first three years at Nebraska, when Dr. Clapp was seriously holding up my work, I had turned to chancellor Avery for help, and he had called Dr. Clapp and me to his office together in hopes that perhaps with our united efforts we might persuade the Doctor to hand the reins for the women's work over to me willingly. But all efforts failed. With a new chancellor I did not know whether I could depend upon such backing and began wondering if I should give serious thought to some of the offers for new positions that were coming my way. But always I felt I could not abandon these wonderfully fine young women at the University of Nebraska until this problem was resolved. For Chancellor Burnett's first year, I felt it wise to

42

suffer things alone, but in his second year, my fifth one at Nebraska, I felt things should drift no longer. The situation had to be settled or I would have to resign. So one day when the registrar's office and the Course of Study Committee both refused to accept reports, records and recommendations concerning professional training work for women with my signature, saying that Dr. Clapp was the recognized head of all such work for women, I went at once to Chancellor Burnett— the first test for his decision as to which one of us he would support.

With the door now open to him on this topic I at last had my first opportunity to tell him the story of my appointment and assurances that I was to be head of all physical education work for women, tea-cher-training as well as the service courses for the general women students and that now into my fifth year Dr. Clapp was still refusing to let go of the teacher-training work and was getting the support of important persons who could block my work. I urged him to go to Dr. Avery for verification of my story. Whether he followed this suggestion I never knew.

One day shortly after this conference the chancellor called me to his office and informed me that I was indeed head over all work in physical education for women and that he would immediately notify all necessary authorities, through letters of verification, that such was the case. But first he wished to put through telephone calls to this effect in my presence to various deans, the registrar and other officials to inform each that I was in his office as witness to his telephone call and he wished to inform each that I was absolute head of all physical education work for women, the professional training as well as all other parts of the departmental work, and that my signature should be honored as official on all departmental reports, communications and recommendations. This finally ended four years of struggle on my part in behalf of the women students to gain control that had been promised me before I accepted the position.

In all fairness to Dr. Clapp, I must add that once the contest ended, he let go completely and at once and seemingly held no grudge. Whenever on rare occasions I found myself seated next to him at faculty luncheons or dinner or even at some private dinner party, I always found him a courteous, interesting and entertaining conversationalist. I was glad that later years gave me opportunity to pay tribute to his wife for her early pioneer work at Nebraska,[26] which seemed to give him much satisfaction.

Chapter III
Divertissements and Dilemmas

The University of Nebraska student body of 1924 numbered around 6,000 and the faculty (mostly men) around 350. There were only four women heads of academic departments besides myself, all graduates of the university. I was the outsider, and from the reception I received from some faculty, I was definitely regarded as an interloper. I soon perceived that my coming was resented at first by all but one of the women heads—the head of home economics who welcomed me warmly and became a staunch friend.

There were a few other women teaching in various departments but the greatest number employed on campus were clerks and secretaries in the administrative offices. In this group were two women heads of offices, the registrar and the dean of women, both graduates of the university. The first received me cordially and shortly became a good friend; the other held aloof initially but gradually became friendly. Practically all other women besides these three ignored my existence. One woman in particular, when she discovered that she could not dictate to me how to conduct sports for women, dropped all friendly advances. She had been more than cordial at first, in fact embarrassingly so, but she later developed into my severest critic, becoming a thorn in my flesh for all the rest of my long tenure at the university, even past her retirement to the time of her death.

At the turn of the century this woman, a graduate of the University of Nebraska, then 10 years out of college and for most of those years a member of the faculty, had successfully organized, coached and managed intercollegiate basketball for women at the university. Since then she had made quite a name for herself in the sporting world through her various local, state and district championships in tennis and golf. In my early teaching years, I had encountered her basketball rules for women[1] and had been placed on the defensive about them. When she first called at my office, she inquired if I was familiar with her basketball rules. So this was the creator of the old controversial rules of my student and early teaching years. I had never known where she lived or who she might be and none of my own profession had the slightest idea.

Apparently she had assumed that with my coming there was to be a revival of the intercollegiate program. To my dismay she immediately took possession of me, told me which faculty members I should cultivate and those I should not bother to cooperate with, even naming the dean of students and the dean of women as persons I should fight at every turn, under no circumstances cooperating with them about anything. I was shocked beyond words but hid my feelings. As tactfully as possible I avoided discussion with her of my plans for sports and reorganization of the department.

By spring she realized I had no intention to revive intercollegiate athletics and, worse than that, I was not going to let her dictate the management of my department. On several occasions when she had tried to interfere with my work, I appealed to the chancellor about how to deal with her as she had much influence with powerful groups in town and on campus, even in the state. I wished at all costs to avoid conflict with her, yet not permit her to disrupt my work.

"So she is trying to pull you, too, around by the nose," the chancellor exclaimed. He was surprised at this turn of events for shortly after my arrival this woman had congratulated him on his determination to have the department reorganized and freed of male domination. She said she was particularly pleased over his selection of me to head up the department.

"In my 15 years as chancellor, bringing you here is the only thing I have ever done that has pleased her. And now you, too, are in her dog house," Then after a long silence, he added, "That woman is a thorn in my flesh." He again pledged his support of my work and urged me to go ahead with my plans, ignoring her disruptions as much as possible and keeping in touch with him. By spring, as she put it to a few students in particular and to many faculty in general, she had found me out "as a sham."

As far as the other women were concerned their indifference and resentment to my presence seemed to stem entirely from the fact that I was an outsider. It was a peculiar sort of loyalty to one's alma mater which was difficult for me to understand and accept. I found it difficult to work on a faculty where there was so much inbreeding. Everything, it seemed, was judged by whether it was the way it had been done at Nebraska in the years past. Nothing seemed to matter except that the status quo be undisturbed. Every move I made to bring about any change seemed to be interpreted by many Nebraskans as disloyalty to the university.

The faculty men, however, were generally cordial and several of them, apparently sensing my cool reception by many women, hastened to smooth my path whenever they could. Chancellor Avery, having persuaded me to come to the university, was ever my friend and supporter, and fortunately he welcomed change.

* * * *

The students at Nebraska were quite different from those I had known in earlier positions. I was struck by the overweight and lack of sophistication of most of these corn-fed girls. Never before had I seen so many fat girls, and our physical examination records verified this fact. These Nebraska girls—fat or thin, short or tall, sophisticated or unsophisticated, whether from the largest city or smallest village, or from a small farm or huge western ranch—all of them for the most part I learned to like very much. It was, for the most part, the students and Chancellor Avery who sold Nebraska to me. On the whole, the students were eager, earnest, sincere, grateful, fun-loving and cordial. The historian, John D. Hicks, spoke of these Nebraska students of the late 1920s as "a constant joy, perhaps the most appreciative students I have ever taught."[2]

In my first few years at Nebraska, women students numbered around 2,500, about two-thirds of whom were underclassmen and required to take physical education. Instead of offering for credit only one activity (gymnastics), as had been the program at Nebraska for the past several years and had been the pattern of the nineteenth century across the land, I introduced this department into the twentieth century. We offered a choice of baseball, basketball, field hockey, golf, gymnastics, riding, rifle marksmanship, soccer, speedball, swimming, tennis, track, tumbling, and volleyball, besides a variety of dance.

* * * *

Mary R. Wheeler, head of women's sports, University of Nebraska, 1924-1927.

Once we had our affairs a bit organized and under control on campus, Mary Wheeler and I began looking about for possible professional contacts in the city but there was nothing organized there or in the state, so we set out to remedy this. Shortly Mary met a physical education teacher from Beatrice, Nebraska who was a graduate of the Chicago School of Physical Education, and when Mary talked with her about the Illinois State League of High School Girls Athletic Association, she showed much interest in it. So with her help Mary organized the Nebraska State League of High School Girls Athletic Associations, modeling it after the first one, the Illinois League, in which she had worked. The Nebraska League flourished for a few years but, after Mary left Nebraska, without Mary's strong leadership, it soon was taken over by the State High School Activities Association and there died from lack of nourishment. It had been a big boost for physical education for girls at the high school level while it was functioning.

At about that same time I was having little luck in a state venture of my own. When James E. Rogers, field secretary of the National Recreation Association, dropped into my office one day in September 1928 from New York City and I complained of the lack of physical education in Nebraska schools, he said, "What you need is a state director of physical education in the state superintendent's office." Always overflowing with energy and enthusiasm, he offered right then and there to help organize a statewide committee to get a state director for us. He said, "You can go farther, faster, if someone from the outside starts the ball rolling. If you'll do what you can to keep the ball rolling, I'll start it."

In no time, he had interviewed the state officers of many important organizations. All were enthusiastic about the idea. They met in my office and organized a state committee to procure a state director. Before I knew it, I was chairman of the committee. We held our first meeting in connection with the State Teachers Convention in Omaha. The group then planned a meeting with State Superintendent Taylor to learn if he would be willing to have such an addition to his staff and if so, what needed to be done to get the person—legislation or what? Superintendent Taylor was delighted with the idea. He informed us that all that was needed was to get him an increased budget to cover this new salary and expenses, and he could then appoint a director without legislation but—and here was the catch—we would have a hard nut to crack to get the governor to increase his budget for such a cause.

Also immediately my detractors in the community began working against the committee simply because I was the chairman. When the chancellor asked why I was so unhappy that I was trying to create a new position for myself at the State House, as he had been informed was the case, I was dumbfounded. When I explained what we were trying to do, I received his blessing to go ahead. The next move was to get a conference with the governor, Charles Bryan, brother of William Jennings Bryan, but it took some time to arrange.

When the day came, we found a polite but cool reception awaiting us. However, when the governor spied the very attractive committee member who had been head of our WAA my first two years at Nebraska and was now teaching, he warmed up a bit. Seeing his interest in her and also that he was quite impressed by J. Stanley Welch, a prominent Lincoln physician, I introduced my committee, carefully mentioning the state group each represented and stated our cause. Then I tossed the ball to Dr. Welch and our pretty young girl to carry on for an opener. Not even they nor all of us combined could make a dent in the governor's preconceived idea that since Nebraska still had so many cows to milk, so much walking to be done, and so many farm chores to be performed by its young people, the schools couldn't possibly need a physical education program. Nothing anyone could say even in behalf of sports, particularly team sports for growing boys and girls, could shake his belief that every boy and girl in Nebraska should get in his own home all the physical activity he needed.

Not even the personnel of our committee swayed him, though they represented the state officers of the American Legion, Red Cross, TB Association, Boy Scouts, Girl Scouts, Camp Fire Girls, Federated Women's Clubs, Parent Teacher Association, High School Boys' Athletic Association, State Girls' Athletic League, State Teachers Association, and many local groups such as Lincoln and Omaha Recreation Boards, Rotary Club, YMCA and YWCA. Even one of the university regents was a member of the committee, besides heads of physical education in Omaha, Lincoln and several colleges.

Although discouraged, the committee persisted and began an educational campaign throughout the state, informing the public of the splendid things being accomplished in 15 states which had state directors of physical education. But the stock market soon crashed, the Depression set in, and our committee folded up, but not until it had performed a useful task in behalf of the state superintendent. A committee of physical educators was set up under the supervision of Windom A. Rosene of the State Education Department and it prepared and distributed a state *Manual of Physical Education* for rural and small town schools[3] throughout the state. It was in use for many years and was issued in many reprints, and upon requests from all over the United States was sent out to state departments of education and to many city departments all over the country. The Chicago Department of Parks and Playgrounds begged for so many copies that Superintendent Taylor ordered an extra printing just for them. Since such a book could not be sold, it may have "put Nebraska on the map" educationally, but it about wrecked Superintendent Taylor's budget. However, for several years afterwards the Nebraska State Department of Education bragged that the *Manual* was the most popular publication it had ever published.

The silver lining to the defeat of our committee to procure a state director of physical education was the opportunity to become acquainted with the leaders of all these state groups. Acquainted with what we were trying to do at the university, they gave us moral support for our reorganization work. Ever since I had experienced the good comradeship of the Oregon state physical education group, I had wondered why we few physical education people in Iowa and later in Wisconsin did not get together. Now, perhaps, we could get a Nebraska group organized to build cooperation between the physical educators in the state and between "town and gown" within the profession.

I prevailed upon Earl Johnson, supervisor of physical education and athletics in the Lincoln public schools, who had given Mary and me a friendly welcome to town on the rare occasions our paths crossed, to stir up the men of the state to join the several women with whom I had become acquainted. I asked Dr. Clapp to interest the male faculty physical educators in this project but he said I was wasting my time and that he was not interested in wasting his, and anyway we didn't need a state organization. So Earl Johnson and I went on alone. We called for an organization meeting in my office at the university in the fall of 1926 at the time of the State Teachers Convention in Lincoln. Catherine Carrick of the Omaha public schools and a few others joined us, and thus the Nebraska State Physical Education Association was born. But it was hard to keep it alive, and it actually didn't get going on a permanent basis until 1931, five years later.

* * * *

At the turn of the century, President DeWitt Hyde of Bowdoin College declared that the program of exercise "is best which reaches the largest number and does the most for the weakest man."[4] This was my belief which I was trying to sell to the University of Nebraska in the late 1920s. But it was difficult because physical education was considered by so many in Nebraska even in the 1920s as merely the equivalent of housework or walking to and from classes. I was fighting a 100-year-old battle in Nebraska. As early as 1825, an educator, William Bentley Fowle, had said that girls in their seminaries should by all means carry on household labors and take walks but that these should not serve as a substitute for their gymnastic exercises.[5]

Not only did I find a widespread belief that physical education was not a legitimate part of education but also a great nuisance imposed upon the students. Even the University Health Service apparently embraced these beliefs. The ruling of the board of regents was that every young woman enrolled in the university was required to take physical education three hours per week for her first two years of residence unless excused by the director of physical education for women. However, there existed the unwritten, yet apparently well-known, provision that the director of physical education for women would be bound in her decision on each petition for excuse on health reasons by what the Health Service advised in each case.

To my amazement I soon realized that any student who did not wish to register for physical education could procure a written statement from the Health Service advising that I give her a deferment for the semester, or for the year, or a reprieve from having to ever fulfill the physical education requirement. No reason was offered for such a demand. I also soon learned that the Health Service considered the reasons for this system to be their own exclusive knowledge. I took careful note of the large number of requests and queried the Health Service about them and was curtly informed to attend to my own business. I insisted that this was my business and, getting no cooperation, took the problem to the chancellor who ordered the Health Service to give me reasons for each request.

According to the Health Service records on file in my office from then on, I was given to understand that an unusually large percentage of the young women who attended the University of Nebraska had such weak hearts that it would not be wise for them to take part in any physical education activity of any nature. They were practically invalids—the great majority of these seemingly husky corn-fed Nebraska girls.

But I had to accept the Health Service pronouncements in each case as well as statements from out-state physicians, knowing from the gossip I was hearing that these excuses were the laughingstock of the campus, most certainly openly acknowledged as such by the students as frauds. I decided not to challenge them but to seem to accept them as sincere, and then do all the public talking I could about the "poor health of Nebraska girls," hoping to shame the perpetrators of this trick into becoming sincere cooperative working partners of my department.

Imagine my joy when in the start of my third year at Nebraska I received a letter from the president of the Nebraska State Federation of Women's Clubs asking me if I would be a guest speaker at their coming state convention to be held in Lincoln. Here was my chance to have a statewide audience for the many things I wished to say about the terrific incidence of physical unfitness of Nebraska girls, as shown by actual records from the medical profession on file in my office. Maybe those Nebraska club women would sit up and listen to my story. Maybe thus it would get wide publicity which might lead to the medical profession doing an about-face in its attitude toward physical education. What if my plan backfired? I decided that it was a chance worth taking if victory might be won. So I accepted this invitation. But because "a funny thing happened to me on my way to the rostrum," I almost lost that chance.

Tailored suits were quite the vogue for street and business wear for women, and I had a beautifully tailored one to wear to this state meeting. Fearful of appearing mannish, especially since I was working in physical education which too many lay persons still looked upon as a calling for mannish women, I carefully selected my accessories to look as feminine as possible. My predecessor was decidedly on the mannish side in build and style of clothes and I, still somewhat a newcomer to the state, was eager to give the public a different picture of what a woman director of physical education could look like. I wore a lacy frill at the neck and a sapphire blue velvet hat which went so well with the long bar-pin of sapphires and pearls I wore on the lacy jabot. I had paid an atrocious price for that hat but it looked so well with my prematurely gray hair and I felt that the visual impression I might make on the ladies, who would come from all over the state was just as important for my cause as whatever I intended to say, so I bought the hat and went without other less important things. Assured by my staff that I looked just right for a "once over" by the ladies, I arrived at the big St. Paul's Methodist Church downtown, where the general sessions of the state covention were held, well in advance of the time for my speech. I had not seen any of the convention committee members nor they me since all arrangements between us had been made by telephone and follow-up correspondence. Arriving early and not seeing an usher, I sailed down the aisle towards the rostrum and at the first row of seats was overtaken by a woman who asked what I wanted.

"I am Miss Mabel Lee, the next speaker," I whispered to her.

"Yes, yes," she replied, visibly irritated with me, "I'll find you a seat."

"Can't I just sit here on the front row?"

"No, you will be in the way there. Follow me," and leading me to the last row of seats in the auditorium, said, "Sit here. We'll call you when we are ready for you."

When it was time for my speech I arose and started down the aisle to be near at hand but the usher ran after me calling, "No, No, it isn't time for you yet. Just be seated here in the back row."

I thought it was strange but I returned to the back seat. The ladies on the platform were obviously upset about something and whispered together and looked out over the audience. Finally they called an usher and sent her on an errand and one of the group stepped to the lectern and began what was obviously an impromptu speech and as she talked she would turn now and then to whisper to the presiding officer. As she droned on and on, I was beginning to grow impatient for the precious time allotted for my speech was slipping away. Several times I arose to go to the platform but each time was pushed down by an usher demanding that I remain where I was. Several ushers were by now clustered at the rear and running from entrance door to auditorium. At last I heard one say to another, "Maybe she slipped in earlier and no one saw her."

"Well, you would think she would have made her presence known to someone, introduced herself at least to an usher!"

A third one spoke up, "I called the university and they said she left her office all of 40 minutes ago." At that I jumped to my feet but before I could say a word the presiding officer flagged down the impromptu speaker and called out to the audience, "Could it be possible that our next speaker is seated somewhere in the audience?"

At this, by now on my feet and shaking off an usher, I called out from the back of the room, "I believe I am the next speaker," at which the presiding officer at the lectern gave an impatient gesture for me to be seated, saying, "Our next speaker is Miss Lee, the head of physical education for women at the University."

"I am Miss Lee," I called back refusing to be seated again and as I started down the aisle the presiding officer called out angrily, "Why didn't you let us know you were here! We have been waiting all this time for you."

By then I was as angry as she and I called back to her from the length of the room, "I did report there at the rostrum and introduced myself and the usher insisted upon my coming back here and staying here until my name was called." By then I was striding down the long aisle, so upset over the presiding officer's displeasure with me that I was having great difficulty pulling my wits together. It was obvious the platform ladies considered me entirely at fault and were more than out of sorts with me. And here was I, too upset to speak at first and with my precious time by then half gone.

After a few sentences I regained my composure and got on with the task at hand but felt I had made a frightful botch of it trying to cut as I talked for it was impossible at that late hour to give my entire speech. After I had finished I learned that some crackpot woman had been pestering them throughout the convention for a place on the program to expound on some pet theme and that all ushers had been warned to be on the lookout for any woman trying to get to the platform and by all means to keep her away.

To complicate matters, all had been commissioned to watch for me and I had been described as an overweight, mannish looking woman—which described my predecessor. The woman who claimed she would know the head of the department of physical education at the university when she saw her described my predecessor to the ushers, not knowing there was a new woman in that position. The usher to whom I introduced myself, not expecting a smaller, non-mannish person, was so sure when I determinedly walked to the rostrum that I was the other bothersome woman that she had paid no attention to my name, thinking only of the necessity to get me chased to the back of the room. It had been a comedy of errors all because I turned out not to be a mannish-looking woman. This sort of thing I have suffered from my entire professional career and it has always angered me for although there are always some women in our profession who are mannish just as in any other profession, the great majority are not.

During my speech, I showed the audience charts giving the actual data (from physicians' reports) showing the high incidence of heart difficulties among our women students. I was confident that a great percentage of these records were not sincere and had been obtained under duress with either the mother or daughter, or both insisting that the doctor give a written, unfavorable statement of daughter's health so she would not have to, as they put it, "take gym," But I accepted these records as sincere and placed them as such before these women. From the figures (almost half of the freshmen and sophomore women were by physicians' reports too physically incapacitated to engage in physical exercise of any nature), I was able to report that I knew no other college or university that had such a high percentage of physical incapacity among its women students as this. Then I dramatically asked why Nebraska girls were in such poor health condition, and I briefly outlined what we would do for these students if given a chance. My audience gasped and what an uproar ensued! But I had actual written reports from physicians from all over the state as well as from our own Health Service to back up my statistics!

Immediately after my speech became public, as it did since reporters from leading newspapers were present, I received several calls from local doctors and letters from out-state doctors to the effect that now with a better understanding of our program, they wished to reexamine their patients who were our students. Delegates wrote in from all parts of the state asking for a copy of my speech, but I referred them to their state office and it finally published the full speech in their magazine.

Newspapers all over the state took up the question of the poor health condition of Nebraska girls as shown from the statistics I had gathered. *The Lincoln Journal* (Nov. 24, 1926) came out with a headline: "Health of Co-eds Provides Problem," followed by a long article reporting my figures. Finally I was asked by a local medical group to produce my figures. This was what I wanted above all things—a chance to place these statistics before the medical profession and at their invitation.

This meeting with the medical organization gave me a rare chance to tell a large group of physicians what we were prepared to do for Nebraska girls who actually were not physically fit, and I begged for their cooperation. With this, victory was won! Resistance toward our departmental work died down. The hundreds of requests for deferments dropped off immediately to a mere trickle and these were obviously for students honestly needing them. From then on the statistics on the health condition of University of Nebraska girls showed that they were as healthy as girls at other universities.

Out of fairness to the Nebraska physicians, I must admit that many were justified in not wanting their patients to take physical education at the university, in light of the work offered in the past, at least in the early 1920s, when the staff for the most part was disinterested in the health protection of the students and unqualified to give proper restricted or corrective work to those needing it. Another dragon slain!

Well not completely slain! The Health Service dragged its feet for some time longer on recognizing us as any more than "Indian club swingers" as the head of that department spoke of us along with other labels as his fancy dictated when he wasn't labelling me in the presence of students in his physiology class "that half-baked woman." The dragon also was not completely slain with many faculty members who liked to please their apple-polishing women students by abetting them in their requests for physical education reprieves which were no longer theirs merely on demand. But gradually, with infinite patience and a lot of stubborness, we won this battle. The cooperation of the medical profession meant rapidly building special classes to accommodate all the students the doctors wished us to take care of. This, in turn, meant that I, myself, must teach all these special classes which I did until I could bring to my staff a trained woman.

Gradually, although most begrudgingly, the Health Service began to recommend correctives (as such special classes were labelled then) instead of reprieves from the department requirement. Gradually, too, the students and some of the student faculty advisers began to recognize the value of this work. Soon local parents began dropping by my office and out-state parents began writing to express their gratitude over the improved physical condition of their daughters. We were merely following a philosophy for our departmental work put so well by Dudley Sargent when he said:

> Let us give less attention to the exploitation of the strong and more attention to the instruction of the weak. Let us give courage to the timid, energy to the feeble, grace to the awkward, and hope to the despondent.[6]

That was also my belief—my plan.

For several years past many students made up their minds they would not take physical education because they didn't like physical activity or didn't like to dress an extra time or being nonconformists they didn't like requirements for anything, because they were the special privilege seekers. There seemed to be about as many reasons why such persons should be excused from the requirements as there were persons to think up reasons. Some that particularly amused me were: I am married and live with my husband; I have to walk so many blocks each day and therefore should be excused; I am overweight and physical education would be damaging; I am underweight and physical education would be damaging; my weight is just right and therefore I do not need physical education; I play the piano and must protect my hands; I wear glasses and physical activity would endanger them; I have fallen arches and physical education would make them worse; I am a Christian Scientist and cannot take a physical examination; I am modest (my mother has particularly brought me up so) and I cannot dress and undress any place but in the privacy of my own home; I like to be alone and I would not be alone here; I can't afford to pay the locker fee; I cannot wear a gym costume for men might come into the building and see me thus attired; I belong to a sorority and it says it is silly to take physical education; and many other such excuses long since forgotten.

I sympathized with students who wished to avoid physical education as it had been offered for the past several years, a program outdated for almost 25 years. I knew, however, that if I were ever to build a good department to serve all well, I had to stem the great tide of deferments which had been keeping teaching schedules light. The first term I was there, 21 percent of all the students supposed to be taking work had been excused the spring before, and as much as 50 percent of the underclass women of one popular sorority and from 23 to 45 percent of nine other sororities were excused. Within a few years I was able to cut this demand for deferments to a mere trickle but it was a great struggle to educate the university authorities, physicians, parents, and students to the fact that the department of physical education for women existed for a real purpose and had something of value to offer.

56

It was a battle royal that I had to wage at Nebraska to put across the idea that a college degree should stand for physical as well as mental efficiency. Willistyne Goodsell, a well-known woman educator, had just written a widely acclaimed book, *The Education of Women*, and I conspicuously posted copies of the following statement from her book and referred hesitant students and colleagues to it:

> Perhaps the determining factor in developing an attitude of social approval of physical training for women has been, or is, the tremendously enlarged social opportunities and responsibilities of women which make exacting demands upon their self-control, self-reliance, and physical and nervous endurance. No physical weakling, undeveloped of muscle, deficient in nervous control and hampered by uncorrected bodily defects can ever hope to grapple successfully with the complicated situations of modern life as they arise in a vocation, in politics, and in the give and take of strenuous social living.[7]

Physical education for men and boys had been dominated for years by coaches who knew little of physical education and were interested only in the good athletes; hence arose the perverted idea that physical education was for the physically fit only. Having fought this battle 14 years earlier at Coe College and 4 years earlier at Beloit College, I now had to start all over again to convert not just a college campus but, since this was a state university, the entire state as well. As I found ever-increasing opportunities to talk to women's clubs and men's service clubs, I had captive audiences and slowly began to crack that surface of resistance to understand physical education's real aims and objectives. Finally we could refuse to give deferments to the physically unfit without stirring up all sorts of hornets' nests and could instead register these girls for corrective and restricted work and educate them physically to be able to live in a world of normalcy instead of one of invalidism. The hundreds of girls who later came to thank us for our special attention to their physical needs and inadequacies were ample reward for the unpleasantness we had to suffer in this battle to educate the university and the public to our aims.

Strange as it was, the university Health Service as then organized was the most difficult department to persuade to cooperate with us, and yet we were so dependent on its cooperation. This became a struggle of several years, victory never completely won until the head of the department, a man wedded to the status quo, retired, and the doors were opened to progress and a new day in that department.

* * * *

In 1927 Dr. Avery, who had held the chancellorship since 1909, resigned because of ill health. Before leaving he did what he thought was a favor to me. He learned that it was difficult for me to get new courses passed on favorably by the faculty of the Arts and Sciences College, to which all physical education was assigned and whose faculty was packed by Dr. Clapp's cronies who voted against any recommendations once they got the signal from him. He advised me to ask to have the normal training course transferred to Teachers College where he believed my wishes would receive better reception. The dean of that college at the time was most friendly to our department. This I consented to since it was teacher-training work. After a conference with my staff who approved the idea, I put in the request for a transfer and Dr. Avery piloted it through the proper channels to success.

What a furor that precipitated among the parents and friends of several women physical education majors. They quickly beat a path to my office door weekdays and to my home on Sundays, protesting that a girl could not possibly be considered really educated if she didn't graduate from the Arts and Sciences College and most certainly not if she didn't "make" Phi Beta Kappa, and to be eligible for that she had to meet Arts and Sciences College requirements. I recall asking one mother, "Are you sending your daughter to college to get a Phi Beta Kappa key or an education?" and she replied:

"If she gets a Phi Beta Kappa key, I will know that she got an education and if she doesn't, she will have failed."

I felt sorry for that student with the threat of that key hanging over her head, hung there by a falsely ambitious mother. Yet on the other hand I was all for heavy doses of cultural courses for my majors. Some years after that, under a new dean, I was ordered out of a Teachers College faculty meeting by the dean following a too impassioned speech on my part in behalf of cutting back on requirements in so-called "education courses" to make room for a requirement in history in the hopes of working in more cultural subjects for our captive students. I took his shouted order literally, "If that's the way you feel, you are in the wrong college—get out of here!" I replied, "That's exactly the way I feel" and immediately gathered up my briefcase, purse and coat, and as the rest of the faculty sat in stunned silence at this clash, I proceeded out of the room and down a long hallway with (as I was told later by one who saw and heard the entire episode), my heels clicking determinedly the entire length of that long walk, clearly heard by the others stunned into silence. That was not the only occasion when I regretted having been forced into Teachers College by Dr. Clapp's intransigence; there were many, many more.

So the department of physical education for women was divided with all courses for teacher-training work placed in Teachers College under the dean of that college and all other departmental courses left in Arts and Sciences College under the Arts and Sciences Dean. For administrative work (budget, staff, facilities, etc.) I was still directly responsible only to the chancellor.

The new chancellor, Dr. Edgar A. Burnett, a University of Michigan graduate, for the past several years had been dean of the Agricultural College. I worked under him longer than under any other of the eight college and university presidents of my entire teaching career—11 years in all, his entire period as chancellor of the University of Nebraska, 1927-1938. He had to be sold on the values of physical education as a part of an educational curriculum. Apparently he had no brief against it although he apparently had none for it either. However, he accepted me with an attitude as if saying "I suppose we have to have physical education for women. Well, if so, I am glad to have you running it. I'll just leave you alone and let you chart your own course."

As Chancellor Avery before him, he gave me his support and I was happy about that. In him I found a man who was somewhat reticent, and with women, even shy, or at least ill at ease, as if unsure how to deal with them. Although he seemed to want to be enthusiastic about my department work, he gave me the impression that he didn't want to be bothered any more than was absolutely necessary. I missed Dr. Avery's enthusiasm and kindly concern about my work, yet felt that Chancellor Burnett was equally friendly and enthusiastic but not capable of being demonstrative. I was thankful that he was always kindly, courteous and considerate.

*　*　*　*

Before accepting the position at Nebraska, I had been assured that a new building exclusively for the women's gymnasium was to be erected "in the near future" if I would only come and make the plans for it. Shortly after my arrival, I found the Coliseum in the planning stage as a new facility for men's sports. When I inquired what that meant for the women I was informed that since the new buildings would house all men's athletics and physical education, and the various other organizations such as ROTC and the college paper, the women could in a couple of years have all of Grant Memorial Hall, both wings, to themselves. Therefore, the new women's gymnasium would have to wait a while longer.

59

For two years we suffered it out sharing Grant Memorial Hall with the Military Department, men's athletics, men's physical education, university band, student newspaper staff, university convocations, university luncheons and dinners, and university dances, trying at the same time to offer a good program of our own to the women students.

Acquiring all of Grant Memorial Hall in place of the promised new gymnasium did not seem altogether unreasonable since it would mean for our own exclusive use one large gymnasium floor, one smaller one, and considerable locker and dressing room and office space besides other odds and ends of spaces to convert into auxiliary classrooms for correctives, golf and other individual sports practice rooms. It meant at least triple office space and double shower and dressing room space over what the women had before. I saw great possibilities for expansion of department work even with the old building, and since considerable money went into its renovation we happily accepted it with the understanding that this was to be a temporary arrangement.

So large a building gave us a variety of exercise rooms, even though all awkwardly arranged and obviously makeshift. An old boiler room had been made into a physical examination room, an old storage closet into an office, an old shower room into a rest room, the football equipment room (which, with its north private entrance door, had been the girls' very own in the 1890s) into a study room for the majors, an old bowling alley into a dressing room, and similar strange adjustments throughout. We were "making do" quite well and happily, but we felt that this couldn't go on forever.

At last with Chancellor Burnett's blessing we worked on plans for a new building. But before I had plans far enough along to ask for a conference, the chancellor sent me word that he would like to discuss building plans with me. I was jubilant at this message and hastened to set an appointment, hoping that my request for one large gymnasium floor, one smaller all-purpose floor, a dance studio, a swimming pool, a correctives room, plus accompanying necessary dressing and shower rooms, several offices, a general departmental office, a lecture room and a study room for majors, to start on, would not be asking too much. Imagine my surprise when we met and the chancellor unrolled a set of blueprints, saying, "If you will give me your written endorsement of these to submit to the regents I believe we can get at this building right away. I find on a quick estimate it will not cost nearly as much as I feared you would feel that you need. I see our way to find funds for these plans at once."

As I walked over to the table to inspect the blueprints, filled with curiosity as to where they had come from, a queer sense of frustration

60

and defeat took possession of me. As I inspected them in alarmed silence and saw that they called for one basketball court with large space on both sides for spectators, a small swimming pool, also with space for spectators at the expense of the size of the pool, two or three offices, and small dressing and shower rooms, and nothing else, I could not speak for some moments for shock and astonishment. Sick at heart, I asked where he had procured these blueprints. To my amazement I learned that the faculty sportswoman from another department who on various occasions had taken an interest in our department had submitted these plans backed by a group of prominent women in the state. A letter accompanying the blueprints said the women "wished to restore to the university the days at the turn of the century when its women's basketball teams triumphed over high schools of the state and the neighboring universities."

The chancellor, thinking I had helped draw up the plans, was surprised when I informed him that the project was not only unknown to me but also that the plans were inadequate for current and future educational purposes.

"You won't endorse these plans, then?"

"Oh, no! I couldn't accept a new building as inadequate as this. We have much more space in Grant Memorial Hall now that it is all our own."

I explained to him our needs, insisting that any new building must take care of the physical education and recreational needs of all women students, not just those highly skilled in basketball and swimming.

"We can't meet such demands as yours as of now. You can have this building now or for the present give up your desire for a larger building. Which shall it be? Take it or leave it."

Without one moment's hesitation, I replied: "We will leave it and keep our dreams."

When word spread that I had rejected plans for a new women's gymnasium which would be built at once, I was accused not only on campus but also in the city and even in the state of "selling the university women down the river." In fact, this accusation was made even in St. Louis at a Saturday luncheon meeting of the American Association of University Women when the faculty woman who had presented the plans was the guest speaker. A close friend of mine, a member of AAUW, living in St. Louis was present at this luncheon. Blissfully unaware that a close friend of mine was in the audience, the speaker mentioned the new director of physical education for women at

Nebraska who was holding up progress. But she admonished her listeners not to worry because a committee of prominent women throughout the state was organized to get rid of me which they hoped soon to accomplish.

Although my St. Louis friend was greatly incensed at this, she let no one there know that she knew me. Instead she called me long distance that evening and reported the incident. The following Monday I reported to the chancellor about the state committee to get rid of me, and when this committee (for indeed there was one) later called on him to start their campaign for the sake of the women students, he gave them a cold shoulder and nothing more was heard of such a committee until many years later. It apparently was resurrected to influence a later chancellor about another matter concerning me. I was told that he, too, gave them an equally cold shoulder.

As to the building plans, these militant feminists, fighting for the best interests of a privileged group of women students over the best interests of the great mass of women students, had "beaten me to the draw." Although I was deeply interested in getting for all women students their just desserts and was in that respect a wholehearted women's rights exponent, these militants looked upon me as a reactionary whose struggles were to be discounted. I had to learn not to let such disapproval bother me unduly. The struggle between myself and this "influence peddling" group followed me to the end of my active career and even into my retirement years. This willful group of women wielded much influence not only on campus and city-wide but even statewide. In the years ahead I paid a bitter price for my views. Fighting against their usual behind-the-scene attacks it seems as if I stood alone. Fortunately the constant support and loyalty of the great number of women students as well as of the chancellor and many faculty members were compensation to weather these storms. I learned the hard way that there are many different facets to the struggle for women's rights. For what rights? For which women?

Later I learned that the year before I came to Nebraska, with women despairing of ever having their interests given a hearing, the noted sportswoman on the faculty had indeed organized a committee of prominent women in the city and state to push for a woman's gymnasium at the university. When this committee asked for a conference with Chancellor Avery he suggested that they draw up plans for the sort of building they felt was needed. The following year when I came to reorganize the department, he had assumed that this group had solicited my help. But such was not the case. It was not until my fourth year that this committee submitted its plans to Chancellor Burnett. These plans (I was told later) had been hastily drawn up when the group learned that my staff and I were at work on plans not including large space for spectators for girls' basketball.

Surprised that it was a member of another department, not I who had submitted the plans, he had sent for me to discuss the project. The chancellor stood by me and rejected the inadequate plans. My staff also stood back of me 100 percent on this decision to hold onto our dreams.

* * * *

If I was having trouble getting the men's physical director to enter the twentieth century along with the rest of us, others were also holding up progress that affected my department. The head of the Health Service, also wedded to the past, intensely disliked having anything brought to his attention that might interfere with his closing up shop at the regular hour. I was disturbing his routine by asking that more attention be given to medical examinations for our pupils. I was also against his ruling that no one but an M.D. render first aid to students. I had insisted on the right of my staff members who held American Red Cross First Aid Certificates to give first aid to pupils needing attention at hours when the Health Service was closed—which was always from mid-afternoon on and all day long on Saturdays, the very hours we had much activity in our department.

Following these irritations, and not knowing of Frederick Luehring's efforts of 1920, as related earlier, I began pressing for the university to establish an infirmary open at all times and staffed by full-time doctors and nurses. This was apparently the last straw for the head of the Health Service who exploded violently when I first broached the subject and ordered me out of his office, shouting:

"What do you think we are running here? In case you don't know, I will tell you that this is a university, not a hospital. You and your wild ideas!! Bah!"

The next hour following this outburst he met a physiology class for which several of our majors were registered. Apparently he was still irritated with me for he opened the class period with a tirade against me, naming me right out so all would know whom he was talking about.

"I have just had a very disturbing experience. That half-baked woman running the woman's gymnasium next door thinks we should have an infirmary here at the university. She should tend to her own speciality [here doing mock arm bendings and stretchings to the great amusement of the class] and leave such ideas outside her realm to those of us who have been educated to know about such things."

At this, one of the women physical education majors rose from her seat and started to walk out, followed by all the other women majors. Once clear of the lecture room, they ran to my office, bolting in upon a conference and exclaiming in one voice what the angry doctor had said. They were furious and rightfully so, for he had been rude and unethical, but I burst out laughing. To me his remarks were so ridiculous, I thought them funny. This calmed the girls. We then discussed the possibilities of an infirmary some day, and I pledged then and there to keep up the effort to get one. (Just for the record, it was to be many years before this dream came true—in fact, not until that director of the Health Service had retired and a young, energetic physician, Dr. Samuel Fuenning, took his place.)

Troubles, troubles, troubles! "Why did I come to Nebraska?" I asked myself day after day in my first few years there. The intransigence of a few I had to work with closely all but broke my spirit on several occasions. But then those wonderfully fine girls who needed my help and welcomed it so heartily would come to mind and I would have courage to carry on and fight to get things righted for them. Then, too, there was ever present the loyal support of the chancellor and his kindly interest in everything I did. To my great relief I received a friendly reception from the newspapers, except from an angry young photographer from some Omaha paper who called me a prude because I would not permit him to go into the girls' dressing room to take pictures of girls emerging from the showers either "towel-draped" or in "angel robes" as he "generously" said he would accept them.

However, our department reorganization plans got a good press for a statewide springboard to educate the taxpayers to the sort of a physical education department I hoped to build for them. On March 6 and 13, 1927, the Lincoln Sunday papers carried a half-page spread about our Women's Athletic Association program and the very next Sunday a full-page on our overall departmental program.

Once I was able to bring to my staff young teachers who were not only well trained but also interested in doing a good job, not afraid of hard work, willing to go "an extra mile" when necessary, personable and cooperative, things began looking up at once. The campus began taking notice and gradually gave us recognition as a worthy part of the university family.

The staff, year by year, increased in size so that in five years it had grown from 2 full-time and 5 part-time teachers to 10 on full-time. These teachers were graduates of Wellesley College, Beloit College, the

Universities of Minnesota and Wisconsin, Columbia University, Nils Bukh School of Gymnastics in Denmark, Central School of Physical Education, and the Boston School of Physical Education. At last we were turning out graduates of our own reorganized department and shortly I kept one or two for my own staff.

Bringing in these young people from other schools posed a problem for I soon sensed that as "outsiders" they were as socially ostracized as I was. So I did what I could to organize some social life for them on weekends. When I enlarged my project to include single men on the faculty who also were out of whatever social life there was, I was summoned to the office of the dean of women and informed that I was furnishing much amusement to the rest of the faculty with my "matrimonial bureau." I was furious! No one else on campus was doing anything for these young, unattached faculty members. Refusing to let this jibe deter me, I went ahead organizing Friday evening sports nights for the faculty singles. At the gymnasium they came together for dancing, volleyball, table tennis and badminton, and in the spring and fall, picnics. The fun they had was reward enough and sufficient antidote for having fun poked at me about it.

Although it had never been so in my other positions, grading became a major headache for me. Early on my arrival I was advised by the staff members I inherited that I should quickly learn which students were sorority members and to which group various ones belonged. "Why?" I asked in innocence, only to be informed that if poor grades were given to sorority girls we would have not only their local chapters but also their "alums" to deal with because all were constantly striving to get a good scholarship rating for their group. "What about the non-sorority girls?" I inquired, trying to keep a poker face. I was informed that since they had no one "to make it hot" for us if we gave them poor grades it didn't matter. I was told that a poor grade could be given occasionally to members of certain sororities but never to girls belonging to the four or five leading groups. As my chief informant said, the leading socialites of the community were "alums" of these groups and would stand for no nonsense from our department.

This was anathema to me and the first time in my life I had encountered it although there had been sororities at all three of my previous teaching positions. I immediately gave orders that we should lean over backwards not to know about students' sorority affiliations, that students should not be aware of our sorority affiliation, and that no girl was ever to get any grade but that which she had actually earned.

What a price I paid for that stand! But I stood firm and, although it took several years, I finally got the sororities and their alumnae and also the parents and some professors who kowtowed to the "correct" sororities, educated to the fact that we didn't "give" grades but instead the students "earned" them. In this educating process I received in my office many an irate "alum" and irate teachers from other departments and also prominent social leaders of the community who were used to having people bow to their whims. All of them berated me roundly for ruining a sorority's scholarship rating by poor grades which I permitted to go out of my office over my signature. I informed all groups that if their members wished good grades, they would have to earn them. Needless to say, I soon became persona non grata among certain sorority alumnae. I resisted all efforts to persuade me to change grades to fit into their plans and thereby gained a reputation for being stubborn when I was only standing for what seemed to me to be right and honest.

Not all these interviews ended in displeasure. A nationally-known author came to see me one day in dismay over the poor grade her daughter had received in a tennis class. "We aren't used to poor grades in our family," she said. But she wasn't accusing me of wrongdoing. She merely wanted an explanation of how we had arrived at the grade and to know if her daughter had been in error.

"My daughter tells me that she was never absent," she informed me.

"But just being present doesn't mean that she will get a good grade," I replied.

"What else is there to go on?"

"Her performance in class, her grades on the tests."

"You mean you give tests?"

"Certainly, just as other departments do!"

I sent for the daughter's records and was able to point out that despite faithful attendance she had not improved her tennis playing or even passed some tests in fundamental skills nor had she learned the rules of the game. The mother was surprised and delighted to learn that we had expected her daughter to learn something and to acquire some skills in her class just as in other departments. The interview ended on a friendly note, the daughter was to accept the grade without complaint and was to be informed that after this she had to "produce" in her physical education class if she wished a good grade. Thus one important citizen was educated about our educational philosophy on grading and became a friend of the department—indeed even of the head of the department for frequently after that we met for lunch together. Many other fine citizens, once we had a chance to explain, accepted our department's new philosophy with good grace, not asking special favors, but some social leaders in the community never did forgive me for not bowing to their requests to have poor grades within their sorority changed to good ones.

* * * *

In the twenties, as an aftermath of the Great War, various parts of the country were suffering attacks of Americanism of peculiar, even sinister forms, and Lincoln, Nebraska was one victim of this obsession. As late as the mid-twenties many main street stores carried in their windows placards with inscriptions such as: "We serve only real Americans here," or "America for Americans only," and the like. To add to the confusion, the Ku Klux Klan was riding high, waging secret war against Catholics. The instructor I brought to the university with me was Catholic, as was also one of the women students majoring in physical education. The very first Sunday after meeting the instructor, the student encountered her at services at the Cathedral. A club of Catholic university students was planning a dance just then and needed chaperones who were supposed to be faculty members, but the faculty was short on Catholics. The chaperones didn't have to be Catholics but the students complained that they could persuade no Protestants to chaperone for them. They were glad to discover that my new staff member was Catholic, and she accepted their invitation to chaperone, persuading me to attend with her. The local papers carried the news of the dance, naming the two of us as chaperones. Immediately it was assumed we were both Catholic.

This was about the time I asked the university purchasing agent to call for bids from various merchants in town with the idea of giving the order for women's gymnasium suits to the local firm that would offer the students the lowest price. When it became known which firm had made the lowest bid and would carry the new costume for the department, representatives of several main street firms called on me and the purchasing agent, putting on pressure to get us to split the order among all the firms although all had had a chance to make a bid. In the midst of this pressuring I was called upon by a professor (one who chanced to know that I was not a Catholic) who informed me that the chosen firm was owned by Catholics which had not been known to me, and if I did not want the Ku Klux Klan after me I had better not swing university business to that firm. That led me to stand firm on the first decision. Nothing in the world could make me switch for a reason like

67

that and the purchasing agent stood with me. This became one more count the Ku Klux Klan had against me.

Mary Wheeler, our new instructor, definitely known to be a Catholic, was under constant false attacks about her work, all made known to me in such a way that her real attackers always managed to keep hidden, and her religious affiliation was never even hinted at. I had been placed on the defensive about her from the very first report that she was attending Catholic services, but I had managed fairly well, so I thought, to keep my experiences in her behalf unknown to her.

After three years she left for an excellent position elsewhere so the attempts "to run her out of town," as I was once told the KKK intended, were no longer necessary. Now they could concentrate on me. Not even Mother escaped their machinations. She frequently received anonymous letters, even telephone calls, complaining about my work at the university. Thus I came to realize first-hand how members of minority groups are sometimes persecuted.

Dr. Burnett had just taken over the chancellorship in July 1927, and one October Saturday morning he called me to his office to tell me that I was being investigated by the chief of police because of complaints by some citizens and that the chief would be asking to see me shortly. The chancellor wanted me to be forewarned and also to know that he had confidence in me and was standing behind me. I asked what the charges were and he said they were too ridiculous for him to even discuss. I would get it all directly from the chief. He felt sure I could answer the charges but I should know that apparently I had acquired serious enemies in the short time I had been there, and he was concerned in my behalf.

"What is back of it all, I simply don't know, and I do not like it," he said as he dismissed me.

I didn't have long to wait. Within the hour the chief called for a conference. Shortly after the lunch hour he appeared at my office. I was glad that it was Saturday afternoon when I was alone in the building. However, I felt deep concern for I couldn't think of anything anyone could honestly complain about to the police and therefore it had to be some trumped-up charges, and this seemed sinister. And sinister it turned out to be. I had been reported as taking photographs of women students in the nude and selling them to young men on the campus. I was too stunned to say anything until I suddenly thought of the silhouet-tograph machine I had introduced into the department for our posture work. I explained this to him and showed him a few of the shadow-graphs of body outlines on sensitized paper—not photographs at all such as I would have liked but could not afford. He inspected the file drawers where these were kept and noted that they were kept in drawers with locks and in a cabinet in an inner private office with a lock. These bore no names, merely code numbers for protection from inquisitive ones. Some "before" and "after" silhouettographs showed marked improvement in posture after class work, and he became interested in our posture program. He was a real convert to what we were trying to do for the women students. Seeing that it was impossible to make copies of these silhouettographs, he assured me he was on a fool's errand and he was very apologetic. All the time my mind was in a whirl of questioning—why this trumped-up attack on me? And by whom?

I had shortly before learned from Catholic friends that there were people on campus who offered to bet that I was a Catholic and they could find no takers, so sure were all others that I was. This had merely amused me at the time as trivia, but now I decided this police investigation must be stemming from the Ku Klux Klan. I asked the chief the names of those complaining against me. Before he could answer I added, "I wish my father were still alive. He and his Masonic friends would come to my defense against this evil thing."

"You mean that your father was a Mason?" the Chief replied in astonishment.

"Yes, I am the daughter of a Mason."

At that he slapped his hands vehemently on the arms of his chair and jumping up, exclaimed "Wait until I take this news back to those complaining against you. This will shut them up!"

He asked if he might take a sample shadowgraph to show to one person in particular. As he bade me goodbye I felt sure I had one more friend in Lincoln, one who gave me the impression that he would cheerfully have pitched into those who had sent him on this foolish errand. He apparently wasted no time for the following Tuesday he returned the shadowgraph with a statement, "I wish to state that it has served its purpose. The rumor has quieted down."

Almost immediately after this I was told by a faculty woman that it was rumored that the local chapter of the Ku Klux Klan had drawn up a list of persons it felt it should run out of town but after some police investigations they were revising it. And seemingly casually she added:

"I hear you are a Presbyterian."

"Yes, I am," I said

"Well, why didn't you let people know that when you first came?" she asked with a bit of a note of irritation in her voice.

"Why should I?" I countered, surprised at the question.

"Oh, I guess there is no real reason," and the subject was dropped. At the time this conversation puzzled me.

From then on, other faculty members became friendly, as if sensing that perhaps I needed a friend or perhaps to my great disgust, because they had gotten the news about my not being a Catholic. Although this police investigation had cleared me of some sinister charge and incidentally opened a friendly door at the police station, it had been an unpleasant and disturbing experience.

Later on the department could afford an actual camera for our posture work. Students, pleased over their improvement, begged me to let them have copies of the photographs to show to their parents, but remembering the earlier charge, I went to the chief of police for advice about it. He sent me to the postmaster. This dignitary assured me that an enemy wishing to make trouble for me could accuse me of giving a student "obscene" material to send through the mail even though the photographs were taken of girls in bathing suits. He asked to see sample photographs and when I returned with them he decided that it would be best if I posted the photographs for the students from my University office, and to protect me he would have on file in his office a permit signed by him for me to send such material through the mail. Thus alerted I got the necessary protection and through the years many a set of parents throughout Nebraska and neighboring states saw the potentially "obscene" literature and rejoiced over this proof of their daughter's improvement and wrote me grateful notes.

Immediately after the chief of police informed me that the case against me had died out, I called on him and asked if I might have the name of one of the persons who had first made the charge against me. He said that it was a student at the university and her parents whose names he did not have but he gave me the name and address of a person he thought might be helpful. When I called on this person at his downtown office he received me courteously and after consultation with persons in another room gave me a name and address of the person who made the original charge. It turned out to be both a fictitious name and a fictitious address. I let the matter rest since it seemed useless to pursue it further.

* * * *

By then I was caught up in turmoil with a student with whom the whole department, it seemed, had been in conflict all of the previous year. She made unreasonable demands and refused to attend classes

70

and then was violently angry at us for reporting her failing in her work. Only five days after the police chief had told me the charges against me had died out, I was confronted by this girl's father. He informed me that because of my refusal to give his daughter a permanent excuse from taking physical education, although there was no legitimate reason for granting such a request, he was retaining two lawyers to sue me.

Since the earlier confrontation came through a student and her parents I wondered if this could be the same people picking up in this way to harass me as the other try failed. If they were one and the same group, did the KKK refuse to go along with them any further? I never knew the answers to these questions. But I felt it quite possible that they were one and the same and now the parents were determined to proceed on their own, no longer being able to hide behind the skirts of the KKK.

At any rate I was alarmed enough to take this threat to Dean Foster of the Law College. He laughed and advised me to ignore it. "Do nothing," he said. "They haven't a leg to stand on and they know it. The father is trying to scare you into giving in to his demands."

Six days later Dean of Student Affairs Theos Thompson told me some man, naming the very man who threatened to sue me, had been in his office complaining about me. He advised me to call on the girl's physician to determine if there might be an emotional situation we should know about to determine future action. When I saw her physician three days later, he declared that there was no reason why the student should not profit from taking physical education, in fact she seriously needed to get into some team sport and learn how to "give and take" with others. This I reported to Dean Thompson. Nine days later the dean called me to his office for a confrontation with the father who was in his office making serious charges against me. The dean had insisted that he repeat them in my presence with himself as witness. I dashed to the dean's office. The father immediately became so abusive and threatening toward me that the dean rose and went to my chair to stand by me in a protecting manner and ordered the father from his office until he could behave like a gentleman. Following this I received such abusive anonymous telephone calls which I laid to this man's door, that when I informed Dean Thompson of them he went with me at once to Dean Foster's office to report them to him. The dean said to stand firm and the father would surely soon tire of it all seeing that he could not intimidate us.

Now the harassments increased and the father sent word to me that he was going ahead with his suit against me. At this, Dean Foster decided it was time the chancellor be informed—the chancellor said to stand firm. As harassments increased still more the chancellor decided the regents should be informed of the trouble. They said to stand firm, especially so since Dean Foster reported that ever since 1891 when the rule was set up by the regents requiring every woman student to take physical education three hours per week for the first two years in residence, the ruling had not been challenged in the courts and there would never be an easier case to win than this one. So Dean Foster then sent for the father whom he informed in my presence that since I was acting as an agent for the university he could not sue me personally but would have to sue the university if he wished to pursue the matter. The father again became abusive and threatening toward me. Finally he shouted,

"Don't think for one moment we haven't been investigating you," and he concluded, "I will give you until midnight next Saturday to give my daughter a permanent reprieve or the Sunday morning papers will be out with big headlines giving the full story of your shady past." Turning to Dean Foster, he added, "I'll be suing the university." He than stalked out angrily. I was too stunned for words and was by then on my feet. Dean Foster immediately stepped up to me and placing a kindly hand on my shoulder looked me intently in the eye:

"My dear, is there anything at all in your past that he might have found out that you wouldn't want known?"

I sensed at once that he had to ask that question and I answered:

"Absolutely nothing! Anything that he gives the papers of any shady past of mine will have to be lies."

"Well, then, you'll not give in to him?"

"Certainly not!"

"We couldn't have an easier case to win. I hope he does go ahead and sue," the dean added jubilantly.

Later the dean, worrying in my behalf, realizing that even lies about some imaginary past of mine could be hard for me and even the university to live down once they were out in headlines in the newspapers, went to the chancellor to ask what he thought we should do.

"It's pure blackmail," the chancellor said. I hope Miss Lee is willing to stand by her decision to fight."

And he called me in. "Yes, let's fight," I said. Then the chancellor got to worrying about what the regents might say. They, too, hoped I'd be willing to go on with it. Again I said, "Let's fight."

Then one regent became concerned about how lies in the newspapers about me might affect my mother, and they asked me to discuss it with her. I had thus far kept word of this unpleasantry from her. As I told the story to Mother, I noticed her spine stiffening and I said, "What do you think I should do, Mother?"

"What would your Father say if he were here?" she asked.

"He would say 'fight.' He would never give in to blackmail."

"Indeed not!" Mother said. "And I, too, want you to fight."

And so it was. We refused to give in. We had one last conference with the father during which the dean warned him that if he gave one untruth about me to the newspapers the university, for whom I was acting as an agent, would sue him for libel. That Saturday night, Dean Foster called me at bedtime, wishing me a good night's sleep and begging me not to worry over what might appear in the Sunday morning paper. As he said,

"Just remember you have the 100 percent backing of the chancellor and regents."

But it was a long, wakeful, worrisome night for both Mother and me. Morning came with no headlines of my "flaming" past, and Dean Foster called me early, exclaiming:

"I was never so disappointed! I thought that at last I was going to find out all about your unsavory past, and I find nothing in the paper." And with another chuckle he added, "From now on, watch your step."

The angry father had backed down completely when we called his bluff. But we lost the chance to try out in court the regents' rule requiring physical education for all women students.

As the years passed by, the university was threatened several other times with lawsuits because of various exigencies connected with departmental work and always the dean rose to the occasion, as if he were mounting a white charger, lance in hand, to defend some maiden threatened in her castellated tower. Grant Memorial Hall did have castellated towers of sorts to make such fantasy seem a bit real. Dean Foster always took keen delight in these threatened legal skirmishes as if to say, "Now we are living!" And if perchance I hadn't been over to seek his advice and help for quite some time, when he would meet me on the campus he would break into a broad grin with merry wrinkles about his eyes and in mock seriousness would exclaim:

"What, no troubles! Surely you haven't been behaving yourself!" He was such a joy to work with. This was the end of such harassments.

Chapter IV

The Turbulent Twenties and Professional Concerns

If the times brought turbulence in my work at Nebraska, they also brought rumblings of change within the various organizations of my profession. Men were not only pitted against other men in argument over curricula, philosophies and principles of physical education, but women, encouraged by the 1920 victory of equal suffrage, were beginning to press for greater attention to their needs and rights for physical education and for a place in the sun in professional organizations.

The Women's Division of the National Amateur Athletic Federation, founded by Mrs. Herbert Hoover in 1923, was rapidly extending its influence throughout the country. In several states where interschool sports for girls were running wild under promotion by men coaches, other groups of men (high school principals, school superintendents and men physical educators) were giving increased support to the Women's Division, urging that correct sports programs advocated by the women be supported to replace the unfavorable type of sport. But the men promoters of girls' sports were not giving up without a fight. They accused us women of trying to ban all competitive sports for girls. Nothing was further from the truth. We were fighting to correct abuses and to abolish only the wrong kind of sports.

For the 1925 Women's Division spring convention in Chicago, Mrs. Hoover invited me to be one of the speakers at the opening session.

This was the first time I met that very interesting woman. I was now drawn into the inner work of this group, which was to concern me deeply for the next 15 years.

At the 1925 meeting of the Women's Division it was reported that my own survey of the women's intercollegiate athletics situation, published in two periodicals in 1924 and in reprints sent all over the country by the Women's Division, had led several colleges to give up their intercollegiate contests in favor of Play Days. So the Women's Division standards were making an impact.

* * * *

In my last year of teaching at Coe College in 1917–1918, I had become interested in the one-year-old organization, the Middle West Society of Directors of Physical Education, for College Women and had joined in its second year of existence.[1] This interest I had carried on while at Beloit College, when similar eastern and western groups had joined with the Middle West Society to create the national organization in 1924. In the spring of my first year at Nebraska I was elected president of the middle west group, following the presidencies of J. Anna Norris of the University of Minnesota, Blanche M. Trilling of the University of Wisconsin, Louise Freer of the University of Illinois, and Lydia Clark of Ohio State University. Lydia Clark was president when the national organization was born in Kansas City in 1924. Because of the peculiar arrangement for selection of officers, she automatically became the first national president. This arrangement was that whenever the national group held its annual meeting in a given territory, whoever was president of the host district group automatically became the national president. In other words, this national group (NAPECW) at first was not an entity in itself but a federation of these three district groups. When the second annual meeting was held in the East, Alice Belding of Vassar College, as president of the Eastern Society, became NAPECW's second national president to carry on until the site of the next national meeting was chosen. When the group accepted the invitation of Elizabeth Halsey, who had recently become director of physical education for women at the University of Iowa, to meet at Iowa City in 1927, I, being the middle west president, automatically became the third national president.

When word of this national presidency for me reached Lincoln, the university administrators were most generous in their congratulations. The student paper carried a headline and article about it, the local paper had a writeup, and the Lincoln branch of the American Association of University Women (AAUW) sent me special congratulations. With such felicitations I entered what was destined to become over 50 years of service to my profession on the national level.

In a way, I felt uncomfortable about this NAPECW presidency for I had not been elected on a national vote. Thus, at that early date I came to feel that this rule was ridiculous and embarrassing to the office holder. I resolved that if in my presidency we did not get any other thing accomplished, we would change this rule, and after long discussions in Iowa City we did just that, calling for a vote for officers nationwide. Other changes in the constitution set this new national group on the path to become completely a national entity on its own— not just a federation of district groups. (It was we midwest directors who held out the longest but finally a few years later swung into line to change from a directors' organization to one open to all women college teachers of physical education.)

Thirty years later, the historian of the Mid West Association of Physical Education for College Women, in writing about this conference at Iowa City, failed to do her research in depth and, before rushing into publication, did not submit the material to us older ones still on the scene, especially to me who was president of both the midwest and the national group at the time. I could have given her the full story of that three-day conference from my thick folder of records and from the many pages in my diary. Instead the final, supposedly accurate historical material referred to the conference as merely a one-day affair:

> On April 12, 1927, the Mid West Directors' Society held its 10th Annual meeting at Iowa City on the day preceding the Des Moines meetings of the Mid West Physical Education Association and in some form of conjunction with the National Directors Society. This was at the conclusion of the first decade, and this would have been a good time for taking stock but apparently in the hustle of scurrying off to Des Moines, no such idea occurred to the governing board. Meetings were held over the luncheon table and at other odd moments and nothing of much consequence appears in the minutes.[2]

To put the record straight as against this official but inaccurate report, it was a three-day meeting, and the meeting in Des Moines was a meeting of the American Physical Education Association (APEA) not a midwest one, and the Iowa City gathering was indeed in some conjunction with the national directors' society, for we of the middle west were playing host to the national group for the first time to put on a program. We thus had voted to give up our own regional affairs and concerns in the interest of the national group. Therefore with much of consequence of a national order on the agenda, the middle west governing board, which then was also the national board, took up only the bare necessities of its own business, working its meetings around those of the national board. And whatever "scurrying" took place to get off to APEA convention in Des Moines must have been quite subdued since the train we took to Des Moines did not leave for almost 24 hours after our last midwest business meeting. So much for accuracy of some historical research!

We spent much time changing the national constitution. For one thing, we agreed that it was important to elect our national officers without regard to where the conferences were held. The original rule was an outgrowth of an era when people, especially women, didn't dash all over the country attending conventions as Americans soon came to do. At that time, to ensure that the national officers would be present at a conference, it seemed necessary to have them located in the area of the conference. But within three years, with the sudden increased use of automobiles by women traveling alone, we saw that we could change this policy. After much discussion and prodding, especially from Lydia Clark, Alice Belding and myself who had experienced firsthand the original type of organization, we elected the officers on a national basis with the district groups to be affiliated and the presidents of each district to sit on the national board to assure coordination.

For the record, this 1927 meeting at the University of Iowa was held immediately preceding the larger APEA convention in Des Moines so that NAPECW members could participate in both conventions in the one trip to the Middle West. At the NAPECW founding meeting in Kansas City in April 1924, 17 directors of physical education for women from throughout the country attended; at the next meeting at Vassar College, 32 attended; and at the 1927 conference in Iowa, 76 were registered. It was a growing organization from the very start, and this first three-day meeting was an ambitious, serious affair, thanks to our hostess and program chairman, Elizabeth Halsey.

Taking part in the program was a distinguished group of educators from the University of Iowa as the main speakers, including Dean Seashore, a well-known psychologist; Dr. Bird Baldwin, director of the Child Welfare Research Station; Dr. Arthur Steindler, director of the University Orthopedic Hospital; and Dr. Fritz Miller, a gynecologist. These last two talked on posture training from the specialist's view.

Considering that only nine years before, the midwest group had met for one day only and in a bedroom of a roominghouse at the University of Michigan with seven physical directors from six states, it was a big step forward to meet for a three-day program with 76 physical directors from across the United States. I soon discovered that a national presidency brought problems and annoyances. Immediately following the convention, newspapers across the country carried a *United News* syndicated article—a purported interview with me as president of the National College Women's Directors Society of Physical Education, as many called it. My first knowledge of the purported interview came from a San Antonio, Texas paper, but clippings from all parts of the country later were sent to me. In this so-called interview I was reported as having said:

> Because the modern college girl takes prescribed courses in physical education, she is better looking than her mother .... She actually trains for beauty .... We must not allow [men] to exploit American womanhood, Miss Lee declared with an emphatic crack of her athletic fist on her desk.

> Hockey has become the most popular outdoor sport for women, Miss Lee said, predicting that co-ed hockey games between universities would come into vogue within five years.

Utter nonsense! I never made such a silly statement as that first one to anyone and I was never guilty of cracking a fist (athletic or not) on any desk as I talked and never in my wildest frame of mind would I have uttered such a statement about co-ed intercollegiate hockey. This initiation into syndicated newspaper reporting was very embarrassing but nothing to what I was to suffer in later years at the hands of other untrustworthy reporters. But for this first time I was utterly amazed, particularly so because I had not been interviewed by a single soul.

* * * *

At last I was becoming acquainted with both men and women workers in my profession. In the early 1920s we college women directors were a small, closely-knit group content just to attend women's gatherings and talk only with one another about our teaching problems. However, I had attended my first convention of the Middle West Society of Physical Education in 1918 in Detroit, and again in 1923 in Chicago where I made my first speech before a mixed group on intercollegiate athletics for women. I had served as chairman of the College Women's Section of that organization for the convention of

78

1926 in Minneapolis, thus attending the next meeting of the council as representative of that section. But I had become acquainted with none of the men in that one opportunity. Now at the APEA convention in Des Moines (my first such convention), I was getting acquainted with a few men in our profession. C. H. McCloy, recently returned from many years in China and now at the University of Iowa, I met for the first time.

Another outgrowth of the NAPECW presidency was the invitation from the International Race Betterment Association to be one of the speakers at its Third Conference, January 2-6, 1928, to be held in Battle Creek, Michigan. There were 87 speakers in all—78 men and 9 women—called upon from every imaginable discipline in the world that had anything to offer toward race betterment. They were from several European countries, Japan, Russia, Mexico, and the U.S. I was asked to represent the field of physical education and athletics for women. Amos Alonzo Stagg of the University of Chicago represented physical education for men, and Fielding Yost, then coach at the University of Michigan, men's athletics. We three carried the ball for our profession. I had met Coach Stagg a few years earlier at a Women's Division-NAAF banquet in Chicago.[3]

It was a heady experience to eat three meals a day at the Battle Creek Sanitorium with these visitors from all over the world—the 87 of us guests of Dr. John Harvey Kellogg at his Sanitorium. Coaches Stagg and Yost, both old enough to be my father, fell into the habit of saving a seat for me at their table at mealtime. They carried on much teasing at my expense, labeling me, to my great amusement, "Miss Nebraska," a title which stuck all the years to follow whenever our paths crossed.

On one memorable evening when Henry Ford entertained the conference at an evening of square dancing, I was fortunate to do the first dance in a square with him and Mrs. Ford, my partner being Irving Fisher, the famous economics professor of Yale. At Mr. Ford's urging, Professor Fisher had joined in but protested that he had not square-danced since his youth. I happened to be nearby and turning to me he asked if I knew square dances. When I said that I too had square-danced a lot in my youth but not at all of late years, he asked if I would be his partner and pilot him as safely as possible through the steps. Henry Ford and his wife were letter perfect. Dr. Fisher and I got lost in the steps now and then but we managed to recover with Mr. Ford helping me and Mrs. Ford swinging Dr. Fisher into line. I have never forgotten their patience with us.

* * * *

79

When I learned that Jesse Williams, M.D., of Columbia University was to be the guest speaker at the 1928 Middle West convention in Detroit, I determined I must go if for no other reason than to hear firsthand the profession's "firebrand" from the East. He was becoming the recognized leader of the progressive education group within the profession of physical education. At the same time Carl Schrader, Massachusetts State Director of Physical Education, and Charles H. McCloy of the University of Iowa were coming to the front as the leaders within our profession to hold the line for "effort" and disciplined education.

Jesse Williams was born the same year as I, as was C. H. McCloy. In his mid-thirties he received national attention in our profession through his book, *Organization and Administration of Physical Education*, published in 1922. Dr. James Huff McCurdy, editor of the *American Physical Education Review*, reviewed the book in the February 1923 issue of this magazine, saying in part:

> The author seems unduly critical of the older methods [of gymnastics] and assumes that the older methods still in use are used from choice, when, in many cases, the more formal types of work are used more largely because of lack of adequate equipment for any other type of work .... The book summarizes and arranges much of the best material which has appeared in the *American Physical Education Review* and other magazines during recent years, as well as giving a definite contribution from the author on the subject of administration of physical education.

This review elicited a scathing letter from Dr. Williams to the editor in which he attacked persons who would write a critical review without signing it and demanded that his letter be published in the *Review*'s next issue. The editor complied and in a note following the Williams' letter claimed the critical review as his own, saying it was not the custom to have a name signed to a book review unless it was written by someone other than the editor. Then in the same March issue (pp. 118–122), the editor published a statement from J. F. Williams:

> It is not customary to read in the *Review* comment on articles that appear therein. I know of no valid reason why a professional journal, such as ours, should not only print but even stimulate correspondence concerning questions presented by the papers published.

Then Dr. Williams went on to say he wished to raise some questions about an article by Mr. C. L. Brewer of Detroit in the December 1922 *Review*, entitled "The American System of Physical Education." Then he attacked Mr. Brewer's defense for formal work on the basis of "thoroughness, discipline, mental and physical alertness, and correct bodily growth." Following that article was a letter signed by both the president and secretary of the North American Gymnastics Union, protesting Dr. Williams' slighting remarks in his recent book to the effect that "many instructors of the Turnverein type do not have even a high school education."

> What we protest against is the slur contained in the words quoted. We think that this is entirely uncalled for and we point with perhaps pardonable pride to the many men who have come from the Turner Associations and who are now holding a high rank in America among educators in all lines.[4]

Battle lines were definitely being drawn publicly through the pages of the *Review* and from the sidelines I watched with much interest the clash between proponents of the old forms of gymnastics and the bold challengers of the twenties.

Then at the national convention in Springfield, Massachusetts in the spring of 1923, Dr. Williams made remarks in a speech before the Public School Section which angered many people. He belittled physical education teachers' long practice of using breathing exercises in their day's order of exercises, presenting physiological support that breathing exercises, as such, are not necessary, and he attacked formal gymnastics of all varieties.

> There can be no such thing as German truth, or Swedish truth, or Danish truth, or American truth! There is truth! Scientifically determined truth![5]

But he seemed unwilling to admit that perhaps some German, some Swede, some Dane might discover a truth which some American could accept.

William Stecher of the Philadelphia public schools, in particular, had been so angered by this speech before the Public School Section that he replied to it in the same issue of the *Review*,[6] saying that hundreds of thousands go gladly to gymnasiums all over the country to do formal gymnastics and like it. As he said, they go voluntarily and pay for the privilege, and do not hate the formal work as J. F. Williams says they do. Stecher said, "Some people like cherry pie while others would rather eat caviar." In that article he also attacked Dr. Williams' upholding of psychologists who speak for interest versus effort, saying:

> In growing children, "effort" as well as "interest" is needed— yes, I am not afraid to say that in education it sometimes is wise to demand effort even when interest appears to be lacking. Life after all isn't all fragrance and moonbeams, and at times a fair dose of wise compulsion is beneficial . . .

It isn't the type of work but the type of teacher .... that determines the result.

At this time Dr. Williams was chairman of a subcommittee of the Committee of the Children's Bureau of the U.S. Department of Labor set up to study "intensively the problem of physical fitness and physical vigor of children."[7] He also headed a subcommittee of this overall committee to work on functional tests. With such important recognition in his early years, he was probably beginning to "feel his oats." He was also showing a propensity to take concepts of others and, mounting a platform which the originators of the concepts seemed hesitant to do, would declare these concepts to the world. He pronounced them over and over again and quickly rushed into print through speeches and books proclaiming them still more insistently so that soon he was accepted by many in the profession as the apostle of the new creeds. Thus ideas advanced by him were accepted by his fervent followers as his, although they were apt to be the original ideas of Thomas D. Wood and Clark Hetherington.

In June 1922 I had first met Clark Hetherington, early pupil of Thomas D. Wood, and with a large group of women physical educators had sat at his feet and listened to his firsthand report of these new ideas of physical education for America. So I was not one who was hailing Jesse Williams as the true "John the Baptist, crying in the wilderness." Yet because of the controversial material involving him in the *Review*, I was curious to hear him. I found him a dynamic speaker.

Up to then Thomas D. Wood, in an effort to bring physical education into line with John Dewey's philosophy, had quietly been advocating the use of "natural gymnastics," as he called them, in place of the old-world German and Swedish forms. In 1927 Jesse Williams had replaced Dr. Wood on the Columbia University faculty as head of physical education when Dr. Wood took over there as professor of health education. Whereas Wood had quietly stressed the positive, not so much attacking the old formalism as advancing a new idea to replace the old, Williams immediately mounted an out-and-out war against the old forms of gymnastics in particular, offending deeply all who had ever championed the old, and they were legion throughout the country.

The battle between the two sides raged for many years in all facets of education. The extremists of progressive education got the upper hand and finally succeeded in deleting discipline and effort from education to bring us to the undisciplined, effortless form of society of later decades from which we now are struggling to extricate ourselves. How little we sensed in the late roaring twenties to what extremes this philosophy, if not checked, would lead us.

82

We middle-roaders who wished to break with the extreme formalism of gymnastics of former years, gladly embraced this challenge but were frowned upon by those who rushed to climb on the bandwagon of the Progressives, who regarded us as obstructionists and devotees of horse-and-buggy days. (Now that the automobile was taking over in our national life, this derogatory term was coming into vogue.)

In his 1928 speech delivered with dramatic flair, Jesse Williams held up to scorn all forms of physical education which involved drill or directions imposed from without, demanding that children be freed of the drillmaster. As I gathered from his speech he would throw out the window not only all formal activities but also the teacher, leaving the children to grope for themselves to find ways satisfying to themselves to partake of physical activities. Following his speech a storm of protest went up from the floor and from then on at all informal gatherings throughout the rest of the convention, delegates argued the subject. Most declared that not all children have ability to do creative thinking and that with this permissive method most children in any group will become mere onlookers as the few exercise. As someone said: "Selfish children will dominate and become more selfish and timid children will withdraw and be inactive."

At this convention, President Clarence C. Little of the University of Michigan was a guest speaker, using the topic "Extra-Mural Athletic Competition for Women and Girls." He was critical of the role college girls were playing in the world of men's intercollegiate athletics, as he said:

> ... yelling their heads off over men's games, wasting their time and energy following men's teams, and making fools of themselves over men athletes.

This struck a responsive chord in me who had so recently gone through unpleasant experiences of trying to chaperone "football specials" (quite a tale for another day). But neither I nor any of the other women agreed with his proposed solution to this unsatisfactory situation—to organize for the women their own intercollegiate games to follow and get excited about.

How little he knew the schoolgirls of the 1920s. The very girls who were "making fools of themselves over men athletes" and "wasting their time and energy following men's teams" were the very last girls who, if offered intercollegiate games of their own, would ever come out for them. Needless to say, however, he aroused much controversy and enlivened the convention meetings. But we women refused to take him seriously.

* * * *

Not being a member of the Council of the Middle West Society of Physical Education, I knew nothing of what transpired at its 1928 spring business meeting. In fact I left the convention before the council meeting was held and was not present at the closing session when the newly elected officers were announced. I also missed the announcement that the Middle West Council had voted to publish a monthly magazine, *The Pentathlon*, with Professor Elmer D. Mitchell of the University of Michigan as editor. The first issue was to be off press in October and sent to all midwesterners registered at the convention.

Having spent the summer of 1928 touring Europe with three friends (we did some bicycling in England and climbed Mt. Snowden in Wales), I had no occasion to encounter professional friends who might have enlightened me about the closing events in Detroit in May. However, one October day I received my copy of Vol. 1, No. 1 of *The Pentathlon*. Since I had heard not even a rumor that there was to be a new magazine, it came as a great surprise. On first glance, I saw at the bottom of the cover the words, "Journal of THE MIDDLE WEST SOCIETY OF PHYSICAL EDUCATION published at Ann Arbor, Michigan." "How interesting!" I thought, and turned to page 1 where, to my great surprise, my own name jumped out at me. I blinked and looked again. There it was unmistakably in the list of Middle West officers for 1928–1929:

President—L. M. Post, Detroit
Vice-president—Mabel Lee, University of Nebraska
Secretary-Editor—E. D. Mitchell, University of Michigan
Retiring President—E. C. Delaporte, Chicago

How could they have made such a mistake? What woman's name belonged there in place of mine? I hoped she wouldn't be angry! Of course it was a woman, vice-presidents almost always were women!

Almost immediately the October issue of *The American Physical Education Review* arrived. It, too, listed my name as an officer. I then wrote the Middle West president, Loren Post of Detroit, calling his attention to the error. A few days later, James E. Rogers of the Playground and Recreation Association of America came to Lincoln and his first question was, "What plans are being made for the midwest convention next spring?" (He spoke of it as midwest, a shortened version that was shortly to replace the older designation.) When I said I knew nothing of any plans, he was surprised and said, "Why, you are the vice-president" and I said, "Oh! that is an error in *The Pentathlon*!" But Mr. Rogers said it was not an error for he had sat in on the council meeting in Detroit in May and was present when I was elected. In fact, when they were hunting for some woman to put up for vice president, someone said it was time they nominated someone from west of the Mississippi River or better still even farther west and that he, himself, had suggested my name and they accepted it. So it was no mistake!

It was almost two months later before President Post replied to my letter, informing me that the listing was no error and that he had his committees set up for the year and plans for convention were underway so there was nothing for me to do. Should anything arise which he felt I should do or should know about he would contact me. It was obvious that the vice-president of the Middle West was not considered even a member of the executive committee. All plans were made and I had not heard anything. He did not even let me know what city was being considered for the 1929 convention or the dates for it.

I decided not to let it bother me. But why did they have a vice-president if there was nothing to do? Then there came to mind the thought that a vice president would be needed in case the president should be compelled for some reason to be absent. What a thought! To have to take over as president and not know one thing about any inner workings of the organization and without being permitted to know about the president's aspirations or plans for the organization. I dismissed the whole thing from mind the best I could, embarrassed to hold such a queer office.

This first issue of *The Pentathlon* proclaimed that it was not born to challenge or compete with other periodicals. However, many in the Midwest and some in the East, too, hoped it would compete with and challenge the *Review* if for no other reason than to wake it up. To start this magazine had not been a fly-by-night decision. In 1926 when Margaret McKee of the Des Moines public schools was president of the Middle West Society she had appointed an editorial board to carry out the council's wish to study the possibility of establishing an official midwest periodical. Dr. J. Anna Norris of the University of Minnesota was chairman of this board, with Elizabeth Halsey of the University of Iowa, W. P. Bowen of Ypsilanti Normal School, E. W. Everts, Minnesota State Director of Physical Education, and Floyd Rowe, then of Cleveland public schools, as her board members. *The Pentathlon* was the result of this board's initial efforts.

The magazine was a success from the first issue. It was the sort of thing so many midwesterners had hoped the *Review* would become. It carried many illustrations and eye-catching advertisements. It also had photographs of the authors of the leading articles. The first article in the first issue was J. F. Williams' controversial address at the Middle West convention the preceding spring.

* * * *

At the last meeting of the American Physical Education Association Council in Baltimore in connection with the spring 1928 national convention, there had been 22 members, 21 men and one woman, Florence Somers, representing the Women's Athletic Committee which was then generally spoken of as the Women's Athletics Section, although unofficially so. Of the members, 17 were easterners, 2 midwesterners, and 1 each from the West Coast, the South and Canada. It was glaring proof that the rising charges of women were true that APEA was merely an eastern organization catering almost exclusively to men. A small group of APEA leaders were determined to change this situation.

One thing decided was to invite a large number of women, who would be likely to be in New York City at the next Christmas holiday to attend the Women's Division of NAAF meetings, to come a day or so earlier and lunch with the APEA Council as an advisory group to suggest ways of increasing women's participation in the Association's governing affairs.

On January 2, I went to New York City to attend the meetings of the Women's Division of NAAF. I had been invited to share the platform for one session with Dr. Lillian Gilbreth, the much talked of woman in the engineering profession who was greatly interested in the work of the Women's Division, and with Mrs. Henry Breckenridge, wife of the president of the National Amateur Athletic Federation. I had been assigned the topic, "Sports—An Educational Dynamic Force," and was apprehensive about my part of the program.

This was the fifth year the Women's Division had put on a winter conference in New York City during the Christmas holidays in order to gain the much-valued attention to their work from the leading men of the profession. As in years past, the men were in New York City at this time of year attending the annual meetings of the Football Coaches Association, the Council of APEA which through the years had been largely a men's group, and the College Physical Education Association which, born in 1897 under the leadership of Edward Hitchcock of Amherst, was recognized as that day's top group of men leaders in physical education.

No sooner had I arrived at the Pennsylvania Hotel in New York City (in those days, a glamorous hotel and the most popular conference site in that city for educational groups) than I was discovered by Edith Gates, Marjorie Bouvé and Florence Somers, who had attended the APEA New Year's Day luncheon put on by the Council of APEA at the

86

City Club. They took me to task over the troubles the Middle West group was supposedly making for the American Physical Education Association.

I had heard rumors that the APEA luncheon had made a grand gesture toward the ladies and was curious to know who had been present. As gossip reported the event, a group of leading men in our profession had drawn up a list of the 12 leading women of the physical education profession as of 1928 who would probably be in New York City. As a matter of passing interest, the list was as follows: Marjorie Bouvé, Ethel Bowers, Edith Gates, Mary Gross, Germaine Guiot, Signe Hagelthorn, Marguerite Hussey, Helen McKinstry, Ethel Perrin, Mazie Scanlon, Florence Somers, and Agnes Wayman. Lydia Clark, Alice Belding and I—the first three women to hold the presidency of the National Association of Physical Education for College Women—as well as Blanche Trilling, J. Anna Norris and Mary C. Coleman were all in New York City to attend the Women's Division meetings but none of us had been invited. Lydia in particular was quite upset about this list, which Marjorie Bouvé had given to me.

These three women who accosted me had quite an indictment against the Middle West Society of Physical Education and, as its vice-president, I was being taken to task. Although Mr. Post was listed as a member of the APEA Council as the Middle West representative, he did not attend this January 1 meeting. As his vice-president I could easily have served as his proxy since I was to be in New York City for other meetings.

It developed that Emil Rath of the North American Gymnastics Union School in Indianapolis, unknowing of Middle West plans to hold its 1929 spring convention in Chicago, had invited the APEA to hold its spring convention in Indianapolis and his invitation had been accepted. Learning of the Middle West plans, C. W. Savage of Oberlin College, who was just completing his third year as APEA president, had used his influence as a midwesterner to persuade the Middle West group to abandon its plans for a convention in Chicago and to join forces with the national group for a joint convention in Indianapolis. But Loren Post of Detroit, the new Middle West president, and E. C. Delaporte of the Chicago public schools, the outgoing president, were adamant, insisting that the Middle West would have its own convention alone in Chicago. I was shocked to learn that there was much ill-will against APEA on the part of several Middle West leaders and that, with that faction at the helm, they apparently meant to let APEA feel their displeasure. I disclaimed all knowledge of any of this and informed these women that thus far I had been completely ignored as the vice-president.

Besides this complaint I was informed that Mr. Post had accepted appointment by the APEA president as chairman of a national committee to study the possibility of enlarging the national council with the thought of making room for more women, but he sent no report to this meeting. Dr. McCurdy informed the council that he had sent Mr. Post, as chairman of this study committee, a letter recommending the following: (1) that each district society be represented on the council by its president plus two others (at least one of the group to be a woman); (2) that the Women's Athletic Section have three representatives instead of just one; and (3) that the Public School Section have two representatives, one man and one woman. (This is interesting in light of criticism that it was Dr. McCurdy who wished to hold down female representation on the council.)

These women also informed me that Dr. Frederick Maroney, supervisor of physical education for the public schools of Atlantic City, had been elected APEA president for 1929 and urged me to contact him immediately since he had declared that APEA needed many changes and he hoped to undertake a reorganization at once. This was the hotheaded fiery Irishman, Fritz Maroney, whom I had heard much about and was destined shortly to meet—the man who was to launch me unceremoniously into the limelight of my profession.

* * * *

The December issue of *The Pentathlon* which reached me belatedly announced the midwest convention site and dates for 1929. I waited until the last of January to hear from President Post about plans for it. He did not contact me so I wrote him on January 30, telling him I had heard in New York City that all was not well between APEA and the Middle West Society and that I hoped he would invite President Maroney of the APEA to attend our conference and discuss frankly any difficulties between us. Then I wrote to our new APEA President as follows:

Dear Mr. Maroney:

While attending the meeting of the Women's Division of NAAF in New York City during the holidays, I learned that there has been some misunderstanding between the APEA and the Mid West Association resulting in the giving up of plans for an APEA meeting this spring. I also understand that the National Council is drawing up a plan of reorganization.

As Vice-President of the Mid West Society, I feel decidedly concerned about this. . . .

Frederick W. Maroney, president of the American Physical Education Association, 1929 and 1930.

Please understand that in any reorganization plans you may have, you will receive loyal support from a large circle of members of the Mid West Society.

If there is anything I can do, please let me know.

I received a reply from Mr. Post dated February 5, thanking me for the suggestion and saying that he was asking E. C. Delaporte, the Chicago convention manager, to invite the national president. The same day I received a reply from Dr. Maroney, which said in opening and in closing:

My dear Miss Lee,

Thank you for your cordial and helpful letter of January 30th. I assure you that I appreciated the splendid spirit which prompted your writing so frankly to me. . . .

I would appreciate an invitation from the Program Committee of the Mid-West Section to appear before the Convention and make a plea for national unity within our ranks.

Two days later, I received a telegram making me president of the Middle West Society of Physical Education! I knew practically nothing of the Society's history and absolutely nothing of its inner working. I knew only a few women members and practically none of the men members. I was vaguely aware that there was dissatisfaction of APEA within the midwest group but knew none of the details. I knew not the slightest detail of any of the convention plans, not having been informed on one single item or even asked for an opinion or idea. Never before had I realized the absolute *nothingness* that a vice-presidency could mean.

This telegram instantly disrupted "the noiseless tenor of my way,"[8] suddenly catapulting me into professional organization work that led to wider responsibilities. It marked a great turning point in my life. I realized that from that moment on I was president of the Middle West Society of Physical Education with the burden of all these problems suddenly transferred to my shoulders. It couldn't have happened to anyone less prepared.

The telegram informed me that Loren Post had died suddenly from pneumonia after a very brief illness. I had received a letter from him written only four days before. Exactly one year, ten months, and three weeks later, the events precipitated by that telegram landed me in the national presidency of my professional association—an office no woman had ever held.

One thing I quickly decided upon. That was to conduct the Association affairs as democratically as possible. I had been a member of the Mid West Council once before (1926). In 1927 I had been a member of the National Council and, since May 1928 supposedly was a member of the Mid West Council again. In all three of these experiences I had never been told anything that was going on, yet a person or persons somewhere had been making decisions and getting things done—but autocratically. I was determined to put democracy to work in our Mid West Council and I found most were delighted to be consulted and to be made to feel a part of it although all were surprised and one or two also bored. Why these last had accepted office, I didn't know.

I found this method laborious and time-consuming but it paid off in building up fine esprit de corps within the group. Those who refused to work, even the little task of answering a letter, I soon put on my blacklist as persons who let themselves get elected to office with no intention of producing. This method involved tremendous correspondence but it bound us all together since we could not meet personally except at convention time.

In thinking it through, I decided that since all convention plans were complete, I had best accept them and carry on with whatever the convention committee had planned for the president to do. But the council meetings themselves would be mine to do with as I thought best. I would indeed be president there, and if I got nothing else accomplished I would ferret out, if possible, what the midwest people were unhappy about with APEA and try to resolve those difficulties. But first I had to meet my 12 council members face to face and get a bit acquainted with them. Two I had seen before (E. C. Delaporte and Dudley Reed, past presidents), but I had never met them or any of the other ten members.

I wrote at once to Elmer Mitchell, the secretary, asking that I be sent a copy of the constitution and any written material available, and to let me know the duties of the president, but he had nothing to send me. There was not even an extra set of the minutes of the last meetings which I could look over. As vice-president, I had never even received a copy. Apparently the Middle West Society just ran along without written plans and with little inner organization. Elmer Mitchell was in his first year as secretary-editor and as I learned later, also wondering what it was all about. Each year, as I soon learned, there was a convention chairman and he was apparently a law unto himself. No one had left any written records, not even of do's or don'ts for their successors. The secretary was so involved with the added duties of editor (all volunteer work) that he had no time for secretarial work beyond bare necessities, so his work, too, was a law unto itself. There were also some vaguely known committees, each apparently a law unto itself. There was little coordination and no written plans or orders for incoming officers and chairmen to go by. Everyone before me obviously had started out in the dark and did what he could purely by trial and error and did not bother to pass on any advice to his successor.

Later I was to learn that the national association was run similarly.

Each apparently tried to function as well as possible with as little correspondence as necessary. This unwillingness by early officers to carry on wide correspondence resulted in their making all the decisions themselves except when the council met. This resulted in feelings (and rightly so) that the organization was run by a few officers and not by the officers *and* the group of people elected to represent various other groups and interests. This prevented the district and national organizations from becoming businesslike and effective. Of course in the earliest days, all correspondence had to be written in longhand and it must have been laborious!

I also soon learned in the Middle West organization that people west of the Mississippi River thought that those east of the river controlled it too much. I thought a lot about all of this between February 9 and April 24 when we came together for convention. I took what time I could to delve into early *Reviews* to try to learn what I could of Middle West and national history and proceedings at council meetings. I decided that before the convention began, I would make sure that the national president would be there to talk with us. Before I would step out of office with a new president taking over at the conclusion of the convention, I would do what I could to bring out in the open all criticism of the American Physical Education Association. We would learn what we could of APEA and discuss what our proper relations with it should be. I was determined that each council member would be given every opportunity to speak out. Also I resolved to throw the council meeting open to all members who cared to attend, with all free to speak even if without a vote. I wanted to get at the bottom of complaints and to force complainers to speak up.

There was no one in Lincoln with whom I could talk over such matters. I felt professionally stranded in Nebraska. So I thought out my problems alone. Later, when confronted with still greater problems, I at least did not have to face them alone. By then I had built up a small circle of professional friends with whom I could correspond for advice and support even if distances from Nebraska were too great for personal get-togethers.

President Post had been as good as his word and did, just before his death, get word to the convention manager, E. C. Delaporte (who was also the immediate past president) that he wished the president of APEA to be invited to the convention. Mr. Delaporte had at once issued the invitation.

Immediately on receipt of the message of Mr. Post's death, I wired this information to Dr. Maroney, and, as the new Middle West president, I renewed the invitation for him to attend the Middle West convention in April with the hope that the two groups would find a way to pull together.

As news of Mr. Post's death spread in the Midwest, letters began pouring in upon me and I began to learn what various midwest people disliked about APEA. As I studied the problems presented, I began to see that I, too, felt APEA needed serious revision. So I entered into the arguments wholeheartedly and began a rushed correspondence with both Middle West leaders and national president, Dr. Maroney, trying to arrive at some conclusions before the April convention.

By mid-March I was able to send Dr. Maroney a list of nine chief complaints against APEA raised by the Middle West Council members, all reasonable and controversial. At the same time, I entered into correspondence with Dr. A. D. Browne, first president of the newly-organized Southern District Society (my old friend of World War I days in Oregon, then at Peabody College in Tennessee) and learned that they, too, in the Southern District were making about the same complaints against APEA. I also drew into correspondence on the subject Mary Channing Coleman who was serving as first convention chairman for the Southern District under Dr. Browne. She would become president of this Southern group following Jackson Sharman of the Alabama State Department of Education and Elliot Graves of the Virginia State Department.

As soon as I received a typed copy of the main outline of the Middle West program for the Chicago convention and learned the dates and hours set for council meetings and the name of the convention hotel, I sent Dr. Maroney a copy and informed him that when he arrived in Chicago I would let him know the day and hour when my council planned to have a special meeting with him to discuss APEA and Middle West mutual interests. As it was by then almost convention time, he wired his thanks and said that since he could not arrive for the opening day he would send the national secretary-editor, Dr. James Huff McCurdy, to represent him at the first council meeting set for that date. This bothered me considerably for I was not inviting the national president or any representative of his to attend my first of two council meetings.

I worried all the way to Chicago as to how I could politely yet firmly let both Dr. McCurdy and Dr. Maroney know that I wanted to talk with my people alone for my first meeting with them. I was ashamed to confess to them that I knew none of the Middle West Council members, even by sight, and wished some chance to get a little acquainted before taking on the national officers who were also strangers.

Dr. McCurdy was in Chicago ahead of me and contacted me. As I checked in at the hotel I had to tell him he could not attend my first meeting. I deeply regretted my seeming rudeness for Dr. McCurdy, although not angry, turned away with a look of hurt and disbelief. I sensed that he was a gentleman of the old school. He was of my father's generation and I was deeply uncomfortable over this incident, as if I had been rude to my own father. But I felt that the midwesterners would not talk freely of their displeasures with the national association were he present and that I must learn their true feelings before meeting with the national officers. It was many years before Dr. McCurdy was at ease with me, although I tried to assure him that this was not an unfriendly gesture.

As I turned away from him, I approached some men in the lobby who looked the athlete type and asked if they would point out Elmer Mitchell to me were he in the lobby. They did so and I was able to walk up to him nonchalantly and say, "How do you do, Mr. Mitchell, I am Miss Mabel Lee from Lincoln, Nebraska." I did not want him to know that I didn't know him by sight, and my scheme worked well. He was equal to the occasion for he answered at once, "Yes, indeed, Miss Lee! I am glad to see you again!" I was sure he had never seen me before but he, also, did not want me to know that. So the ice broken, he introduced me to several men I was supposed to know but did not.

I had my private session with my council the next morning, after which Mr. Mitchell and I hunted up Dr. McCurdy and President Maroney for a talk with them before the Council would meet again.

I had been warned that Dr. Maroney was a hotheaded Irishman and I was certain that unpleasantness was in store for me when he learned from Dr. McCurdy that I had closed the first council meeting to him. I was not wrong. He obviously had a chip on his shoulder. He introduced himself to me quickly and immediately blew up over my treatment of Dr. McCurdy. I told him I regretted the incident but would do it over again because I had a legitimate reason and I would like to explain it to him. His anger only increased, so I took him firmly by an arm and, looking him intently in the eye, asked:

"Did you come here to quarrel with me or to try to find a friendly way to settle our differences?"

He looked at me with open-mouthed disbelief and I saw the color rise in his face. Though my remark angered him further, he bit his lip, stood silent a moment, then threw back his head and burst into hearty laughter, "Spoken like a prince," he said, and then corrected it to "like a princess." Appalled at my own temerity to speak to him so and relieved at his sudden change of mood, I, too, burst out laughing. At

Elmer Dayton Mitchell, *editor of* The Pentathlon, *1928–1930 and of* The Journal of Health, Physical Education, Recreation *and* Research Quarterly, *1930–1943.*

this he extended a hand, saying, "Let's be friends," and we shook hands. From then on Fritz Maroney and I got along famously as we worked together to try to make APEA over to· be a more truly democratic and national organization.

To my delight I found that all my hasty correspondence with council members of the Middle West group had paid off and, united, we were able to present a solid front before the national officers, our invited guests. The convention closed with a second council meeting when the two national officers were present. It ended on a friendly, hopeful note with both parties agreeing that each was in error in some directions, that the ax should be buried and that APEA should be reorganized to make a place for the district groups as integral parts of its organization. Fun-loving yet fiery Fritz Maroney was won over to our point of view, and meeting as strangers we parted as friends and partners committed to wage a war. Thus began one more deep professional friendship that lasted until his death 29 years later.

* * * *

The convention delegates were full of talk of formal versus informal activities, and prophets were beginning to arise to beg for a great middle course between those who, as one of our guests from the East, Carl Schrader, put it, look on physical education "merely as an anatomically functioning muscle exercise" and those who look upon it merely as a medium of expression. Also arousing much discussion was the speech of another guest, Frederick Rand Rogers, New York State Director of Physical Education, when he threw a bombshell at his audience. He advocated putting all athletic coaches in the bleachers and off the field at contests, thus "giving sports back to the players." At another session, Avery Brundage, president of AAU, spoke in favor of women entering the Olympics, a timely topic. But Dr. Percy Dawson, noted physiologist of the University of Wisconsin, coming into prominence at the time as an advocate of simplified spelling, spoke out against women's entrance into the Olympics. He pointed out the differences between the Greeks, who sought the development of all youth, and the Romans, who excelled in spectator sports with the few highly skilled developed for the entertainment of the multitudes. He begged us in all of our work to remember the Greeks rather than the Romans. He won the day for us women who were trying to keep women out of Amerian Olympic teams of 1932, so that when the resolution against participation of women in the Olympics was placed before the delegates it passed by a thumping majority, almost unanimously, and the newspapers broadcast our decision to the public.

But the papers weren't so kind otherwise. Reporters naively expected presiding officers to hold up the opening of meetings while they interviewed the upcoming speakers and thus would not have to stay for the speeches. When their requests were refused, they wrote fabricated interviews that were so sensational that none of the speakers or presiding officers in the wildest, off-guard moments would have uttered. Anything for a sensational story. I blush even today for the things I was quoted as having said. After one session, a Chicago paper came out with a large headline:

FEAR FOR U.S. OF PALLID MEN, STURDY WOMEN

Then there followed a lengthy article of how the men delegates deplored the puny American men "weakened by lack of exercise, stunted by long hours of work ... sallow, anemic, palsied creatures" but how they "rhapsodized" about American woman "as a dynamic combination of Diana and Venus beside whom man will cower shamefully." The article closed with this:

> But while the men educators were fearful of what will become of manly physique in the future, Mabel Lee of the University of Nebraska, acting President of the Association, grew lyrical in picturing the feminine beauty of 1950 ... Outdoor sports now so popular among women and interpretive dancing are serving to develop both the minds and bodies of women so that ugliness is becoming decadent and pulsing beauty the order of the day.[9]

Utterly ridiculous! Neither the men nor I had given any such interviews or said any such things.

At the convention banquet, for the second time at a physical education meeting, I found myself seated next to Amos Alonzo Stagg. This time he was the speaker and I was the president of the group. Thus a friendship started a few years earlier was given another push. He was always a delightful dinner companion.

At the closing council meeting the group would not take "no" for an answer. They insisted that I had started a cleanup campaign and that now I must carry on, and so I was elected president of the Middle West Society of Physical Education in my own right for the coming year, the fourth woman so honored in 17 years.[10] And a fine group was elected into the council, not mere figureheads but workers to carry on with me. By now all were acquaintances and more than that, friends! We agreed to push constructively for radical changes in APEA, chief of which would be to incorporate the district societies as integral parts of its own organization but all with freedom of action within their own districts. The Middle West Council voted to pay the expenses of its president after this to the annual official APEA Council meeting, held for so many years past during the Christmas holidays in New York City. This meant the Middle West would have no excuse not to be officially represented and to have its voice heard.

97

Therefore, during the Christmas holidays of 1929 I attended the annual council meeting of APEA as the representative of the Middle West Society of Physical Education. (The council meetings held at APEA conventions in the spring were not the annual official business meetings with election of officers.)

* * * *

At the APEA Council meeting I encountered much ill will towards the so-called illegal, yet winked-at, Women's Athletic Section under which the Women's Athletic Committee functioned. I soon learned that some of the men of the profession were causing quite a furor over their discovery that the Women's Athletic Committee had quite a sizeable treasury which came from the royalties from the *Athletic Guides* which it produced and which it used to cover the expenses of its publications. There had never been any intent to keep the existence of this treasury a secret; it was known to the officers of APEA, but apparently not to the men who were quarreling with the women. They seized upon this as still another great irregularity within APEA since no other Section had a treasury of its own. The cry was immediately raised that the women should turn this treasury over to the APEA treasury and that APEA should budget the committee's work. This gave the women deep concern. It also became apparent that there were some women in the profession who were complaining to some of the men leaders that the Women's Athletic Section was a "self-perpetuating" group and a "closed door corporation." This increased the resolve of some of the men to bring this group of women to task.

President Maroney had hoped during his first year in the national presidency to iron out difficulties with both the obstreperous mid-westerners and the determined ladies of the unofficial Women's Athletic Section through informal get-togethers at a national convention, but the Middle West Society's insistence on meeting alone in Chicago in 1929 forced APEA's cancellation of plans for a national meeting at Indianapolis. However, at the December 1929 official national council meeting, Dr. Maroney was elected to a second year in the presidency. He promised a complete reorganization of APEA with all parts of the country, and women as much as men, given a voice in the reorganization.

* * * *

98

As the new President of the Middle West Society of Physical Education, I felt strongly that it was all wrong for the midwesterners to criticize the national organization without at the same time trying to do something constructive about changing the things we did not like. Therefore I hoped I might at the Christmas holiday council meeting of 1929 have an opportunity to "put the middle west cards on the table" for all to see in the hope of bringing our disagreements out in the open for discussion. But the full agenda allowed no time to discuss middle west displeasures. As we were running behind time, the meeting came to a close without a chance to say the things that weighed heavily upon my mind and which I felt it was my duty to say.

Before closing, the officers for the next calendar year were elected. Dr. James Huff McCurdy, then 64 years old, who had been secretary-editor for the past 23 years, had resigned during the fall, and Elmer Mitchell of the University of Michigan, who had for a year been putting out the Middle West's very popular *The Pentathlon*, had been elected by mail vote to take his place. This threw the door wide open for a complete revamping of the national association's magazine. Its name was to be changed to *The Journal of Health and Physical Education*, beginning with the January 1930 issue.

These were the days when people were not asked ahead of time if they would permit their name to be submitted as candidates for office. Now, I, the gadfly from the Middle West Society, prodding for complete reorganization and radical changes in the national association was chosen vice-president, as if they weren't having enough trouble with the women. But perhaps they thought this might at least put me on the team that was on the defensive. However, after my recent Middle West experiences, no one knew better than I the utter futility of a vice-presidency, the complete lack of any responsibility, so that when my name was presented I made no protest. This office had been handed around among the women for many years as a polite gesture, with the presidency, that holy of holies, reserved exclusively for the men. But I thought I might find worthwhile work which a vice-president might do.

I was disappointed in not getting a chance to present some grievances at the council meeting but luck played into my hands at the open luncheon meeting that followed the council meeting. There was, besides the council members, a rather large attendance of friends and members of the Association, mostly men, who were in New York City for various holiday meetings of men's groups. President Maroney introduced me as the new vice-president, saying jokingly that he had been having quite a time the past year trying to handle the obstreperous midwest folk. To my surprise, he added that perhaps I might like "to say a few words" in their defense. There wasn't a moment to collect my wits, but I knew I couldn't let this opportunity slip by. So I arose saying I felt that APEA's sins in relation to district organizations were inexcusable and needed correction. I confessed that I had attended but one national convention and that I knew little of APEA and had much to learn. I said that I felt the Women's Athletic Section problem was going to be hard to solve. I congratulated the former editor for granting the women a permanent page in the magazine starting with March 1929, for the Women's Athletic Committee and the Women's Division to use jointly on topics related to athletics for girls and women. I added that as much as I was interested in the work of that group I could also see that many women had little appreciation of the larger overall problems of an organization that had to serve men's interests as well as women's. I tossed in the remark that I felt the organization had pampered the men entirely too much and too long, forgetting the women. At all this I was met with hearty but friendly laughter.

So here was I, January 1, 1930, as the Terrible Twenties came to a close, caught up in undefined, unexpected duties as vice-president of APEA and as president of the Middle West Society of Physical Education, with the national convention scheduled for Boston immediately following the middle west convention in Milwaukee the last of March.

* * * *

In many ways the twenties were a disturbing decade. There was much unrest in all segments of society. The Great War, catapulting the United States into world politics, had been an upsetting experience for the entire country, and the recovery period seemed to be dragging out indefinitely. Many young people, although a noisy minority, even many middle-aged people, were "kicking up their heels" and having a great fling at life as if to make up for time and opportunities lost during the war. They made enough of an impression with their "goings-on" to give the decade the names, The Roaring Twenties, The Terrible Twenties, The Disturbing Twenties, and so on.

As for myself, then in my early forties, life, as far as the professional side of it was concerned, was indeed beginning at 40, as a popular book of that era proclaimed to be the case for all.[11]

At this time there was just beginning to be talk on campus about college girls smoking back East so why not in Nebraska? I firmly believed from my earliest teaching days that elders owe it to youth to take a clear open stand on issues affecting them. Here was a serious issue I felt deeply committed about, to warn all young girls coming under my influence against the harmful physiological effects of smoking. There were many of the medical profession who were furnishing proof enough of the dangers of smoking. My staff of that day supported me 100 percent on this issue.

Since no smoking was done as yet, at least not in the open, I decided that as the director of physical education for women, I should take a stand so that the girls would know right from the start that I was at least one woman on the faculty who opposed it and why. However, before I did anything, I checked to see if the Health Service might be thinking of promoting a non-smoking campaign on campus and if so, to offer my department's cooperation. I was received by the head of the Health Service with amazement that I would be willing to give time and energy for "these unnecessary things" and it was suggested that I "tend to my own business." So I decided to carry on with this project alone.

Although I personally opposed smoking not as a moral issue but entirely from a health standpoint, I now realized that here in Nebraska, where many people still objected to dancing, even folk dancing, on moral grounds, I would get more support from the moralists on this issue than from the University Health Service. However I was happy to find support from any group although I raised a loud voice about the harmful physiological effects of smoking.

I opened the campaign by asking for a few moments with each physical education class during which I called the girls' attention to the fact that smoking was becoming a fad among college girls back East and that if any Nebraska girls were thinking of taking it up I hoped they would give serious consideration to the fact that it is habit-forming and when it becomes a habit is a serious menace to health. Fortified by all the physiological facts I had been able to muster about smoking and quotations from nationally-known physicians, I kept my talk strictly on a health basis. Then I followed the talks by huge posters against smoking plastered on all the bulletin boards in our own building. Within two days I had reached practically every underclass girl and many upperclass women. This talk triggered one big topic of conversation at all the sorority houses and rooming houses (so I was informed) and, from reports that seeped back to me, also in many private homes about town as well. *The Omaha Bee*, hearing of my campaign, sent a reporter to interview me and the newspaper came out, November 1, 1925, with a headline:

This was followed with a lengthy writeup of my views against smoking. It was for me the first shot fired in public in a battle I waged for many years, most of the time a lone battle, and ever a losing one against the tide of public acceptance of smoking by women, regardless of consequences.

It has always been amazing to me to discover through the years that, of the many who believe in a thing, few will ever take a public stand on it. As I recall, not one faculty member outside my staff joined my crusade publicly, although many of the men and one or two of the women called me at once to congratulate me on my stand. However, the student leaders in the Women's Athletic Association enthusiastically joined the campaign at once and immediately adopted a training rule of "no smoking" for all its teams, making the following public statement in explanation:

> Not that University of Nebraska girls are inclined to smoke but there is a slight tendency for the girls in many schools and colleges to exploit the new so-called "right" and we are simply nipping the idea in the bud.[12]

Almost immediately the Lincoln newspapers asked for interviews on the subject, and the editor of the State Parents Teachers Association magazine asked me to write an article on the subject for them. The Lincoln papers, not to be outdone by the Omaha paper, now carried articles on other health campaigns that we were promoting for the education of the university girls in the hopes of getting them to discard high heels in favor of low heels for school wear and milk-drinking instead of so much candy-eating between meals. For the sake of the many girls who could not afford silk stockings for school wear (and there were indeed many of them) we tried to persuade all university women to wear lisle hosiery for school wear, as I did to set an example. With almost every underclass girl on campus registered in our classes we had a large captive audience for our campaigns.

But I paid a price for all this, especially for my stand against smoking by women. Shortly the dean of women informed me that I should know that I was the laughingstock among the few faculty women and faculty wives who were themselves taking up the fad, but that she herself and many others were glad that someone was speaking against it. I wondered why she and the others were not helping us. I soon came to see, however, that it was my staff and I who were looked to for this unpopular task. But we stuck to our guns and kept up our somewhat lonely crusade, and I in particular immediately became persona non grata with the faddists who themselves were smoking.

Chapter V
A Depression And Other Annoyances

Who of those persons who lived through them will ever forget the difficult years of the Great Depression? They were years of deep worries to all. Many of the young people who did get to college came at great financial sacrifice of their parents. There was a constant stream of emotionally disturbed girls in my office (at times, boys, too) seeking advice as to whether they should continue with their studies or return home to help with family finances, or at least to ease the load of expenses. Never before or after did I so frequently have to replace the box of tissues always on my desk for girls with colds but now for weeping girls, too. Also never was the studio couch in my private office so frequently occupied by weeping students seeking solace there, shut away from the prying eyes of classmates and other teachers. The students of these years missed the experience of happy carefree years such as I had known in my college days at the turn of the century.

The Depression took a great toll of education. Speaking at the opening of the Citizens Conference on The Crisis in Education held in Washington, D.C., January 5-6, 1933, President Hoover said:

> Above all, may I ask that throughout your deliberations you bear in mind that the proper care and training of our children is more important than any other process that is carried on by our government. If we are to continue to educate our children, we must keep and sustain our teachers and our schools.

Despite this warning, President Hoover had no more than stepped down from high office when the full fury of the Depression broke and the need to sustain our schools was forgotten by too many.

The need to curtail expenses came to mean doing away with "frills," cutting salaries, and reducing the size of staffs. Music, vocational education, home economics and physical education (in the order listed) were named as the chief frills and, therefore, suffered the most from cuts. Coming to the defense of physical education was a National Commission on Physical Education composed of Jane Addams of Hull House; Harry Emerson Fosdick, a noted New York City clergyman; Stuart Chase and Norman Thomas, both well-known political theoreticians; the superintendents of schools of Chicago, Philadelphia, Detroit, Providence and Denver; the presidents of several leading colleges and universities; and the presidents of the American Medical Association and the American Public Health Association. This group issued a statement[1] imploring the public to realize that in these trying times physical education was more essential than ever in our schools if youth were to be trained for worthy living and if serious social problems were to be avoided in the years ahead, youth must be trained in functional motor skills and interested in wholesome play.

At this same time, H. L. Mencken, editor of *The American Mercury*, and John Dewey, professor of philosophy, Columbia University, took public sides on the question, "Shall We Abolish School Frills?" Mencken spoke facetiously, as was his habit, but Dewey, taking the negative side, said:

> The schools represent the interest of the young. The young do not constitute a vested interest; they are not organized nor powerful. But they stand for what is most precious in American life and for the future country that is to be. For these reasons I do not think the ridicule of literary folk nor the direct assault of big taxpayers will be successful.[2]

Statements from the National Commission on Physical Education and John Dewey plus many more from leaders of the physical education profession stemmed the tide to the extent that physical education was only eighth on the list of subjects that suffered most from elimination of staffs at this time.[3]

Many of us wrote articles for the lay public defending physical education as a necessary part of education. We also seized every opportunity to speak before school boards, men's service clubs, women's clubs, PTAs, and other educational groups wherever we could find them and could "get a foot in the door." It was a disturbing time but through these efforts we won a fairly good victory. When it came to a final decision, most laymen by then could not visualize a school functioning adequately without sports, and this recognition carried with it the other activities of a physical education program. Physical education actually suffered less from cuts than did other subjects also not considered academic.

* * * *

Practically all salaries as well as operating budgets of schools took a big cut during the Depression, reaching their lowest in the year 1933–34 from the top figures of 1928 and not returning to the 1928 levels until around the late 1930s, if then. It was a 10-year worry but almost everyone was in the same boat. A few of my colleagues who were heads of college physical education departments weathered the storm without cutting salaries but most of them did so by cutting staffs, thus adding to the great mass of unemployed since it was almost impossible for anyone out of a job at that time to find another. However, some schools and businesses took the humanitarian way and reduced their staffs by not filling vacancies, retaining all others and giving a salary percentage drop to all alike.

When orders went out from the chancellor's office at the University of Nebraska that all salaries were to be cut 22 percent across the board, and that each department was to delete a percentage of its staff to correspond with the percentage enrollment drop in the department, we department heads were plunged into serious difficulties. It was up to us to decide which staff members were to be dropped—this with a great certainty that those dropped would not find other positions. What sleepless nights followed that order!

A tragedy befell the Romance Language Department as a result of that order! I just happened to be standing at one of the north windows in our west gymnasium one morning when an instructor in that department ran from behind another building into a grassy plot of lawn in my line of vision and shot himself to death. Only a few minutes before, the instructor had dashed into the classroom of the head of his department and, before the astonished and terrified students, shot the department head, catching him in the wrist as he tried to duck behind his desk. Then the attacker ran out of the building and into the grassy plot under a shade tree and killed himself. Needless to say, the campus was in pandemonium for quite some time. When we later learned that this man, a bachelor, was the sole support of his invalid mother, it was easy to surmise the panic he experienced when notified that he was to be dropped from the staff to meet the department quota of deletions.

106

Just previous to this I had the unhappy duty of deciding which one of my own staff was to be dropped—thankful that it was only one. I had been through a somewhat unpleasant experience for, after long deliberation, I had selected one of the latest comers and was sick at heart over the whole business only to be met with angry protests and accusations that I "had it in for her." Adversity is hard for anyone to take and when my interview with the chosen one was over, the load weighing heavily on my heart was immediately somewhat lightened by her turning the situation into charges that I was attacking and firing her without cause. Her quickness to see nothing but evil in my action made me realize that my choice was, after all, a wise one. She scarcely spoke to me again, sullenly finished the term, and walked out of my life completely.

My sister, Ferne, a buyer at Marshall Fields in Chicago, had at this same time been summoned to her head office and informed that before the closing hour she was to decide which of several workers in her department were to be told that their employment would end that very day. Several of the young girls were the sole supporters of invalid parents or of younger brothers and sisters. That experience of having to decide which employees to drop was so traumatic that she was almost sick in bed from it. In fact, both of us wound up with bad cases of the shingles which we then attributed to our unhappy responsibilities.

Completely ignorant about shingles, I finally went to my doctor with my sores and pains in hope of securing relief.

"What is your trouble?" he asked.

"Well," I replied, "I would swear that I have been bitten all around my waist by spiders and that a mule has kicked me in the ribs."

With a roar of laughter the doctor said, "You must be the world's best diagnostician! I'll wager at once that you have the shingles. What has been bothering you?"

And so it was—I had the shingles. The world must have been full of people with shingles those worrisome years even if shingles are caused by a virus as my physician today assures me is the case.

It was to be many years before the size of our staff returned to its pre-Depression total. By the end of the 1930s we were still down to 78 percent of the salaries we had at the opening of the decade.

At Nebraska, as no doubt in most schools, salaries of women teachers on the whole were lower than those of men teachers. Not until the 1940s did I, as a full professor, receive as much as the minimum salary for that rank, even though I was also head of a department. It was a struggle to bring any salary on my staff up to the declared minimum for each rank. The minimum, maximum or average salary for any rank was information very difficult for me, a woman head of a department, to obtain. When in some years I was able to learn of these figures it was always because a male department head in chance conversation let information slip to me, not realizing that this was apparently supposed to be privileged information for men only.

Worried about going out to teach at Depression salaries, if they were so fortunate as to get a position, the upperclass students majoring under me were frequently asking how they were going to manage on such low salaries. I decided that the time had come to work into one of my upperclass courses a special talk on budgeting one's money. I went to a banker to ask advice for this talk and he gave me three sample budgets to represent three types of persons: the tightwad, the spendthrift and the thrifty. Since these were made out for a man with a family to support and so would in many details not meet budget needs of a professional single woman, the students and I worked them over, falling back on my own experiences of earnings and savings. Together we drew up what seemed a reasonable budget for a woman teacher without dependents. The bankers' budgets were as follows:

	Living	Education	Recreation	Giving	Saving
Tightwad	37%	1%	1%	1%	60%
Spendthrift	58%	1%	40%	1%	0%
Thrifty	50%	10%	10%	10%	20%

Together the students and I worked out a budget for the unmarried woman teacher without dependents: living 50 percent (covering board, room, clothing, laundry, health needs, transportation, taxes, personal gifts, and the like); education, 7 percent (covering professional expenses, travel for professional business, advanced study, professional books and magazines, and the like); recreation, 8 percent (covering social clubs, travel, amusements, recreational reading materials, entertaining, and the like); giving, 10 percent (covering church, college, community and charity donations and impersonal gifts); and saving, 25 percent (covering life insurance, funds for retirement, savings accounts, stocks and bonds, and the like). From this we moved into a study of budgeting for buying clothes and for travel, both worrisome items if to be held in balance.

Although I couldn't give much time to this in actual class, the girls were always so interested that we had several non-required, out-of-class followup discussions on the topic. Usually most of the students turned out, so interested did they become in personal budgeting. For many years after these girls had graduated I received grateful notes from many, particularly those who had married, telling me how grateful they and their husbands were for these budget charts as a guide as they were establishing their homes and families. And usually there was an added, "My husband says no one ever mentioned such a topic to the fellows in any of their college courses and he is as grateful as I for this help."

Times have changed so that I wonder what today's bankers offer for suggested budgets. Then we had not yet entered the period of widespread going into debt for luxuries—the "dollar down and a dollar a day" era. We still felt, as did the generations before us, that we should not only live within our income but also save some of it. These budgets carried no item for paying interest on loans. Also, taxes were neither high nor numerous and we knew no such thing as paycheck deductions as today. We also knew nothing of government social security and little of pension funds. What financial security we were to have for the future we knew we had to save for on our own.

* * * *

For most of the 1930s I worked under the kindly but somewhat uneventful leadership of Chancellor Burnett. A few high spots of these years cling tenaciously to my memory. How well I recall a certain November day in 1930 when he stood up firmly for women's rights against a group of women questioning them. The ladies arrived in his office without an appointment to complain about an aspect of my department work. Imagine my alarm that morning when the chancellor's secretary called me to his office to answer to complaints of the state officers of the Women's Christian Temperance Union who were there in a body, deeply wrought up over one of the courses our department required of its majors.

I ran over to the Administration Building a bit breathlessly, wondering, "What now?" The indignant ladies had plenty to say about our department's requirement that the women majors take a course in human anatomy. As they said, it was bad enough to require a woman to take such a course but worse still from a man teacher and with men students in the class, and worst of all they were even, heaven forbid, doing laboratory work in dissection, so they had just learned, and with men present.

I had understood that the battle for women's right to study such subjects had been fought and won years before. In fact, over a 100 years before, Emma Willard in New York State had fought and won this very battle. Now I had to wage this war all over again in Nebraska and against the admirable ladies of the Women's Christian Temperance Union, this time not a group of dissenting men.

Without previous warning I had to prepare my impromptu defense as I stood before those irate ladies. Their arguments against the course were indeed time-worn. Mrs. Emma Willard herself no doubt would have recognized many of them in the 1820s. But I played in better luck in the 1930s than she did for I had back of me a chancellor who spoke for all men educators of the new day when he defended the requirement of this course. I was glad when he informed them that ever since 1900 the University of Chicago had been offering such a course to other than medical students and in coeducation classes. Together we stood firm in favor of the course and I went to lengths to explain why the course was required. Finally satisfied, the ladies agreed that perhaps after all the course should be continued. My informing them that my father had for many years been an ardent worker in Iowa for the cause of temperance and a staunch supporter of the Iowa WCTU did no harm in softening the belligerency of the opening moments of the interview.

* * * *

In the midst of these alarms and disturbances there was the ever-present concern for the students and their recreational needs as an outlet for their worries. As the Depression deepened, students had ever-decreasing allowances for movies, dances and the usual weekend diversions. Recalling what fun I had during my undergraduate years at the fun nights at the gym, I enlisted the help of my staff. For long stretches of time our department put on Friday and Saturday night coed fun nights at the gym for any students who cared to come. This project helped hundreds of young people in mixed groups to find recreational outlets free of cost and available on campus under university auspices.

A well-remembered memory of the Depression years is of the day when I asked Coach Dana X. Bible, head of men's athletics, if he would be interested in joining my women's department in putting on co-recreational evenings open to all interested students. He was happily disposed toward the idea but, being quite busy at the time, said that he would give the project his enthusiastic backing in every way other than being personally drawn into it. If my department would do all the planning, organizing and running of the program, his department would do what it could to put the idea across to the fellows, would let us use whatever of their facilities and equipment would

110

be free at necessary times and above all would give our efforts their hearty blessing.

I had previously approached the director of physical education for men to seek his cooperation, but he assured me that such an undertaking could not possibly succeed without a desire for it on the part of the students which he was sure I would find non-existent. So, bolstered by Dana Bible's enthusiasm and offer to help, my department went ahead with the plans and for several years this project was a great success. We were happily surprised at the numbers of both men and women students who came out to bowl and to play volleyball, ping-pong, badminton and tennis together. We furnished the setting, equipment and facilities for much good fun for several hundred students.

* * * *

It was in this decade that I published my first book—a college text. What an experience it was—not only in the writing of it but in events leading up to it and also to the strange circumstances that transpired after its publication.

Nothing was farther from my thoughts in my early years of teaching than writing a college textbook, but after a few years in teacher-training work I sensed the great need for a book on organization and administration of physical education done by a woman for the girls' and women's departments. Although a few men had tackled the topic supposedly for both men and women, nevertheless any young, inexperienced teacher had to search those textbooks to find aids for good organization and administration procedures in behalf of girl's and women's work—also had to digress somewhat when it came to the consideration of the philosophy and principles guiding girls' and women's work as differentiated from that for boys and men.

Among the professional courses offered to our majors, I was extremely protective of three courses in particular—orientation in physical education for underclassmen, philosophy and principles of physical education, and organization and administration of physical education of women's work for upperclassmen. Others could teach techniques and methods courses, history of physical education, kinesiology, physiology of exercise and all the other courses, but I, the head of the department, clung zealously to the teaching of these three courses in particular. I was determined to start all entering majors with an immediate taste of my own philosophy about physical education in the hopes of quickly weeding out the misfits and of starting the others immediately on what I considered a "right path"—call it orientation, propaganda, brainwashing or anything else. I wanted every girl to feel from the very start my own enthusiasm for the profession, an understanding of my beliefs, hopes and dreams about it, and the firm knowledge that it would be hard but rewarding work.

Disillusioned over the inadequacies for women teachers of the texts on organization and administration prepared by men, I began toying with the idea of doing a textbook for my own students. It would make teaching the course much easier and would send my students out to teach with a guidebook at hand. Also by now I had become recognized as somewhat of an authority on women's physical education. Heads of girls' and women's departments in colleges and high schools and YWCA leaders had begun writing me that they could find no satisfactory published guides for organizing and administering their own departments and, in their own training they had taken such courses taught by men, all aimed in general at boys' and men's departments. They asked if I would kindly write them how to do this and that. But most of all I received letters from Nebraska schools at first and gradually from schools in neighboring states and after a while from far-away states, saying, for example: "I am an English teacher (or home economics or history or whatever) and have been assigned to teach physical education part-time. Please tell me how to get started (or what to teach and how to teach it)."

These letters asked as many different questions and called for as many different types of help as there were writers. No two ever seemed to call for the same thing so, as desperately as I wished that I could formulate a few form letters to send out in reply, I never could. I couldn't bear to let these calls for help go unheeded. The sum total of these evergrowing numbers of letters clearly called for a textbook. Finally many letters began to come saying: "Enclosed is a stamped and addressed envelope. Please write me whatever I need to know to organize and run a girls' department of physical education." They proved the last straw. I decided that if for no other reason than pure self-defense I had to do a book.

I had moments of doubt about it. Who was I to write such a book? I had never in my own professional training years had the benefit of such a course. When I went out to teach I knew absolutely nothing about organizing and administering a department for girls other than what I had learned by observing my own college physical director at work, and yet I stepped at once into the directorship of a department. The organization and administration of the Boston Normal School of Gymnastics was no guide for me as it was purely a small professional school. So I had learned on the job by trial and error. But I had learned a lot and why not share this knowledge with young teachers who, some professionally trained but inexperienced and some totally untrained, were nevertheless out teaching physical education and asking for help? I had had no one to turn to for help. All of us teachers in the early 1900s were feeling our way on our own and without benefit of textbooks. But we had learned many things by that method and now were in a position to guide the new generation to save them from too much error in their own efforts. So this book became a crusade with me. The only time I could work on it was Saturday afternoons, Sundays and vacations (for in those years I scarcely had a free evening during the week). It took me three years to complete the project.

The three summers of 1934, 1935 and 1936, except for a few weeks each summer in Estes Park for hiking with family hiking enthusiasts, I was in my study at work almost daily from 6 a.m. to dark. Mother brought me mid-morning and mid-afternoon snacks of cookies and milk to cheer me on and insisted to all inquirers that I could not come to the phone—bless her understanding that I should not be disturbed. With her guarding my time, I had the entire book in first draft by the end of summer 1935 and in second draft by the end of summer 1936. On weekends and vacations of the school year 1936–37, I put it into third and fourth drafts and had my *Conduct of Physical Education* in the publisher's hand by commencement time. The first publisher I approached took the manuscript—beginner's luck!

The November day after I received the first copy of my book, Mother had a surprise dinner party for me inviting my entire staff to celebrate the occasion. How happy she must have been to realize that at long last home life could return to normal. My staff decided to make the celebration a hilarious occasion. On the staff were some clever young women who could stir up the most jovial parties, and this was to be an extra-special one. They had persuaded Mother to slip them copies of the book's table of contents listing all the chapter titles and went quickly into production of a book of their own, a spoof on my book to present to me at the dinner party.

Shortly before the dinner hour on that evening, Mother sent me on some errand to keep me away for some time. In my absence the staff, parking their cars at a distance from our house, helped Mother set the table for 12 guests. As I was always most unconcerned about what went on in the kitchen until dishwashing time, Mother had had no difficulty in keeping that part of the dinner secret. When I returned what a surprise awaited me! But that was nothing compared to the after-dinner surprise when my staff solemnly presented me with

113

their "book," entitled *Staff Simple Supplement* published by Foolish Ness, Inc. It was bound in pink cardboard with lavendar decoration, copying the design, if not the color, of my own book cover. The author was listed as C. Nalj Temp, a fictitious name from the initials of the staff members. The pink and lavender cover served as a gesture to my love of pastel colors.

What a treat awaited the opening of that rare volume—a one-copy edition. The frontispiece carried a picture of me with dedication of the *Supplement* to "that other famous work," *The Conduct of Physical Education.* The preface was a Pre-Face followed with a statement that "Page references are not necessary because the pages are not numbered." The table of contents declared five chapters numbered in the authors' own inimitable way of handling Roman numerals I, II, III, IIII, IIIII.

Chapter I dealt with "Appraisal of Activities" with subheading "Euthanasia through Physical Education." It offered besides profuse illustrations of anatomical charts and the like, the following as part of its subject matter:

> And now we have reached the class designed to meet the needs of that large group of delinquents who have heart trouble. The prerequisite to this class is a fraternity pin. Splendid instruction in "lassooing" technique is given here to show the girls the ropes . . . .

> Now, you take the subject of flat feet—oh, no—you take it— I'm tired of it all and in closing may we quote Wilma Haynes' article in the *Research Quarterly,* March, 1931, page 215, "After College, What?" So what!

The third chapter was on "Marks and Marking—Grades and Grading" and to match my use of a quotation to head each chapter, it carried the admonition, "Of two evils, choose neither." It offered several methods of grading such as the Monte Carlo, the Red, White and Blue, the Share-the-Wealth, H & W or Soak-The-Rich, the Greek or Please-All, and the Rubber Elbow or N.M.B. The authors claimed these methods to be "free of precedents, standards, norms, statistics, and the warping, binding, biasing influences clinging to traditional educational procedures;" also that "they are fresh, untried and unsound, being less than 24 hours old."

The chapter on competition is full of zany advice to teachers and offers among its more classic statements the following:

> As exemplified at the University of Nebraska, 90 percent of the women students give no thought to becoming Miss America . . . .

About 50 percent have been elected some sort of a sweetheart, and authorities express their faith in declaring that the rest will be elected as soon as more traditions can be concocted.

This unusual book is profusely illustrated by paste-in cutouts from all kinds of magazines, lay as well as professional, all of which may or may not have any bearing on the subject matter. The illustrative climax is reached with silhouettographs of all staff members and the janitors and dressing-room matrons, offering all imaginable representations of "before and after" postures. This pink and lavender bound limited-edition book is one of my choice mementoes.

Later I turned the tables on the authors of this limited edition. During the Christmas vacation I took a sadly needed rest at the seashore at Galveston, Texas. I had worked on the manuscript on vacations and free days, many a day from 14 to 16 hours at my desk, and on nights when university work claimed my day and early evening hours until 1:00 and 2:00 in the morning. I was dead tired! What a surprise awaited me on the beach at Galveston—sand dollars! They gave me sudden inspiration. I brought back a great box full of these dollars. Mother put on a second "book" party for me and my staff. With these dollars I paid them unexpected royalty on their *Supplement*—to their surprise and great hilarity.

I had guessed correctly that there was a need for a book on organization and administration of physical education written by a woman for girls' and women's work. My book was adopted as a text in colleges and universities across the country and to my surprise and pleasure by men's professional training departments since many men would go out to head up girls' and women's departments as well as those for boys and men, and the training schools were glad to have a guide for this purpose. It also enjoyed good foreign sales chiefly in England (where it was reviewed in a British journal) Australia, South America, Japan and China. It was reviewed in many state education journals as well as in the *NEA Journal* and the American Medical Association's *Hygeia*, and was voted by NEA as one of the 60 best educational books published in 1937. Within five months it went into a second printing. It was a somewhat heady experience since it was my first book but I was shortly brought down to earth about it by queer experiences related to it.

The first peculiar experience came closely on the heels of completion of the first draft. By then word had gotten about that I was writing a textbook and when I received a call from a local educator asking for a conference on a personal matter, imagine my surprise to learn that he wished very much that I would take his wife, who had had some training in physical education, into partnership on my book. I protested that all the research work was completed and the manuscript in first draft, all entirely my own personal work and that I would not consider adding any name to mine as co-author. But the husband protested that his wife could now take all the rest of the responsibility off my shoulders—she would put it through second and still later drafts as I would think advisable and attend to all other details of getting it published. Surely such work would warrant adding her name to mine as co-author. Never have I encountered such insistence. He had an answer to each protest I could offer. The fact that I had produced this book entirely on my own all based on my own years of experience and that now it was past the stage where I could have used a co-author to do half of the drudgery meant nothing to this man.

He pleaded with me—in the end almost tearfully—saying that his wife had a great ambition to be an author and this would give her an opportunity to make that dream come true. But I was adamant— as his friends said, stubborn—and insisted that this effort was to be mine and mine alone. What I didn't tell him was that I was by then well-known nationally within my profession, and that alone would surely help considerably to put my book across without adding the name of his wife, an unknown beyond local areas. Also I refrained from telling him that his wife had no professional experience to bring to the writing of such a book that could possibly mean anything at all to me. Before her marriage she had had a few inconsequential positions and had not made herself felt in any but a small professional circle. Her training in my field had been at a school known to me and at a time when its professional course offerings were decidedly run-down. Since graduation she had no training anywhere else to bolster her poor training.

When the husband finally gave up trying to break down my resistance, his friends took over the project. I was annoyed for several weeks by telephone calls, interviews at my office, evening and Sunday calls at my home, all demanding to know why I was unwilling to accept this woman as co-author of my book, and persistent that for the success of my book I surely needed her help. But finally, at a great expense of time, energy and patience, my stubbornness won out and this peculiar annoyance ceased.

Still greater and most unexpected annoyances were awaiting the actual publication of the book. No sooner was it off press (and given a most generous review and acclaim in the local city press) than I was hailed to the chancellor's office to answer to the charge made by an unnamed accuser that I had had my manuscript typed by my department secretary on university time and therefore at the state taxpayer's expense. Astounded at such a false accusation, I could only beg the chancellor to take my word for it that the charge was not true until I could have time to produce proof of its falsity. He insisted that my word alone was proof enough as he most certainly would accept my word against that of my accuser, but I insisted on producing tangible evidence.

The next day I returned to his office to show him the cancelled checks on my personal banking account with which I had paid my typist. The chancellor admitted that he was glad to have this evidence to produce in addition to my word as he, too was under attack by the same person who was attacking me. It was well for us both that he be armed with concrete proof. My accuser had up to this time been the only woman on the faculty whose publications hailed her as a recognized author in her field (although none of her writings was used as textbooks); apparently she was jealous of that reputation as the only woman author on campus and my book was now a threat to it. I had meant her no harm but apparently she took it as a personal insult. And troubles did not stop there.

I had written the book in the first place because I wanted a textbook for my students so naturally as soon as it was off press I designated it as the text to be used in my course on organization and administration of physical education. However, I felt some embarrassment since it meant that I would be profiting personally from the sale of the book. I got around this possible criticism by ordering the copies for my class on my own personal order at author's discount, which would cancel out the royalty payment and charge the students just what I paid for them. Also, I paid all express charges myself instead of adding them to the students' payments. Thus the students bought the book at a greatly reduced cost and I profited nothing from the use of the book financially.

Soon someone went to the manager of the university bookstore that handled required texts for students and complained that I was in the bookselling business, cheating the store out of legitimate business. He went to the chancellor and I was called in about this. When I explained what I was doing and why, he laughed and said I was leaning too far backward in trying not to profit personally at my students' expense and advised that I place my textbook order after this with the usual channel—the university bookstore. This I agreed to do but with the provision that I would reimburse each student 10 percent of the cost of the book so that I still would not profit at the students' expense. The chancellor laughed at my persistence to be above reproach but I reminded him that when one had detractors such as both of us had, constantly watching for some fault to accuse us of, one had better be wary.

This care was not enough to appease those determined to keep me from using the book, at least on the University of Nebraska campus. The next attack took a different direction. This time a person whose name was never known to me (although guessed at) complained to various members of the board of regents and apparently painted so black a picture of me abusing my position that it was agreed to make a ruling that no faculty member could use a textbook which he had authored or co-authored. The ruling took this form no doubt to avoid pointing a biased finger at any one person. I was told that it caused much debate for several professors had published textbooks used by their students. Although no faculty member mentioned the ruling to me or asked me to join them in protest, several did join together and sought a hearing with the regents which ultimately resulted in a quiet cancellation of the ruling. Thus, local unpleasantness over the local use of my book finally died down.

One happy occasion to counterbalance the unpleasantness was a luncheon which the A. S. Barnes & Co., my publisher, gave in Atlanta the following April to celebrate their 100 years in the publishing business and to honor the president, John Barnes Pratt. Since I was one of their newest authors I was seated at the head table at that large luncheon party that filled the ballroom of the large hotel.

In later years the young women of my profession came to speak of my *Conduct of Physical Education* as their professional bible. It had filled a real need of that period.

* * * *

As women in ever-increasing numbers began to smoke in the 1930s, following a start in the twenties, the habit, to my amazement, engulfing more and more women of the physical education profession, I was increasingly caught up in a personal crusade against it. It was so out of keeping with every tenet of a quest for physical fitness, which to my way of thinking was one of the great cornerstones of any physical educator's credo.

Unlike many of my friends who entertained the same objections to smoking as I did, I was not content to keep quiet. If I were to influence young women to avoid tobacco, I needed positively to let students know that I myself did not smoke—not to leave them wondering if I did so in secret as many did at first when smoking by women was still tabu in the teaching profession. To be in the strong position of practicing what I preached, I made an effort to have on my staff only young women who did not smoke and were interested in using their own example and influence in preventing students from taking up the habit.

So in the thirties, even more vigorously than in the 1920s, I waged war against smoking by women and thereby became persona non grata among many women in my profession—not that I preached to them, for I strongly felt it was none of my business what any of my peers or older acquaintances did about the problem. My responsibility, as I saw it, lay entirely in my work with young girls who came under my influence. Nonetheless several old friends who had taken up the habit (and by so doing had sold their birthright to try to influence young girls not to take it up) began avoiding me. Friendships I had previously enjoyed with some of my women professional co-workers in particular I thus lost. At first it hurt, but I soon realized that any friendship that could not survive a difference of opinion was not a worthy one.

This public stand against smoking, as did a later one against drinking, brought me surprising support from a most unexpected direction. I had not given the slightest thought to what the men co-workers, either in or out of my profession, might think of this battle. I was merely doing what I felt was right for anyone working in the health field without thought as to who may or may not take the same stand. Had I stopped to think it through, I would have realized that the great majority of men in physical education and athletics did not themselves smoke and would not approve of it, but since I had not given a thought in that direction I was agreeably surprised to discover after my first public outburst against smoking that some of the women and almost all of the men present gave me a hearty round of applause.

Through the years our professional meetings were almost totally free of smokers until women took up the habit. From then on, smoking at our professional meetings became common, with almost all of it done by the women. And although through the years many women congratulated me for having the courage to take such a public stand against smoking, it was usually the men who gave me the heartiest support in this crusade.

Holding office in three different national professional organizations, as I did in the 1930s, enabled me to speak out frequently in many different parts of the country. I made the most of these opportunities, becoming deeply entrenched as the recognized woman leader of the group deploring the bad habit of smoking. If my stand cost me some friends, it brought me new ones. It also brought me, within the educational world, a reputation as a woman leader against smoking, judging from the many letters I received throughout the thirties from college presidents, school superintendents and YWCA secretaries, asking me to recommend teachers for their physical education departments who did not smoke. They added that they had turned to me for help since they understood that at the University of Nebraska I took a strong stand before my students against smoking.

At this time the national YWCA was so strongly against smoking by its staff members that word was passed throughout the country that there were two colleges where they could turn for help in procuring physical education staff members who did not smoke—the University of Nebraska, and Oberlin College where Gertrude Moulton, M.D., was head of the department of physical education for women. So for a while some of us were trying to prepare teachers who did not smoke and others were trying to find teachers who did not smoke. But it became a losing battle as more and still more women took up this habit.

I have understood why many of my co-workers were unwilling to forego smoking themselves for the sake of the beneficial influence they might otherwise have exerted over their pupils and young friends. The thirties were critical years for those decisions since before then smoking by women was frowned upon as a moral issue, so there was little temptation for most women to experiment with it. But now aware of the growing addiction of the drug habit by women, I protected the influence of my department on the women students on our campus by advising all applicants for staff positions not to apply if they smoked or drank since they would find themselves misfits in our local situation. Thus I was able to keep our department staffed fairly well only by young women who practiced what we as a group preached.

In the early thirties I was suddenly catapulted into professional notice on the national level (as related later) and took the first opportunity to speak out as a recognized leader who was against both smoking and drinking. Drinking as a growing problem for women was just then beginning to rear its ugly head, but it was still quite unthinkable that a teacher would so demean herself. When it first came to my notice at a professional gathering there was such immediate denunciation, that I have never forgotten it. The incident occurred in the ballroom of the leading hotel of one of our large cities. Our national professional association had held the opening session of its annual convention and the convention manager had asked the audience to withdraw while the floor was cleared for dancing. When the group came together again it soon became apparent that out of a small group of men and women who had returned together, one woman was inebriated. Her companions quickly abandoned her and she roamed about the ballroom, an embarrassment to the other delegates. Immediately a small group of young men, so young they must have been attending their first convention, searched me out and begged me to remove the woman from the ballroom. I demurred thinking that her companions should be held responsible for her.

"But you are the one woman here whom everyone recognizes as one who would disapprove of her behavior," one earnest young man exclaimed. "It is a disgrace to the profession for her to be here in such condition."

I was in hearty accord with his last statement and said I would do what I could about it. So I turned to a group of older men to discover that they were all equally indignant. They agreed that one of the group who had first been with the offending woman should escort her to her room. When buttonholed, her companions objected to assuming this duty but the group of protesting men grew ever larger until at last one man and one woman took their unsteady companion to her room. Never have I seen a group of men so indignant over the behavior of a woman. I knew then where I could find hearty support within my profession for any campaign against drinking. I was indeed flattered that the younger men in particular just entering the profession would single me out as someone they could turn to in this situation.

All my life I had known of men whose lives and families' lives had been ruined by drink. I decided early in life that when it came to habits that ruin health, I *was* my brother's keeper. My example was to cause no one to fall. However I soon came to realize that my presence was unwelcome in many small get-togethers such as I had previously attended and enjoyed. I soon learned that frequently lonely is the crusader but I accepted that as a price one pays for "taking a stand."

To me teaching has always seemed to be a "pedestal" profession where young people look up to the teacher for guidance. Thus it behooves the teacher to be worthy of being "looked up to."

Chapter VI

Progressive Education Movement Takes Its Toll of Physical Education

---

Those of us who were not in sympathy with the extremes of the Progressive Education Movement were disturbed by theories coming out of Columbia University as experienced particularly in the heyday when methodology became all-important. A teacher must know how to teach whether or not well educated in the subject matter to be taught. To protect the educational interests of my own department, I locked horns many a time with members of this group. There were some teachers college faculty members who chiseled away at college requirements in disciplined learning to increase requirements in their "education" courses, thus producing the gradual lowering of standards in the curriculum. This erosion pushed for the dropping of difficult courses—courses which as a rule do not appeal to most American college girls, such as chemistry, physics, laboratory work in anatomy and physiology—all courses needed in the preparation of a well-educated physical education teacher.

I was constantly on the defensive with many teachers college faculty members over the retention of these requirements in my department's curriculum. This group seemingly had control of state departments of public instruction so that in order to get a certificate to teach in a public school one had to take as many of these "education" courses as dictated by the teachers colleges to the state departments.

The educationists made a great assault in this era on the old liberal arts education, casting aside the old general requirements in foreign languages and much in sciences and mathematics, history and literature, and replacing these with "education" and life-adjustment courses. The liberal-arts teachers were fighting for their very existence in the lives and education of those who were to become teachers.

Having been brought up in the liberal arts tradition, I was heartsick at what I saw unfolding. Although I was one preparing students to go out to teach, I found myself at great odds with educationists who called the shots on how teacher training was to be carried on. It was to be carried on to prepare all prospective teachers to go into the public schools only and to teach according to the educationists' limited ideas of education. The greater percentage of our physical education majors were planning to teach in colleges, YWCAs, recreation departments, and such—not in the public schools. (Few public schools of the 1930s offered opportunities to teach in this field.) They would therefore not need a public school teaching certificate, yet all had to conform to the public school certification requirements to get their bachelor's degree— an inexcusable rigidity that was finally escaped by the creation of schools of health, physical education and recreation within several universities, most of which were free of teachers college ties. Those students who were not preparing to teach in public schools no longer had to meet the certification requirements of public school teachers.

I was thankful that the certification "racket," as I called it, did not reach into the college field so that college students other than those in teachers colleges and schools of education could be taught by persons who had specialized in the field in which they were teaching, not in so-called "education" courses. I was also thankful that all my own teaching years fell into the college category, thus saving me the need of taking those education courses, instead of psychology, philosophy, anthropology, French and German, etc.

My struggle against the extremists of both the Progressive Education Movement and the educationists as they affected my own profession of physical education came to a head in the thirties. By then the Progressive Education Movement had taken on new impetus and new ideas. The lower schools were to furnish guidance, facilities and equipment, but the children were to educate themselves. Teachers were not to offer information except as students asked for it, and, to cut the teacher down to size after many decades of enthronement on a raised platform, the pupils were to call him by his first name.

Caught in the rush to make teacher education as well as public school education easy for everyone, I found myself in the ever-decreasing minority fighting to maintain high standards of disciplined education. How I suffered when, as head of a department caught up in the philosophy of teachers colleges of the 1930s, I was forced to give in to a majority vote, first on this and then on that requirement, in order to substitute more and ever more courses of teaching and the like. These were the sort of courses which, if he were entering the field of physical education, anyone with a head on his shoulders could figure out on his own and learn on the job unless he were going into professional sports or on the stage for a dance career. But the fundamental sciences, which are the "roast beef" for which the "milk toast" courses were substituted, a student can never readily pick up on his own if deprived of well-educated teachers and the use of science laboratories.

Although I highly approved of holding onto these disciplined requirements for their own values, I had one other reason for wishing to retain them—a psychological one. In earlier years, Mary Lyon at Mt. Holyoke had clung obstinately to her household work plan because, as she said, "the domestic work would prove a sieve that would exclude from the school the refuse, the indolent, the fastidious, and the weakly ...and leave the finest of the wheat, the energetic, the benevolent and those whose early training had been favorable to usefulness, from whom you might expect great things."[1]

What a sympathetic response Mary Lyon's reasoning called forth from me, who was struggling 100 years later to weed out the weaklings and hold the requirements of chemistry, physics and modern languages, and laboratory work in both physiology and anatomy, in the curriculum for young women preparing to teach physical education. Although I was in complete accord with the other reasons for holding to these requirements, I was also conscious of the need to retain these courses as a sieve to weed out those not in earnest about an education in my field. But the philosophy of many so-called educators was too much for me. I frequently went down in defeat before their onslaught to make education as palatable and easy as possible for everyone.

According to the theory that you teach children, not subject matter, there developed now in our teachers colleges the "ear-to-the-ground" technique in advising prospective teachers about their major subject-matter fields. When word went out from the placement bureau that there was a shortage of English teachers, students were advised to prepare to teach English; if a shortage in mathematics teachers, then the specialization must be pushed in that direction. It mattered not at all whether the prospective teacher was interested in teaching English or mathematics. All were to become educational "opportunists."

At this same time, Teachers College was giving all its entering students a vocational test in which the student was to check on a long list the subjects he liked to study and then he was matched up with a vocation in which he supposedly should make good according to the particular subjects he checked. Our prospective women majors in physical education were deeply frustrated for physical education was not on this list; only nursing was matched for women with a liking to study anatomy and physiology. All these hopeful physical education majors were called in one at a time for a serious conference and informed that their schooling would be wasted if they did not prepare for the field of nursing. I had to console many weeping girls and give them courage to stick by their desire to be physical educators.

* * * *

More students than ever were going into graduate work in the 1930s and standards also began slipping here. A graduate degree that supposedly stood for advanced work, with greater depth of learning than at the undergraduate level, now in some areas came to stand merely for more work of the undergraduate level.

As early as 1903, William James decried the lack of real learning involved in too many Ph.D. programs, speaking of the growth of this threat to education as the "Ph.D. Octopus."[2] By the 1930s the octopus had grown to much larger proportions than James had known. As the schools demanded higher degrees for higher salaries, graduate programs proliferated across the country to meet the demand. It was a source of great annoyance to me when certain teachers college professors at Nebraska began pushing for graduate work to be offered by the department of physical education when it had all it could do financially to offer excellence in its undergraduate work. I also felt strongly that our undergraduates should go on for graduate work to other schools for wider experiences, and that they should specialize in advanced work in those disciplines which contribute to the advancement of physical education, such as anatomy, physiology, psychology and sociology.

Shortly after his arrival at the university in 1938 to succeed Dr. E. A. Burnett as chancellor, Dr. Chauncy Boucher, former dean of the Graduate College of the University of Chicago, called me to his office to inquire indignantly why I had not discussed with him my project to push for graduate work in physical education instead of his having to learn of it through a group of Teachers College professors who had interviewed him in behalf of such a program. My amazement at learning of this for the first time was matched by his learning that I knew nothing of such a movement and therefore was not a party to it.

"Good heavens," I said to him, "we are not yet doing the high quality of undergraduate work we should be doing, hampered as we are by limitations in staff, equipment and facilities. How can we ever offer proper graduate level work until this other fault is remedied?" And catching my breath, I hastened to add:

"Anyway physical educators should study for their advanced degrees in the fields of physiology, sociology, psychology, and the like—not take more physical education courses. Many physical education courses some schools give for graduate credit are merely at undergraduate level. There are already too many schools offering graduate work in physical education when they are inadequately prepared to do it properly."

He was indeed surprised at my outburst, also delighted and he called out: "Bravo! I didn't know there were people like you in the physical education profession!"

"Ah! There are lots of us. You should get acquainted."

He assured me he would block this push to get physical education set up at graduate level at Nebraska. I was amazed when I later found out who made up the little group that proposed it and yet had never approached me on the subject—some people who probably thought they had discovered an easy way for some of their friends to pick up an advanced degree with little effort. My stock went up materially with the chancellor from that day on and later I felt that my stand on this won me victories in other unexpected and important directions with him.

With the great proliferation of doctor's degrees—doctors of education as well as doctors of philosophy—many people were awakening to the realization that the top degree without a good personality plus social consciousness to go with it cannot of itself produce a good teacher.

* * * *

If the Progressive Education Movement was creating general havoc here and general advances there in various parts of the country, depending upon whether it was the education "crackpots," the liberals or the conservatives in control, it was also creating extremes here and moderation there in way of changes in my own profession.

126

In the early post World War I period, all activities that did not give the child opportunity to plan movements for himself became suspect to the progressivists as not contributing to his personality and social development. Dr. Thomas D. Wood had from the 1890s advocated exercises that simulated activities which were an outgrowth of needs of everyday life, such as running, jumping, leaping, throwing, wood chopping, sawing, lifting, carrying, stooping and the like. From these evolved a form of class activity which he called "natural" gymnastics. He urged substitution of these gymnastics for the "foreign" systems brought to the United States by the Germans and Swedes—gymnastics originally intended to develop fitness for military service. To Dr. Wood, the objectives of these gymnastic systems were wrong for American physical educators whose aim was to develop young people to be physically fit to enjoy life in a democracy.

Clark Hetherington, a member of the first freshman class at Stanford, had become an ardent admirer and loyal follower of Wood, and later a co-worker to advance this philosophy in America. Hetherington had also been influenced by the great psychologist, G. Stanley Hall, who took an early interest in physical education. Hetherington worked with him at Clark University in the late 1890s. In his book, *Adolescence*, Hall stated that gymnastics need "radical revision and coordination of the various cults and theories in the light of the latest psychophysiological science."[3] Wood and Hetherington had been aiming at this revision through the early decades of the twentieth century but it was not until the late 1920s and early 1930s that their views began to receive attention from the profession as a whole. However, schools were slow to adopt the new natural gymnastics, not because of any inherent fault in them but simply because there were not sufficient leaders prepared to teach them.

How well I recall the fiasco at the APEA convention in Boston in April 1930 when at last we were to be given a demonstration of natural gymnastics as taught in a high school by a graduate of Teachers College, Columbia University, who had received her professional training under Jesse Feiring Williams. We had heard much talk of this new form of gymnastics and I was quite intrigued and most receptive, even wondering where I could find a teacher for my staff who would be properly trained to teach it. Particularly did I desire it for our professional training students, and I was eager to see specialists at work. No doubt many others went to that demonstration as expectantly as I.

But alas, the demonstration was a dismal failure—at least most of us felt so since we saw nothing but a large group of high school girls enter the gymnasium and seat themselves in a semi-circle about their leader. As soon as an announcement was made of what they proposed to do and how, the girls began discussing something with the teacher; the audience did not catch what was being said. Now and then, a girl would rise and run to a piece of apparatus and the leader would follow her. After the student's question was answered, both resumed their seats on the floor. When the period ended, there had been much talk, but no one had had any physical activity. It was a great anti-climax. As far as I was concerned that was the death knell of natural gymnastics as demonstrated by one of the supposedly top-notch teachers. And from the disappointed "buzzing" on all sides, I was not alone in my let-down feelings. All these years since I am still wondering what Thomas Wood and Clark Hetherington, had they been present, would have thought of that demonstration. It certainly could not have portrayed what they had in mind as a class hour spent in natural gymnastics.

Although some forms of natural gymnastics were offered in some schools about the country (in fact at Amherst since the 1860s), Wood's excellent theories languished from lack of proper leadership. Hence the profession was left at the mercy of two groups waging war against each other—one group calling for a complete overhaul of physical education programs in favor of permitting each child to determine for himself what he wished to learn and how, while the other group clung to the old disciplined formal activity, with the pupil submerged in group action executed at the teacher's commands.

Advocates of the new philosophy overlooked the fact that most children have more physical likenesses in common than physical differences and therefore can be developed physically through activities based on their common needs to which formal gymnastics can contribute as they exercise in unison. On the other hand, many advocates of the old system refused to see the needs for social training. The quiet leadership of Wood and Hetherington now gave way to a militancy previously unknown as Jesse Williams struck out violently at all opposition to his ideas and at all who advocated the old gymnastic forms.

Since formal gymnastics had been the core, in fact almost the entire body of the school physical education program before World War I and even into the 1920s in many places, it was, of course, formal gymnastics that bore the brunt of the progressivists' criticism. Once the Great War was over, people were in no mood to have any activity in the schools that smacked in any way of foreign authoritarianism, and what did so more than the old formal gymnastics? Because of Williams' militancy, in some extreme situations the very word "gymnastics" became almost a dirty term within the profession.

As the slogan "America for the Americans" became popular after the war, so, too, did the idea of "American ideas, American ways for

128

Americans." Then, too, Wood's advocacy of natural gymnastics as a peculiarly American idea compared to the old foreign forms was catching on, at least in theory, to further the transition. But failure to produce the necessary teachers of this new form was the stumbling block to a successful launching of natural gymnastics.

It soon became apparent, however, that even this form was not fulfilling the purpose since this type of exercising did not come to children naturally in the gymnasium but had to be demonstrated and taught by a teacher, just as with exercises of the old German and Swedish forms. Hence, as many saw it, the old was merely to be replaced by new teacher-contrived, teacher-controlled, teacher-imposed exercises under a new name. When taught by poor teachers, full of theory but short on practical and creative skills to arouse pupils' recognition of a need to ask for assistance, little happened other than a lot of talk. There was little exercising which after all was the main purpose of the class meeting in the first place. This stirred up much contention since many teachers clung to the idea that a teacher should teach and a leader, lead. Carl Schrader, Massachusetts State Director of Physical Education, was one of the most outspoken defenders of this idea in our own profession.

*　*　*　*

As the battle line was formed, there came to the front to wage war for their beliefs the old German and Swedish gymnastics proponents versus the progressivists. It was a battle that waged within the profession throughout the thirties and into the early forties. It took nothing less than another world war to resolve it—the war of course didn't settle the dispute but it claimed everyone's attention in other directions and the battle died from lack of support from either side. In the end, neither side won. Yet in a way both sides won for in the sixties there was a vigorous revival of gymnastics in the schools—an entirely unique form consisting partly of the early progressivists' ideas, partly of the old foreign forms in use of apparatus in particular, yet even that in a form quite different from the old.

But while the battle raged in the 1930s, it created much excitement, particularly at the physical education conventions. Never was the name of the recognized fighting leader of the progressivists, Jesse Feiring Williams, listed on the program for any convention meeting that he did not draw a large crowd for everyone knew there would be fireworks. Williams affected people in decided ways—either one liked him very much or disliked him very much. Yet in another way he affected almost everyone the same way—almost everyone feared him. He was a highly intelligent man and his thrusts at an opponent could be impressively vital. Also he could be bitingly and cleverly sarcastic to anyone who dared disagree with him, so that unless one could "stand the gaff," he thought it over seriously before entering the arena against him.

The opposing side had no one recognized leader, probably because there was no single teacher-training institution recognized as the leader in preparing teachers to teach according to the old ways. The old Boston Normal School of Gymnastics, perhaps more than any other institution, had prepared women teachers for Swedish gymnastics but it had long ago, as had the department of physical education and hygiene of Wellesley College, given up the old Swedish form for an Americanized version under Dr. William Skarstrom, a Swede who had worked in earlier years at Columbia University with Thomas D. Wood. Swedish gymnastics, even Skarstroms's modified form, had all but vanished from the schools by the thirties, and no voice was raised to espouse it.

The Normal School of the North American Gymnastic Union at Indianapolis, however, was still loyal to German gymnastics but Emil Rath, its director, was a kindly, friendly soul who would never willingly have tangled in a public argument with anyone. There were many enthusiasts for German gymnastics in the public schools of Cincinnati, Milwaukee, St. Louis, Kansas City and Chicago, to name but a few. These people were willing to argue, but it was the person in the teacher-preparation field who was in the strategic position to influence the situation by indoctrinating the teachers sent out across the country, not the public school person. Lacking the strategic position enjoyed by the progressivists through their support by Columbia University, nevertheless, the opposition usually mustered a few fighters who took turns entering the arena against Dr. Williams—Carl Schrader, a native-born German transplanted to America in early childhood, Charles H. McCloy of the State University of Iowa, William Streit of Cincinnati Public Schools, Strong Hinman of Wichita, Kansas public schools and August H. Pritzlaff of the Chicago schools. Now and then, Jay B. Nash of New York University or Neils P. Neilson of the California State Department of Education would get into the act, although they were not diehards for the old formal gymnastics.

But no matter how many were ready to wage battle on the one side it was usually the indomitable Jesse Feiring Williams who took on all comers singlehandedly for the other side. Every time I saw him step forward on a platform sensing a fray, the hairs on the back of his neck bristling, his every muscle seemingly tensed and an expression on his face that most certainly declared his assurance of victory, I thought of Sir Walter Scott's lines in *The Lady of the Lake*:

Come one, come all! This rock shall fly
From its firm base as soon as I. [4]

The greatest debates were of the Williams versus McCloy variety. Whenever these two were listed in a convention program, the convention manager knew he should book the largest auditorium available since everyone wanted to be present for the excitement.

In those days physical educators flocked in huge numbers to Teachers College, Columbia University, for their advanced degrees and apparently, as far as I knew, never did a degree candidate in that department ever openly oppose the head of the department or publicly take issue with him on any subject. Dr. Williams was a man who brooked no differences of his opinions. Everyone, except a small handful of brave souls who had never been his pupils, stood in great awe of him and were fearful of opposing him in any way—that is, everyone apparently but C. H. McCloy.

Not only did Dr. Williams castigate the Old World gymnastics in school programs and also those who taught it, but he even berated setting up exercises such as Walter Camp's "daily dozen." He held up to scorn C. H. McCloy in particular who defended them for certain people unable to exercise otherwise, although he disclaimed their use for a school physical education program.

Dr. McCloy took all criticism in easy stride. These two were well matched. Although Dr. Williams was past-master at the use of sarcasm, what Dr. McCloy lacked in sarcasm he more than compensated for by sheer down-to-earth logic and common sense and his pretense not to notice the sarcasm. Each had a large following. However, many of McCloy's followers were hesitant to speak out publicly, fearful of the invectives, taunts and sneers that would come from the opposition. Followers on the other side had no such fears of Dr. McCloy to deter them, so that from public display of support the sides seemed unevenly matched. While McCloy stuck strictly to the issues, refusing to indulge in personal invectives, Williams freely castigated and ridiculed everyone who dared take side against him. While he, too, always put on a good show—he was a brilliant and polished speaker—he left his audience chilled by the taunts and sneers levelled at all opponents. It was indeed an intrepid soul who was willing to cross swords with him.

Although C. H. McCloy was not adverse to natural gymnastics, provided the children actually got worthwhile physical activity (which seemed doubtful from all he had seen of it as it was taught), he could

131

not accept complete rejection of the tested good of the old. In this he had strong backing from the German, Swedish and Danish Americans. In many speeches McCloy stood his ground against Williams' attacks on his person as well as on his views, and now and then handed back a bit of subtle sarcasm of his own, such as the following:

> I hope that the next 50 years will show physical educators to ... seek for facts proved objectively, to supplant principles based on average opinions of the people who don't know but who are all anxious to contribute their averaged ignorance to form a consensus of uninformed dogma.[5]

* * * *

Jesse Williams' idea of a cure for the wrongs of the physical education programs seemed to be to kill gymnastics completely and, with the aid of his ever-increasing body of followers, he fairly well succeeded in doing just that, not, however, without a protest from gymnastics enthusiasts. The most influential leaders among the women who felt that the Swedish and German gymnastics had served their day also advocated a change, but not a killing. During the summers of the late 1920s, Helen McKinstry (later president of Russell Sage College) organized groups of American women to study Danish gymnastics at Nils Bukh's school in Ollerup and bring this form back to American schools. Radcliffe as early as 1925, and following its lead, Barnard, Wellesley, Wells, Mt. Holyoke, Bryn Mawr, Vassar, Smith, and Goucher Colleges (all women's colleges) by early 1930s had adopted this form of gymnastics in their physical education programs. Graduates of the professional training courses at Wellesley and Smith Colleges soon carried it into the women's departments of other colleges and universities and large high schools of the country. Thus, the women quietly discarded the old German and Swedish gymnastics for the Danish form, but the great run of men who clung to gymnastics in their programs doggedly held to the old forms.

While the new progressivists in the 1920s were demanding the breaking of all ties with gymnastics of the old formal forms, the Columbia University group was by the late 1930s no longer pushing even natural gymnastics. It had proved of too little value unless taught by teachers who were creative and talented in this new form of teaching. Such teachers were entirely too scarce for the movement to spread. Apparently such teaching leadership, actually non-teaching and entirely pupil inspired, was too difficult to attain. Now this group was calling for the elimination of all forms of gymnastics from the school physical education programs, with sports, dance and related activities (camping, etc.) to make up the entire program. In many women's departments in colleges, far in advance of the men's department, sports and dance had long held the spotlight, with gymnastics a small side show, if offered at all, so that the war was being waged mainly to win the support of college men's departments and the program builders in the lower schools.

But proponents of natural gymnastics did not give up readily and while the struggle lasted they were the targets of McCloy's claims that much that they included in natural gymnastics was not "natural" after all but, like the old formal forms, was teacher-imposed. On the other hand he boldly attacked his opponents' criticism of apparatus work, which was an important part of every gymnastics class, as an activity unnatural to youth.

Recalling the free play of my own childhood years, much of which was most certainly a form of natural gymnastics, I could not understand what this rejection of apparatus work was about. Vaulting over the box and boom was certainly a continuation of childhood experiences of vaulting over the fences which surrounded almost every yard in town; walking the balance beam, a repetition of walking the picket fence; swinging on flying rings a continuation of swinging on wild grape vines down in the woods; swinging on travelling rings a simulation of swinging from branch to branch of a tree; wriggling in and out of the rungs of the Swedish ladder but an aftertaste of the joys of squirming in and out of the inviting openings in Aunt Mary's ornate porch railing; vaulting the low buck but a sequel to hilarious games of leap frog; climbing swinging ladders a postscript to climbing shaky ladders leading to haylofts. McCloy and his followers understood all this clearly and could not for the life of them understand this rejection of apparatus work in a gymnasium as something unnatural and therefore taboo in an educational program. But then maybe Dr. Williams and his followers never knew the joys of such free play in their childhood. If so, it is understandable that they did not see the connection between the apparatus work of a gymnastics program and this natural free play of childhood.

I also couldn't understand the great cries of anguish from Jesse Williams and his followers over offering even the free standing exercises (calisthenics) of gymnastics in a physical education program. That group claimed that all youth hated gymnastics and those who did partake of it did so only under coercion. My own personal experience as a teacher rejected this claim. I had taught Swedish gymnastics to college

133

women students for many years and with few exceptions they liked it. But then I liked teaching it and I had received my training in teaching it from a master teacher. Maybe these two things were a large part of the reasons for its acceptance. However, by the end of the 1930s gymnastics had almost completely disappeared from our physical education programs—Danish and Finnish (which had come in belatedly after the Danish) as well as Swedish and German—particularly in women's programs, to be replaced entirely by sports and dance.

While this battle to rid education of gymnastics was raging on the grounds that children should not be subjected to an un-American activity requiring group action at commands of a leader, I could not understand why the same objections were not aimed at bands, orchestras, glee clubs and choruses which also require submission within a group and obedience to a leader. I decided that these activities would have been objects of equally unreasoning attacks if the musicians had developed within their group persons who misinterpreted Dewey's philosophy as violently as did the extremists among physical educators who hated old world gymnastics.

The advocacy of sports to the exclusion of gymnastics in a physical education program drew fire from many who held that a good gymnastics program was far better than a poor sports program such as many schools put up with. The extreme progressivists seizing upon John Dewey's philosophy twisted it to fit their own likes and dislikes while the extreme conservatives, refusing to accept the new, were stultifying our program. In spite of the uproar, as usual, the great numbers of calm, middle-roaders prevailed, and physical education moved forward quite sanely.

In the end it was largely economics, not the scorn of Jesse Williams and not the Progressive Education Movement, that rang the death knell of old world gymnastics in the physical education programs of America. When school boards found that they could support programs of sports and dance on a less expensive basis than gymnastics (for gymnastic apparatus was more costly) they gave up gymnastics readily.

* * * *

The would-be killers of the so-called "fads and frills" of education and the extremists of the Progressive Education Movement did not hold the stage alone in the 1930s. There were the pessimistic writers and speakers of this period who proclaimed that there were no new frontiers to challenge the youth as our fathers, grandfathers, great- and great-

great-grandfathers had known. "No more worlds to conquer." It was a great topic of conversation for speakers in the depression decade.

A group of women in our profession became excited over the idea of teaching children to live wisely in a democracy. They seemed to think that the idea was entirely new with them, discounting all that had gone on quietly for many years before under the guidance of wise teachers, not only in our own field but in all fields of education. But now this group of women physical educators with their "new" ideas was going to make over at least the entire profession of physical education if not all of education. They talked endlessly of the democratic process. One woman in particular amused the rest of us considerably when her eternal talk on the subject was pitted against her undemocratic behavior, bordering on the dictatorial in conferences, committee meetings, and the like. In theory she had all the answers about the democratic process but in practice she set a poor example.

Then there also arose among the women of my profession a vocal group that became enamored of the idea of counselling students which took on such importance with some that it seemed to take precedence over all other objectives and aims of a physical education program. From the way this group promoted the topic, they seemed to think that they, too, had been the first to discover this facet of education. They also amused many of us considerably, especially those of us who had been counselling students for 20 and more years but doing it without fanfare as a side issue outside our classroom work. Now under the tutelage of the promoters of this "new" idea we were, to save time in private counselling, to use our class periods for group counselling, which even we older ones did see as a new technique. But we objected to it when used as a substitute for activity in classes.

These overly ardent crusaders lost all sense of proportion, forgetting that many teachers in other departments were also interested in these same pupils and were also counselling them. They also forgot that in many schools there were deans of girls and deans of women who looked upon their own function as primarily counselling. To these physical education zealots hoping to build a new world of education, counselling was apparently the one thing that would get the job done and they alone were to do it. And they would do it by having girls don their gymnasium suits and sit on the gym floor in a semi-circle about the teacher while she extolled the values of democracy and moved on to discuss their group personality problems. The class bell rang and, in extreme cases, the girls would return to the dressing room and doff their gym suits without having had any real physical activity. Yet these were the only teachers in the entire school who were prepared and hired to give them physical activity. When they neglected this part of the school program it was a total neglect but if they did not do the counselling there were many teachers in several other departments who made up for the neglect.

In these years of tensions I argued with many a young physical education teacher that she must not, in her eagerness to take over in the group counselling field, lose sight of her main job which was to teach physical education. Anyway most were totally unprepared to do group counselling even though the idea held much fascination for them. Some who had taken some graduate work, met up with new theories and had become enamored with the idea of the dramatic presentations by groups to bring personality conflicts out in the open, psycho-dramas they were called. These ideas were much talked of and tried out at some physical education conferences. A few women leaders of the "new thought" went to summer seminars and picked up a little learning on the subject which they palmed off on delegates to our own conferences as the last word in the techniques of effective teaching. As I sat in on these demonstrations, I was always conscious of the old saying, "A little knowledge is a dangerous thing." After a while this fad passed over and we came back to earth and presumably again taught physical education.

I was glad I was by then anchored in the safe harbor of administrative work. Nothing remained of the exercise program I had been taught to teach in my own professional training days. Gymnastics which we knew best of all were out, as was esthetic dance. Even sports classes now were taught from an altogether different (and I must say better) angle with drill in the fundamental techniques preceding actual playing of a game. In my school days we played at the game until we learned it—"learning by doing" as people spoke of it later but with a somewhat different connotation. It was a greatly changed world of physical education by the late 1930s and I must confess (for all I disapproved of the extremes of progressive education) a better one.

The pull of the extremists had brought us out of a rut and stopping short of the extremes, physical education had been greatly improved. In the mid and late 1930s it became impossible to bring to my staff good gymnastics teachers since the professional departments in colleges no longer gave training in gymnastics. But dance had settled down into a form accepted all across the country, known as modern dance, the successor to esthetic, nature and interpretive dance of earlier years. It offered such splendid physical developmental activities (not for their own sake as the dance teachers were quick to point out) that I seized every opportunity to see that every student under my direction registered for modern dance some time during her college years at Nebraska. Although a sports enthusiast, I recognized that sports alone could not replace the physiological values of gymnastics which I felt strongly were fundamental to sports. Therefore I gladly adopted modern dance through its fundamental exercises as a fitting substitute for gymnastics for our women students.

By the 1950s several books were published that proved to be effective attacks on progressive education.[6] The opposition of the far left, far right, and in-between were all calling for a return to academic discipline, with all children required to study history, English, sciences, mathematics, and foreign languages as their birthright and for teacher training to be reunited with the arts and sciences faculties, and the schools to be removed from the control of professional educationists with a de-emphasizing of pedagogy. In reality they were objecting to the excesses of Dewey's followers who had not only misinterpreted his philosophy but also had not developed a body of teachers who could adequately handle their ideas. The result for the schools in far too many places had been merely chaos.

The pendulum had swung back leaving in the schools much of Dewey's own philosophy but divorced of its ill-fated trimmings which were added by extremists whose views he himself did not share. Dewey did point the way to something much better than our schools knew in the nineteenth and early twentieth centuries. Who today is not sold on the idea that in the education of the child there should be a recognition of individual differences, opportunity for personality development and for proper social and emotional growth as well as for proper physical growth, yet woven through it all discipline? The transition period of the experimentation of the twenties and thirties led to something much better in the education of the child than anything the pre-World War I period offered.

By 1940 the movement had come under such criticism that the Progressive Education Association died in 1955 with its magazine, *The Journal of Progressive Education*, holding on two more years before it, too, folded, thus ending a tense, controversial period in the history of education.

Chapter VII
Petticoat Rule Comes To One National Professional Organization

In its infancy in the late 1880s and 1890s, the American Association for the Advancement of Physical Education had served well the northeastern seaboard of the United States where physical educators were for the most part concentrated. By the turn of the century, it had begun to draw an increasing number of members from the middle states and then from the Pacific Coast and as far south as the Gulf of Mexico—in other words, its membership had become truly a national group. But it was still provincial in its outlook, still very much ruled and controlled from the East, so that by the 1910s there were discernible rumbles of impatience from the hinterlands.

It took 35 years for the Association to elect as president one who was not working on the Eastern Seaboard, Dudley B. Reed, M.D., of the University of Chicago. He served as national president for three calendar years, 1920 through 1922. By then the workers in the profession in the Middle West, largely ignored by the workers in the East, had already set up their own independent professional organization, and soon became a challenge to the older supposedly national group.[1]

A "late bloomer" in so many ways throughout life, I had been unusually slow in the first years of my career in involving myself in professional concerns beyond my own little teaching job. However, my profession had done little before The Great War to reach the young roots at the local levels. We young teachers were awakened slowly to broader professional interests. I had been teaching eight years before I plunged my first irons into the professional fire when I discovered in 1918 first the Middle West Society of Physical Education and then the Middle West Society of College Women's Physical Directors.

The 1920s offered still more irons for my professional fire when I discovered the Women's Athletic Committee of APEA, the Women's Division of the National Amateur Athletic Federation, and the National Association of Physical Education for College Women; into the 1930s these several irons glowed warmly as with each passing year I was drawn ever deeper into the inner work of these groups. Now in the 1930s I added two more irons, the Nebraska Physical Education Society and APEA. In 1931, Earl Johnson of the Lincoln Public Schools and I revived the Nebraska State Society of Physical Education, following the 1926 unsuccessful attempt of the two of us to get a permanent organization going. In the late 1890s there had been other unsuccessful attempts at organization, unknown to us.[2]

Elmer Mitchell, editor of the new *Journal of Health and Physical Education* turned over the editorial column of this first issue January 1930 to Frederick Maroney then president of APEA and to me then president of the Middle West Society, the two groups whose magazines had been merged to create the new one. President Maroney wrote of "American Physical Education at the Crossroads," calling attention to the early workers who had laid a strong foundation for our profession saying that all teachers of physical education must work together, "for a better understanding of our program and we must keep faith with the men and women who were the pioneers of our subject in the schools of the land." In my part of the editorial I said that the Middle West Society was proud to contribute its magazine *The Pentathlon* and its editor to the national association and that "we are more earnestly than ever before committed to national unity."

Upon my election as president of the Middle West group, I seized the initiative and kept control of the Middle West convention as president. In previous years, the convention had been in the hands of a convention chairman. Presidents and their councils had been looked upon, as far as conventions were concerned, as mere figure-heads. The presidents gave their addresses, presided at any business meeting that might be called (although in the national association the official business meeting was held in New York City during the Christmas holidays apart from the convention), and, aside from these two tasks, were only sideline guests. The convention chairman was the head person at the convention and his will was the law. Whatever programs were offered reflected the philosophy and wishes of the convention chairman, not those of the president of the Association and his Council.

Frederick Maroney, a young fire-brand, was not afraid to upset the *status quo* whenever it seemed necessary to do so. He had been cheated out of a chance to have a convention during his first year in the presidency (1929) because of the Middle West's obstinate insistence upon holding its own convention in Chicago although APEA desired to come into its territory at Indianapolis. This caused APEA to give up all plans for a convention for that year altogether.

With the national slated for a convention in 1930 in Boston with Dr. Maroney elected president for a second calendar year, the Boston Physical Education Society, upon signs of his intentions of running his own convention, demanded that previous custom be observed and that the entire responsibility be placed in the hands of the local person it would name as convention chairman. Dr. Maroney reluctantly consented to this. Carl Schrader who as a past president had himself been a mere figure-head during three conventions (1923, 1924, 1925) was named convention chairman, and if Frederick Maroney was not being allowed to run his own convention at least Carl Schrader was now having his chance to put on a convention, and since he was a close friend of President Maroney he did naturally talk many things over with him. But this inability to make the convention his, added to the many unpleasantnesses met up with earlier in dealing with the Middle West, gave Dr. Maroney a great feeling of inadequacy. He was a man used to success, to having his own way and to having his plans carried out. He encouraged me as president to keep the reins of the Middle West Society in my own hands if at all possible, and it was easily possible because although the Milwaukee people wanted to have the convention there in 1930, the person they named as convention chairman was apparently none too eager for a lot of extra work.

When J. E. Rogers of the National Recreation Association dropped into Lincoln early in 1930 I checked plans with him and asked him for advice, for he had helped put on many Playground and Recreation Association conventions. When he asked what arrangements had been made with the hotel for complimentary rooms for top officers, I was astonished. It had never entered my head that there might be such a possibility. As acting president at the Chicago convention in 1929, stepping in at the eleventh hour to fill the vacancy caused by Mr. Post's sudden death, I had paid for my own room. It had never occurred to me to ask for a complimentary room as acting president, and apparantly it had not occurred to Mr. Mitchell, the secretary, or Mr. Delaporte, the convention chairman, to ask in my behalf. I never have known if the Morrison Hotel in Chicago furnished complimentary

140

rooms for them in 1929. I never could bring myself to ask. So I was learning the hard way. And Mr. Mitchell was learning, too.

When I now wrote Mr. Mitchell asking what he as secretary was doing about contracts with the Milwaukee hotel for 1930 and to investigate the possibility of complimentary rooms for the president and secretary, he replied that it was highly doubtful if the hotel would consider complimentary rooms, so I dismissed the idea. Later I wrote the hotel making a reservation for one of their lower-priced single rooms since I was going on from there to the national in Boston and, with allowance for traveling, only to one out-of state meeting the two-convention trip was going to be quite expensive. So when convention time came around I found myself settled in a very small and undesirable inside room, next to a freight elevator, and from there carried on as president of the organization. Then when I reported to pay my bill when checking out the hotel manager made the "magnificent" gesture of writing on the room bill "complimentary to the president of the Middle West Society." If they intended to give a complimentary room, why not a decent one instead of a mere hole in the wall! And why was I not so informed ahead of time or at least when checking in? Again I couldn't bring myself to ask Mr. Mitchell what his experience had been as secretary.

Caught up in the details of putting on a convention by correspondence, I was meticulously making a record of every piece of work to be done to pass on to my successor with warnings of "Do's" and "Don'ts," as I was learning entirely from trial and error. Not one scrap of paper had been turned over to me from my predecessor's files. I was determined that never again should a person in the Middle West Society come to the presidency with no guides.

* * * *

The members of the Middle West Society of Directors of Physical Education for College Women went to Milwaukee early to attend their own private conference preceding the larger Middle West Society convention, so that all of us were safely tucked away before the March 25th blizzard struck. Mr. Mitchell had had all the programs printed in Ann Arbor and had sent them to Milwaukee by a staff member going by auto. But they got caught in the blizzard. Although Mr. Mitchell and President Maroney and all the east-of-Chicago crowd traveling by train were held in Chicago for hours because of the storm, they did finally arrive most belatedly, but the auto with the programs and

141

association records did not arrive until the closing morning of the convention. Most delegates who had ventured to go by auto were stalled at farm houses across Iowa, Illinois, Minnesota, Michigan and Wisconsin, as we learned later, and many as soon as they could get out of the snow turned back home. So it was a sadly depleted crowd that did manage to get there. But those who arrived made a great holiday of it. Without printed programs, everyone had to gather every two hours in the hotel lobby to read the large bulletin board announcing what would take place next and where. Fortunately, we officers had our typed copies of the program. And as each meeting closed, announcements would be made of coming events. No one could plan for anything in advance and as some speakers never did arrive, all sorts of impromptu substitute programs were arranged. As everyone took the emergency in good spirit, it all made for much merriment and there developed among the delegates a wonderful, unforgettable spirit of camaraderie.

Traffic signals were just then coming into vogue in our cities and were something of a novelty. Our convention chairman persuaded the city traffic manager to let him have a stop-and-go lantern set on a post which he installed on the platform to be controlled by hand. The idea was that as soon as a speaker was introduced and arose to begin speaking, the head time-keeper would flash on the green light and when the time alloted for that speech was up, he would flash on the red light which came on accompanied by the loud ringing of a bell just as happened in the street connections. I was dismayed at the prospect of running our meetings this way, for although I was all for friendliness and informality, I felt that this bordered on rowdyism, but I held my tongue when I saw how gleefully everyone was accepting the innovation. But the speakers, fearful of not finishing on time, watched the traffic signal post nervously along with the audience.

Finally, a woman guest speaker, annoyed by this loud ticking signal, stopped in the midst of her speech and pointing an accusing finger at the signal, called out angrily, "Take that thing out of here!" At this I stepped up to the platform and called for the convention chairman to get help and cart it off the stage. And Dr. Maroney, our guest from the national association, looked as though he might be going to have a stroke from his efforts to keep from bursting into the gales of laughter that struggled to possess him. At heart one of us Midwesterners not attuned to the reserved, sedate and formal ways of so many Easterners, he was having a hilariously good time among us unpredictable, unconventional, and outgoing folk from the Midlands. And the merriment and informalities seemed to dispel the last of any hard feelings left over from the 1920s between the Middle West Society and the National Association.

142

When I invited Dr. Maroney to sit in on our last Middle West council meeting he thanked the Middle West Society for giving the national its new secretary-editor, and then turning to me, he bowed, and added, "also its Vice-President who is to be the next president of APEA." I was astounded at this as apparently were the others for all sat for a moment, as did I, in stunned silence. No woman had ever been president of APEA. How ridiculous could he be! Seeing my embarrassment and the surprised silence of the others, he hastened to add: "Of course I have no power to control such things but you all now know my wish!" I was speechless! When I regained my composure, I ignored his remarks, sensing for the moment no other way to handle such an embarrassment, and hastened on to the business matters at hand. As soon as the meeting was over, I cornered Mr. Mitchell and procured his promise to persuade Dr. Maroney that there were to be no more foolish statements, particularly none the next week in Boston.

* * * *

With the convention at an end, those of us Middlewesterners who were going on to the national convention in Boston made up a jolly group for the railroad trip east. From a furious last of March blizzard such as is well known in the Middle West at that time of year, we stepped directly into spring in Boston. There I attended the second APEA convention I had ever attended. Put on by Carl Schrader, Massachusetts State Director of Physical Education, as convention chairman, and Marjorie Bouvé of the Boston School of Physical Education, Boston, as hostess, it was a brilliant convention, meticulously correct from section meetings to formal banquet.

Presented at the general session as vice president of the organization, I began enlarging professional contacts to include Westerners as well as those of the Middle West and East.

True to his promise to the Middle West group that he would do what he could to get APEA reorganized on more democratic lines and functional lines, President Maroney had announced at the December 30, 1929, council meeting that all sections and affiliated groups were to be discontinued temporarily. Each was instructed to think through its reorganization plan and apply for re-admission through the constitution committee, Clifford Brownell of Columbia University, chairman. These groups wishing to be re-admitted were to meet certain standards to be established and announced shortly. The year 1930 was to be a reorganization year.

143

Also at this December 1929 council meeting the president announced that a group of women had persistently demanded recognition as a group to put on a program in swimming for women, at the spring convention in Boston, apart from the program put on of late years by the unofficial Women's Athletic Section (WAS), saying that they ultimately hoped to establish an independent Section on Swimming for Women. Since the earlier group, WAS, had been permitted a program at conventions for the past several years, it also petitioned for a place on the Boston convention program and, when there was some hesitancy about granting the request in light of all the reorganization worries, a few of the WAS women became naggingly insistent, knowing nothing as yet of this other group of women pushing for a separate swimming program.

This nagging insistence of two groups of women proved too much for President Maroney and having reached the end of his patience with all of his other nagging worries, he°exclaimed, "Okay, we'll have a program on athletics for boys and men, too," and he announced that both programs would be set up as subgroups under the Public School Section and that all must understand that this was but a temporary arrangement for the Boston 1930 convention only and that neither group was to elect chairmen at the program to carry on for the following year because, as he said, there were no official sections on either men's or women's athletics and that "this nonsense has to stop." However, Dr. McCurdy, always a friend of the Women's Athletic Committee and its programing counterpart, WAS, had in the March 1929 issue of the *Review* started a permanent page on athletics for girls and women to be a special feature of the magazine conducted jointly by the Women's Division of NAAF and the WAS. So he as secretary-editor of APEA had publicly recognized a section on women's athletics.

Then at the December 1929 council meeting, President Maroney announced that as the newly elected vice-president I would be a member of the program committee for the next convention. Immediately after this council meeting, the chairman of the Public School Section approached me in alarm because he had his program plans well underway and he did not want these two sub-groups wished off on his program. Also, the women began pressing me to overrule President Maroney's decree about their place on the program. Feeling that a president's decree could not be set aside lightly, I refused the request of both groups and thereby won the enmity of a few women although the Public School Section Chairman took it in stride and conceded he could not see how I could have ruled otherwise. I urged the women to be more patient but a few of them declared later, in reporting the meeting, that I had "sold the women down the river."

144

* * * *

The following December the official annual business meeting of the APEA Council was held, as in the past, in New York City, in connection with meetings of groups of men of our profession, such as the College Physical Education Association (then 33 years old) and the Football Coaches Association. These two groups alone called out many physical educators, so that most of the APEA council members, predominantly men, were coming to New York City anyway for other meetings at the holiday season. The Women's Division of NAAF, then seven years old, had also established the habit of meeting at this same time in New York City. With deep interest by now in both the APEA Council and the Women's Division, I joined the holiday pilgrimage crowd headed for this winter professional Mecca.

During this year of my national vice presidency, I was in a position where I could advance the cause of a large group of women pushing for recognition for the unofficial Women's Athletics Section. To protect the interests of the Section (meaning to put it in a position where it would have a vote in the council, a move bitterly opposed by some of the men), I was actively fighting a little sub-rosa group of women who were opposing the other women with the secret backing of a little group of men who hoped to defeat the Women's Athletics Section through this sub-rosa group. These were men who felt the women were pushing for too much but, unwilling to come out in the open about it, were working through this little group of dissident women. Also I had learned that some of the *status quo* men were critical of Dr. Maroney's propensities for breaking with tradition, and his seizing every opportunity to insist that I was to be the next president surely became an irritation to this group.

There was no movement of women to push for a woman president. It was much more geography, than sex, that set whatever battle lines existed within the profession. From the very year of APEA's founding in 1885, women had been elected to the lesser offices. Only the presidency itself was considered the prerogative of men only, and that apparently had never been challenged. In fact, Dr. Maroney had been taken seriously by no one, not even the women, and least of all by me. Whenever he dropped his little bombshell of an announcement, there was no denying the expression on the faces of the listeners as if saying in the idiom of a later day, "You've got to be kidding!" In 1930 no one but Frederick Maroney and his little group of followers seemed to think it possible to have a woman president of this national organization.

When the official business meeting of APEA council was held December 30, 1930, in New York City, I never dreamed that Frederick Maroney would have his wish confirmed. Nothing could have been more casual than the circumstances surrounding the election of officers. They used no nominating committee in those days. The president merely announced it was time for election of officers and he was ready to receive nominations from the floor whereupon Carl Schrader arose and said, "Mr. President, I feel it is high time we have a woman president and I nominate Miss Mabel Lee." As I recall it, it was Dr. Arthur Lamb of McGill University of Montreal who seconded the nomination. Since no other name was offered, the call for nominations was declared closed, and I was elected by unanimous vote of those present. I was too stunned for words. It had all happened in a moment—no remarks by anyone in support of my candidacy, not one word to the effect that a tradition of 45 years was being broken, just the barest formality! Equally casually and informally, Jesse F. Williams was elected vice-president, but it could have been no surprise for he, although a controversial figure, was well known across the country as a popular author and much sought-after speaker in our field.

I was as surprised as everyone else especially because up to two years before I was virtually unknown within the profession except by the group of women physical education teachers in colleges. Serving as vice-president was not looked upon as a stepping-stone to the presidency. Only twice before had a vice-president stepped to the top position and both occasions were in the early 1890s, so holding that office some 40 years later gave no encouragement towards moving into the top office.

Even though Dr. Maroney had been warning me that I was to be the next president I was totally unprepared for it. I was at first so completely stunned that I was practically speechless and perilously near tears. However, when called upon for a few words, I managed to get to my feet to thank them for the confidence they had placed in me and to ask for their loyal support. On sudden thought, I reminded them of my speech just a year before when elected vice-president when I had pleaded for complete reorganization of APEA on a more logical and grass-roots-watering basis. Now I expressed my delight and the delight of the entire Middle West Society that had been demanding changes which, under Dr. Maroney's fine leadership, were showing signs of beginning to come true. And I pledged myself to advance the work.

Of the six women on the national council at that time (Edith Gates representing the National YWCA physical educators, Helen Hazelton of Purdue University representing Women's Athletics Section, Ruth Elliott

Author in 1931 when she broke the sex barrier for the top office in her national professional organization.

of Wellesley College, Gertrude Moulton of Oberlin College representing NAPECW, Natalie Wilson unknown to us other women, and myself as vice-president) only two were present besides myself (Edith Gates and Helen Hazelton). So one woman (the WAS representative did not have a vote) and 31 men, representing other APEA memberships, elected the first woman president of the American Physical Education Association. Two other women were present as visitors (Marjorie Bouvé of Boston and Mazie Scanlon of Atlantic City). Thus petticoat rule (as the coming of women into high office replacing men was commonly spoken of in those days) came to one national mixed-sex organization to take over for the calendar year of 1931.

At this council meeting Clifford Lee Brownell, chairman of the constitution committee, presented plans for almost complete reorganization of APEA, meeting the major criticisms of the Middle West group. The changes were accepted by a large majority. Not only were the district groups to become integral parts of the organization from then on, each with representation on the executive committee, but the annual official business meeting was to be held in connection with the annual convention, making the December 1930 gathering the last official council meeting of the past 20 years to be held apart from a convention.

The official meeting of the council elected at that time for the calendar year 1931 would be held April 1, 1931, marking the close of that regime preparatory to swinging into a pattern of spring meeting to spring meeting from then on.

As soon as the meeting adjourned all flocked to congratulate me. It was a tremendous outpouring of friendliness, enthusiasm and desire to help. So the presidency of the first woman was off on a happy note. Everyone seemed pleased and the men most of all. But then as usual they were in the great majority and they seemed to want to strut over their achievement of having elected a woman. This had not been a campaign of women against men with the women, at long last, putting their candidate over. My election had been proposed by a man and sponsored by the men. I had been nominated by a man and the nomination was seconded by a man, and the men held the controlling votes, so that in a sense I was elected by the men although there was no opposing vote. The first woman was stepping into the presidency seemingly with the complete backing of the men who had been in absolute control of the Association for 45 years. They were happy because it was their idea and their doing. The women were happy because at last a woman was recognized. As some of us talked it over later, not one of us knew at the time a single mixed-sex national organization other than the National Education Association that had ever had a woman president.

Surely never did a woman president enter office under more favorable circumstances. However I sensed that although it was an auspicious beginning it would take some maneuvering to keep the waters calm, and I prayed I might be equal to the occasion. Indeed I entered upon this new era for the national association happy that for the moment everyone else seemed to be happy over it. I saw that the day had come (if only I did not blunder too much) when women could at last have an equal place beside the men as partners in the professional work—no longer looked upon as a minority group to be shunted in and out of vice-presidencies at the will of men and permitted nothing more.

One of my first undertakings was to appoint Dr. J. F. Williams, who had been elected vice-president, to serve as chairman of a committee to study the problem of allocating the various states to the districts so that this work would be completed in time to incorporate the allocation into the new constitution by April, 1931. I had been flattered to have Dr. Williams as a member of my team. I wrote Mr. Mitchell, January 16:

> Dr. Williams' name added to the list of officers adds great professional color. His name alone is an asset to any list.

This I wrote in all sincerity for I felt as practically everyone else seemed to at that time that he was the acknowledged scholar of the new group coming into prominence.

Then I entered upon lengthy communication with Secretary Mitchell over the constitution. We had served as a team together when I was president and he was secretary-treasurer-editor of the Middle West Society through two conventions. Now we were entering upon the same relationship in the national office.

However it was the forward-looking and liberal Middlewesterners who had first opened the door to the top position to a woman within our profession. As early as 1917, this regional group, then five years old, having had two men presidents, elected Ethel Perrin of Detroit as its first woman president. A graduate of my own professional school, the Boston Normal School of Gymnastics, she was one of the few women in the country then head of physical education in a large city school system. She was the first woman in our field to be recognized by the top office by even a district group. Five years later, J. Anna Norris, M.D., of the University of Minnesota (also a BNSG graduate) held that same presidency for three successive years. Immediately following her in that presidency was Margaret McKee, reared and educated in England, head of physical education in the public schools and city recreation in Des Moines, Iowa. These three dynamic women set a good pattern as women presidents of a mixed group in the Middle West from 1917 on at the district level. Now in 1931 the national group had its first woman president (I, also a BNSG-Wellesley graduate).

A few months later the Eastern District Society, then 12 years old, having had five men presidents, elected its first woman president, Marjorie Bouvé (another BNSG graduate). At the same time the Southern District Society, then four years old with three men past presidents, elected its first woman president, Mary C. Coleman (BNSG-Wellesley graduate). Three years later the North West District Society fell into line—after four years with four men presidents, it elected Ruth Weythman of Washington State College at Bellingham. The Central District Society, born in 1933 by a division of the old Middle West group into sections east and west of the Mississippi River, elected a woman, Clare H. Small (BNSG graduate) of the University of Colorado as its first woman president in 1934. In that year the South West District was born, and its third president was a woman, Louise S. Cobb (another BNSG-Wellesley graduate) of the University of California (Berkeley). From 1912 to 1934, the entire country was covered by district societies within my profession, and in the period 1917 to 1938 women came into their own in the top offices in all these regional groups.

Except for a few isolated unpleasant experiences with a few women, prompted in all probabilities by envy or jealousy, and with a few men prompted no doubt by a desire to dominate over women, I do not see how any woman could step into a national presidency as the first of her sex under more auspicious circumstances than did I nor how one could have on the whole a happier experience from it. (I have often wondered how it was in 1911 with Ella Flag Young when she became the first woman president of the huge National Education Association after many years of none but men presidents.)

At this time the American Physical Education Association boasted a membership of almost 6,000 from a start of 49, 45 years earlier. Ninety years after its founding, (1975) it had 46,782 members and in 1977, 46,854 members.

Now I had a task to perform. I couldn't let all these people down— the men who had the power to hand me this honor and the women who were happy about it and were offering me their loyal support. Since the election had taken place during the Christmas holidays of 1930 I had only three months to prepare for the national convention and to carry on the reorganization of our national association which Frederick Maroney had started in an effort to meet the many criticisms of the Middle West group. Now one of the Middle West's own was at the helm. I simply had to make good!

Fortunately things on the whole went well for it immediately became an unwritten law that men and women should alternate in the presidency of this national organization, a custom breached but twice in all these over 45 years since, and then without question from the women. Had I failed it would have been a long time before a second woman would have been given a chance at the presidency.

As word of my election spread, the women were rather dazed. Had there been a women's movement to push for reorganization any one of several women who were well known in the profession would most surely have been pushed for the office—most certainly not I. But after they got over their first surprise and astonishment, most women accepted me as the first woman president in fine spirit and with great loyalty. I was besieged with telegrams, letters, notes of congratulation, pledges of loyalty and offers of assistance—from men as well as from women—so that it was a heart-warming experience.

Just before the spring convention of my presidency opened, a Middle West woman who was almost a total stranger to me, wrote the following:

> Whatever you believe or whatever you do, I hope you are conscious of the fact that the women in physical education are overwhelmingly proud to have any woman as president of the national association, but when it is possible to have someone we admire and respect professionally and personally as we do you, the women physical educators are almost certain to bust a button during the first week in April. [Referring to the first convention with a woman president][3]

I knew I was being watched and tested in the name of all women of our profession. I had to make good or it would be a long time before the men would entrust a woman again with the Association's highest office.

* * * *

The first of the two spring conventions which I put on as president was held in Detroit in April, 1931, at the somewhat new Book-Cadillac hotel. As president, I had been assigned a suite of two twin-bed rooms, each with its own bath, plus a connecting large living room and entrance hall. During the winter I had spear-headed a drive among Boston Normal School of Gymnastics alumnae to finance the trip to this convention for Miss Homans long-time director of this school who was to be honored and who was then 83 years old and seriously failing in health. A few of us had been informed that she was living in greatly restricted circumstances financially—pensioned niggardly by Wellesley

151

College. This situation surely would have been far from the thoughts of Mrs. Mary Hemenway of Boston when she stipulated in her will in the 1890s that her legacy should not only finance the Boston Normal School of Gymnastics through affiliation with some collegiate institution but should also, as we understood it, finance Amy Morris Homans, her trusted co-worker through her directorship of the department of physical education in this collegiate tie-up and her later retirement. My dear friend, Marion Watters Babcock of my own BNSG-Wellesley Class of 1910 had volunteered to go from her home in Philadelphia to Wellesley to accompany Miss Homans to Detroit and back home by train and to be her constant companion throughout the stay in Detroit. I was able to have both in one of the bedrooms of my suite.

From that vantage point Miss Homans held court in the flower-bedecked parlor. Besides floral tributes to Miss Homans, a great number of people and organizations sent flowers to celebrate the presidency of the first woman so that the suite of rooms was festive. There Miss Homans received her former pupils and a great circle of admirers. It had been many years since she had attended an APEA convention. Every morning Henry Ford sent a car and chauffeur to take her and her friends for a drive but I was never free to accompany them. And each afternoon one or both of his two sisters (old friends of Miss Homans) called at the suite. Miss Homans had a last wonderful reunion with many old friends and former pupils.

In my maiden speech as president, at the opening general session, I made reference to the historic Boston physical education conference of 1889 which had been organized and directed by Amy Morris Homans—because of her presence with us that evening. As I spoke from notes rather than a manuscript, I do not have a record of my exact words but whatever they were they unfortunately gave the impression that I looked upon that event as the beginning of our Association history, for no sooner was I off the platform than the first critic called my attention to this error, pointing out that it was W. G. Anderson who had founded the Association and the year was 1885. Two or three others kindly but firmly set me straight also, so I really had bungled that statement all unintentionally. And this faux pas must have been reported (no doubt gleefully by some people back East who looked upon us Midwesterners as somewhat uneducated) for in May, I received a courteous letter from Dr. W. G. Anderson, then long retired from his position at Yale University, sending me a souvenir of the birth of APEA and telling me briefly the story. The souvenir was a copy of the letter of invitation sent out by him calling the first convention. I was delighted to have it and even more so to have this courteous friendly letter from our founder. That letter turned out to be the beginning of many years of delightful correspondence with a charming, friendly gentleman. However, it was not until four years later at our Golden Jubilee Convention in Pittsburgh that I had an opportunity to meet him but by then we were well acquainted as "pen pals."

My presidential address had been kept short for there was an unusual and important ceremony to take up most of the evening. For the past two years, at Frederick Maroney's instigation, the Association, through a special committee, had been at work on a plan to honor leaders in the profession. An Honor Award had been agreed upon, the honorees had been selected, and the first presentations were to be made by me at the opening session of this 1931 convention. As these were the first awards in our 45 years of conventions, it was decided for this year to recognize a large group consisting of early outstanding leaders still living as well as exceptional leaders still at work but nearing retirement. Forty-eight honorees had been selected and 24 had signified their intentions to be present in Detroit. Thirteen (all Easterners) who could not be present were to receive their awards at the Eastern District Convention which would follow in a few weeks in Trenton, N.J. and 11 would be honored at Detroit *in absentia*. So with 35 citations to read at that opening session, the slate was full. Since there were no precedents to go by, Elmer Mitchell and I were faced with dozens of questions to be answered quickly as to the details of the ceremony. We were establishing precedents ourselves.

Among the more notable of the honorees besides Amy Morris Homans (with her elegant tortoise-shell trumpet-like hearing aid, quite the vogue in those years before something better was invented) were James Naismith, creator of basketball, and Amos Alonzo Stagg, both well known nationally in sports circles as well as in physical education. From the platform I could look over the array of honorees as the 24 of them were seated in the front row of seats—12 on each side of the aisle. As Detroit's Mayor, Frank Murphy (later to become attorney general of the United States and still later a justice of the Supreme Court) and Superintendent of Schools Frank Cody made their addresses of welcome, I sat back and studied this group. It was, indeed, a remarkable group. This first Honor Award ceremony had brought together all the great of our pioneer days who were still living and could get there. Most were but names to me and I was glad they were seated alphabetically, so I could identify each from the printed program.

I was happy to be the one to confer this honor not only on Amy Morris Homans, the director of my professional training school, but also on three of her earlier graduates, all by then friends of mine— Lydia Clark, J. Anna Norris, and Ethel Perrin, besides Blanche Trilling a later graduate and for extra measure of joy, a recent friend, Elizabeth

Burchenal, a Sargent School graduate, head of the American Folk Art Society.

Dr. Maroney, our immediate past president, was to receive the award and was to be present at both the national and Eastern District conventions. In deciding whether to receive the Honor Award from me, the new president whom he had championed as the first woman to hold that office, or Dr. Jesse Feiring Williams, his close friend who held the vice presidency of the national and also the presidency of the Eastern District Society, he finally chose to wait until a few weeks later so that it would be Jesse Williams who would make the presentation.

Since the conferring of these first honor awards was such an historic event within the Association, a listing of the 1931 honorees seems appropriate here. The single star before the name means the award was presented at the national convention in Detroit, a double star means it was presented in Detroit *in absentia,* and all other awards were presented by Dr. Williams at the Eastern District convention in Trenton, New Jersey, a few weeks later. The list is as follows:

1. W. G. Anderson	*25. Gertrude Moulton
** 2. Jessie Bancroft	*26. James Naismith
3. Howard Braucher	*27. J. Anna Norris
* 4. John Brown, Jr.	28. Henry Panzer
* 5. Elizabeth Burchenal	*29. Ethel Perrin
* 6. William Burdick	30. J. E. Raycroft
** 7. Joseph Cermak	*31. William Reuter
* 8. Lydia Clark	*32. Charles W. Savage
* 9. Louis J. Cooke	33. John Schmidlin
*10. Gertrude Dudley	34. E. C. Schneider
**11. Delphine Hanna	*35. Carl Schrader
12. Oliver Herbert	36. Herman Seibert
**13. Clark W. Hetherington	37. George Seikel
*14. Amy Morris Homans	**38. William Skarstrom
*15. Eugene Howe	*39. Amos Alonzo Stagg
*16. Henry Kallenberg	40. William Stecher
**17. W. H. Kilpatrick	**41. Thomas A. Storey
*18. A. M. Kindervater	*42. Henry Suder
**19. William Kopp	*43. Blanche M. Trilling
**20. Joseph Lee	*44. Jesse F. Williams
21. Frederick W. Maroney	*45. George Wittich
*22. James Huff McCurdy	**46. Thomas D. Wood
23. R. Tait McKenzie	**47. August Zapp
24. George L. Meylan	*48. Carl Ziegler

Since Miss Homans was the oldest of the group present and severely handicapped by hearing difficulties, we decided to call her first so that she could be escorted from the ballroom if she became tired. All others were called in alphabetical order.

In the group at Detroit that April evening of 1931, there were past presidents of the Association, the creator of the game of basketball, the country's most talked of football coach, 7 retirees, 8 women and 16 men, all ranging in age from 45 to 83, the youngest being Jesse Feiring Williams who had risen quickly to national recognition within the profession. Of the 7 women in that group besides Miss Homans, 5 were in important positions at prestigious colleges and universities and 2 headed up national organizations.

Of those honored *in absentia* that evening (two women and nine men), five, both men and women, were retired, and four men were still at work. The names Bancroft, Hanna, Hetherington, Wood, almost 50 years later, still mean much in our profession as does that of Joseph Lee, patron saint of the playground movement in America.

Of the group of 13 upon whom the national Honor Award was conferred at the Eastern District convention that same April, the three stars of the occasion were W. G. Anderson, founder of APEA, R. Tait McKenzie, president for four years (calendar years 1912 through 1915), and George L. Meylan earliest of all living past presidents of that day.

With these two lengthy ceremonies, APEA united its past with its present, starting a tradition that almost 50 years later is still going strong.

The spring before, the Bostonians had put on the national convention to my liking in its social amenities which seemed to come easily to them but were difficult to sell to the Middle West. In the few years I had been attending conventions I had become used to being one of a very few women who donned dinner dress for dinner and formal evening dress for later social affairs. Many women arrived at the conventions in tailored suits and wore them morning, noon, and night, and the men, too, wore only business suits all the time. And with men usually at the helm and oblivious of the fact that they should be setting the tone, we seemed destined to remain socially inept as a professional group. I had stoutly maintained that if our profession was to be accepted on a social footing with other professions (and a social acceptance seemed to me important as well as a professional acceptance) we must show that we know how to hold our own in the social world. But I had no "platform" then from which I could make my voice heard.

So now, spurred on by the memory of the lovely social touches of the previous year's convention by the Eastern District hostesses, I was determined to do what I could to bring the Middle West physical educators around to an improved social consciousness. So I quietly passed the word around that I expected everyone to be in formal attire at our banquet. Some of the men exploded and said I would kill the affair. But enough of them assured me I could count on them and on their swinging the others into line that I stuck to my guns backed by Vaughn Blanchard, our Convention chairman. This does not mean that Middle West folk had never before dressed up. There had always been, as far back as I knew, a small core of both men and women who bowed to social custom and came to the banquet in formal attire. But they were conspicuous among the much larger group who obviously couldn't be bothered. This lack of leadership in social direction had always annoyed me a great deal with our professional leaders, and now that I was thrust into a leadership role I intended to make my influence felt.

So practically every letter that went out of my office to professional workers the last few weeks before convention carried a long-hand post-script, "Formal dress, please, for our banquet." And never had a professional banquet in the Middle West had such a big turn-out. The huge ballroom of that lovely hotel was packed with tables for six to eight except for the small space reserved in the center for dancing, for the Detroit banquet committee had begged to have it a dinner dance, then a new social fad taking the country by storm. By far the great majority of men and women were in formal attire. But everyone was timid at starting the dancing between courses. After the orchestra had played its first number to an empty floor, Miss Homans seated near me at the head table whispered to me, "My dear, I think everyone is waiting for you to start the dancing!" Such a thought had never entered my head. I was not yet used to this strange new role, nor to having Miss Homans say, "My dear," to me. And as if he had been in league with Miss Homans, Fritz Maroney seated at her other side excused himself to her asking if I would lead off with him for the next dance. Terrified at the thought of dancing with all those people watching, I knew I must forget my fears and accept the invitation. So I replied, "if the orchestra will give us a waltz," for, after Gilbert's strenuous coaching, I was always best at waltzing. So word was passed along to the orchestra. Immediately when we whirled onto the dance floor, other couples joined us and soon the floor was crowded. The ice was broken and the dinner dance was a huge success. As we passed Miss Homans on our return to our seats, she motioned to me and whispered, "My dear, you dance very well." Praise from her who had scolded me un-ceasingly for two worrisome years of schooling!

Never did a banquet of our Association have more brilliant speakers: Carl Schrader, a skilled toast master; Dudley Reed, of Chicago University one of the profession's greatest wits, who gave a never-to-be-forgotten spoof of our research workers who at times were taking themselves too seriously; and Agnes Wayman and Mary Coleman, both quite clever at repartee. All let me in for a lot of "ribbing," proclaiming this a new era of "petticoat rule." Who but Agnes would have the bravado in 1931 to say "petticoat" right out in a mixed audience?

When the dessert was brought on, it equalled any imagined setting of an Arabian Nights Tale. Although in later years I was to see variations of this dramatic idea, this was the first any of us had seen it. The lights were turned off in the great banquet hall and there marched in a long procession of waiters bearing aloft trays of iced desserts, their fancy shapes and designs fantastically outlined by hidden electric lights glowing through the icy forms, the only lights in the great ballroom. For the moment it was a breath-taking fairy land! When the lights came back on in the ballroom Vaughn Blanchard announced this had been a special surprise for APEA's First Lady!

For our closing Saturday morning session we offered "fireworks" in the form of two debates on currently controversial topics. For one, Dr. J. F. Williams proclaimed that we are becoming too health-conscious, while Dr. John Sundwall, Director of Public Health of University of Michigan denied the allegation; for the other, Frederick Rand Rogers, the New York State Director of Physical Education who had recently eliminated all state school athletic championship tournaments in his state, proclaimed that all state athletic tournaments for high school boys should be abolished, and Dr. William Burdick, Maryland State Director of Physical Education, defended such tournaments. These two debates held a large crowd over for this closing session.

I had had a very difficult time persuading the last two to debate publicly even though each was an ardent advocate of his side of the question. But I had acted on the great urging of a large number of men. We immediately got into heated argument over the conduct of a debate. Frederick Rand Rogers insisted that the affirmative has the closing speech and Dr. Burdick insisted as vigorously that the closing rebuttal goes to the negative side. When I checked with our University of Nebraska debate coach and was informed that the affirmative should be last and so informed both speakers, Dr. Burdick wired me that we might follow such a custom "in the West" but Easterners did not accept such a pattern. Then I turned to a debate coach who had prepared teams for contests with England, Australia, Canada and other sections of our own country, and I found that the University of Nebraska coach had informed me correctly and I was not being provincial. Thus fortified, I settled the pre-debate debate by ruling that Dr. Rogers, as the affirmative, would have the last word. At last Dr. Burdick conceded the point but only most reluctantly. It was apparent he was greatly displeased with me. However as far as I was aware the debate went off quite well; a lot of heat was generated and a lot of men had a chance to let off steam over the topic afterward. But I didn't learn until later that the debate opened old wounds and that after the meeting was adjourned many lingered on to prolong the debate into arguments that left new wounds that were many years in the healing and some never healed.

This made me wonder if a convention should be used to offer the setting for quarrels within a profession. In reviewing later my long correspondence with Dr. Rogers and Dr. Burdick over these arrangements, I came to agree with both that although controversial topics should be presented, they should not be set up as debates, inviting "free for alls" immediately after when tempers had been aroused. Both speakers had objected to the debate idea but the many men in the profession who insisted upon having the topic presented thus had been too much for all of us. I still had a lot to learn.

One unexpected incident during the convention filled us with dismay but the executive committee could do nothing about it, taken by surprise as we were, when two or three black delegates were refused permission to eat in any of the hotel dining rooms, public or private. On checking with the hotel management, we learned that a black delegate could not room there either but could sit in at convention meetings that were not held in connection with meals. Although we had very few black members at the time, we were deeply disturbed by this. Whether this was the first that such a problem had arisen within our profession or that black members of our profession had registered at a convention, I was never able to learn from any past records.

In late March, 1976, LeRoy T. Walker, vice-chancellor of North Carolina Central University and head coach of the USA Olympic Track and Field Team for 1976, became the first black president-elect of the American Alliance for Health, Physical Education and Recreation. None but white males held the top office for 45¼ years, fall 1885 through December 1930, when the election of a white woman broke the sex barrier. Now 45¼ years later the election of a black male president-elect broke the color barrier for the top office. Today blacks room at the same hotels as do we white members and are received in all dining rooms, but it took federal laws to bring this about. As far as I was able to learn, the acceptance of blacks in hotels never was a problem of our profession's making. We were victims of rulings by hotel managements. Gradually, succeeding groups in control learned to clear these things

with hotel managers before naming their hostelry as convention headquarters.

* * * *

The convention program was the frosting on the cake. The real work
came with the official business meetings of the executive committee and
council which, as related earlier, were for the first time in 20 years to
be held in connection with the national convention instead of during
the Christmas holidays in New York City. There were to be two official
council meetings at annual conventions after this, the first to be the
official annual meeting when the old council would elect officers for the
new year and conclude its year's work, and the second when the new
officers and new section chairmen elected during section meetings of
the convention would meet with the officially recognized representatives
of affiliated organizations and districts to plan the work for the coming
year. A difficult task lay ahead.

Earlier, as vice-president I had spoken quite freely of changes that
needed to be made in the national professional organization. Now as
the new president I had been given the go-ahead signal to put the
changes into effect. Almost at once I began striking snags. My ignorance
was colossal about how some people cling to the *status quo* as something sacred; how persons long entrenched in an undertaking are loathe
to give way to newcomers; how the many Easterners lacked confidence
in Middle Westerners and Westerners; about the queer satisfaction that
a few stubborn men get out of opposing women no matter what the
issue and that some women get out of challenging and defying men just
for the game of fighting them; and last of all my ignorance was also
colossal about the queer quirk of human nature that leads a few women
to demand greater recognition of women, and then when one is
singled out for recognition to turn on her and criticize her every move.
I had much to learn.

Now I learned the truth of things which I had only surmised before.
Surely no one with less experience could have been catapulted into the
presidency. It was only four years earlier that I had attended my first
national convention and at that time had sat in on a council meeting as
president of National Association of Physical Education of College
Women. Then two years later as president of the Middle West Society
of Physical Education I had attended the official holidays council
meeting where I was elected vice president. Three months later as vice

president I attended my second national convention and a third council meeting and my first executive committee meeting, and nine months later attended my fourth council meeting at which time I was elected president. So I had had little opportunity to learn of the inner workings of the national organization. I had no commitments to earlier factions, I was the unknown quantity on whom the organization was taking a great chance.

Working out in Nebraska somewhat alone professionally, I had not been drawn into any factions and had little opportunity to make enemies or friends.

The reorganization of our national association embodied the district organizations as integral parts, not as opposing organizations, and the doors were opened to spread responsibilities for expanding the profession to the various sections of professional interests.

I knew rather vaguely that the women had been quite unhappy for the past several years over the men's lack of interest in permitting them to expand interests in behalf of women's athletics. I also was somewhat aware of the struggles of the college women teachers to set up a college women's section only to be forced by majority rulings to make it an overall women's section which the women did not desire. The men had been adamant and had kept out a college women's section. A running battle about this had been going on for several years and now we women wanted this nonsense brought to an end. With a woman in the presidency and a complete reorganization going on anyway, it was easy to see that at last the women should have their way on this since it was the college women alone, asking for such a section. Moreover the fact that the college women had their own separate national organization by now still did not alter this wish in relation to APEA since the new organization catered to heads of departments and an APEA's college women's section would cover the concerns of all women teaching physical education at the college level. Shortly the college women directors group opened its doors to all women teaching at college level.

But this 10-year struggle by the college women for recognition as a college women's section was nothing compared to the equally long struggle of the women in general to gain recognition of a women's athletic section within the national set-up. They had been for the past several years asking to have their heretofore unofficial Women's Athletic Section (an outgrowth of the earlier National Women's Athletic Committee) legitimatized so they would not have to beg favors of the men for recognition of their work and for the privilege to put on programs at conventions. I first had to acquaint myself with the story back of the women's efforts. As a teacher of course I knew that this group put out the official rules for women's sports and I had learned a little of their difficulties in the early 1920s when I had been drawn into one of their programs to present the topic of intercollegiate athletics for women, but my work had been with the Women's Division of NAAF rather than with them, and so I knew little about the history of the group. Now I frantically fought for free time to dig into old records for the story of this group so I could make decisions. However the records were discouragingly meager.

At the first council meeting on the opening day of convention (April 1), the last under the old constitution, there was much final spade work yet to be done to get ready to swing into the new type of organization at the next meeting scheduled for closing day (April 4), when a new council would take over. For one thing the council declared that the officers elected December 30, 1930, to serve for 1931 according to the old constitution under which they were elected should complete the full year's term and then since there would not be a regular official meeting again until April, 1932, they should carry on from January 1, 1932, through the 1932 spring convention when the next official annual business meeting would be held. Therefore, the officers of 1931 had an extra short term of three to four months to make the transition to a new fiscal year. This meant a second convention for the officers of 1931 to put on and with a full 12 months to put the new constitution on trial.

A committee had been set up, under Jesse Williams as related earlier, to divide the USA into districts with the states allocated to the various districts. Much of the country was already functioning under districts except for the far west states. The allocation of states of 1931 stands today except for one state, Wyoming, which was assigned to the North West District but later transferred to the Central District as a result of a division of the old Middle West Society into two units for the sake of better grass-roots tending.

There was one real skirmish over this allocation work when it was learned that Jesse Williams' committee on allocation of states had assigned Colorado to the South West. Members of the Colorado State Society of Physical Education were immediately up in arms over this, insisting that they had belonged to the Middle West Society for all its 20 years of existence and had no intention to be tossed out of it without a hearing. But the Easterners were a majority on that committee. Also their chairman had a reputation for bull-dog tenacity for his own points of view. It was a real battle for a brief period, but finally thoughts of what a barrier the Continental Divide could be, coupled with the fact that the vast majority of Colorado physical educators lived east of that

Divide, swung the decision in favor of leaving Colorado to the group with which it had long been associated.

With allocations made, the districts were to be officially represented on the Executive Committee from then on. From a previous canvass of all existing state physical education societies and the Canadian one, it was found that Canada and 28 state groups met the new requirements of 25 members of APEA, plus other considerations, and all were thus permitted representation on the new Council.

All sections under the old constitution were instructed that the year of April 1931 through April 1932, was to be a trial period of the new plans, and at the convention in 1932 final plans would be drawn up and accepted and the new APEA constitution was to be in effect from then on. In other words, the new constitution was to be on trial for the coming year. The following old sections were accepted at once as meeting the requirements of the new constitution: Public Schools, Therapeutics, Teacher Training, and Research. And a new section, Dancing, was accepted on trial. The omission of the Section on Women's Athletics from this list does not mean that it was rejected but that because of its peculiar functions it required special consideration, to be carried on by a special committee throughout the year.

At the Detroit 1931 convention, the new council stayed on Saturday afternoon to organize for the new year and to review the changed situation. The national Association was entering a new era under a completely new constitution—a constitution aimed at making the national really nationally minded and to unite all parts of the country and all district societies. The changes were radical. For one thing, this new council was the first since 1907 set up to serve from spring convention to spring convention (a custom renewed in 1931 and still followed today). Under the old set-up there had been for the calendar year 1930, 8 women on the Council out of a total of 40 members—20 percent women. Now for the new year 1931–1932, there were to be 16 women on the Council out of a total of 61 members—26 percent women.

One drastic change we all hoped for was the breaking of the stranglehold that some of the old guard in the East had on the Association. They were dying hard over this new constitution and its greater democracy which spread the privileges and responsibilities throughout the country. The newcomers went to this first council meeting under the new organization curious to see who would turn up with official records to show their election according to the new rules. When I asked the secretary to call off the names of the sections now recognized and for the newly-elected chairman of each to announce himself and present his credentials, we were delighted at the new faces that were appearing.

162

When a particular section was called, a young member from the Middle West claimed the chairmanship and the secretary verified that he was the new duly-elected official representative of that section. After these formalities were finished and we had moved on to other business, one of the old guard entered the room and before taking a seat came to me and asked that I pardon his tardiness and record him as present representing this particular section. This presented a serious difficulty. He had been chairman of that section continuously for many years. It was reported that he never bothered to hold an election (just dismissing the meeting year after year without an election), and that he reported himself to the new president as the chairman of the section. This same slipshod procedure had been going on for years in other sections, too, so I was informed. Now we were cleaning house. No one objected to any person holding any office provided he was properly elected. We merely wanted to put the affairs of the Association on a business-like, legal and democratic basis.

So here was a ticklish problem. Had it been almost anyone else I would have said that there must be some mistake but one didn't handle this particular man that way. He was already at odds with me over my "standing up to him" when he was unwilling to let the women control their own affairs in the Women's Athletic Committee and over other matters, and now it was up to me to stand up to him again by refusing to let him hold on to that section chairmanship any longer unless he had been officially elected. I couldn't have a scene right there before all the council anyway, so I did not at the moment challenge his statement, thinking to have a conference first with the person claiming to be the newly-elected chairman and with the secretary, Mr. Mitchell. Later a check proved that the new man had indeed been officially elected as official representative at the business meeting which had been called by the secretary at the close of the program when the chairman had absented himself before the program ended and did not return to conduct a business meeting himself. It must have been a shock to him to give up the chairmanship after so many years in possession of it.

I asked this gentleman to remain after the meeting was adjourned for explanation, at which time he accused me of "high-handed" methods. But I stood my ground. He finally angrily bowed to my ultimatum and departed. Later he wrote me a highly indignant letter of protest over the "shabby way" he had been treated after 20 years of faithful service to this section.

Apparently these men were firm believers in the divine rights of kings. But we new officers at the helm were not. One old guard member frequently at my second convention in 1932, so I was told, called attention to little groups of delegates to "the sorry mess" a woman president was making of things.

In the end this man maneuvered to hold a seat in the new council by persuading his state's Society of Physical Education to appoint him its representative. Since we were dropping all city-level organizations from our national council, all those previously representing these groups were dropped from our rolls. There couldn't help but be many hurt feelings over this too.

At the Detroit meeting I appointed Jay B. Nash to represent APEA on a National Olympic Committee which was planning to have an International Congress on Physical Education at the time of the Olympic Games in Los Angeles in 1932. Also it was decided upon Dr. Maroney's motion that the constitution make provision for Dr. James Huff McCurdy, former secretary-treasurer-editor for many years, to be a permanent member of the legislative council. Most organizations petitioning for affiliation under the new set-up were accepted. However, all sub-groups of a national organization were rejected. For instance, the National Association of Directors of Physical Education for College Women was accepted as a new affiliated group but not the district associations of that mother organization on the grounds that as a national we affiliate only on the national level.

Beginning with the new year 1931–1932, all APEA district presidents were to be members of the executive committee along with two other persons elected at large by the Council. At last one more of my *musts* on reorganization to tie the districts together and to tie all to the national in important relationships transcending state representation had become a reality. At last, too, I had seen the local societies dropped from representation on the national council—another pet aversion of mine of the old organization. I felt that these locals should function only through their states to strengthen the state groups.

Mr. Blanchard reported an unprecedented take of $2,200 from exhibits and urged election of a permanent exhibits manager; the matter was referred to the executive committee with power to act.

In closing the meeting I reminded all that there would be no more annual business meetings apart from conventions, that there could be special called meetings at other times but not for transaction of routine annual business. I also called their attention to the fact that under the new constitution we hoped each state would soon have a state physical education society with enough APEA members (25) for representation on the national council and that we hoped each district would sponsor the state groups within its territory and each state group would sponsor local groups within its boundaries. I also informed them that with this new constitution we were entering a new era in which we hoped sections would function not only at conventions by putting on programs but that all would appoint working committees and further the cause of their interest through the year.

* * * *

As Miss Homans told me goodbye that April day of 1931 in Detroit, she kissed me and said,

"I hope that some day you can forgive me."

"Forgive you?" I asked in great astonishment.

"Yes, I greatly misunderstood you when you were a student, also your family and the part of the country you came from."

Recovering from my amazement at her remarks I insisted that it was I who should be asking to be forgiven for never having taken the time to tell her how grateful I was for all the attention she had given to me in my student years to help make me an acceptable teacher. Thus we parted. I never saw her again. Two years later she died—October 29, 1933.

After she and Marion had gone and I was packing to leave, as I took the large photograph of my mother from my dresser, I recalled that when I showed it to Miss Homans she had seemed to be unbelieving that it could possibly be a photograph of my mother. It was one taken by Harris and Ewing of Washington, D.C., only three years before, in which she was wearing the black evening gown with the bodice encrusted in rhinestone designs which she had worn at a reception at the White House during the Coolidge administration. Then I realized that no doubt Miss Homans had all the years since my student days still pictured me as coming from a backwoods setting, my parents uncouth settlers of the wild and wooly West. Mother, sixty-six years old when this photograph was taken in 1928 was a handsome woman of much poise and dignity which the photographer had caught. Miss Homans had gazed at it silently with a puzzled look and finally said, "She is lovely. I fear I greatly misjudged you!" And now several days later she had again repeated that statement.

A year following the Detroit convention when Marion visited her in Wellesley, Miss Homans talked about the changing educational scene and expressed worry over what was happening in the Depression years to physical education in the schools, finishing with the remark, "I should not be surprised if Mabel Lee is the one among us to handle the situation." I would have been elated beyond words to learn that after our reunion in 1931 she had at last accepted me wholeheartedly as a worthy worker in our profession and beyond that even had unreasoning faith that I might be able to put professional affairs in order. But Marion, busy at the time with her famous surgeon husband and four little children, and the cares of servants in a town house, country house, seashore house, and mountain house, could not keep close contact with school-day friends, so that it was 34 years later before she passed on this remark to me, reminded of it when we were having a reunion and enjoying together her diary.

* * * *

Before election to the presidency of APEA, I had promised my mother that I would take her on a trip to Europe the summer of 1931. Such a trip was the great dream of her life. Not to have the entire three months a complete loss professionally, I searched out the address of a leading professional school of that day in England to visit and, armed with a few sheets of APEA social note paper headed "Office of the President" which I naively considered sufficient for advance introductions for use in Europe, I confidently set out. But what a humiliating experience awaited me first in France where I quite by accident stumbled on the head officers of the national French Physical Education Association, an experience which at the time I blamed on language difficulties, and later in England. Embarrassingly, I had to blame my own stupidity in not realizing that France and England of the early 1930s were not prepared to believe that a woman would hold the presidency of America's national physical education organization.

In both countries I was given the full treatment reserved for imposters of the first order. What a surprise, what a humiliating experience, the second one in England all the more amazing because there was no excuse of language barrier to explain it. More astounding still was the snubbing given me there by women and not by men as was the case in France. In the summer of 1931 neither men nor women physical educators of Europe could believe that any woman claiming to be president of the American Physical Education Association could be anything but an imposter—in short, a liar! And I was given full treatment reserved for such! Never can I forget it!

In 1972 when Charles E. Lee, Director of South Carolina Archives and History, introduced himself in Vienna to the President of the

Society of Austrian Archivists as the President of the Society of American Archivists, he was given a warm reception.[4] I wonder if the same thing would have happened had he instead been a woman and the year, 1931.

Chapter VIII
Presidential Concerns

Encouraged by the successes of my first year of national presidential work, I buckled on my armor a bit tighter for there was a second convention to put on. And it was well that I tightened the armor for serious troubles lay ahead. By then the honeymoon with a first woman president was over and a few storm clouds had gathered.

One very serious storm developed over Bernarr McFadden, the notorious physical fitness exponent, who was trying to curry favor with our national professional organization for the advantage it could bring to his questionable magazine, *Physical Culture*. This caused serious trouble within the executive committee and for a few others resulting in unhappy confrontations which left long-lasting wounds—almost a half-century later I am still well aware of the scars of those wounds. As one person caught up in the very center of all this unpleasantness and as one who kept a lengthy personal written record of the affair, I am leaving a full report of it for posterity as a bit of AAHPER history that should be preserved, even if at the time the majority ruled that it should be covered up. The cover-up was so complete that official records of that day reveal nothing of it. Following that there was an appeasement move to preserve peace of which I also highly disapproved but I was again on the losing minority side.

Only three of us, of all who were drawn into the conflict, still live and of these three, I am the only one who knew the full story first hand. My records of this will become the property of AAHPER Archives after my death, to be available to research workers but only after the date specified.

There was one last big reform to finish, if possible, before writing "fini" to my adventures at reforming our national professional organization. I had been shocked to learn that the elections of officers were casual, controlled by a small Eastern clique, and undemocratic. I resolved that never again, if I could help it, would officers be elected without a nominating committee, open call to all members to suggest names of candidates, a slate of at least three nominees, and a secret ballot. When I proposed this in the 1931 reorganization to be put into effect in 1932, I was met with what may literally be labelled as cries of anguish from the old guard in the East and accusations from a few that I was playing "dirty politics."

So it goes down in history that this democratic procedure finally was voted in under my successor's presidency to go into effect in 1934 but it was I who fought desperately and at times it seemed almost single-handedly the two years before to put this idea over. In fighting for it, I lost one or two of the very friends who had put me into office. But in the end I won. It was without a doubt the force of the Middle West group pulling together that finally put it over, and it was only fitting therefore that the first president to be elected by this democratic process should be one of our own Middle West group—Strong Hinman, the man who made the presentation of the plan to the council for consideration. It was equally fitting that the chairman of the first nominating committee should be an Easterner but as one appointed by the president, Mary Coleman, a Southerner, that Easterner was carefully chosen. He was Dr. John Brown, Jr., head of physical education for International YMCA, who had no sympathy with the Eastern bloc that had for so long run things. He was all for real democracy and the protection of the rights and privileges of the rank and file of our members. Political wire-pulling was out!

In 1933, Mary Coleman, my roommate of Boston Normal School of Gymnastics days, the vice-president, was moved into the presidency (to my delight).

It was quite a platform I had set for myself for my presidency—not a publicized one, yet nevertheless one I was determined to carry out. There yet remained to do: (1) bring all the district groups into the fold, (2) establish a rotating system for conventions throughout the several

Mary Channing Coleman, "Coley," of North Carolina College for Women, the second woman to hold the national presidency in the American Physical Education Association.

districts, but entering a district for convention only on invitation of the district society and in conjunction with it, (3) establish the policy of placing on all important committees a representative from each district in order to reach down to the grass roots for all types of work, (4) investigate the informal but persistent rumors about a possible tie-up with the Department of Physical Education of the National Education Association, and (5) procure section status for women's athletics and for dance groups. I believed in these matters and felt committed to them so I went after their acceptance with all the influence I could muster. Most I accomplished but not without a bitter fight over certain features of number 5 above, which developed into a real contest of the women versus a small group of determined men, as related later.

As to district organizations, the East, Middle West, South, and North West were organized, the last less than a year old then, but the South West was still out of the fold. (It was to be another three years before it would organize, delayed because of the very large and independent California State Society which, out-of-step through the years with APEA, felt no need for expansion, thus leaving Nevada, Arizona, Utah and New Mexico unorganized and needing at least California's help.)

As to rotating national conventions throughout the various districts in order to reach the grass roots frequently, there had been up to then 36 national conventions in the 45 years—22 in the East, 10 in the Middle West, 3 in the South West, and 1 in Eastern Canada. This may seem unfair but in the nineteenth century and at the turn of the twentieth there were not enough grass roots anywhere to support a national convention except in the East. However, since the Great War, physical education had spread rapidly and grass roots were developing fast in other parts of the country. Since that war there had been 11 conventions: 5 in the East, 4 in the Middle West (2 in today's Mid West and 2 in today's Central), and 2 in the unorganized South West. Now the South and North West were to be given national consideration.

The day needed to be past when the national organization could put on a convention in a district uninvited and in competition with that district's own convention. Such action had been a bone of contention more than once.

* * * *

In the 1890s a Department of School Health and Physical Education was set up within the National Education Association.[1] APEA President, Edward Hartwell, M.D., head of physical education at Boston public schools had taken an active interest in it. Later, Thomas D. Wood, M.D. had been interested in it, and still later, (1910–1911) Clark Hetherington had held the presidency of the Department,[2] and more recently Jay B. Nash, a protege of Hetherington, had held that position. All three of these last named men had worked in the Department of Physical Education of NEA rather than in the APEA. All three started their professional careers in California and through the years California workers in the profession had dragged their feet with APEA in favor of work in the profession through NEA. In 1917 these Californians approached APEA with the suggestion that APEA merge with the Department of School Health and Physical Education of NEA for the common good. (The discussion of this was to develop into a 20-year project.) But Dr. William Burdick, then president of APEA, was not interested enough to push discussions.

By 1926, Jay B. Nash had followed Wood and Hetherington to New York City and as head of physical education at New York University he was once more pushing the Department of School Health and Physical Education of NEA. When Charles W. Savage of Oberlin College became president of APEA for the calendar year 1926, Nash, an Oberlin graduate, made the most of that contact.

At the December 31, 1926 annual business meeting of the APEA Council in New York City, Jay B. Nash, representing the Bay Cities Society but by then of New York University, reported that the far West was not friendly toward APEA and he was trying to do something about it. He said that the Physical Education Section of the California State Teachers Association was getting 500 to 800 out to their meetings and they had no dues. He added that APEA should be one with the Department of Health and Physical Education of NEA. He then moved that a committee be appointed to study with Dr. McCurdy the interrelationships of the sections of APEA and the teacher groups of NEA. The motion passed and President Savage appointed a committee with Carl Schrader as the chairman, and Frederick Maroney and Jay B. Nash to work with him. But it was three years before the committee brought in a report and it called merely for further study. The delaying game was developing. In 1929 the new APEA president, Frederick Maroney, under pressure of the former Californians, appointed a new committee to carry on the investigation with William Burdick of Baltimore its chairman, and Carl Schrader, C. W. Savage, Jackson Sharman, Ethel Perrin, and James Huff McCurdy as members. Nothing came of his committee work either.

As I stepped into the APEA presidency, January 1, 1931, Jay B. Nash began pushing for committee action on this NEA merger. I began an investigation and discovered that it was doubtful if Dr. Burdick had ever called a committee meeting, merely reporting each year, "no final report as yet" and thus holding the chairmanship and control of the committee firmly in his own hands. At the time I put this down to procrastination. However, I had been learning about persons who accept important assignments, do nothing, and yet cling to the appointments for whatever place in the sun they might get. This was one more such case I decided, and not wishing to carry dead timber in my administration I tried to move the chairman to action and when that failed threatened to discharge the committee. I had already become involved in arguments with this one die-hard Easterner of the old guard over my championing of the women pushing for an officially recognized Women's Athletic Section, over his 1931 debate with Frederick Rand Rogers, and now over this APEA-NEA affiliation committee. In this matter I was not opposing any stand he was taking—in fact the committee had been so inactive that I didn't know what its stand was; I merely insisted upon action. When I used the threat to discharge the committee as a prod to action, he disarmingly countered that the committee could not be discharged until it brought in its final report and that was not as yet ready. So I gave in, wishing no more trouble with him.

In the meantime, Dr. Nash, then chairman of the NEA Department of School, Health and Physical Education, was pushing me to appoint a new committee and he offered to appoint one from his NEA group in the hope that the two would become an official joint committee to push for affiliation. He assured me that several state physical education associations were dissatisfied with APEA and were ready to withdraw from it and join NEA instead. Investigation seemed to prove that the states of the Southwest were never going to be loyal APEA territory until we did have a tie-up of some sort with NEA. This was the one section of the United States not organized as a district within our national association organization, and this was a worry.

On October 8, 1931, Dr. Nash wrote me a long letter which said in part:

> I believe that some plan could be formulated to preserve the traditions of the American Physical Education Association, to finance our activities and at the same time to tie up in a very advantageous way with the leading educators in this country. It seems to me that now is an opportune time to take these various trends and unite the strength of all of them in one big movement.

The more I looked into the matter, the more I became convinced that affiliation of APEA as a whole with NEA was not logical and until I could round up a following for my point of view I came to see that it quite suited my purposes for Dr. Burdick to stall a bit longer.

While NEA's interests were widespread in the field of education, they were limited to the public school sphere. On the other hand, APEA's interests were confined to the field of physical education alone and encompassed many spheres of action outside the public schools. Our organizational interests lay not only in the public schools but also in the college world, in the YMCAs and YWCAs and recreational domains, in the medical sphere of exercise, and in the world of sports and dance. How could we become merely a department of NEA and foster all these other interests? Also we supported a Public School Section which paralleled NEA's interests in physical education through its Department of Physical Education. Here as I saw it was the answer to the question of affiliation.

I got in touch with our secretary, Elmer Mitchell, about Dr. Nash's long letter and my reactions to it, and on October 14, 1931, Mr. Mitchell wrote me as follows:

> As you know, there has always been a strong sentiment in the Far West to affiliate the APEA with the Physical Education Section of the NEA. I think you have analyzed the situation most remarkably and perhaps your suggestion to affiliate the Public School Section with the NEA Physical Education Section is far the most practical solution of this problem.

Before Mr. Mitchell's letter reached me, I had written to Dr. Nash that Dr. Burdick had been chairman for the previous few years of a somewhat inactive committee on NEA affiliation and that I had asked Dr. Burdick to get in touch with him. I also told him quite frankly where I stood on this issue and that I, personally, would be interested only in an affiliation with our Public School Section. Now when I learned that Elmer Mitchell approved my idea about our Public School Section, I felt better about my stand. From the pressure building up about NEA affiliation, I had begun to wonder if I stood alone in my opposition. Then gradually I discovered others who were with Elmer Mitchell and me in what was beginning to look like a very small minority group. Now obsessed with the thought that we should affiliate with NEA only through our Public School Section, I got the idea that we should develop departments and make it a Public School Department of APEA instead of a Section; then it would seem logical to others for our Public School Department of APEA to affiliate with the School Health and Physical Education Department of NEA. Thus we would not seem to be completely taken over by NEA.

But I was filled with questions as to the various personalities I had to deal with. I regretted that I knew these men so little. They were all comparative strangers to me. Although I was getting acquainted

174

rapidly with the men leaders in our profession, I still knew next to nothing of behind-the-scenes personalities and their conflicts. And Elmer Mitchell, a person not given to small gossip and personality probings as I was finding out, seemed to know no more about such things than did I. So he was no help to me in trying to get at the bottom of why some people acted as they did. I found I *needed* to know about people so I could counter their actions well in behalf of APEA work.

Alden Thompson, Michigan State Director of Physical Education, was by now the new chairman of the APEA Public School Section and I wondered if it would be wise to appoint him as a new member of Dr. Burdick's APEA Committee, but I suggested to Elmer Mitchell that he have a personal conference with him first to alert him to our joint thinking on the NEA affiliation matter. On October 29, 1931, Mr. Mitchell wrote me as follows:

> Mr. Thompson has been to see me concerning your suggestion that the APEA affiliate with the NEA through the Public School Section. He seems to favor this suggestion and everyone else with whom I have talked thinks that it would be a big mistake to affiliate the APEA as a whole because we would lose our present support from the college, private school, recreational YWCA and YMCA people. Your solution seems absolutely the ideal one and I hope that we can go ahead on that basis.

It was later that I learned that up to then Jay B. Nash had not worked in any way in APEA but had worked enthusiastically in the Department of School Health and Physical Education of NEA instead and that not only was he enthusiastic over this department of NEA but also downright hostile toward APEA. I hoped to break down this hostility and to enlist his support for the new APEA which we Middle-westerners were helping the Easterners contrive out of the old. In a way my earlier ignorance of these undercurrents was a help for I blundered along "where Angels fear to tread" and this blind blundering, recognized as such, was forgiven and my advances accepted.

At this time, a Lincoln, Nebraska woman, Ruth Pyrtle, was president of NEA and I talked with her about affiliation and from her learned some very surprising things. I had asked the NEA office repeatedly for a list of persons of our profession who were interested workers in NEA's Department of School Health and Physical Education and had gotten no place with these requests—probably not from intent but from failure to take care of correspondence. So now, at my request, the president of NEA immediately sent copies of the minutes of recent meetings of the group, as well as the list of names. On December 9, I wrote Mr. Mitchell as follows:

> To my very great surprise I have learned that A.W. Thompson is vice-president of this Department [of School Health and Physical Education of NEA], J. E. Rogers, secretary-treasurer, and Ethel Perrin, F. W. Maroney and William Burdick members of the executive committee. Dr. Burdick and Ethel Perrin are both members of our committee on NEA affiliation and I had wanted A. W. Thompson to serve on that committee since he is chairman of our Public School Section, but now that J. B. Nash has named him chairman of his NEA Committee to confer with our committee, I feel that we should therefore not have him on our committee. I really feel that our APEA committee should be made up of persons who are not in any way connected with the Department of Physical Education of NEA so that we would get an absolutely unprejudiced viewpoint from them. Now I discover that even our own chairman (Dr. Burdick) is a member of their executive committee.
>
> Now I find in their minutes that they are definitely committed "to accomplish, if possible, the immediate consolidation of the two organizations into one Department." To me this puts an altogether different light upon the whole proposition.

I was, indeed, upset to discover that the chairman of our own APEA committee to investigate NEA affiliation was a member of the executive committee of the other group and as such committed to a definite course and as chairman of our committee in a position to push APEA into that course. Mr. Mitchell and I both felt that this APEA Committee should consist of disinterested persons entirely so that they would look at the matter from APEA's own best future good. And here unwittingly I had placed Mr. Thompson, chairman of our Public School Section, on our committee only to learn now that he, as well as the chairman and other committee members, are members of the other group's executive committee. It was a surprise to find that even J.E. Rogers, whom I felt I knew quite well, was NEA's group's secretary, and I had not known it. And Dr. Burdick, Dr. Maroney, Alden Thompson, J.E. Rogers, and Ethel Perrin, all committed in behalf of NEA to push APEA into "immediate consolidation of the two organizations into one." It all smacked too much to suit me of what in a later day we call a "CIA operation," infiltrating the enemy's camp. But was APEA infiltrating NEA's committee or was NEA doing the infiltrating? I felt quite sure the CIA operatives were APEA personnel and I was very unhappy about it.

How could our APEA members at large expect a disinterested investigation of the NEA affiliation from a committee seemingly overweighted with persons already committed to a set course? If only I could have disbanded the APEA committee without a fight but Dr. Burdick, although he refused to correspond with me about it, held onto it with bull-dog tenacity. I wanted no one on our APEA committee who was also on the NEA Executive Committee.

With all these worries on my mind I awakened suddenly one night to recall a whispered joking remark I had overheard a few years ago to the effect that the NEA affiliation matter would always be safe as long as the chairmanship of our committee was in Dr. Burdick's hand. At the time, a few years before, the remark meant nothing to me. Now it came to me in a flash. Dr. Burdick and the president who appointed him were not in favor of NEA affiliation and his committee set-up was merely their subtle way of playing politics to keep the matter from coming up. Dr. Burdick would hang onto that chairmanship, do nothing, and thus kill it. When was I going to learn to play the game of politics? How naive I was! Well I wasn't for NEA affiliation either but I had been willing to have the topic discussed and settled by a majority vote. I had tried to push Dr. Burdick into action. I had referred Dr. Nash to him. Dr. Burdick and Fritz Maroney had probably purposely gotten themselves onto that NEA Department Executive Committee to block things there. Well, I had a bit of a chuckle over their clever way of operating, and I decided that since I had so many other worries just now (the MacFadden affair was taking on bothersome proportions) I would just let Burdick and Nash "slug it out" alone.

On December 14, 1931, I again wrote Mr. Mitchell that I was still unable to get any reply from Dr. Burdick after five attempts. But I had had correspondence from others which led me to say in this letter:

> I am afraid we are being railroaded into absolute consolidation and the more I think about it the more I am sure that is not what we want.

Mr. Mitchell replied at once that "there are a number of things that warn me that we should go very carefully into this matter." But there seemed to be no way at this point by which we could get rid of Dr. Burdick's old committee without causing bitter dissension. As I wrote Elmer Mitchell in that December 14 letter:

> It has been a hard struggle to swing the Middle West and the National into friendly relationship. I do not need to remind you of that. We must seize every opportunity to make the bonds between the two groups strong.

And as Mid Westerners, we both knew that whatever errors we

committed would be chalked up against the Mid West in particular even if against APEA in general. So we decided to let "sleeping dogs" sleep even if this committee work didn't get done.

Quietly I began a campaign of sounding out the college physical educators, sports coaches, YM and YWCA physical directors and a few physical therapists; I found utter lack of interest in such affiliation, but a willingness for our Public School Section to so affiliate. However, most were willing to let things drift and therefore they felt Dr. Burdick's inactivity was to our advantage. But we were up against Jay B. Nash's push. Finally Dr. Burdick reported in late December that his committee was at work. However the affiliation matter continued to drift.

Many years later I learned indirectly through Dr. Burdick's widow that he purposely played a delaying game since he did not wish affiliation and had concluded that I was for it by my letting Dr. Nash push for action. Therefore he wished to put off action while I was at the helm. Apparently knowledge of my campaign to limit the affiliation to our Public School Section did not filter through to him, and he was too disgruntled with me on several other counts for easy communication. It was too bad that we didn't get together on this topic. As it happened, in spite of Dr. Nash's nudging of us, nothing came of the matter with the next two presidents, both working in the college field. The next president, Strong Hinman of Wichita, Kansas public schools, who was a great admirer of Jay B. Nash and had drawn him into our Association work, was completely sold on the idea of the Public School Section affiliation only and also on delaying tactics and he, too, let the APEA-NEA merger plan ride. Then Agnes Wayman of Barnard College succeeded to the presidency and, although working in the college field, for some reason I never understood, she was interested in the merger idea and reopened the question. Her vice-president, William Moorhead, Pennsylvania State Director of Physical Education, was an ardent follower of Jay B. Nash and may have swung Agnes Wayman to his way of thinking. When he succeeded her as president he made her chairman of a new committee with instructions to get down to business about an investigation of the possibilities of a merger. This she did, going to Washington and conferring with NEA officials, after which her committee drew up actual terms for a merger and pushed her plan through to acceptance by APEA to go into effect under the next president, C.H. McCloy of the University of Iowa. Although Dr. McCloy had been one of the small group in favor only of merging through the Public School Section, yet an ardent supporter of Jay B. Nash in most projects, he readily fell into line on acceptance of the complete merger and he did put it into effect during his APEA presidency.

The APEA office was transferred in 1938 to the NEA building in Washington, D.C. Jay B. Nash, a loyal worker in APEA, four years later became president and was from then on an acknowledged top leader of APEA, his interest and labors never flagging until his death in 1965, 13 years after his retirement. But within 30 years after affiliation, many in the profession were having after-thoughts about the merger. Prodded by NEA, it expanded to take on first health education, then recreation, then safety education, driver education, school nurse education, spreading itself ever and ever thinner as it grew ever and ever larger—fast approaching 50,000 members by the end of the sixties—until our original function of promoting and advancing physical education became greatly watered down. Of the minority group that tried to swing the affiliation only of the Public School Section, only a few of us are still living and I, for one, as I hear the discussions on all sides that we are too fragmented for the protection of our original cause am tempted to say: "I told you so." But as I hold my tongue I think that my idea about affiliation of the Public School Section only was a good one after all, and when I am reminded of a remark of Dudley A. Sargent in 1920, I realize I would have had a supporter in that project had that great leader still been alive. His remark was:

> I am a little bit concerned for the good of our cause when I see so many subjects brought forward under the head of physical education.... This (referring to the American Physical Education Association) is the parent organization of physical education and we should stick strictly to physical education.[3]

Perhaps it was a natural thing to tie health education with physical education administratively although they are two totally different fields of education. After World War I, pressure was put on the schools to take on health education. Most schools could not afford such specialists and where would they have found them anyway at that time? Since physical educators were supposed to have had some training in the fundamentals of health education, it was the path of least resistance to appease those pushing for health education by assigning this work to the physical educators. So there grew up in the public schools an acceptance of the two as joint responsibilities whether the persons were qualified or not. It was easy to wink at this bit of pretense in the name of education since the public had become accustomed through the years to have sports coaches assigned physical education work even though most of them had no training in physical education—other than a small piece of it concerned only with coaching sports. This was so common a practice that to the general public the term "sports coach" was synonymous with "physical educator." Now the physical educator became a health educator, at least by title if not in fact, and for administrative purposes in every public school system of any size the department of physical education became the department of health and physical education. So a clamor arose in APEA in the late 1930s to add health education to the title and in 1937 as it was merging with NEA, APEA became the American Association for Health and Physical Education (AAHPE). A year later, the Association changed its name once more—this time to the American Association for Health, Physical Education and Recreation (AAHPER) which title has survived to today except that since 1974 the word Association has been changed to Alliance. Thus the fragmentation was started under NEA.

The authentic health educators were dismayed at this appropriation of their functions forced upon physical education by educationists unknowing of the differences in the two fields, or sometimes uncaring of the criticism as long as they put on a show to the community of having a health education set-up in the schools. Of course in many places genuine health educators were hired and many were placed over both health education and physical education, with the latter suffering from the health educators' lack of understanding of physical education. In other situations genuine health educators were employed but placed under the physical education experts, with health education suffering from lack of understanding of its functions. Soon, large segments of the medical profession were up in arms about this marriage of the two forced by the school administrators. It was an unhappy marriage at first until time eased the situation by health educators becoming knowledgeable about physical education and physical educators becoming knowledgeable about health education. These many years later both parties seem to have found a way to live peacefully and effectively together and the medical alarmists have largely disappeared. But there were troublesome years when our AAHPER was in great disfavor in many directions, not escaping also the displeasure of the several recreation associations. But these have by now become so fragmented themselves and so numerous that AAHPER is no longer looked upon as the villain intent on disrupting their private world. In 1974 all official relations with NEA were severed, and AAHPER since then has been a separate entity.

Chapter IX
Women's Lib—1930s Style

Groups wishing to set up new sections within APEA for official recognition under the new constitution had to make formal application for permission to function, presenting organization plans to conform to the new rules for such groups. This meant new hope for the women's group interested in promotion of correct athletics for girls and women, which had been clamoring for official recognition for the previous 10 or more years. As Dr. Maroney left the office of president, December 31, 1930, this group of women, along with all other section officers, were informed to get busy, draw up plans, submit them at the Detroit convention of April 1931, and enter into a trial year for 1931–1932 with hopes of final official acceptance as an official section at the convention of April 1932.

On January 1, 1931, I stepped into the presidency and thereby inherited the task, also the privilege, of being the one to see the old unofficial Women's Athletic Section officially become a bona fide section of our overall national professional organization. The struggle to accomplish this one step in equality for women seems almost unbelievable today in light of what has transpired in the way of women's rights and privileges during these intervening 45 and more years. A brief review of events related to this struggle leading up to the 1930s seems to be in order.

This is the story.[1] In 1894, Senda Berenson of Smith College, and then other women, modified Naismith's basketball rules for use by girls and women. When confusion arose about the several variations of rules, Miss Berenson asked the officers of APEA to appoint a committee to be officially recognized on basketball rules for girls. This suggestion was accepted. At one of the monthly council meetings held in June 1899, Dr. Dudley A. Sargent, then president of APEA, set up such a committee naming Alice Foster, then of Oberlin College, its first chairman with Senda Berenson as one of the members to edit the rules. This committee produced the first official rules in 1901, published for it by the American Sports Publishing Company.

In 1905, when Dr. Gulick was president of APEA, the women asked that their rules committee be expanded into an overall basketball committee to widen its field of action. This move was made and Senda Berenson became chairman of the National Women's Basket Ball Committee. By 1917 the need was felt to encompass more than basketball in the committee's work. Prodding by the women resulted in APEA, under President William Burdick, changing the old committee to the National Committee on Women's Athletics, which became generally known as the Women's Athletic Committee. (Had this occurred 15 years later in the days of alphabetized groups, it would have become known as the WAC, anteceding the more widely-known military title— the WAC of World War II years.)

At this time Senda Berenson asked to be relieved of her over 25 years' work in promoting and making basketball rules for girls. Elizabeth Burchenal, executive secretary of the Girls' Branch of the Athletic League of the Public Schools of New York City, was appointed chairman. It is interesting to note that although both Presidents Sargent and Gulick had given the women the reins completely (1899-1917), President Burdick appointed two men to the new committee, Dr. L. R. Burnett of the Sargent School of Physical Education and Dr. E. A. Peterson of the Cleveland public schools, thus setting a precedent which caused considerable trouble in later years. The other members of this overall sports committee were Elizabeth Bates of Brown University, Florence Alden of the Baltimore Public Schools Athletic League, Ethel Perrin, head of physical education of Detroit public schools, Blanche M. Trilling of the University of Wisconsin, Winifred Tilden of Iowa State College (Ames), and Maude Cleveland of the University of California— Berkeley. It was a most representative committee with both private and public schools and colleges representing the East and West coasts and the Middle West.

This committee had been appointed in January 1917 so there was time for it to plan a program for spring convention, but it had been informed that committees were not recognized as programing groups.

182

So they contented themselves with a paper by Florence Somers, then of the Cleveland public schools, on the *Standardization of Athletics for Women,* which they sneaked into the Women's Section meeting with the blessing of Gertrude Dudley of the University of Chicago. Gertrude Dudley was chairman of that unofficial but winked-at group which had won the privilege of a program because of the influence of immediate past-president Dr. E. H. Arnold of the New Haven School of Physical Education, who, like Sargent and Gulick, was not loathe to open doors to women.

Under President Burdick they did not fare so well. The following year they offered no program but resolved to call an open committee meeting the following year. There is no record that they did have such a meeting but the lack of a report does not prove that they did not. Blanche Trilling, talking informally from memory just before her retirement, claimed that the first meeting of the Women's Athletic Section was held at a national convention in Chicago in 1911. There is no record of an APEA convention in Chicago in 1911, and at that date the Women's Athletic Section was not yet born, even with sub rosa status. There was nothing then but a six-year-old Women's Basket Ball Committee. However, there was a national convention in Chicago in 1919, the very year the Women's Athletic Committee was determined to have an "open" committee meeting as a program feature. It is highly probable that Miss Trilling was speaking of this convention. If so, it did mark the first program of an unofficial group on women's athletics. It is also possible that 1911 is a printer's error in *The History of National Section of Women's Athletics,* by Eline von Borries, published in 1941. So much for historical research!

For 10 years (1917–1927), as chairman of the National Committee on Women's Athletics, Elizabeth Burchenal, Blanche Trilling and Katherine Sibley tried continuously to get a place on convention programs to discuss the problems of women's athletics but they met with constant rebuff from the majority of the men who were continuously in control of the national association.

Peace-loving, fun-loving, outgoing Elizabeth Burchenal quietly steered the National Committee on Women's Athletics from 1917 to 1921. Blanche Trilling, her successor, won important skirmishes with the men in the committee's favor and did get the door opened at least a crack. These were the years just preceding and following women's victory for suffrage when some men who had been against that movement bull-headedly were unwilling to grant women any rights which they had it in their power to withhold. Some women still could not resist the temptation to be militant in demanding rights, which irritated even the men who were not inclined to oppose them, losing even their support.

* * * *

In 1925 the chairmanship of this committee fell to the very tactful Katherine Sibley of the University of Syracuse. No doubt President Schrader welcomed the change from the militant Middle West Blanche Trilling to a less militant Easterner when Katherine Sibley took over. She carried on the struggle for an official seat on the APEA Council for the Women's Athletic Comittee for two years. In her first year, she won recognition for her committee as an unofficial section within APEA, but for program purposes only. Even this was not automatic. Permission to attend council meetings depended upon invitation, year by year, as each president cared to handle it.

Dr. McCurdy, the secretary-editor of APEA, sent her an invitation to attend the council meeting, January 1, 1925, "as a guest," saying that he felt that the National Committee on Women's Athletics should be represented there even though it was not officially recognized as a Women's Athletic Section as yet. The door was opening a bit more for the women. They now had a voice in council meetings if not a vote; it was at least a step toward recognition and apparently fully concurred in by President Carl Schrader. It was not so much the Association presidents who held out against the women through these years as other men whose votes and influence counted heavily. (Incidentally, at this meeting, Miss Sibley was elected vice president of APEA for the year 1925, which meant she did have a vote.)

The 1925 convention was held in June in Los Angeles. The absence of records of a women's meeting leads one to conclude that the women took a holiday this year from attempts to further the women's athletics cause. However, encouraged by the 1925 show of friendliness, Miss Sibley requested a place on the 1926 convention program in Newark, N. J., for a discussion of women's athletics. The new president, C. W. Savage of Oberlin College, set up a temporary unofficial Women's Athletic Section, naming Jessie Bancroft, then assistant director of physical training of the public schools of Greater New York, as temporary chairman. Jessie Bancroft then turned her meeting over to Katherine Sibley and her National Committee on Women's Athletics.

To protect himself from possible charges of favoritism towards the women, Mr. Savage set up a temporary unofficial Men's Athletic Section, too, with Elmer D. Mitchell of the University of Michigan as its chairman. The two groups then were given permission to set up programs. For the fourth time now, women had managed to get the topic of women's athletics on the program. But this was the first that a section on women's athletics had been mentioned even though temporary and unofficial. At least it meant a toe in the door.

The part of the program given over to the Women's Athletic Committee was later reported as having Grace Jones of Summit, N.J. as chairman. This was most certainly an error as Katherine Sibley was still chairman of the committee, and Grace Jones did not come into that position until five years later. It may have been that Grace Jones was presiding at that part of the program as a substitute for Miss Sibley and so was listed as chairman instead of merely as the one who presided. (The APEA *Review* of those years was full of such errors.)

In the spring of 1927 I attended the APEA convention in Des Moines, Iowa. The delegates were friendly and, trained in a variety of physical activities, seemed to like to dance (ballroom, square or folk type of dance) so that in joining in the social mixers each evening following the speeches, I began to get acquainted with others beyond the college women's group. Here I first learned that all was not harmony among the women leaders working in the field of women's athletics and some of the men of the profession.

As an utter greenhorn at professional organization maneuvering, I sat in on the council meeting as the representative of NAPECW at this convention and from the sideline voted for whatever the Women's Athletic Committee was fighting for. They won long sought-for open recognition of the committee as an unofficial Section of Women's Athletics, but were given verbal warning before the council members that the Section was to have only guest status at APEA Council meetings and the privilege of putting on programs at convention only with special permission of the president, year by year. This was actually nothing new since this situation had existed for the previous few years. The only difference was that now it was more out in the open. It meant that the door was pushed a little farther open.

When Florence Somers of the Sargent School of Physical Education was appointed by President Savage to take over the chairmanship of this committee in 1927, she seized the bull by the horns and applied to the council for her committee to be recognized officially as a section so that it would have voting membership on the council. The women working in the interests of women's sports were tired of their many years of hard work without official representation on the council or voting privileges.

Since agreement could not be reached, the women decided to let sleeping dogs lie and went ahead planning programs as if they were a section, but not holding elections. It was a strange situation openly winked at by the leaders among the men to arouse as little friction as possible. The editor, Dr. McCurdy, even listed the new chairman's name in the *Review* as if she were an official member of the council representing WAS.

Florence Somers was a quiet, tactful, non-militant, yet forceful leader, who steered a sure but quiet course ever nearer the desired goal. Open acceptance by the council of this new section status, even though still unofficial, was at least one more step forward, even though a sort of lefthanded salute to the ladies. Now Miss Somers began the fight for that next step—recognition as an official section.

The one big reason for the holdout of the men against full recognition was the fact that the women were not willing to permit their officers to be elected annually and most certainly not by APEA members who happened to sit in on the program when the election was held, as was the case for all sections within the Association. This group, unlike practically all other sections within APEA, was a year-round working group committed to the task of putting out the official rules for women's sports. This called for selection of highly skilled and trained workers. For this reason the women felt strongly that it could not be subjected to the whims of such elections of officers. This proved a real stumbling block to negotiations since the men held the majority vote in the council, and many of them, wedded to the past, refused to recognize this essential working difference between this group and other sections.

Under Florence Somers' chairmanship, the Women's Athletic Section (the WAS as it became nicknamed) put out a series of syndicated articles through the National Newspaper Service of Chicago which was carried in papers in all parts of the country. She also persuaded Dr. McCurdy to give the section, jointly with the Women's Division of NAAF, space in the *American Physical Education Review* for articles of interest on girls' athletics.

Finally a compromise was reached. The chairman of the National Committee on Women's Athletics, appointed by the president of APEA for a term of two to four years, would automatically become chairman of an unofficial Women's Athletic Section and thus would have a voice in the council and would be empowered to arrange programs for conventions without annual need of permission. Even more important, the members of the Committee on Women's Athletics whom she could appoint would become her executive committee. This protected the group's right to select its own skilled workers for rules-making free of political elections. Since this section was as yet unofficial, it did not have to elect its chairman annually at conventions. Thus, Miss

Somers, a presidential appointee, was able to carry on for three years (1927–1930) while the problem was being negotiated of how to reconcile differences and become a legitimate section.

A Baseball Rules Committee was added to WAS with Helen Hazleton (then of the University of Minnesota) as its chairman. Under her, Gladys Palmer of Ohio State University did for girls' baseball what Senda Berenson had done 35 years before for girls' basketball–modified the men's rules. All of these women had to stand up against a group of determined men who were pulling strings behind the scenes, making a last stand against change. The 1920s were exciting years for women trying to get what they wanted and thought they should have within the American Physical Education Association!

* * * *

As Frederick Maroney of the Atlantic City public schools stepped into the presidency of APEA January 1, 1929 the battle lines were being drawn between one large group of determined women representing all parts of the country on the one hand, and a small but die-hard group of men on the East Coast on the other. At the same time, a small group of women, never clearly identified, complained to the die-hard group of men that the Women's Athletic Committee was a self-perpetuating group and a "closed-door corporation." This only increased the resolve of these men to bring to task the unofficial WAS and dissolve it if possible.

At this time a delegation of women who never identified themselves used Jesse F. Williams as their "front man" to present a petition to put on a women's swimming demonstration at the spring convention in Boston with the openly declared intention of organizing a Women's Section on Swimming which would be no part of the Women's Athletic Section. This was a complete surprise to the WAS leaders. It placed their entire project in jeopardy were it to develop that the women themselves were divided. The women who signed this petition did not appear in person to plead their case nor had they even approached the WAS leaders with a hint that they wished swimming to be isolated from all the other women's sports. The petition was refused. Their absence at the meeting puzzled me since they were known to be in New York City at that very time. I have always been suspicious that the swimming group was put up to this by a few men just for the sake of producing a rift in the Women's Athletic Section.

187

At that meeting I was elected vice-president of APEA, and upon adjournment one of the ringleaders of this new women's group, whose identity I did not get at the time, besieged me outside the meeting room, to back them and use my influence in their behalf. When I refused she bitterly attacked me and began a campaign of innuendos against me and the WAS, swinging to her side a few men who were only too eager to have a cause for fighting this particular group of women.

Following this meeting President Maroney informed me that the day was past when a vice-president had no responsibility. He asked me to try to find out what needed to be done to mollify the Middle Westerners and to swing the Women's Athletic Section leaders to get the demands of both women's athletic groups into line with APEA's best interests as the over-all mother group. Many men hailed this development as a definite rift in the women's ranks and made the most of it.

As I took over the vice-presidency of APEA for 1930, President Maroney also assigned me the task of looking after his interests on the program committee for the coming Boston convention with special orders to "calm down the women." This was a disturbing task and in the end, in trying to protect APEA's best interests as I saw them, I had the hot-headed ones of both groups angry with me. Some of the WAS group were naggingly impatient and, because I did not give them a full, clear and immediate go-ahead, accused me of betraying their interests. At the same time the naggingly insistent women of the other group (who I strongly felt should be granted no consideration since they seemed interested not so much in having a women's swimming section as in using such plans to cause a rupture in the women's ranks) passed the word around that I was holding back progress. Thus I was caught in the middle between two hostile groups of women.

I was in luck when the calm, clear-headed Helen Hazelton of Purdue University took over the chairmanship of the WAS from equally calm, clear-headed Florence Somers. Helen soon quieted down the excitable ones of her own group. She carried on with the task of devising some plan of organization that would be acceptable to both the women and the die-hard men, and she sought advice from Mr. St. John, Ohio State University Athletic Director, whose opinions and advice were highly sought on sports matters by the men of the profession. No clearly-defined woman leader emerged from the other group. Just who they were no one knew for sure. Their displeasure with WAS leaders and with me was made known to us now and then in a roundabout way by the die-hard men opposing WAS. I never had an opportunity to deal with these women directly. It developed into a sort of cloak-and-dagger affair that I have never ceased to wonder about. Why didn't they come out in the open and negotiate with us? Soon this group evaporated and we heard but little from it until another two years as related later.

At the 1930 convention in Boston, President Maroney, in keeping with his promise to the Middle West group that APEA would be reorganized along more democratic lines, announced that all old sections were disbanded and all groups wishing to continue as sections and all groups wishing to create new sections should present their recommendations at the December 1930 Council meeting following the new pattern set for such groups. The big stumbling block to official recognition of this woman's group was selection of the chairman. She could not be selected at the whim of an audience or on a popularity basis but instead should be chosen carefully for her expertise in sports, her sports philosophy, and her drive to get the rules revised and published on time. There were constant publication schedules to be met following long and important committee meetings on rules revisions.

By 1930 these publications were bringing in a good financial return; 85 percent of the royalties came from the *Basketball Guides* alone.[2] Their budget stood at around $4,000, quite a fortune that day in re-

Helen Hazelton of Purdue University who piloted the women through to final victory in their over 10-year struggle to win national section status for women's athletics within the American Physical Education Association.

189

lation to the APEA treasury. This, too, was a stumbling block to the group's acceptance. Some of the men insisted that no section should be allowed to have a treasury of its own. The women at first adamantly refused to enter into any agreement with the APEA Council as to how the group would earn, control and handle its money.

Most of the misunderstanding between the men and women arose over this publishing question. The men in APEA had no such concerns since all sports rules for men had from the very beginning been put out by separate committees for the various sports. Each was an independent group and practically all were functioning before APEA came into existence. There had been no rules for women's sports published before Senda Berenson and her group started girls' basketball in the 1890s and set up their rules under APEA. Gradually they took over rules for other sports. No other groups entered this field until after the APEA groups were already well established.

During the Boston convention of 1930 the women involved in the Women's Athletic Committee and others interested in setting up, under the reorganization plan, a section to be officially recognized and called the Women's Athletic Section (such as had been functioning since 1927) did a lot of conferring. Some went so far as to suggest that the Women's Athletic Committee disband as a committee of APEA and organize as an independent organization and then ask for affiliation with APEA.

On July 30, 1930, the APEA Constitution Committee had a meeting in New York City, then sent out copies of the first draft of a new suggested constitution to all council members to study. Upon receipt of it, Helen Hazelton of Purdue University wrote me:

> As far as I could make out, there is still no provision for our body recently known as the Section on Women's Athletics but inaccurately so known for we are not a whole section and would not want to be. We have a special, unique function to formulate rules and edit *Guides*. The problem is to name and legalize us. There are two prerogatives which we want to insure to ourselves— the right to elect our own officers and committee members, and representation on the National Council.

On August 15, 1930, Miss Hazelton wrote Dr. Brownell, then chairman of the APEA Constitution Committee, that her group was a rules-making body in the field of women's sports and that it would not want to become an organization apart from APEA as had been suggested by some. She wrote him that perhaps the Women's Athletic Committee should become a standing committee of APEA on rules for women's athletics and that there should be established a Women's Athletic

Section with this standing committee under it. She also wrote to me for my opinion of this procedure and told me that "it has been suggested to me that we become a standing committee or commission." She did not say where the suggestion came from. I approved the idea and wrote Dr. Brownell calling for his careful consideration of the idea that in organizing a Women's Athletic Section the peculiar functions of the old Women's Athletic Committee should be kept in mind. This committee must be kept separate so it could carry on its work, including provisions that the committee could select its own officers and experts to carry on its work. As vice-president of APEA and the only woman on the Executive Committee, I pledged to Miss Hazelton my wholehearted support of her plans.

By November 1930 a group of women supposedly from Columbia University, who had the year before petitioned to be recognized as a Women's Section on Swimming, came to life again. They had been refused on the grounds that one Section on Women's Athletics was sufficient. This refusal was strongly supported by the women of WAS as they considered this new group an attempt to weaken their position. They suspected that it was being promoted behind the scenes by a few men who wished merely to cause trouble for WAS. After the 1930 convention in April, the swimming group, enlarged and more determined, began bringing pressure upon President Maroney to be given a place on the 1931 convention program. Although he had appointed me as chairman of the Program Committee, he ordered the new chairman of the Public School Section, Strong Hinman of the Wichita public schools, to make a place on his part of the 1931 convention program for these women to offer an "on-trial" Women's Swimming Section program.

Since Mr. Hinman had his entire program planned, he refused claiming that there was no reason why his section offerings should be the scapegoat to support this "fly-by-night" women's group which the WAS women were not promoting. He turned to me as chairman of the program committee to support him. I did, but I had quite a battle on my hands with our president. "Fritz," as every one called him once they became acquainted with him, was a hot-headed Irishman, quick to anger. More than once in the two years I worked closely with him, when he exploded into sudden wrath over some problem I would, as if his big sister, seize him by the shoulders and give him a shake.

"Stop that," I would exclaim, "you are acting just like a spoiled little boy who needs a spanking. Calm down and let me explain to you just what it really is that the women want and why." His explosions most frequently came over what he called "women pushing too hard for power."

If he was quick to anger, he was equally quick to repent, and he would calm down and shamefaced would turn on that Irish charm and beg to be forgiven for the angry outburst. I would explain the women's point of view the best I could on whatever problem was the cause of the outburst and he usually came around to the women's side. Then he had to placate the men who were dragging their feet over letting the women "have any more power," as they put it.

On December 8, 1930, Miss Hazelton sent to all working members of the National Section on Women's Athletics a suggested new form of organization proposed by her committee on reorganization–Marguerite Hussey, Florence Somers, Gladys Palmer and herself. The group had done a complete about-face in its thinking. In August they did not want to become a separate organization. Now they proposed again that they become a separate organization affiliated with APEA, thus preserving their freedom to handle their own affairs and their own funds. In addition they offered a Women's Athletic Section within APEA, which would be apart from this other rules-making new organization, for the sole purpose of putting on programs at conventions.

On December 15, 1930, I informed Miss Hazelton of my approval of the latest plans and assured her I would use my influence to get them accepted. Miss Hazelton then said she had approval from the Constitution Committee for her group to go ahead with the plans. At the December council meeting she would apply for recognition by APEA as an affiliated organization to be known as the Women's Athletic Rules Association.

By the time of the annual council meeting in December 1930, when all petitioning sections were to report their plans, the former unofficial WAS proposed a new section and also the Women's Athletic Rules Association. This independent association would take over all sports rules-making functions and have its own treasury. When this plan was reported to the council, there was enough of an outcry from several of the men that the council as a group expressed displeasure. In a sudden gesture of irritation with the women, President Maroney appointed a committee (one of his last acts before stepping out of the presidency) to get the old unofficial Women's Athletic Section reorganized to the better liking of APEA. He named three men to the committee, with one of them as chairman: Carl Schrader. Serving with him were Dr. William Burdick, an outspoken critic of the women promoting WAS, and Ralph LaPorte of the University of Southern California, who was just then finishing his term as president of the College Physical Education Association (a men's organization then over 30 years old). The other two members were Helen Hazelton, the new chairman of WAS, and Marguerite Hussey of New York University. Even though Mr. Schrader was generally considered a champion of the women, this sudden appointment of such a committee angered most of the women. I still feel to this day that Dr. Maroney was trying to appease the die-hard men to make them think that they were still in control with a clear majority in sympathy with their wishes. But many of the women refused to see it that way. Helen Hazelton took on the responsibility of trying to "calm them down." All the past year's hard work of the WAS women was now seemingly swept aside by the men.

By presidential decree, the whole thing seemed to be taken out of their hands and placed in the hands of another committee with a man as chairman. To be sure, the two women members were their own leaders, but why this sudden action and why, if the council wished such a committee set up, didn't it wait until the new president, who chanced to be a woman, was elected only a few minutes after this committee was announced? Also why was there a special APEA Committee set up to reorganize this section alone of all sections? Miss Hazelton told her executive committee later that the men had explained to her that the committee had been appointed because the men might wish some day to set up rules committees too and this new committee should work out a scheme of organization that would hold for both men and women. Although it was obviously a subterfuge of face-saving on the part of the men who were back of this scheme, Miss Hazelton politely accepted the explanation and determined to make this new committee work effectively for the sake of peace and progress.

So the year 1930 ended with seeming peace except for the serious problems of bringing the Women's Athletic Rules Association and the Women's Athletic Section into an acceptable relationship with each other and with APEA. The problem was serious only because a group of obstinate die-hard men made it so. On January 1, 1931, as related in Chapter VII, I took over as president of APEA.

To meet the requirements for reorganization of sections, the new chairman of the old WAS–from 1931 on known as the National Section on Women's Athletics (NSWA)—was for the first time elected at an open meeting from the floor of the 1931 Detroit convention. She was Grace Jones of Summit, New Jersey public schools who had for the past few years been working on various committees of WAS and thus was a welcome choice of the women. For the coming year of probation (1931-1932) it was decided that the APEA president should appoint the chairman of the Women's Rules and Editorial Committee (a new name now adopted for the proposed Women's Athletic Rules Association), which would take on this special function while Carl Schrader's special committee would continue its work on final organization plans of NSWA. When earlier at the 1931 convention I announced that this committee had now concluded its work, such an uproar ensued from a few men that I felt it wise to reappoint it to carry on through the 1932 convention, by which time the Association would be ready to function entirely on its new constitution. Anything to keep the few belligerent men mollified. It had been proved anyway that the women's interests had been well served under Carl Schrader's chairmanship of this illogical committee. It preserved the peace and got a good job done. Grace Jones tactfully accepted it as had Helen Hazelton before her.

* * * *

At the official annual council meeting held at the 1931 Detroit convention (the first in 24 years held in connection with a national convention instead of during the Christmas holidays in New York City) Carl Schrader was called on to report for his ad hoc committee on the reorganization of the WAS. He reported that they had produced two plans and he asked that Helen Hazelton, the chairman of the Women's Athletic Committee, be called to explain the favored committee proposal. Miss Hazelton presented both plans. She reported that the Executive Committee had approved the favored plan which was for the former Women's Athletic Committee to carry on for the coming year as a standing committee of APEA as it had been functioning since 1917. Now it was to be known as the Women's Athletic Editorial Committee with all monies to be turned over to the APEA treasury instead of to the committee as before. The committee was to be put on a budget which should be drawn up by the committee and approved by the APEA Executive Committee. The plan provided that the work of this editorial committee was to be completely divorced for the trial year from the Women's Athletic Section which Mr. Schrader's ad hoc committee proposed should be given official sanction on the year's trial basis. The council approved these suggestions.

In order to give the newly approved Women's Athletic Editorial Committee official sanction as a standing committee of APEA, Gertrude Moulton of Oberlin College moved that the president appoint it as an on-trial standing committee for the coming year. The motion carried, and I immediately named Helen Hazelton as chairman with the following of her selection to serve with her: Harriet Rogers of Virginia, Eline von Borries of Maryland, Harriet Brown, Amy Howland, Marguerite Hussey and Ethel Bowers of New York, Florence Hupprich of Texas, Katherine Montgomery of Florida, Doris White and Marjorie Camp of Iowa, Helen Sheddon of Pennsylvania, and Gladys Palmer of Ohio. Except for Marguerite Hussey, the secretary of the Women's Athletic Committee, the members of the committee were the current sports subcommittee chairmen.

Following that, Grace Jones announced that she represented a group of women who wished to present a petition for the creation of a National Section on Women's Athletics, to function for the coming year on a trial basis and to present its final organization plans at the next convention meeting of the Council. Immediately some man moved that the petition be rejected, but his motion was lost for want of a second.

Upon questioning, Miss Jones assured the council members that the group she represented was known to the Women's Athletic Committee and that this petition met with their approval. This allayed worries that the women might not be pulling together. Miss Jones explained that the petition coming from a group other than from the Women's Athletic Committee itself meant that the women were organizing for a complete separation of the function of the rules-making body and the convention programming work. The new National Section on Women's Athletics (NSWA) could carry on as did all other sections, with elections from the floor at program meetings without interfering with the continuity of the rules making. This seemed to answer the criticisms of many men and the petition was granted with the admonition that since there was a program of a Women's Athletic Section for the next day, that group should elect a chairman for the coming year. They agreed to this. After the program meeting on Thursday, April 2, presided over by Elmore Biggs who had been elected at the unofficial section meeting the year before to produce a program at this convention, Grace Jones, as related earlier, was elected chairman of this on-trial section for the coming year.

On June 2, 1931, Grace Jones wrote me that she was at work on the new constitution of NSWA for presentation at Philadelphia next spring. She presented a plan for the Women's Rules Committee (which was to function independently the coming year during reorganization) to become a standing committee of NSWA. The plan called for an executive committee of 10 members—1 each from the 5 APEA districts; 2 at large; 2 representing Women's Division of NAAF, and the chairman of the Rules Committee. She asked for my advice and suggestions on this. She informed me she had appointed a constitution committee of Grace Davies, Helen Hazelton and Agnes Wayman and that the treasury from the Women's Athletic Committee had been turned over temporarily to the new Editorial Rules Committee. She asked how she should get necessary funds for her NSWA work in the interim.

Technically the reorganization ad hoc committee set up for the old unofficial Women's Athletic Section by Dr. Maroney in December 1930 should have died with the old constitution. It would have been easier for all of us if it had, for it now served no useful purpose other than to mollify a group of foot-dragging men. All other sections were reorganizing on their own without special committees set up to reorganize for them.

Prolongation of this committee seemed utterly ridiculous! I disliked carrying this farce any further, but when I intimated that this committee no longer was needed, one of the men members immediately denounced me as being autocratic for declaring committees disbanded before they had completed the work for which they had been appointed. So I sought advice and it was decided that rather than further alienate the small group of men ready to attack me on any move since their animosity would in this case be turned on NSWA, it would be better to continue to recognize the committee until the period for trying out the new constitution ended in April 1932. So I begged the women for their own best interests to acknowledge this ad hoc committee as still the over-all committee to propose reorganization plans for NSWA.

We all agreed that the chairman, Carl Schrader, and Mr. LaPorte, one of the other two men on the committee, were friendly to NSWA's hopes. Only the third man, Dr. Burdick, might make trouble for them. So at Grace Jones' "I am green and would so like to get started in the right direction. I will be grateful for any help which you may have time to send me," I wrote her, June 8, explaining that this old committee was the official committee to reorganize NSWA but I was appointing her as a new member of the committee. I was sure Mr. Schrader would welcome all of her suggestions.

Because the reorganization of the National Section on Women's Athletics had developed into such a ticklish business, I decided to have a preliminary meeting with Grace Jones representing the NSWA, Helen Hazelton representing the Women's Rules and Editorial Committee, Agnes Wayman representing Women's Division of NAAF, and Marjorie Bouvé, the other woman member of the APEA Executive Committee before my special meeting of the Executive Committee, December 29, 1931. I wanted Miss Jones to brief us on her group's final plans in the hopes that we women could present a united front to put the plans over. I had great confidence in both Grace Jones and Helen Hazelton and was eager to do what I could as president of APEA to put their wishes into effect. The men on that committee were in an embarrassing position, too, and were eager to get the committee assignment over.

An unofficial Christmas holiday meeting of the Council had been called at the urging of the men for December 1931, but no official business could be transacted. We could only discuss, but discussion could clear the air and by December 1932, maybe the Eastern old guard would be weaned away from the old-time December meetings in New York City.

Before this December meeting I was able to work in a brief preliminary meeting with the four women as planned. When the executive committee met, Carl Schrader reported that the women had consented to have their finances placed under the APEA treasury and that they would present a proposed budget. Grace Jones reported that her NSWA executive committee wished to present the main outlines of their proposed reorganization and if it were approved they would then proceed to work on minor details before the spring meeting. The main outline she said had been approved by the Women's Rules and Editorial Committee through its chairman, Helen Hazelton, and by the chairman of the Women's Division of NAAF, Agnes Wayman, and by the NSWA officers represented by herself. It had also been approved by me as president of APEA. The executive committee of APEA expressed confidence in the plan presented and advised her committee to proceed with details. Then Helen Hazelton gave a report on her committee work and called on Marguerite Hussey to report on the treasury of the Women's Rules and Editorial Committee. Then Grace Jones reported that whereas this editorial committee was now functioning as a standing committee of APEA appointed by the president of APEA, the women agreed that after April 1932, they wanted it to become a standing committee of the NSWA instead. The executive committee of APEA received the idea favorably.

At the Philadelphia convention of April 1932, all sections presented their final petitions for readmittance into the American Physical Education Association under the new constitution.

It soon became noised about that Carl Schrader's committee on reorganization of the Women's Athletic Section was not unanimous in its decisions and that in all probability a minority report would be presented which would please a large number of the men who were members of the new legislative council. This deeply concerned the women. After their hard work of the many months past, it had seemed that at long last they were to get approval of their desired plans. I also was told that the women's group that had earlier proposed the formation of a Women's Swimming Section was reviving its plans and would now appear before the council to petition for its acceptance. At the time this proposal first came up, the women of the Women's Athletic Section were greatly disturbed thinking that such a section would invade their field of work. For some reason the proposal died down and now two years and three months later it bobbed up again. Nita Sheffield of

Columbia University was given as the person who was representing this group of women. It was reported that their petition had the endorsement of Dr. Jesse F. Williams.

I was asked to put Miss Sheffield's request on the agenda of the April 20 council meeting. I did so, but with misgivings, because some members of this group had been recently causing much needless unpleasantness. We had great difficulty scheduling the proposed Women's Swimming Section program at days and hours to suit their whims.

Aroused by this turn of events which might cause a break in the women's heretofore united front, and by the insistent rumors that all was not in agreement on Carl Schrader's committee, I was worried about the possible failure of the National Section on Women's Athletics to get its proposed plan through the council for final approval. I realized that if it failed it would be because of lack of support by the men since they were in the decided majority on the council. So I set out to try to find out where the heart of the opposition lay and why.

I discovered that an ardent supporter of the women was Dr. John Brown, Jr., a council member representing the National Association of the YMCA Physical Directors. He was equally concerned when I told him my worries and he resented as much as did I the attempt of the other group of women to split the women's efforts by proposing another women's athletic section. All these 40 or more years later I do not know yet whether or not this other group from Columbia University was acting in good faith.

In my conferences with many men, I discovered that there were some men in APEA who were opposed to a Women's Athletic Section since they saw no need for a Men's Athletic Section. Others felt that the women "busied" themselves too much throughout the year and magnified the importance of their work when the affairs of APEA had moved along nicely all the previous years without groups working between conventions. Others were said to resent women's increasing importance in Association affairs. Some even resented having a woman president and although they said they had nothing against me personally, they hoped my election was not going to set a precedent. Some even asked where this was going to lead to if this tendency were not checked.

After hearing my explanation of what it was the women wanted and what they were working for, not one man with whom I talked was opposed to their petition. Practically everyone told me that the affair had not been represented to them in that light by the men who were trying to organize enough strength to defeat the women's plans. All these men now pledged their support for the women.

198

At the council meeting, April 20, at the 1932 APEA convention in Philadelphia I called for a report of the Committee on Reorganization of the National Section on Women's Athletics. Carl Schrader, the chairman, presented a majority report calling for council approval of the plans which the women themselves proposed. Then he announced that the committee had not been in agreement; Dr. Burdick of the committee requested the privilege of presenting a minority report, a plan unanimously rejected by the women on the committee. Immediately it was moved and seconded by two men that the minority report be accepted and approved. A split second ahead of calls of "question," John Brown jumped to his feet demanding recognition and launched into an impassioned speech insisting that the women be allowed the plans they desired and that if after trying them out the Association found fault with them they could later be forced to change their organization to meet Association wishes. He also made some scathing remarks about men who were unwilling to give the women a place in Association work and were thus obstructing progress. This silenced the opposition and gave the women a victory. The earlier unofficial Women's Athletic Section now became the official National Section on Women's Athletics (NSWA), with a Women's Rules and Editorial Committee set up as a standing committee within the Section. This protected the need to appoint specialists in this group rather than have the work done by persons elected at random.

When later I called on the group requesting a Women's Swimming Section to present its petition, no one rose to speak for it. The petition was lost by default.

Thus ended a 15-year struggle of one group of women to gain their rights to a place in the sun within the official working of one national organization. The fact that there had to be such a struggle seems strange today, but the retelling of this story should give hope to other groups still fighting for their rights. There is always, so it seems, a hard core of die-hards to defeat before rights of any kind become a reality.

Following this final victory the program meeting of the NSWA was offered. The audience was so large that it filled the ballroom of the Benjamin Franklin Hotel. It was reported to the audience that there now was an official National Section on Women's Athletics (NSWA) and that the former Women's Athletic Editorial Committee of APEA was now the Women's Rules and Editorial Committee, a standing committee of NSWA. These announcements were received with great enthusiasm. At the election that followed, Grace Davies was elected the new chairman to succeed Grace Jones. The women of our profession should never forget the wonderful work done during those trying times by Helen Hazelton and Grace Jones, assisted by their many fine committee members.

At the legislative council meeting on April 23, under the new council the women's group asking for consideration of creation of a Section on Swimming for Women withdrew its petition which resolved that problem. At that same meeting, Grace Jones, as the outgoing chairman of NSWA, presented the treasury of APEA with a gift of $200 from the funds of NSWA as a token of goodwill, adding the hope that the women's work would always prove an asset to APEA.

Thus ended a bitterly contested battle—now NSWA was recognized as a legitimate section of APEA. I was happy to have been the president of APEA to see that battle for the women through to a victory when so many men fought it vigorously, but it would never have been accomplished without the final plea of Dr. John Brown, Jr., who swung enough men into line to assure the final majority victory vote.

At the conclusion of the NSWA program, Agnes Wayman presented a resolution which was passed unanimously by the section. The copy given to me by the chairman, Grace E. Jones, is one of my cherished mementos and reads as follows:

> In as much as the APEA is just finishing its first year under the leadership of its first woman president, and in as much as Miss Lee has contributed much to the cause of physical education through her constructive leadership, her graciousness and her ability, and in as much as this is a woman's section, I would like to suggest that we give a rising vote to show our appreciation of Miss Lee and her accomplishments. I would further suggest that this be spread upon our records and a copy of it be sent to Miss Lee.

Twenty-seven years later this women's group, grown into a large organization, was granted division status within the national association where it had unquestioned equal rights with all other seven divisions. Today it has advanced to the status of National Association for Girls and Women in Sport (NAGWS). It offers service to the nation, districts, states and local grass roots in the field of girls' and women's sports; it sets standards for all women's sports and publishes sports guides and official rules of women's sports. Today hundreds of women trained in our profession toil the year round in its many projects, just as did a smaller group from the turn of the century on.

No more would the women have to resort to all sorts of subterfuges to carry on important work in behalf of women's sports. It had been a 16-year struggle since the section's birth under President Arnold in

1916 as a mere committee. Recognition of that group as a full-fledged section had been so bitterly fought by so many men that I seriously doubt if the wishes of the women would ever have been achieved until a woman was in the presidency. 1931 and 1932 gave them their chance and at last they made it.

Grace Davies carried on as chairman of NSWA 1932–1934, and Eline von Borries of Goucher College from 1934 to 1936. Under both, NSWA prospered and settled into quiet acceptance by APEA. After so many years of struggle for a place in the sun it was a relief to have peaceful cooperation.

* * * *

At the same time the group of women was fighting for rights of women's athletics within the Association, another group of women was also asking for recognition. This group wanted a section within our new national organization to advance the interests of dance in the schools. They had much enthusiasm and push and like the group for women's athletics, they chafed under the man-made restrictions that did not hamper the other sections since they were composed mostly of men and were not year-round working groups.

Throughout the years I had come to sense a difference between the drive of most women working in the profession compared to that of most men I had encountered working in this field in the opening years of the century. Many men resented a second group of women pushing for "a place in the sun," as they spoke of it, especially another group intent on year-round work to promote their professional interests. The pattern of bestirring themselves only once a year to put on a convention seemed to many of the men to be sufficient extra work for the year. They didn't like to be stirred up too much for the advancement of physical education. The original title of the professional organization had been the American Association for the Advancement of Physical Education (AAAPE) but at the turn of the century the word, "advancement," was deleted and the title became American Physical Education Association (APEA). Many men seemed content to forget about that word, "advancement," but not the women, and now another group was pushing for attention.

At the Middle West Society convention in Milwaukee in 1930, a group interested in dance got together informally and discussed the possibility of creating a Dance Section within APEA. Ruth Murray of the Detroit Teachers College was named their organizing chairman. At

201

the national convention which took place the following week in Boston, there was a place on the program for a discussion of dancing in the elementary schools, which was set up under the sponsorship of the College Women's Section.

This section, by the way, was another unofficial section which year by year throughout the 1920s had been allowed to sponsor programs for women's interests. One year it was called a College Women's Section, another, a Women's Section, depending upon who had the upper hand—Mrs. Persis McCurdy, assistant editor of the *American Physical Education Review*, who wanted such meetings to be for all women, or Gertrude Dudley or Blanche Trilling, or someone else of the college women directors groups who wished a chance at conventions to discuss their own college-level problems. This was in the years before the National Association of Physical Education for College Women. Mrs. McCurdy resigned in 1929 so there was no conflict in 1930. But by then NAPECW was quite well established and the need for a College Women's Section was no longer felt so that this group let the unofficial women's section die with the 1930 Boston meeting.

At this last meeting of the unofficial College Women's Section, the leaders asked Dorothy LaSalle, then a graduate student at Columbia University, to present the topic of dancing in the elementary schools. It was a logical topic since the college directors were heading up teacher-training work for women in many colleges by then. At the close of that meeting the chairman was asked to present to the APEA president a request for the appointment of a committee to study dancing in the elementary schools and suggested that Miss LaSalle be appointed chairman of this committee. President Maroney honored the request and added this committee to the long list of booklet committees which he had previously created to prepare monographs on a great variety of topics published by APEA and distributed about the country on calls for help.

As vice-president of APEA and chairman of the program committee for the next spring convention, I asked Miss Murray and Miss LaSalle to get together to put on a program on dance in the schools at the 1931 convention, and to include Miss LaSalle's report on her study of dance in the elementary schools. Miss LaSalle was asked to act as temporary chairman to plan for a permanent organization of a Dance Section, with Miss Murray as secretary. Miss LaSalle could not accept the chairmanship because of her responsibilities under Dr. Thomas D. Wood for his part of the 1930 reports on the White House Conference on Child Health. I then appointed Ruth Murray to take over the chairmanship of an unofficial Dance Section, to procure signatures of 25 APEA members to a petition for official recognition as a section, and to set up a program for the 1931 Detroit convention. At the close of that convention program it would be necessary to hold a business meeting, effect a permanent organization and elect a chairman for the year 1931-1932. Miss Murray accepted the appointment, prepared a program and arrived at the convention in Detroit with a petition with the necessary signatures. At their business meeting, Mary O'Donnell of Columbia University was selected chairman for 1931-1932.

At the 1931 Council meeting the petition was presented and the group was instructed that the Dancing Section was accepted on a year's probation (as was the case with all groups asking for recognition under the new constitution). At the next annual business meeting they were to ask for official recognition as a permanent section. So two women's sections were at last functioning with full official blessing for a year's trial by the close of the Detroit 1931 convention.

All this was going on with considerable opposition from some men who wanted no more women on the council with voting power and from others angered by this group's taking over Miss LaSalle's monograph on *Dancing in the Elementary Schools* insisting that it be published by a commercial publisher with the royalties accruing to the Dance Section to build up its own treasury. There had been enough difficulty getting acceptance of the idea of the women's sports group having its own treasury, and now another group of women was asking the same privilege. Even though they had given up their commercial publication idea and stepped into line with the other APEA booklet committees and had their monograph published in APEA's *Research Quarterly* (December 1931 issue), some of the men were still angry at them for demanding special treatment and were using this as an excuse to get enough votes to deny the women a Dance Section.

In order to save the day for them I had urged the women to give up graciously this commercial publishing scheme but my efforts were taken by some of that group as opposition to their total plans to establish a section. In the end I got most of the opposing men and some of the women calmed down but it was quite a struggle because Miss O'Donnell, their chairman, was temperamental.

The group seemed to want to do everything its own way, regardless of patterns of action set up for all such groups. It also seemed greatly indisposed to live by any rules laid down by APEA. The many booklet committees set up by President Maroney had been warned to run up no expenses without authorization. The Dance Section appropriated the booklet committee on dance as its own special project, to which no one really objected, except that it ignored the dictum about expenses. All these monographs were to be published by the Association but the

Dance Section turned its monograph over to a commercial publisher with royalties to be paid directly to the section. This was unknown to us officers until the publisher, thinking the arrangement a bit out of order, called our attention to it.

The executive committee decided that the manuscript must be reclaimed from the publisher. To head off a quarrel with this group of women, the Association paid the expense of the monograph's preparation even though the expense had not been authorized. This brought down upon my head in particular (since I was a woman opposing them) the anger of Miss O'Donnell and her group. Their leader was obviously under the influence of the little cell of die-hard men which backed them to make trouble for me. (The author of their monograph was not one of this angry group, and her monograph *Dancing in Elementary Schools*, which was published in the *Research Quarterly*, proved to be one of the most popular of all the series of monographs.) It was quite enlightening to learn in this unpleasant way how naggingly insistent some women can sometimes be in their determination to have their own way regardless of common decisions for the common good.

I came to realize later how deep was the curiosity of some of that group about what I had written on these difficulties to others. Someone took from my office in Lincoln, Nebraska, my complete file of correspondence concerning the Dance Section. Shortly after I stepped out of the presidency, I discovered this entire file was missing. For almost 30 years I never knew what became of it. Then, when in the Washington D.C. national office in 1962, as the Association's first archivist, I was going through old file drawers of materials accumulated before 1938 and stored away in the sub-basement. I came upon a package still wrapped and tied just as it had been posted to Washington. It had never been opened, but the postmarks and name and address of sender were all obliterated by smudges so that it was impossible to tell who had sent it or from where or when it had been sent. So I opened the package and to my utter amazement found it was my long-lost file of Dance Section correspondence and records. Who had pilfered it from my office? To whom had it been sent? And why? And who had sensed its later historical value and sent it to the National office? And what a queer circumstance that of all people, the very one whose property it was, would chance to be the AAHPER archivist these many years later and would be the one to find this collection of my personal papers in Washington, D.C. The thief and the recipients of the thievery, if perchance they still live, will no doubt be surprised to learn that at last I found my lost papers.

In the end, by April 1932, the group had enough favorable votes in the council to accept the Dance Section as a permanent group. The monograph was also in such demand that the council gave permission for it to be published by A. S. Barnes & Co. with the royalties accruing to the section through the APEA treasury.

However, I, who fought so hard for this group of women to have their wishes come true, had to bear the brunt of the displeasure of many men over their lack of patience. Since I was in the position of authority at the time I was the one who had to say "No" to them on occasion, thereby acquiring the enmity of some of the women, too.

Today, the Dance Section has become the National Dance Association with a large following of both men and women. It is a very active member of our national organization.

Chapter X
Delights and Leftover Cares

In spite of several deep-seated worries and many little concerns, I found some time to enjoy the Philadelphia convention of 1932, the second convention over which I presided as president. This time I knew better and arranged ahead of time for help in my suite of rooms at the headquarters hotel, the Benjamin Franklin. A former secretary of our department at the University of Nebraska who was married and living in Philadelphia moved into the hotel with me and became my secretary-maid-telephone and door-answering service. My Philadelphia friend of Boston Normal School of Gymnastics and Wellesley College years, Mrs. Wayne Babcock, came each day with her car and chauffeur and took me for a drive. No matter how little time I could spare she firmly insisted that I go with her if only for a few blocks or for a cup of tea at her town house in Rittenhouse Square nearby. This proved a veritable life-saver since the MacFadden affair had cast a gloomy mantle over everything as far as we top officers were concerned and we were working under great tension.

For another diversion, the Philadelphia Physical Education Association and the Second Alarmers Association (Philadelphia's famous fire followers) gave all convention delegates a trip to Valley Forge and a picnic supper in a beautiful park. The weather was beautiful. Grover Mueller, supervisor of physical education for the Philadelphia public schools, as our convention chairman was a superb host and manager.

In spite of our fears (the Depression was beginning to be felt), we had a splendid enrollment of almost 2,000 delegates—more than at

Detroit. The many letters of congratulation which I received from all parts of the country after convention was over indicated that the program was an unusually fine one. Nellie Lee Holt, who had made a great hit at the Detroit convention the year before, again was a guest speaker at a general session and again she pleased the men as well as the women. (Two years later she returned to Philadelphia to make her home as the wife of Judge Curtis Bok.) Bill Streit of the Cincinnati public schools, our song bird of the Middle West, organized a male quartet which performed throughout the convention. They gave us frequent interludes of music and led the delegation in song, making a lot of fun on several occasions.

At the banquet Frederick Maroney was the toastmaster and never was there a more witty one. When he introduced me as "Our Mabel," he was first met with astonished silence. In 1932 a woman was not addressed by her first name in public. It was a bit of daring which only Fritz would attempt and hope to get away with. Not only daring but audaciously presumptuous! It seemed that every eye in that large ball-room was riveted on me to see how I was taking this bit of impudence. As soon as I recovered from the first shock of it, amused at Fritz's impertinence, I threw back my head in hearty laughter. The whole room full of people burst into relieved shouts of glee. The appellation "Our Mabel" stuck for many years but, of course, only with close friends. Dr. R. Tait McKenzie would not be a party to such informality. When he arose to address the gathering on "Benjamin Franklin and Physical Education," he first made me a courtly bow befitting the gentleman of the old school that he was and addressed me as "Our first lady," a title by which he addressed me from that evening on until his death six years later.

That banquet was a brilliant affair. After my insistence that all wear evening dress for the banquet in Detroit the year before, which was a great success, I issued no further orders for the Philadelphia banquet trusting the more formal Easterners to set the pattern. Again practically all dressed for the occasion and gave our banquet dignity befitting a national organization of educators. President and Mrs. Gates of the University of Pennsylvania were our guests that evening, and also Mrs. R. Tait McKenzie whom I met for the first time.

The following day Dr. McKenzie called for me with a car and driver and took me to the University of Pennsylvania to show me his collection of autographed photographs of APEA leaders through the years and also the original molds for his many pieces of sculpture. On the way to his office he asked the driver to take us to his statue of *Benjamin Franklin* on the campus. I told him that four summers before I had seen and deeply admired his Scottish-American monument *The Call* in Princess Street Gardens in Edinburgh, when the monument was less than a year old. The preceding summer I had seen and admired his statue *The Homecoming* in Cambridge, England, which was nine years old. He protested that I had "done penance enough" as he put it. When I exclaimed about his wonderful collection of autographed photographs of professional friends, he asked if I would permit him to present me with an autographed photo to start a collection of my own and I proudly said "yes."

When I arrived home, the promised photograph, a large one, was there ahead of me. It bore the inscription, "To Mabel Lee, First Woman to fill the President's chair of the APEA. 1932. Sincerely yours, R. Tait McKenzie." All these years it has been a cherished possession from a man of culture and refinement, internationally known in the world of art as well as in medical and physical education circles. He was a little younger than my mother and I was happy to have this opportunity to become a bit acquainted with him. We had before this met only most casually. I found him at once a most cordial and friendly person. Would that I had come to know him earlier. He would have been one to whom I could have turned for comfort, sound advice, and support in the difficult recent months.

All of a sudden, it seemed, my presidency was over. There had not been a dull moment—the first presidency with a woman at the helm. Looking back at it from today's perspective, I see that my second short term, the transition period, was a disruptive, disturbing period. As if anticipating later national unpleasant history, we had our own APEA "cover-up" operation; a few years ahead of Britain's Chamberlain our own private APEA "give-in" to appease an offender to buy "peace in our time"; and even by 40 years foretelling "Watergate" by our own APEA type of CIA operation "break-in" to steal papers.

After a man had followed me in the national presidency of this double-sex organization, Mary Channing Coleman, my old roommate of BNSG days, followed him, thus setting the pattern, still honored, of having alternately men and women presidents. This I look upon as a great compliment to both Coley and me. Only twice has the pattern been broken, during the merging with NEA and during the World War II years when we were dealing with our contemporaries all around the world—lands where women were not yet recognized in such top professional offices. It was a wise and understandable move to have William Hughes of Columbia University at the helm at that time.

* * * *

Home again after convention, a second year's outpouring of congratulatory letters awaited me as I stepped out of national office with women's place at long last acknowledged not only in the presidency but in women's groups with official voting power in the council. A letter from one man in particular (Carl Schrader) I have never forgotten. It said in part:

I have enjoyed working with you, and the history of the Association when again written will refer very definitely to its first woman president. I have great admiration for you. The sea was not always calm. But anyone can sail a boat in a still pond.

Indeed the sea had been rough at times but I had good luck and wonderful support in most ventures and so brought our craft safely to harbor although seriously damaged. I had learned a lot and surely had grown a lot, too!

One reward was to gain back once more Christmas Eves and Christmas Days with my family. Every Christmas Eve, and many New Year's Eves also, 1927 through 1931, found me tucked away in some lower berth on a Pullman coach headed for or from New York City and meetings of the Women's Division of NAAF and/or the council meetings of APEA. Christmas of 1932 was the first in six years that I was able to spend the actual day with Mother and my sisters and their families.

Shortly I began to sense the price I had to pay for this honor, fortunately a price set by but a few; nevertheless a price that hurt. Immediately, I began to realize that gone were the days when various women friends would write to arrange for us to meet to take the same train to convention or the same train home, or at convention would call my room to arrange for us to go to meetings and meals together. I now had to roam about by myself except for a few deeply loyal friends. When I entered a dining room alone where a group of former friends were together there were no longer calls to me to join them. So I usually ate alone until a group of men would discover me alone and call for me to join them, or until my new women friends happened along. As old friends dropped away new ones with larger hearts and greater understanding now discovered me—women whose friendships have remained true and firm all these years. So it worked both ways! I was not too aware of all this at first, for at conventions I was swamped with business which tied up almost my every moment so that I had not time to look about, little time to be alone.

It had been a wonderful experience even though a handful of willful men, fearful of granting women too much, made it very uncomfortable for me and for women leaders in general and a handful of jealous women had also made it uncomfortable for me in particular. But the great majority of the men stood staunchly by me and the other women and won the victory for us, for it was they who had the majority vote. We were entering a new era in national association affairs. The feuding between the Middle West and the national Association groups was at an end.

A year later after still more women had become members of the council, a small group of men complained jokingly to me that now the women did most of the talking in council meetings, to which I replied:

"But you men have done practically all of the talking for 47 years, surely you don't begrudge us our turn!"

"Of course not," one replied, "it is good that at last the men and women of our profession are talking together." And all present nodded ready assent.

Now in one more segment of our national life the struggle for women to have an equal place in our professional organization was over!

* * * *

Frederick Maroney had set the ball rolling for the new constitution in 1930. It had gone into effect on January 1, 1931. My council and I had put it on a one-year trial and in April 1932, saw it through its final form and acceptance.

The committee that had drawn up this new constitution consisted of 22 persons: 10 from the Eastern territory including the chairman, Clifford Brownell; 6 from the Middle West group including me (then APEA Vice-President); 3 from the South; 2 from the Southwest; and 1 from the Northwest. The six representing the Middle West group had forced the issue for a new constitution. Never before had a constitution been drafted for this organization by a committee with representation from all parts of the country. The chairman had given all members opportunity to be heard repeatedly. He had carried on laborious correspondence in order to get this work done. It was democratic procedure to the nth degree. Because of the nation-wide representation and the democratic procedure followed in the committee work the new constitution was happily received and adopted by an overwhelming majority. Not until this 1931–1932 constitution was representation on the executive committee given to specifically defined districts as an integral part of the national Association.

Under my presidency, five new interests were recognized as sections: teacher training in 1931, and recreation, men's athletics, camping, and dancing, in 1932. Under my presidency the Women's Athletic Section had at last achieved legal status as the National Section on Women's Athletics.

I had one big task to complete after the 1932 convention—one that I assigned to myself—to revise the Convention Guide which I had prepared the year before following an earlier Middle West one I had prepared in 1929-1930. I had entered national office in 1931 as had also the secretary and the convention manager without as much as one sheet of paper of "Do's" or "Don'ts" to go by, without a guide of any kind—not even a convention budget or a list of precedents to follow.

There is a record that during the presidency of Charles Savage in 1926, Jay B. Nash had spoken up for a record of "how things have been done before" as a guide to local people when putting on a convention. He was backed up in this request by E. H. Arnold, a former president. It was moved, seconded, and passed that the secretary should prepare a statement of precedents as a guide to those who put on conventions. However nothing came of this.

After Frederick Maroney and I had lamented together in 1930 over the lack of written guides for action, he had appointed a Convention Guide Committee which finally in December turned in a report of two or three pages of mere generalities—an utterly useless piece of work.

On October 23, 1930, I wrote President Maroney complaining that the 1930 Convention Report was most inadequate and that as vice-president I was still finding myself lost in a sea of unanswered questions. He replied October 28, reminding me that he hoped I would be the next president and that I would keep records to pass on to the next convention chairman. In that day when teachers in general were at last driving cars in large numbers, he closed with:

> I hope that I may pass the wheel of control to you with the ignition in fine condition, the battery charged, the tires well inflated, the upholstery renovated, and the brakes well adapted to national driving conditions.

And he reminded me that he had come into office two years before with absolutely no records on file to go by as guides for action. He in turn left me nothing.

I decided then and there that if I did not do one other thing during my presidency I would myself make as a contribution to APEA a minutely detailed Convention Set-Up Guide from my own 1929-1931 experiences.

So starting from scratch, I had devised a set of procedures. It developed after the 1931 convention into a sizeable booklet and now as I stepped out of office I brought it up to date and turned over to our national office a booklet of 34 typed pages of instructions. This was the first such record, and my successor was the first president to step into office, with any procedures to go by thanks to much burning of midnight oil. Since then these procedural guidelines have been kept up to date and as changes in procedure have developed, a great volume of material is now on file in the national office as constant guides.

I am proud that it was I who made the first real start in that direction. It was an important piece of work, first for the Middle West District and then for the National.

Strong Hinman brought the Middle West procedures up to date in 1933. Following the split of this large district into the Midwest and Central Districts, C. H. McCloy worked the procedures over throughout the year of his Central District presidency so that he stepped out of office with even more minutely detailed procedures for the conduct of Central District affairs. Thus the ball, started rolling in 1931, snowballed until by 1934 not only the Midwest but also the national and then the Central District had developed convention guides from my small start.

There was another task which I felt was as important as the Convention Guide. As soon as people saw the value of that piece of work, they began clamoring for a guide to cover the many precedents and traditions which the workers needed to be cognizant of but were not proper for the constitution and bylaws or as convention set-up material. So I was drafted by President Mary Coleman to draw up a set of traditions and precedents which had been in effect through the years as the result of council and executive committee actions. It was as time-consuming to start that work from scratch as it was to start the Convention Set-Up, but I got a fine committee together to help me and from 1934 to 1939 we slaved away at it.

This committee was composed of one representative from each District: Grover Mueller (East), Margaret Bell (Midwest), Paul Washke (Northwest), Mary Coleman (South), Winifred Van Hagen (Southwest), and me as chairman representing the new Central District.

At the San Francisco convention in 1939 we were ready with our report which started out as follows:

212

Recognizing that while the Constitution and Bylaws give us the foundations for our main procedures, there are constantly many details and minor actions to be considered if our organization is to function effectively and according to the wishes of the majority, President Hinman appointed a committee in the fall of 1934 to compile a list of precedents and traditions for guidance. The committee made a study of the precedents that were already a record of official action, of those that were in use informally but not authenticated by official approval, and of such as might well be inaugurated for the sake of more effective functioning of our Association affairs.

As a result of this work, some earlier actions of the council were rescinded as no longer in keeping with the times. Many precedents already in practice were given official sanction, and a few that needed to be established for smoother functioning were adopted. This report of many pages was ordered printed in booklet form and made available to all workers.

* * * *

Having been so very deep into the struggle to keep the East (under the guise of being national) from dominating the Middle West, I was quickly sensitive to the fact that the Middle West group east of the Mississippi River in its turn dominated the Middle West Society. Dr. J. Anna Norris of the University of Minnesota, Margaret McKee of the Des Moines public schools, and I of the University of Nebraska (strangely enough, all three women) had been the only presidents out of a total of 13 from west of the Mississippi in all its 21 years of existence. And in all those years there had been but four conventions west of the river.

For 1932–33 there was at long last one more president, Strong Hinman, and one more convention, at Wichita, for this section, so this seemed a good time for C. H. McCloy, Strong Hinman, and me to raise the question of dividing the Middle West into two districts with the Mississippi River as the dividing line. Unlike the APEA-Middle West argument, there was no hard feeling between the two groups. In fact we three who thought up the split and engineered its acceptance realized we would be in a way cutting ourselves off from our good friends on the other side of the river. Practically no one from west of the river attended even a district convention except when it came west of the Mississippi, and that had been at most only once in five years. We saw a great potential for professional growth in this territory through a division and so we started our campaign.

At first most of the small group west of the river who were accustomed to going to district conventions and working in the Middle West Society upbraided us soundly for even suggesting such a move. Four leading women, in particular, bitterly opposed the division. It was difficult to get them to see the possibility of new friends in the new group nearer home or the need for missionary work at home.

Sensing the intensity of the opposition from a few directions, we three, jokingly adopting the sobriquet "The Three Musketeers" among ourselves, met in secret for several sessions. Our plans and proposals were very hush-hush until we had worked out every last detail of the reorganization with all possible arguments, both for and against, outlined for a united front before "going public" with the final proposals. We rushed the plans and presented them to enough forward-looking westerners to assure success and then presented the idea to the Middle West group as a whole. Dismayed at first, the group east of the Mississippi asked what we were unhappy about and what they had done to hurt our feelings. Once we explained our missionary zeal and a complete absence of any hard feelings about anything, all quickly caught the idea as one for progress. Except for the few vociferous die-hards from some of the prairie and plains states (Colorado, Iowa, Minnesota, Missouri), all women who dreaded the divorce for personal reasons alone, the plan was voted in by a big majority. There remained only the task of getting the split officially approved by APEA which came about quickly.

The very next year (1933-34) found the two new groups, the Central and Midwest District Associations, peacefully and happily at work. (The title Midwest now replaced the old Middle West.) In a very short time the new Midwest District Association was far larger than the old Middle West even when it included all the states of today's two districts, and the new Central alone had as large a membership as the old Middle West. Our predictions came true quickly and our hopes were more than fulfilled.

One strange outgrowth of this split has been the different way the two groups have looked upon their combined history of 1912-1933 when they were one unit. The new Midwest considers its history to have started in 1912 and considers as their past officers, those who served from west of the river as well as those who served from the eastern section. But the Central District considers its history as starting with the year 1933-1934, ignoring the years when all these states, both east and west of the Mississippi River, were organized and functioning as one group.

It was not as if the states of the Central District had not been organized in APEA until 1933. I am inclined to think that the fact that one group retained the old name has led all unthinking ones not interested in history to think the years 1912–1933 belonged only to those who retained the old name. When a woman changes her name in marriage she does not consider that she had not lived before that date. (Or does she?) At least she does not claim the date of her new name as her birth year! In 1959 I talked briefly with the president of the Central District about its history and I found him quite surprised to learn that the states of today's Central District had any professional organizational history before 1933.

* * * *

Having taken to heart the fact that as one of the presidents of the national organization I knew little of its history, I resolved to correct that mistake as quickly as possible. At my first chance for such research work in early 1935, I suddenly realized that we were approaching our 50th anniversary and I had not heard one word about any celebration. I got in touch at once with the national president, Strong Hinman, and learned that he, too, and apparently everyone else, was unaware of this important milestone. Grateful for the information, he and his executive committee quickly channelled all plans into a Golden Anniversary convention and were lucky to be able to bring to the program Dr. W. G. Anderson, the founder and first secretary of the Association, then long retired from his position as head of physical education at Yale University.

* * * *

In the late 1920s and early 1930s I had put in many years of continuously demanding work in behalf of our professional organization. I had taken the lead in the settlement of the quarrels between APEA and the independent Middle West Society. I had led in the struggle to get APEA reorganized to function as a national organization in fact as well as in name. Almost single-handedly and with much opposition I started the struggle to put the election of officers on a democratic basis. I had engineered the end of the men's sniping at the women over their Women's Athletic Section. I had raised the question of trying to force hotels to accept blacks the same as whites. I had given the Association its first written set of procedures for putting on conventions and running its affairs, and I had chaired the first committee to collect and put into written form the precedents and traditions of our organization as guides for action. Given power by the men I had opened the door to equal participation of women with men in all organizational work on the national level. By the 1940s the national association had become accustomed to its democratic set-up and functioning—so accustomed to it that the newcomers, the younger generation most probably little sensed that it had not always been so.

Chapter XI

The 1932 Olympics
and Related Excitements

The summer of 1932 brought great excitement to the United States as host to the Tenth Olympiad in Los Angeles. It had been 28 years since the USA had hosted an Olympiad and the entire nation was going all out for this one.

Many organizations were planning their annual summer conventions around the Olympic Games and California. My attorney brother-in-law had such a convention scheduled for Los Angeles preceding the Games and was driving out with his family. The NAPECW planned its meeting for Mills College in the San Francisco Bay Area preceding a conference of the Women's Division of NAAF to be held at the Biltmore Hotel in Los Angeles, which in turn was to precede the First International Recreation Congress in Los Angeles to be held for the entire week preceding the opening of the Olympics—a full two weeks of national meetings in which I was deeply involved.

Since my sister Madge and her husband and 13-year-old daughter were driving to San Francisco to visit old friends before Earl was due at his July convention, they invited me to make the automobile trip with them. It was a great adventure to drive even from mid-America to the West Coast in those days. The countryside beyond the Mississippi was poorly organized for automobile tourists. It was a long tedious trip from Lincoln, Nebraska on, but a fascinating one full of reminders of settling of the West. The night accommodations in what tourist camps were available were of the crudest kind. Off at one edge of the camp there would be a crude shack with toilets and showers for women, and at the opposite edge a matching one for men. The cabins were bare shacks with a floor, four walls, a roof, a door and a window or two, and a bare electric light bulb hanging on a cord from the center of the ceiling. They were furnished with uncomfortable beds or cots, a crude chair or two, a wash stand with a wash bowl and a pitcher of water, and towels hanging on nails. There were shelves in lieu of dressers and nails all around the walls to hang clothing. No rugs, no draperies—just the barest necessities. Many were outfitted with small wood-burning stoves. Some did not even have a lock for the door. If you asked for a double cabin there would be a curtain strung on a wire to divide the space into two rooms. At least it was a place to rest with a roof over one's head.

Filling stations other than in towns were unknown; everyone carried red containers of extra gasoline in boxes secured to the car running boards plus containers of water for car radiators. Cars of those years were outfitted with tool cases for "do-it-yourself" tire changing or re-pairing.

It was another 20 years before I would venture to drive a car alone to the West Coast. The changes in that brief time in highways, cars and tourist accommodations were almost unbelievable.

* * * *

In San Francisco, I went to Mills College where the College Women Physical Directors were meeting for three days under the presidency of Dr. Gertrude Moulton, of Oberlin College. I was booked as one of five speakers for the banquet along with Neils Neilson who was attend-ing the meetings along with Clark Hetherington, the honor guest, Rosalind Cassidy, our hostess, and Dorothy Ainsworth of Smith College with whom I was getting acquainted for the first time.

I had made rail reservations to travel by night from San Francisco to Los Angeles. When I was invited by the Stanford University women's staff to spend a day visiting their campus, I accepted provided I could arrive in San Francisco in time to claim my Pullman reservation. They persuaded me to let them cancel that reservation and drive with them to Palo Alto where there would not be the slightest question about picking up another reservation as that particular train made a stop at

Palo Alto. Arriving at Stanford, I was told by the department secretary that there was not one Pullman berth available for that night. This threw me into a panic for just before I was leaving Lincoln, the Women's Division in New York City had called to inform me that Mrs. Herbert Hoover, our nation's First Lady, had just learned that President Hoover could not go to Los Angeles to open the Olympics and therefore she would remain in Washington at his side. As Honorary Chairman of the Women's Division she was to open their conference July 21st. Agnes Wayman, chairman of the Women's Division, would not be in Los Angeles either. Mrs. Hoover asked if they would ask me to preside over that first evening's meeting in her place. Of course I said, "yes," flattered to be the substitute for Mrs. Hoover.

* * * *

I just had to get to Los Angeles on that night train but later calls to the station to inquire about possible cancellations offered no encouragement. By early afternoon I was greatly disturbed, but, suddenly I had what seemed to be nothing less than a miraculous break. The USA Men's Olympic track team and the All-Western College football team (which was booked to play the All-Eastern College team as a special program feature of the Olympics) had been in practice the previous two weeks at Stanford and were leaving that night on an all-male special Olympic train for Los Angeles. As soon as "Pop" Warner, Stanford's football coach heard of my predicament he assured me that he could and would find a berth for me on that train. He arranged for a berth for me in the same coach with Lou Little, football coach of Columbia University who was at that time also coach of the USA Men's Track Team. He courteously accepted me and personally introduced me to all the men assigned to that coach. They "rolled out the red velvet carpet for me"—the only woman on that long private train full of star track and football athletes, their trainers, managers, coaches, and assistant coaches, and all the paraphernalia required by such a group. What a train journey!

What an experience awaited me the next morning as that train pulled into the Los Angeles station. One glimpse of a woman getting off that train sent the mob into a frenzy of excitement—"the Babe, the Babe," they shrieked—well at least they had to settle for the Babe's mother after they spotted my gray hair. Lou Little asked two of the track stars to escort me off the train and stay with me until a police escort came to get me out of that mob.

* * * *

Thus I arrived safely and on time to preside at the opening meeting of the Women's Division of NAAF, and to introduce Dr. Rufus B. von Klein-Smid, president of the University of Southern California, who was the guest speaker that evening in the ballroom of the Biltmore Hotel. The next day I gave the keynote speech for the conference as Mrs. Hoover had invited me to do a few months earlier since I had been first woman president of APEA.

On July 23rd, the First International Recreation Congress opened at the same hotel. It was a long conference, seven days of it. My part in that program was scheduled for the very last day so I checked out of the hotel. It was an opportunity to visit old hometown and old Coe College friends for a few days before Madge, Earl and young Marjorie came from San Francisco and we took over our reservations together at another hotel for the Olympics.

The American Physical Education Association had aligned itself earlier with an International Congress of Physical Education which hoped to do physiological research on the Olympic athletes. As President of APEA I had appointed Jay B. Nash of New York University to represent APEA at the Congress. But at our executive committee meeting in New York City in December 1931, Dr. Nash reported that the Americans in charge of Olympic athletes (presumably the AAU officers since J. Lyman Bingham was the official general manager of the athletes for the X Olympiad) were blocking all attempts to arrange for any physiological research on any athletes on the ground that it would have a bad psychological effect on the contestants. The American officials, all men of AAU, stood alone on this. Officials of foreign groups were willing to permit it. However the Americans, as the host nation, had the last word and ruled no interviews, no observations, no experiments of any physiological nature with any Olympic athlete.

Later, the International Congress of Physical Education turned to the American Association of Physiologists to try to get permission but it was also unsuccessful. The American Olympic officials were adamantly against any research. Later the medical doctor members of the NAPECW, unaware of these efforts, tried to get permission to carry on physiological research on women athletes for there were to be many women contestants in this Olympiad, Europeans and Asiatics as well as Americans. They, too, were refused permission.

In keeping with the ancient custom, the art, music and drama groups put on exhibitions, some involving competition for prizes. For this occasion, the University of Southern California brought to its summer staff two of Europe's most famous physical educators—Doctor Eugen Matthais, then of the University of Munich, and Doctor Carl Diem, then the dean of the famous physical education school in Charlottenburg, Germany. He was looked upon as the Olympic spiritual successor of Baron de Coubertin.

As one of its chief attractions, the Congress staged an enormous folk festival one evening in the Rose Bowl at Pasadena, engaging many different national groups. But I had bad luck and missed a part of the festival. After the Women's Division conference ended and before I had commitments with the Recreation Congress, I had a reunion with old college friends who took me for a day at the beach. It was a new experience to this land-locked greenhorn and blissfully unaware of what was happening to me as I relaxed on the beach in a scanty bathing suit (at least scanty for conservative me) I picked up a serious sunburn. The next day my family drove in from San Francisco and that evening we drove to Pasadena to attend the Folk Festival in the Rose Bowl.

About halfway through the program I began feeling dizzy and, fearful that I was going to faint, I left my seat and just barely made it to a corridor where I crumpled into a heap, unconscious. An usher blew a sharp whistle (so I learned later) and stretcher-bearers appeared like magic from nowhere. In no time they had me on a stretcher and out of the stadium and were on the verge of putting me into an ambulance when my sister missed me. She heard someone say, "a lady has fainted and the Red Cross is taking her to an ambulance," called to her husband and they ran after the stretcher-bearers just in time to "claim the body." As they arrived I came to and was transferred to their car and taken to our hotel, wondering what under the sun had happened to cause a scene like that.

On the hotel physician's orders I stayed in bed all the next day but the following day was up early to preside at a morning session of the International Recreation Congress, with delegates from 43 nations. I felt quite all right except my legs were so swollen I could scarcely bend my knees. But I had other things on my mind and went on my way walking awkwardly and calling for help to mount the steps to the platform of our conference room.

For that afternoon Dr. Charles LeRoy Lowman had invited the Congress delegates to visit the Orthopedic Hospital with its rather new Memorial Building, a wonder of its day. It was added to the buildings Dr. Lowman had built ten years earlier for what was then an Orthopedic Hospital-School Complex, a unique medical complex in that day for any part of the country west of the Alleghenies. Chartered busses would call immediately after lunch at the conference hotel to transport the delegates to the hospital. The children were to offer a full program of recreational games for handicapped children.

Margaret Andrews, a friend of BNSG and Wellesley years, was on the physical therapy staff. She invited me to come early and meet Dr. Lowman and the staff and have lunch with them before the crowd arrived for the afternoon program. So after dismissing the morning session, I managed to waddle off the platform and get myself to a taxi, by now a bit alarmed at my frightfully swollen legs. As soon as I arrived, Margaret demanded to know what was the trouble. When I told her of my by now burning back and swollen legs and my fainting at the Rose Bowl two days before, she took me straight to Dr. Lowman. Thus I first met that extraordinary man who was the first surgeon specializing in orthopedics in Los Angeles and the first to build an orthopedic center in the Southwestern United States. (In 1971 he was named "Doctor of the Century" by the Los Angeles County Medical Association, and a year later was honored by the establishment of the Charles LeRoy Lowman Chair of Orthopedic Surgery at the celebration of his and the hospital's Fifty Years of Service With Sensitivity—1922-1972. In 1974 he was honored by the President of the United States for his service to the nation.)

Introductions over, the doctor was solicitous about my condition and called his head nurse to take me in tow. She informed me I had had an attack of sun fever, treated my legs and back with some ointment, bandaged both legs from heels to upper thighs, encased my upper back in a bandage jacket, and put me in a wheelchair for the rest of the day. From it, I joined one of the children's wheelchair volleyball teams in the program for the delegates to the International Recreation Congress. The children had been playing in their wheelchairs for some time and managed them cleverly. I was the dub of the team but they gave me a hearty welcome.

Then Dr. Lowman ordered me back to my hotel and to bed for the rest of the day and the next day and to drink orange juice by the quart. Two days later I was able to join the enormous crowd heading for the stadium for the opening ceremonies of the Olympiad. I vowed I would indulge in no more days on the beach.

* * * *

The Tenth Olympiad opened July 30, 1932. The USA teams alone totaled over 500 athletes. Women athletes were housed in the Chapman

Park Hotel downtown, with bus shuttle service for them to the various facilities to be used in competition.

The opening ceremonies with 2,000 athletes from 39 nations were deeply impressive. They, of themselves, gave promise of a brotherhood of man but after the athletic contests began, the inadequacies of mankind to handle such a brotherhood began to show up. The dream that perhaps men and women could come together from all parts of the world to match their athletic skills in friendly rivalry began to fade.

Of the women champions it was "Babe" Didrikson and Stella Walsh who held most of our attention—the "Babe" because of her bad manners, social ineptness, and poor sportsmanship, and Stella Walsh of Cleveland because of her controversial switch to enter as a member of the Polish women's team.

As Baron de Coubertin had from the very first modern Olympiad opposed the entrance of women in the Games, so too did we women of the Women's Division of NAAF, NAPECW and NSWA of APEA oppose their entrance. But since men promotors had proved too much for us we accepted defeat and decided to observe carefully all we could and do whatever we could to learn about the women in Olympics. To this end a group of women of APEA got permission of Olympic managers to go and come at their pleasure at Chapman Park Hotel headquarters and to mingle and talk with the women athletes, except when they were going into or engaged in contests or returning from contests. The women physicians of the group were warned to make no attempt to give contestants medical advice or inspection of any sort.

All this was very limiting but it was better than nothing. Dr. Gertrude E. Moulton was one of this small group and because she was an M.D., she was granted a pass in and out of Chapman Park Hotel and permitted to ride with the athletes in their chartered bus. Later she talked with me at length about her experiences but assuming that she would put it all in writing from her own first-hand knowledge, I never attempted to record what she told me. Now it seems that she never got around to making written record of it. For this I have deep regrets.

Chapter XII
Shorts and Leotards

By the mid 1930s shorts had become generally accepted in schools in place of bloomers which had had a 40-year hold on the world of women's and girls' sports and gymnastics. At first shocked at shorts, the lay world finally adopted them and by the end of the thirties, they had become a common sight on the streets of America's hamlets, small towns and cities—a privilege never claimed for bloomers even at the turn of the century.

As bloomers of an earlier day had been the symbol of a career in physical education for women, so shorts became the new symbol. They were worn by girls and women of all descriptions and ages but, because of such universal acceptance as street wear and house wear as well as for gymnastics and sports wear, they lost much of their significance as the symbol of a career. By the late 1970s shorts were still enjoying great popularity—almost a 50-year vogue, far beyond any popularity bloomers ever enjoyed.

* * * *

As the Depression deepened and the 1930s wore on, dissension developed within the physical education profession over some aspects of women's sports, partly because of misunderstandings and partly because of human nature—jealousies of the "ins" on the part of the "not ins."

224

One of the misunderstandings was between certain leading members of the Women's Division and certain members of a group of hockey enthusiasts who were publishing a new popular magazine, *The Sportswoman*. This misunderstanding was looked upon by some within the profession as a quarrel between the Women's Division itself and the magazine, but I did not interpret it so. It came because of open criticism by a few over-zealous leaders in the Women's Division of the field hockey matches put on by private hockey clubs in several of our larger cities. Personally many of us saw no harm in these matches. In fact I rejoiced that there were women in America beyond college years who loved to play the game enough to support several clubs around the country. As they were all promoted and managed by the women players themselves and, as far as I could see, absolutely free of all taint of commercialization—all matches were surrounded by social amenities and devoid of intense desire to win at any cost—I could see no cause for criticizing these efforts. To me they represented sports in an ideal situation, the sort of thing we all claimed we would not be against if it existed anywhere.

However there was no occasion for anyone to learn how I felt about the situation, and because several of my close friends were outspokenly critical of these inter-club tournaments, some people apparently jumped to the conclusion that I was equally critical. I didn't realize that I, too, was being blamed by a few angry ones in the other camp until in an early issue of *The Sportswoman* (put out by Constance Applebee of Bryn Mawr College) the editorial of May 1931 gave me a dirty dig for some critical remark I was reported to have made at the Women's Division meeting of NAAF as the president of APEA in Detroit the month before. My supporters laughed it off with me, but it angered Mary Channing Coleman so much that she wrote the editor an angry letter or two and finally cancelled her school's subscription to the magazine. She sent me a copy of one of her letters which said:

> Many issues of *The Sportswoman* have proved most disappointing in their emphasis on professional and spectacular aspects of sports. Their rather acrimonious antagonism to the policies of the Women's Division of NAAF has been a keen disappointment to us.[1]

It was this acrimonious antagonism of the group back of *The Sportswoman* towards the Women's Division and its leaders that set many women against the Women's Division, an antagonism not at all deserved. Never to my knowledge did the Women's Division ever officially take stand against Miss Applebee's hockey clubs or her periodical but it got the blame for the unpleasant remarks made by individuals who happened to be prominent in Women's Division work. Many others followed Mary Coleman and cancelled their subscription to Miss Applebee's magazine. I held on to our Nebraska subscription for I wished to be kept informed of their policies and criticism of Women's Division of NSWA and APEA which, along with us women leaders in these groups, came in for frequent abuse.

It was certainly a non-conformist group of women back of the magazine but just who "called the shots" for the editor we were never sure. Whoever they were they hid behind Miss Applebee's skirts and we all knew what a non-conformist she had always been. She was most capable in her specialty, field hockey—an English woman transplanted to America and apparently but little imbued with the idea of democracy in sports. Although I knew nothing of her first-hand, several people told me she had no sympathy for the great mass of girls who were "dubs" at sports but who nevertheless hoped for some place, even though it be lowly, in the sports activities of the day.

Aside from the occasional obvious digs at the ideals of those of us who were fighting for the sports rights of all girls, the magazine was a good one in the field of women's sports and served us for several years. But finally when times grew hard and budgets were slashed I, too, dropped our Nebraska subscription. There was no cash to spare for a magazine that catered so exclusively to the highly-skilled sportswoman—a type we knew so little of in an area where we were still struggling for the bare fundamentals of a physical education program.

Miss Applebee never aligned herself with the profession by work in APEA, NSWA, Women's Division of NAAF, not even in the National Association of Physical Education for College Women even though she was head of the department of physical education at Bryn Mawr College. There was an utter lack of communication between her, the high-priestess of English field hockey in America, and the profession in spite of the fact that so many of us women were promoting her pet game which she, herself, had introduced to America.

Marjorie Bouvé, I felt, hit the nail on the head when she, herself extremely tolerant of the sometimes undue enthusiasm of the hockey clique especially those in and around Boston and Philadelphia, said to me one day laughingly, "Oh well, we just have to make allowances for them. It is a sort of sickness—hockey fever—that they get. They almost make a cult, a sort of religion, out of it." Agnes Wayman of Barnard College always insisted that field hockey enthusiasts had a blind spot for all other sports, all other activities. "They are all a little unbalanced," Agnes said to me one day. "Let's hope they do not ultimately split the ranks of women working in physical education." I never actually sensed this extreme enthusiasm working far away in Nebraska where even the two largest cities in the state couldn't come up with enough women to make two teams. I never was fortunate enough to be near any of the tournament sites when match play was in progress.

However I most vividly recall my own efforts to whip together a hockey club in Lincoln in the late 1920s and early 1930s. There was in Lincoln at the time one of the largest chapters of American Association of University Women in the country but not even among that group could I get out enough women for weekend play, except for a few games with university girls which soon fizzled out. I finally reached out to Omaha, a much larger city not too far distant, in the hopes of organizing a Lincoln-Omaha Hockey Club. Surely the two cities together could stir up enough women who had played hockey in college and wished to keep up the fun. Even this proved but false hopes, and I had to give up my dream of prolonging my love of playing field hockey into middle age.

Throughout all my grown-up years I have met few women who cared to engage in sports beyond school years. Golf and swimming, yes—but these two sports carried social status. My interests stemmed purely from a love of sports for their own life-restoring, life-refreshing, life-enriching values. Social-status values meant nothing to me.

* * * *

In the fall of 1931 as a woman president of APEA, I was deluged with calls for help from superintendents of schools, principals of high schools and men high school coaches assigned to coach girls' teams against their wishes who were being pressured by sports promoters to organize their girls for AAU tournaments. Even boards of education were being pressured when girls' physical education departments and the school administrators failed to arouse enthusiasm for their projects. In one large city of the South the board of education capitulated to AAU pressure. When AAU attempted to force the superintendent of schools to inaugurate at once a policy of interscholastics for girls, he wrote me begging for help in his arguments with the board against this policy.[2]

AAU even tried to draw into their net the few remaining private training schools of physical education, hoping thus to indoctrinate prospective teachers, but they struck a snag when they attempted to pressure Emil Rath, head of the Normal School of the American

Gymnastics Union in Indianapolis. He, like most of us women, was all for lots of good wholesome sports for all girls but he had no interest in the kind of sports contests AAU wished to promote. When the pressure on him became too concentrated, he, too, turned to APEA for help. Pulling together we got him and his school freed of this pressure. He tipped us off that the American College of Physical Education in Chicago "needs help and enlightenment and needs it badly." The manager of a team representing that school roamed about seeking matches with schools and groups who would be willing to play boys' rules—this from a school specializing in turning out women teachers of physical education. When the Women's Division of NAAF became aware of this lack of standards in a professional training school, it raised the question of APEA rating the physical education professional schools and tossed the challenge in my lap as president of APEA. As APEA already had a committee at work on that question, I handed this query to the committee.

Although few statistics were available as to what was transpiring in the 1930s in interscholastics for girls, I have a few figures of my own. Disturbed at what was then considered shocking costumes being worn by girls of high schools engaged in interschool sports, the National Section on Woman's Athletics of the American Physical Education Association asked me in the early 1930s to make a nationwide sampling survey of athletic and gymnastics costumes worn by girls of America.[3] They also suggested that I procure information on extramural sports as of that date. When the survey was completed the information on extramurals made the article too long for publication so that it was deleted. Now over 45 years later portions of it are being published for the first time.

I received replies from 163 high schools across the country in cities and towns ranging in size from 300,000 to 5,000 in population, which I classified A, B, C, and D according to size. Thirty-nine percent of the 163 schools were engaging in extramural sports for girls, with the highest percentage (49) occurring in the Class D, schools of the smallest towns. It is probably quite safe to assume that in these schools the only girls who were entered in the sports program were the highly skilled. Basketball and volleyball were the sports played almost exclusively by girls in these schools.

Some state departments of education, notably those of New York, New Jersey and California, concerned about the welfare of school girls in relation to a growing interest in many towns in winning girls' basketball teams, tried to keep the activities sane by setting up guides for all schools, such as:

1. No varsity practice in the sport before December 1.
2. Only two practices per week each of no more than one hour.
3. Health examination of participants by school or approved physician.
4. No contests until January.
5. No more than one game per week and that in the afternoon and only nine per season.
6. No games that keep students away from home over night.
7. Sport in charge of properly-trained women instructors, but if from necessity a man is in charge, he must have special training in the field of physical education with a woman assistant as advisor and chaperone.
8. No girls' games in connection with boys' games.
9. No girls' games involving commercialism.
10. No admission charge to girls' games—the contests to be financed by the schools.
11. All publicity of games under control of the principal of the school and it should emphasize the sport, not individual players.
12. No participation in games during menstrual periods.
13. Submerge these contests as much as possible in favor of intramurals.[4]

Whereas at the opening of the decade 57 percent of all four-year high schools in New Jersey engaged in interschool sports for girls, by 1933 all had replaced interscholastic sports with intramurals.[5]

Of the small schools offering sports for girls none supported physical education departments for girls. Such departments did not exist even for boys although most assigned some male teacher to offer sports for boys. What few small town schools did offer sports for girls offered them only in an interscholastic setting and most with men coaches. The men refused NSWA rules for girls, either using boys' rules or AAU rules for girls. But these proved unsatisfactory and finally in the late 1930s by which time the Iowa Girls High School Athletic Union had become nationally known, a set of basketball rules was devised for it and copyrighted by a sporting goods salesman. Those rules were quite obviously devised with an eye to creating a sensational game for the public to watch.

In the 1930s when this bit of educational nonsense was just getting well underway across the country we women, trained in physical education and concerned that the type of sports offered to young girls should be educationally sound, busied ourselves writing articles for newspapers and periodicals and making speeches on the subject before women's clubs and men's service clubs. Chief among these were Ethel Perrin, Agnes Wayman and Helen McKinstry in New York, Florence Alden in

Oregon, J. Anna Norris in Minnesota, and Blanche Trilling in Wisconsin (all graduates of BNSG, except Agnes Wayman). I, too, in Nebraska, as well as many others in other states, was writing and giving speeches. It was a bit of work we all entered into with missionary zeal.

* * * *

In an attempt to appear exemplary in the face of criticism from our profession and from lay people who recognized our profession as the one best suited to set standards for women's sports, AAU in the early 1930s set up a National Women's Sports Committee. None of us was able to pin anyone in AAU down as to what it was doing or who were its members. I did find out the name and address of a Chicago woman who was supposed to be its chairman but in spite of offers to meet her for formal or informal chats on various occasions when I was to be in Chicago, I never obtained an actual appointment. AAU wanted the public to think it wanted to cooperate with us women professionally trained to handle women's sports yet avoided actual contacts with us. Apparently to AAU, a sane and wholesome pursuit of athletics meant nothing if it stood in the way of a team's winning. To us women it meant a lot in behalf of girls under our care. Therefore they were not interested in dealing with us.

Imagine our surprise when in early 1932 AAU, through Mr. J. Lyman Bingham, chairman of AAU Women's Basketball Rules Committee, and assistant to Avery Brundage, president of AAU, invited NSWA officials to join AAU's Girls' Basketball Rules Committee to put out a joint set of rules. Grace Jones, then chairman of NSWA, referred the matter to Eline von Borries, chairman of NSWA Basketball Committee, and she at once got in touch with me for advice as to APEA's stand on such a project.

I had heard so much unfavorable talk about AAU in regard to its management of both men's and women's sports that I had no interest in having that organization infiltrate our women's sports organizations and committees. I had a strong feeling that to gain some semblance of respectability they, like Bernarr McFadden, were eager to use any opening as an excuse to seem to be associated with us. I doubted if they had the slightest intent to cooperate with us. In fact at this very time AAU was preparing for its Olympic try-outs in our own University of Nebraska stadium in the coming summer. For the sole purpose of swelling gate receipts (so I was told confidentially by a prominent local businessman who was "in on the know" and unhappy about

230

it) they were planning to import a women's track team for the occasion. Alerted about it, we women were furious since it was pure exploitation of girl athletes. I had whipped together a local committee of prominent women's club and PTA members to try to keep the women's track team off the schedule and out of Lincoln. We were having little success against the power of AAU, so I was in no mood to entertain the thought of NSWA cooperation with that organization.

However when Eline von Borries informed me that Mr. Bingham very much desired at least a conference with her and any others of her choosing I agreed that we should at least talk with him to see if we could convert him to our philosophy about sports for women. Shortly Helen Hazelton, immediate past chairman of NSWA and the current chairman of NSWA Rules Editorial Committee, and I were to be in Columbus, Ohio, attending the convention of the Mid West Society of Physical Education. We thought that Columbus would be a convenient meeting place for Eline von Borries from Baltimore and Mr. Bingham from Chicago, so a conference for the four of us was set up for March 29, 1932, in the suite of rooms which the Middle West Society reserved for me at the headquarters hotel, as guest of the convention. Helen Hazelton was asked by Grace Jones, then chairman of NSWA, to be her official representative.

This historic APEA meeting of NSWA and AAU was held as planned and Mr. Bingham offered NSWA the opportunity to put on AAU's next women's basketball tournament for them in the name of AAU. Without even conferring alone about it, we knew that APEA would never consent to such a move even if we women desired it. The men leaders in APEA had for years been fighting their own private battles with AAU over the control of men's sports. Bingham also asked that NSWA join AAU in putting out women's basketball rules, but he had so many strings attached to his proposals that we were not interested beyond offering to submit his proposals to the NSWA membership for consideration. We knew how such a vote would go and at the national convention a few weeks later in Philadelphia, the members voted overwhelmingly to reject the proposals. AAU was not as eager after all to have a joint basketball rules committee as to have NSWA sit on its committee and be persuaded to try to convert APEA to accept AAU's rules as NSWA's own official women's rules. We had no interest in such a venture.

Following this I was particularly eager to talk the whole situation over with some of our men leaders such as R. Tait McKenzie of the University of Pennsylvania, Carl Schrader of the Massachusetts State Department of Education, Dudley Reed of the University of Chicago,

James Huff McCurdy of Springfield College, and John Brown, Jr., of International YMCA, none of whom was in Columbus at the time but all of whom I would probably see a few weeks later in Philadelphia. In that city I had an opportunity for a long talk with Dr. McKenzie. He was recognized in our profession for his prudence, good judgment and clear thinking, and I told him about the meeting in Columbus with the AAU representative, our purpose for the meeting, and the gist of our discussion. He expressed alarm and warned me as president of the American Physical Education Association not to permit NSWA to be drawn even into AAU committees since, always in the minority, it would never be able to make its influence felt but through its membership would be exploited as seemingly lending approval to AAU actions. He told me of behind-the-scenes experiences with AAU which he and many of his friends had endured for years over the conduct of men's athletics exclaiming that AAU little knows what cooperation is and that it is a supreme dictator, calling all the shots and creating trouble.

> Stay clear of that crowd. You women who want to keep women's athletics clean in America have in this organization the sort of group about which you would not have the slightest knowledge or experience in order to cope with it in your own interests. It does not know what fair dealing or good sportsmanship is. It will be too much for you women with your idealism. You will be sucked in by it, used by it for whatever advantage your good name will give it and in the end your ideals will be besmirched. You will have lost much and gained nothing. Have absolutely no dealings with this organization.[6]

This advice coming from so distinguished a person, an older man of much worldly wisdom and experience and a well-known physician who cared for health considerations in sports, left me shaken. I resolved that we women must do all in our power to keep the girls and women of America out of AAU's grasp.

About this time the Women's Division of the National Amateur Athletic Federation became deeply concerned over sports tournaments for girls sponsored across the country by AAU—tournaments shamelessly exploiting the girl players and bringing in large gate receipts to the men sponsors. I had taken definite steps to use my influence against these tournaments in my part of the country, and the national office of the Women's Division in New York City knew they could count on me for active support when it was needed. Therefore I became accustomed to frequent letters and long distance calls from that office when help was needed in Nebraska or neighboring states.

At the conference with Mr. Bingham of AAU in Columbus, he accused us women of being interested only in a destructive program and against all competition of girls in sports. I decided it was time he was informed about our intense interest in getting the great mass of girls in America into sports programs with much competition for all. So free of APEA presidential duties I wrote him a long letter in January 1933, stressing our constructive program for all girls, not just for star performers, closing with:

> While we women are most interested in THE GIRL herself, you men are most interested in the SPORT and champions. Our differences arise entirely from this difference in emphasis.[7]

* * * *

At this same time AAU was making a big bid to hold its national girls' basketball tournament in Wichita, Kansas. The national office of the Women's Division in New York City begged me to do what I could to stop it, informing me that upon appeal from AAU representatives the Federated Women's Clubs of Wichita were considering sponsoring the tournament. I got in touch with the leaders of that group and told them enough to persuade them to refuse to sponsor the tournament. My letters to them had proved sufficient to raise questions in their minds about the tournament. They were relieved that they had not after all sponsored it. This led to discussion in their member clubs which resulted in the president of the PTA Council calling a meeting and inviting the head of public school physical education to discuss the matter with them. Fortunately for the cause this person happened to be Strong Hinman who was at the time president of the Middle West Society of Physical Education and an ardent champion of everything we women were fighting for in correct sports for American girls and women. The meeting closed (as reported to the Women's Division office in New York City and relayed back to me in Nebraska) with the women strongly opposed to bringing the AAU tournament to their town but realizing it was too late to stop it. They decided that they could influence their husbands to refuse to contribute any money toward the guarantee of $10,000[8] demanded of the group that finally did sponsor the tournament.

Because of speaking commitments, I didn't see how I could be away so much from my University work, so I sent word to the Women's Division that I couldn't observe the AAU tournament for them but that I had arranged for a Wichita woman to act in my place. A determined telephone call from New York City begged me by all means to be there at least for the final evening. I changed my plans and drove to Wichita on Thursday morning, arriving in time for a long and shocking report from the woman who had been observing for me— also in plenty of time to take in the closing evening's events.

A week later I was back in Wichita to attend the last convention of the old Middle West Society of Physical Education which would split into two new groups at its close—Midwest Association of Health, Physical Education and Recreation and the Central Association of Health, Physical Education and Recreation. While there the Kansas State Women's Division representative arranged a breakfast meeting at which I was asked to be the speaker. The local group invited representatives of the leading women's clubs in the city, women who had scouted the recent tournament along with me, and a group of women who had scouted an AAU all-city girls' basketball tournament earlier in Kansas City put on by Miss Pattric R. O'Keefe, an elementary school physical education supervisor in that city. Miss O'Keefe had brought down upon her head the ire of all the local women high school physical educators. (One thing that had bothered them was that in addition to sponsoring the AAU tournament in the first place, she refused to use women officials who had passed NSWA top ratings as basketball officials.) The local arrangements committee had also persuaded the AAU Missouri Valley Commissioner to join us. He came and sat through my speech but hastily withdrew as I was closing and so was not available for the discussion period that followed. But the representatives of the Federated Women's Clubs, PTA, YWCA, Business and Professional Women's Clubs and a national officer of the American Association of University Women stayed on and we had a long and enlightening session which swung these women firmly to our side on the subject of correct sports for women. All pledged to oppose vigorously an AAU tournament for women in their city again.

A week or two later, a group from all over the United States got together at our APEA convention in Louisville, Kentucky. Agnes Wayman, then chairman of the Women's Division, held a meeting in which a group of us women reported on what we had observed of women's participation in the past summer's Olympics. Agnes had persuaded Avery Brundage, president of AAU, to take part in the program, hoping to have him there for the discussion to follow but he was too foxy for us. After speaking, he excused himself on pretext of another pressing engagement, and we could not even find him later for a private conference. He managed to elude us completely. But we were cheered by the large Kentucky delegation that reported that after years of work the women physical education teachers had finally brought about the abolition of the Kentucky State High School Girls' Basketball Tournament.

The following year at our national convention in Cleveland, (when I had to have protection from some anonymous vulgar sports follower) we tried to tackle the problem of AAU promotion of women's sports in that city—it was so contrary to so much that we women fought for in correct sports for girls. The situation was made difficult because the head of all physical education for the Cleveland public schools, Floyd Rowe, was the AAU commissioner for that area. He refused to see harm in anything he was promoting and was making it difficult for women physical educators on his staff who dared raise a voice against his plans. Therefore, to leave the Cleveland women public school teachers out of the argument, the women physical educators in colleges of Ohio were waging the fight against his AAU efforts. dreds of women all across the country were trying to keep the control of women's efforts out of the hands of men sports promotors.

* * * *

If I seem to have been greatly preoccupied throughout my teaching career with dance, it was because dance more than other activities of a physical education program was constantly changing and I felt that I had to keep informed about its development and keep my department up to date. Gymnastics in the 1930s had vanished generally from school programs, and sports changed little from year to year, only a slight modification of this or that rule. Now and then a new sport came along but already set as to rules and form. Swimming took on new forms in "water ballets" and synchronized swimming which affected our swim clubs rather than class work, but dance was always in a state of unrest and change it seemed. It was ever demanding my attention not only in my early teaching years as a dance teacher but also later as an administrator giving it a place in our departmental program.

The soft-flowing draperies and ballet slippers of the World War I era, and the 1920s, were now replaced by a garment which to the amusement of us middle-aged and older teachers, resembled the old-fashioned union suit of the winters of a bygone day. Called a leotard, it was named after Jules Leotard, a nineteenth century French aerialist. Shortly, leotards were universally adopted, taking on all colors of the rainbow after their introduction in somber black. Soon also they came in short-legged, short-sleeved cuts to lend great variety to dance costuming.

Those students who wished to study dance as a creative expression, not as a public display, were dependent entirely upon the forms of dance we offered. I felt strongly that we should offer a form that recognized the spiritual values in life in all its aspects—happiness as well as bitterness, joy as well as frustration, triumph as well as defeat, blessing as well as tragedy, purity as well as decay. Modern dance, as I saw it offered by most leading exponents, depicted life only in its negative forms.

Disturbed about this I asked some of our dance teachers about this interpretion of life. I soon realized that these teachers, reared amidst our American freedoms, had experienced joy more than tragedy and because of their lack of despairing experiences in their personal lives would not emulate the leaders unduly in their choice of themes to interpret. I knew, on the other hand, that youth loves to pretend that life is tragic, certainly not all joy, and I did not object if a teacher led her students into interpretations of life's realities.

With the coming of concert dancers to the world of the performing arts such as Isadora Duncan, Ruth St. Denis, and Ted Shawn, there arose the need to differentiate between the teaching of dance to prepare performers for the stage (since the later stage successes of Mary Wigman, Martha Graham, Doris Humphrey, and Charles Weidman had brought modern dance to public attention) and teaching dance to students so that they might know and enjoy dance as part of their all-round education. From these two altogether different needs there arose the argument as to where the teaching of dance belongs in a college—in the fine arts or physical education department. It seemed to me to belong in either place with each approaching it from its own perception of the needs of pupils.

I always insisted upon procuring for my dance staff only young women trained first and foremost in physical education who would appreciate sports and other activities and beyond that had specialized in dance, not to become professional performers nor to turn out professional performers but to give to our students an appreciation for and some skill in dance as an educational experience. To fulfill this requirement I sought young women who were pupils or pupils of pupils of Margaret H'Doubler who I felt, through the tumultuous years of the coming of modern dance largely from foreign sources, had kept her American feet firmly on the ground for an American form of modern dance.

Although what had been labelled interpretive dance in the late

1910s and 1920s was still being offered in the early thirties in a some-what changed form, the name gradually changed to modern dance. The form of dance, at least that offered in the schools of America was not as yet greatly changed from the interpretative form earlier taught by Margaret H'Doubler at the University of Wisconsin and her pupils scattered about the country. As modern dance developed I could not understand why it rejected the title of interpretive that had been coming into vogue for the past decade. But I suppose each new set of leaders wants its own new titles to indicate in name even if not in actuality a break with the old.

Not until German Mary Wigman came to America in the early 1930s to present her own form of dance, which was quite different from what we had been offering as interpretive dance, did I realize that there were two quite different forms. Repelled as I was at first by Wigman's type of dance, I was glad that the teachers on my own staff stuck to our American Margaret H'Doubler's forms of educational dance. It changed from the earlier interpretive form, but did not go to the extremes of Mary Wigman's ideas. Ultimately it did change and took on the new name, modern dance.

In 1932 I had the pleasure of being seated next to Mary Wigman at a luncheon on the day following her dance recital in Columbus, Ohio. At that time she revealed to me a little of her sad and troubled life during and following the Great War. This in a large measure explained for me why the themes of her dancing were devoted so exclusively to interpretations of unhappy thoughts and I felt moved to forgive her somewhat for the evening of gloom she had given us.

Two years later I saw our own Martha Graham in a modern dance recital in Omaha, Nebraska, and I was repelled by her morbid por-trayal of life through dance forms. Her recital was given in connection with the convention of the Central Society of Physical Education so the audience was largely physical educators. Back at the headquarters hotel following the program, what a scene! Most of the men had been out-raged at calling such an activity dancing, and many of us older women were distressed over predominance of cheerless, depressing interpreta-tions of life. The complete absence of music other than percussion instruments beating out rhythms had been irritating to many. A few men had great fun dashing about the lobby cornering the heads of de-partments demanding to know if we had tossed our pianos out the window. The younger generation of women and a few older ones were enthusiastic about this new form of creative dance.

In one way I was repelled by this new so-called modern dance because of the fanaticism of its apostles. At one period they preached that it was most uneducational to dance a dance already created no matter by how great an artist or to dance to music previously composed no matter how gifted the composer. One must dance only dances one's self or one's co-workers have created, and if to music rather than to percussion instruments, then only to music created for that particular dance (the music accompanies the dance and not the dance, the music, as they put it).

I had many an argument with one dance teacher whose eternal beating of tom-toms during her class hours was driving the rest of us distraught day by day. When she explained why she couldn't use piano music at least some of the time for accompaniment, we got into a discussion of why dancers must dance only dances which they themselves have composed and I asked,

"Then I suppose no singer should ever sing any song except what she herself has composed?"

"Yes, that is so," she replied.

"And no pianist must play any composition except her own?"

"Yes, I guess that would follow," she said.

"And no one person should ever read anything but what she herself has written?"

"You are not being fair," she cried out at me.

"It is you who are not being sensible. Just for the sake of developing creative expression in our students, are we to discard all literature, all music that was created before our day—even all dances? What could be more inspiring for students than to learn to dance to some of Chopin's waltzes or mazurkas?" I asked.

"You simply don't understand modern dance," she countered. I had to confess that I didn't.

* * * *

When this form of dance first came into mode it distressed me to pass through our dance studio. I almost always found the students writhing on the floor rolled up in little balls or crawling about groping for the seeming unreachable. On the rare occasions when I would find them up on their feet, heads thrown back, arms outstretched as if at last they had discovered joy in living—running, skipping, leaping— I would be so pleased and so enthralled that I would forget my errand

238

and stay on for a while. Gradually more action and less grovelling on the floor took over and I rejoiced in the fine conditioning the dance techniques were giving the students—the conditioning students of an earlier generation got from gymnastics, which now, thanks to the progressivists, had fallen into such disfavor that students would never have registered for such a course had we still offered it.

So the real reason I so enthusiastically embraced modern dance in my departmental program I kept to myself knowing how unpopular my reason for acceptance would be with the dance teachers of that time. I had always been an ardent champion of gymnastics as a cornerstone for building physical fitness. So with gymnastics gone from our programs I now gladly seized upon modern dance which in its fundamental techniques was an excellent substitute for gymnastics for body conditioning apart from any other merits.

With the loss from the staff of both of our teachers who handled Danish gymnastics and, without possibilities of replacements, gymnastics were now lost to our program. We couldn't even find a pupil of Finnish Eli Bjorksen, whose gymnastics were so popular in England. I would have been a bit fearful, however, of anyone who might turn our gymnastics classes into the sort of cult worship I had witnessed in the summer of 1931 at a school of physical education near Canterbury, England. As splendid as I thought the form of exercises to be, I was repelled by their almost fetish worship of Bjorksen's gymnastics.

To replace gymnastics I would like to have made modern dance a requirement for all college girls but I couldn't go that far in my support of one activity. I had to content myself with stressing dance all I could, offering many classes and at choice hours. I thought it was a splendid sugar-coated pill to offer the students to make up for the loss of gymnastics, and in a way it was even better since it offered values lacking in the form of gymnastics which we had known up to then.

After a while the craze for drum beating as dance accompaniment passed, the piano was restored to the dance studio, and even music of the masters was heard once more. Lincoln's prominent pianist, Wilbur Chenowith, later to become known as a composer, took an interest in our modern dance classes after a trip to New York City in January 1930 to play some of his compositions for Rudy Valle's radio program. After a chat with Margaret H'Doubler, he consented to compose for our university modern dance classes and produced several outstanding selections for recitals. I soon noted that now and then students would do some dances which others more talented than themselves had composed. And also I noted a bit of cheerfulness, light and airiness creeping back into the dance with Freudian ideas not so apparent in the background.

While the "Freudian period," as some labelled it, was at its height, Ted Shawn from the professional dance world was moved to speak of modern dance, as presented by one of his own former and highly publicized pupils, as morbid. So perhaps after all I hadn't been too far off in my criticism in the 1930s.

*　*　*　*

When a few young men at the University of Nebraska called on me in the 1930s to ask permission to join our modern dance classes I was glad to make room for them. I also pushed WAA to sponsor a recital on the campus by Ted Shawn and his troupe of men dancers. It was a great success.

Shortly after this performance one of the athletic coaches complained that too many of the fellows were soft and needed toughening up, and the word got into the student paper. Immediately I was on the phone daring the complaining coach to send his softies over to the women's gymnasium so we could put them to work in a modern dance class on fundamental techniques that would put them in shape. He scoffed at the idea but I said I was in dead earnest for I was sure that the basic techniques we taught had something worthwhile to offer his men. He came to my office for a talk. In the end he was willing to try my plan provided we kept it a dark secret.

Our dance teacher was enthusiastic and agreed to go to the men's gym and give the football men a sample lesson behind locked doors. The fellows felt sheepish about it but went along with coach's "crazy idea." At the end of their first sampling they were convinced that modern dance had something for them even if only in the way of body conditioning. They fell into line. The teacher gave them a series of lessons and the coach was delighted over the results. Although these lessons were most hush-hush, the coach and the fellows behind closed doors became ardent boosters for men taking modern dance.

Later we brought to the campus Charles Weidman, Lincoln's native son and America's leading male exponent of modern dance. He had started his dance career under Ted Shawn and in 1928 with Doris Humphrey, another pupil of the Denishawn School, opened his own dance studio in New York City.

If I didn't like much in modern dance as an educational form, especially the morbid ideas it so frequently interpreted, I had no quarrel with it as a professional stage-offering to the public in general. The public could take it or leave it. As an educator I wanted dance as well as sports in the schools at least to offer creative expression and self-enrichment forms as well as wholesome exercise for the great mass of girls and women of America. I was not interested in promoting forms that appealed only to the highly skilled or highly emotional.

Chapter XIII
The Local Scene
of the Depression Years

The 1930s were as unforgettable because of the terrible weather, especially in the spring and summer, as they were because of the Depression. Spring after spring we were harassed by terrible dust storms. Never had I experienced catastrophes like these resulting from the terrible widespread and long-drawn-out drought. Many a morning, spring after spring, we found our front door stoop on the south of the house literally buried in red dust that most surely had blown in from as far away as Oklahoma—red dust not native to Nebraska or even Kansas, so everyone said. The summers were distressingly hot, so hot that people talked of frying eggs on the red-hot pavement—at any rate most everyone moved down into their basements. The laundry room double gas-burner originally installed presumably for the wash boiler did yeoman service as a replacement for the stove in the kitchen now deserted for basement living. Evenings we "came up for air," shunning the still hot screened-in side porch for the back garden which also was unbearable without the garden hose spraying nearby on the rare occasions when we were permitted to use our water hose thus.

Trees all over the city died and grass was burned out. The only escape, summer after summer, seemed to be to get out of this part of the country, which Nebraskans could quickly do with the Rockies in the neighboring western state and the wealth of lakes and resorts in Minnesota and Wisconsin. My family in Iowa, Kansas and Nebraska now discovered for several summers Estes Park in Colorado and its wonderful mountain trails.

For a few years we rented a cabin in Moraine Park at 8,000 feet elevation. We could look across the Big Thompson River, not large at that point, and the meadows from our front porch to the front porch of the summer cottage of William Allen White, the nationally known "Sage of Emporia." What all-day hiking trips we had doing the Bear Lake Trail, the climb up Twin Sisters, the trip to Gem Lake, Hallet's Peak, Flattop, to boulder field of Long's Peak, Andrews Glacier, and with always the climax of the trip, the Fern-Odessa Lake hike starting at Bear Lake and ending at Brinwood. These were such wonderful vacations, full of hiking with my sister Madge, my two brothers-in-law (Earl the lawyer and Ted the minister, both born the year I was), and niece Marjorie, plus a retinue of mountain cabin neighbors from Kansas, Texas and points between. I came to feel that a year without a chance to follow mountain trails for several weeks was a year lost.

But the northern lakes called to us, too, and some summers we chose them for Mother's greater enjoyment, and some summers we got in a bit of both mountains and lakes. Then there was the unforgettable summer of 1931 spent roaming all over Europe with Mother and two friends; the auto trip to California in 1932 as related earlier; and the summer of 1933 when a Madison, Wisconsin, friend, Elsa Fauerbach, corralled a young niece and nephew there and I, a young niece in Iowa and we disappeared with them to Elsa's cousin's hunting lodge at Bailey's Harbor across the peninsula from Green Bay. The lodge was miles from another cabin, so we let the three children shed their clothing and run on the beach in the nude to their heart's content (a 1930s sort of children's nudist camp, which we were not too sure we wanted to tell their parents about for fear they would consider the maiden aunties doubtful proxy parents).

Following that escapade there was the trip of 1935 back East getting in a bit of American Youth Hostel hiking in New England with Gertrude Moulton. The summer of 1938 there was a combination of northern lake and Rocky Mountains when Dorothea de Schweinitz of my Glacier Park mountain experiences of the early 1920s and I met, each with her own car, at a resort in northern Michigan, she coming from Washington, D.C. and I from Nebraska. A week later we decided it was the mountains we wanted, not a lake, so we suddenly checked out and headed for Lincoln in our two cars. From Lincoln, we went to Estes Park, Colorado, in Dorothea's new sports car, and climbed mountains for a week.

In 1939 I drove with Mother to Cedar Rapids, Iowa in early June, picking up my Iowa and Kansas sisters and meeting my Chicago sister at Coe College, which was conferring an honorary LL.D. degree on me. After much festivity I headed back to Guthrie Center, Iowa to drop off Madge, on to Lincoln to drop off Mother, on the next day to Lawrence, Kansas to drop off Jean, and then headed alone to Austin where I was to teach at the University of Texas for the first summer session as a guest professor.

Although most enjoyable, this my second fling at teaching in the summer, convinced me all over again that it was not for me. I threw myself into my work so intently the nine months of the year that I saw once more, following a 1922 summer position, that I really needed the

Author with her mother and three sisters in June 1939 at time of conferring of honorary doctorate, LL.D. by Coe College. (Courtesy of Coe College).

summer months free for play, reading, contemplation, travel and relaxation. Patient Mother put up with my erratic hours without a murmur during the regular school year, so I tried to make it up to her in the summer by taking her with me on some trip planned with her in mind. So this Texas summer, the minute the last class was over and grades were in, I headed for home, picked up Mother and a new car that had long been on order, drove to Chicago to pick up my sister Ferne and then drove to the Canadian border for a few weeks of relaxation in a resort near Macinac Island. From there we went East for a brief visit with Mother's brother whom she adored but seldom saw. With the six weeks of teaching, it proved a tiring summer and once more I vowed never to teach in the summer. It was to be another 13 years before I broke that vow.

* * * *

Depression-years students majoring under my direction at the University of Nebraska became my joy in my work like those of the late twenties. I soon realized that as they graduated I could serve them better than the Placement Bureau functioning through the Teachers College. The Bureau seemed to have a one-track mind—all teachers of physical education should expect to teach an academic subject along with physical education—and it was highly critical of students who expressed a desire to teach physical education full-time.

Since my professional contacts had widened nationwide, colleges, universities, high schools large enough to maintain full-fledged physical education departments for girls, YWCAs, recreation departments, and summer camps were turning to me directly to supply them with young teachers. The Teachers College Bureau only showed an interest in openings in public schools and since Nebraska was a state mostly of small towns, this meant part-time physical education positions only. They seemed to regard our department as set up primarily to serve the Bureau so it could fill the incoming demands for teachers of English *and* physical education, or history *and* physical education (whatever academic subject was in current demand).

Every so often the Bureau director would demand to know why I wasn't forcing every major in physical education to take a minor in this or that, whether they had any feel for teaching this or that or any particular interest in it either. He even lectured me on my lack of loyalty to the state of Nebraska, that I was sending our graduates all over the country to teach physical education full-time when Nebraska schools were crying for English (history or whatever) teachers. I constantly assured him that whenever Nebraska schools would wake up and establish departments of physical education to offer our graduates full-time positions, we would gladly urge them to accept these positions.

Finally giving up on me, the director tried a very direct approach. He called the brightest physical education majors into his office one by one and tried to persuade them to drop their major and instead specialize in whatever academic subject of the moment was in great demand. "But I am not interested in teaching history" (or whatever subject was being urged), the girls would exclaim, only to be given a stern lecture on what did her being interested in the subject have to do with it. Most of them weepingly came to me with stories of these annoyances. He left one student very angry and, after repeated calls to the Bureau director's office, she angrily poured out the whole story of these annoyances to me. Since the director was so insistent that she was wasting her time majoring in physical education, I decided that the time had come for a showdown with the chancellor to learn which of us was serving the university better—the Bureau director who felt that the desires of the public schools should be placed above those of the young people who wanted an education, or I, who felt that the desires of the student to get an education which would serve her to go out any place in the entire world to engage in an activity in which she has deep interest and to which she would be prepared to devote full time.

Chancellor Burnett was amazed that there should be a need even to discuss such a matter. "Of course the students who come to the University of Nebraska for an education are to be served first and foremost. That is the main reason for the existence of the University," he replied at once. In fact he was highly indignant that any student would be so annoyed. He immediately phoned the dean of the Teachers College in my presence, reported to him the reason for my being in his office, and said that he wanted this annoyance of students stopped at once. With that these disturbing incidents did stop.

With the subject thus brought up to the chancellor, I informed him of the constant calls I was receiving to recommend graduates of our department for full-time positions in leading colleges and universities, in large city YWCAs and high schools throughout the country, and some from foreign countries. I was pleased with many such requests that ended "We want a young woman who has been trained under your direction, Miss Lee."

As to the young woman whom the Placement Bureau had particularly harassed (Ruth Schellberg), she stuck to her guns, held on to her full major in physical education, and after a few years of teaching in a high

246

school in Nebraska, the University of Minnesota and Macalester College, she went on for the master's and doctor's degrees back East. I finally brought her to our University of Nebraska staff a few years before I retired. After that she headed the women's department at Mankato State College in Minnesota until her own retirement during which time she made an enviable place for herself not only in physical education but also in outdoor recreation, becoming a North Woods guide, taking through the years many canoe parties over the Canadian border following the old trails of the early French voyageurs. (*Life* magazine in its July 14, 1941 issue covered one of her canoe trips including photographs.) She also devoted her summers for many years to camping for girls, working her way from counselling to directorship positions in summer camps across the country. In later years she has taken mixed groups of college students on dance and camping trips in Europe. One memorable summer in the 1960s she took a group of college students who were modern dance enthusiasts on a camping trip through Europe with "Come dance with us" printed on a huge banner on the leading van. Wherever they were camping they found young people to dance with them. While teaching at the University of Nebraska, she also started courses in camp leadership and in canoeing. She has given much time to the National Board of Camp Fire Girls. In 1974 the University of Nebraska brought her back to the campus for Masters Week, when each year outstanding alumni in diverse fields return for meetings with students. In 1973 she was appointed archivist of the American Association for Health, Physical Education and Recreation.

Physical education would have missed one of its finest teachers and exponents of the good life if the University Placement Bureau Director had persuaded Ruth Schellberg to drop the physical education major so she would be prepared to teach physical education part-time with English, history or some other subject in some small town school in our state.

When I was to preside over the first of the two conventions of my APEA presidency and found myself domiciled in a complimentary suite of two twin bedrooms (each with a private bath), a large sitting room, and a good sized connecting hallway, I was quite overcome. There were telephones ringing constantly in all three rooms and continuous knocks on the door for callers and delivery of telegrams, flowers, and messages. By the time the first student from Nebraska called to see if she could help me, she saw at once that she was needed. We soon realized that I needed two helpers to answer the door and telephones, do secretarial work, order meals, help me get ready for this and that, and even in the end to draw bath water, lay out my clothes and help me dress. Several of my physical education majors had come to the

247

convention and when they realized my predicament, they organized an "assistants' squad." They mapped out all the hours in blocks, 7 a.m. to midnight for each day and saw to it that there were two on the job every unit of time. What lifesavers they were and how competent! Never was a president of anything better served! Almost 50 years later a couple of these girls still laugh with me about the fun they had "giving Miss Lee free secretarial and maid service."

Those Nebraska girls have always been a great joy to work with. And how proud I have been of the way they have used the training we gave them, whether as teachers or homemakers.

* * * *

In 1929 Dana Xenophen Bible came to Nebraska as football coach and head of athletics after 11 years of coaching at Texas A. & M. He stayed on for 8 years, winning 50 football games, losing 15 and tieing 7, and then left for a 10-year contract with the University of Texas at Austin. In the sports world he is ranked among football's greatest coaches. I rank him as also one of the greatest for a woman physical educator to work with.

In 1937, the year before we changed chancellors again, we changed the director of men's athletics. It was with deep regrets that I saw Dana Bible leave. The goings and comings of these athletic directors would have concerned me little if the women's physical education department were not dependent upon them for a share in the use of parts of the athletic fields and the swimming pool in the Coliseum, which had been installed in the summer of 1931. Also, our Women's Athletic Association now held, at their pleasure, all concession rights at the football and basketball games, the money from which financed the WAA projects. I had none but most pleasant contacts with Mr. Bible in every way.

At Coe, there had been "Prof", Ira Carrithers and Coach Eby of my early teaching days with whom I shared a gymnasium and athletic field most amicably, although the men always had first choice. Then at Nebraska after an initial start in relations with both the men's physical education and the athletic departments that were none too comfortable, there was the pleasant but brief experience with Coach Berg and later with Dana Bible. Now in 1937 Colonel Lawrence Jones took over as athletic director. "Biff" Jones, as every one called him, was a very different type of man—as much a gentleman as Dana Bible and a charming person to meet socially, but a tough bargainer professionally.

248

He was a West Point graduate and I soon sensed that I was dealing with a military man, and apparently before World War II the military was not used to dealing much with women. He always seemed a bit surprised that I would want to discuss use of the secondary fields— never in our wildest dreams did we women imagine ourselves daring even to ask to step foot, even in girl's soft shoes, on the sacred (varsity) football field.

"What is there to talk about?" he would ask. "I'll just send you a memorandum of what you can have." With that, he would dismiss me, and I would come away feeling quite abused (but hiding my feelings from him) because I had not been given a chance to present our needs and wishes and because there had not been the slightest gesture at arbitrating and adjusting. I was just "told."

Not so with Mr. Bible. He looked over the list of needs for my department and then showed me the list for his department and that of the men's physical education department. Then together we tried to work everything in and agreed upon a schedule for the use of the facilities. Even so, I always came away a bit disappointed, but after all I had checked his needs against mine and felt he was justified in insisting on certain choice times. With Biff Jones I never knew his needs or whether we might have had a better break if I could have queried him on some of the hours he kept for the men. I was merely informed that I could use this or that at such a time. I could take it or leave it.

In later years in thinking back over these experiences I have had a good laugh as I have come to realize that I got just as favorable a schedule of days and hours with Biff Jones as I ever did with Dana Bible—the difference being merely in the way each did it and made me feel about it. The military way left me feeling frustrated, the civilian way as if I were a partner in an educational venture. But I held no grudge toward Colonel Jones for always with business affairs disposed of he was as much as Mr. Bible a charming person. And I guess he held no grudge toward me for wasting his time trying to discuss things with him. Many years later after I had retired, when the Nebraska Rose Bowl football boys of his day were having a big reunion (and he had returned to Lincoln for it,) I dropped in at the Cornhusker Hotel hoping to get a chance to say "Hello." I had no more than entered the lobby, thronged with men, when suddenly one circle broke open and with no one running interference for him, Coach Jones broke loose from the group not for a touchdown but for a pass—at me—for he greeted me with a great big hug, swinging me off my feet. It was a breathtaking "hello."

"My it was good to work here at the university with you," he exclaimed.

"You mean it was good bossing me about, the way you bossed all the fellows!" I countered, and we laughed together, with the football fellows joining in.

Before I came to Nebraska the Athletic Board had given WAA the rights to parts of the concessions (candy and hamburgers) at athletic games on a contract under Coach Dawson that called for WAA to pay 50 percent of the net profits to the Stadium Fund. When Coach Bible came in 1929, the percentage was cut to 25 percent. The Corncobs (the men's Pep Club) shared concession rights with the WAA but, fortunately for the girls, they worked as two separate units under separate accounts with the Athletic Board. I say "fortunately for the girls" because they took their privilege seriously, were organized on a business-like basis, worked hard on the job, and made good money, paying a goodly sum into the Stadium Fund each year as well as into their own treasury.

The boys had no business-like organization, evidently no record of goods turned over to salesmen to sell, no accounting of monies taken in nor of the amounts turned over by individual salesmen. This offered easy opportunity for misappropriation of funds, and finally Coach Bible refused to renew their contract, turning over the entire concessions contract to the girls of the WAA.

During the Depression bank holdups were common, as were encounters on streets with desperados with guns who attacked anyone suspected of having money to bank. By the time the game was over and the salesgirls had turned in their cash and reports and were paid their commissions, and the cash—always a large sum—was in the money bags ready for the trip to the bank, the football crowd would have vanished, darkness would be descending, and the few girls who were heads of concessions would be left pretty much alone in that almost deserted corner of the campus with only the cleanup crews at hand. It seemed an ideal time for a holdup, and I worried for the girls' safety and prodded them to speed up procedures to get out quickly. The minute I saw from my office window the first of the crowd leaving the stadium, marking the end of a game (I never could take time off those Saturday afternoons even for a football game) I dashed to the stadium to help them get off for the bank as fast as possible. I knew that if there ever were a holdup these girls' parents would have every right to criticize the university authorities if no faculty member had been with them, and as frightened as I was at the very thought of encountering a man with a gun, I knew this was a responsibility I could not delegate to another staff member.

What little prayers of relief I would send skyward from that stadium each home football game evening as I saw the girls climb safely into the police car bound for the bank where a teller would be awaiting them. After a bit of a false alarm one evening that left us all shaken, I talked matters over with Coach Bible and John Selleck, who was then business agent for athletics and student activities,[1] and had the cash admission money to worry about, and it was agreed that we couldn't run the chance of endangering those girls any longer. From then on the girls had police protection during the game in addition to police escort to the Coliseum where they turned over their money to Mr. Selleck who from there on looked after it along with the athletic department monies.

By 1938, as business was growing with an easing of the Depression, it was increasingly difficult to get enough sales girls for football games, so the WAA offered a 10 percent commission on all sales. This brought out a large group of sales girls and increased net profits considerably because of increased sales volume. That same year the girls dropped their rights to sell at basketball games because the effort had become scarcely worth the bother. It was about this time that the girls were ordered by the Athletic Board to quit selling apples—one of their best sellers—because of complaints of spectators of being hit by apple cores carelessly thrown (perhaps some purposely so) and of cleanup squads because of the many apple cores strewn all over the bleachers and field. This meant a serious loss to their business but the problem was solved when the Athletic Board compromised by ruling that cored apples could be sold. WAA invested in an apple-coring machine, and Friday afternoons and all of Saturday mornings of home football games, WAA girls and most of the women's physical education staff cored apples. No one escaped this task, and it paid off for apple sales skyrocketed and the cost of the coring machine was soon more than written off. What "mountains" of apples we all cored those years! What apple eaters the Cornhusker crowds were! But then Nebraska was a great apple-growing state!

Under Coach Jones the girls were persuaded in 1940 to give up their rights in regard to the sale of soft drinks to give freshman football squad fellows a chance to earn money. These items were heavy for the girls to handle and they readily gave them up. As far as I could ever learn, this was a chance for these fellows to put money into their own pockets—a rather shocking thing to us women when the WAA girls worked for the treasury of the WAA to serve all women students with only the 10 percent commission going to the individual sales girls. This was one more thing that marked the gulf between men and women over money matters in those years and all the years before. Women weren't supposed to be paid what men earned, or even to ask for such or even to feel they had a right to such. However at this same time Coach Jones got the 25 percent of net profits paid by the girls to the Athletic Board for the privilege of the concession contract reduced to 18 percent.

In 1931 a swimming pool was installed in the basement of the coliseum with the understanding that it was to be shared part-time with women students. This meant providing dressing and shower rooms for women all of which turned into one big headache because although the top men in various departments made us welcome, the lower echelons of coaches, managers and teaching staffs openly rebelled at sharing any part of that building with us. They made constant trouble for us—from student janitors to student men lifeguards who were foisted upon us to give athletes a chance to earn money. But they felt no concern for taking proper care of the pool and dressing rooms or for keeping their scheduled hours for lifeguarding, paid for by the women's department but, on a ruling of the athletic department, not open to women guards. And no one higher up assumed any responsibility for seeing to it that these men athletes did the work assigned them. Sharing facilities with men with vague ideas of good housekeeping and with little feeling of importance for keeping to scheduled hours proved difficult everywhere I ever taught, whether at Coe, Oregon State, Beloit or Nebraska. As far as physical education and sports were concerned, women were always second-class citizens. My several friends teaching in the woman's world of women's colleges played in better luck in these respects.

*   *   *   *

In the fall of 1938 things at the University of Nebraska changed markedly when Chancellor Burnett retired at the age of 72 and Chauncey Samuel Boucher succeeded him. The two men were as unlike as could be. Chancellor Burnett was slow, plodding, kindly, and in failing health; Chancellor Boucher was alert, hard-working, impatient, young, and motivated by some inner drive that kept him on his own toes intellectually as well as physically, expecting that same drive of all faculty members. Dr. Boucher had three degrees from the University of Michigan, had done graduate work at Harvard, and had taught at Washington University, Ohio State and at the Universities of Texas, Wisconsin, Chicago and West Virginia. At Chicago he had been dean of the College of Arts, Literature and Science, and at West Virginia, president. So he brought first-hand knowledge of many universities and no doubt was amazed at the lack of esprit de corps and the slow, easygoing tempo of faculty operations at Nebraska. It was high time, I felt, for someone to stir up the sleepy place.

Those faculty members who liked the easy life, and, no doubt, every campus has some, had been having a heyday and enough of them had succumbed to the enticements of "flowing with the tide" that the ones who wished "to be up and doing" felt under restraint. Now we were to have an awakening. The energetic new chancellor usually arrived at his office at 8 a.m. and from campus gossip it soon leaked out that by 8:01 a.m. he himself was on the telephone calling deans and heads of departments, and when not finding them in their offices, he would exclaim to bewildered secretaries: "What, not in his office yet? A new day has started! When do you expect him?" This last would throw any secretary into a panic in a desire to protect her boss. Then he would ask the secretary to inform her superior that the chancellor had called at 8:01 or whatever time it was and was surprised not to find him in. Word of this checking on the administrative officers soon spread, and the little knots of faculty members clustered together briefly and furtively in front of various campus buildings soon came to mean a checking on who was the latest to be called.

Word got about from the secretaries, too. My own department secretary became apprehensive that any day the chancellor would call and learn that I was one more slacker, for I never made the slightest effort to arrive before 9 a.m. Finally the inevitable call came and I arrived later to find the secretary in a dither of concern over me.

"The chancellor called for you at 8:03 a.m. and was surprised not to find you here yet."

"Did he ask me to call him?"

"No, he just said, 'A wonderful new day has started and she is not here yet?' and hung up the receiver."

"Well, I will call him anyway."

"Oh, I wouldn't do that if I were you. He didn't sound in a very good mood."

"Yes, I'm going to have it out with him right now. There'll never be a better excuse for bringing up the topic of my personal work schedule. He has a lot of things to learn about my work."

And so I called. He answered the phone himself.

"Oh! Chancellor Boucher," I called out blithely summoning courage for such dramatics, "I understand you called me earlier. You are such a busy man that I think I should tell you it will always be a waste of your time ever to try to find me in before 9 a.m."

"You mean, you never come to work before 9?"

"That's exactly what I mean. I wish I could tell you about my schedule and the schedules of my staff. May I come to your office?"

"Well, well," apparently taken aback. "Well—yes, come over right now."

For some queer reason I didn't stand in awe of him as did so many. I felt he was being very cocky—in fact, I had classified him as an intellectual smart aleck who needed to be stood up to, but I kept my thoughts to myself. His tactics had spread a feeling of fear among most of the faculty members (for he had been severe with others about other things), a fear I was determined was not going to get the better of me. He was quite a handsome man, always well groomed and obviously aware that he was putting up a good appearance. And because we were on equal footing age-wise—he being just months older than I—I was determined to make the most of it. I had chanced that morning to don a severely but well-tailored suit and had relieved its seeming mannishness by wearing a little sailor hat trimmed in a band of colorful daisies and a blouse with frilly lace at the throat, so that I felt I could hold my own against his smart appearance, and I sensed this to be important in dealing with him. So I donned my hat and gloves and putting on as jaunty an air as I could summon, fully aware that I was in for a little "rough-going," I breezed into his office. He had recovered from the surprise of my insisting upon seeing him.

"Well, now, let's hear your little story as to why you never come to your office before 9."

"Indeed I don't!" I answered airily. "While most all the other faculty have departed by 3:30 and 4 p.m., my department is just swinging into its busiest hours of the day. All of our recreational, non-elective work comes then and on Saturdays, and my office is filled with girls who take these free late afternoon hours and Saturdays to beg for conferences and committee meetings with me. I never know what it is on weekdays to get away before 6 and 6:30 and frequently even 7 p.m. and then I come back two and three evenings each week for student and faculty committee meetings."

He was amazed at this information, also interested. Until then, it had been impossible to get a conference with him. As I rose to leave he walked with me down the length of his office and at the door paused before opening it for me.

"Now that I understand your schedule, I'll not call you again during the 8 o'clock hour." Feeling a bit cocky, I replied jauntily, "Can I count on this as a promise?"

"Yes, indeed, you can!" And so I won my reprieve and told my secretary she could stop worrying and suggested that this incident be a secret just between us. There was enough talk about his cracking the whip over everyone that I felt it would be better if no one knew of my victory or that I, a mere woman, had stood up to him. That indeed would have caused gossip.

Actually I had won more of a victory than I had guessed for I did not know until later that he had been well imbued at the University of Chicago with Robert Hutchins' skepticism about the merits of physical education. In fact at one conference he openly boasted to me that it was he rather than Hutchins (who got the credit for it) who had thrown out football at the University of Chicago, at which I leaned forward, looked him straight in the eye, and said:

"I don't think that is anything to brag about."

He looked at me for a split second in amazement at my temerity and then relaxing, threw back his head with a great roar of laughter which must have carried to his outer office for when I emerged a few moments later the sedate deans, lined up waiting their turns at interviews, looked at me as if thunderstruck. I can well imagine that roars of laughter emerging from that office were rare so that all were amazed and brimming with curiosity as to who was enjoying relaxed chatter with the chancellor.

But he didn't forget my brashness. A few days later when our paths crossed on campus, he demanded to know what I really meant by that remark, for surely I held no brief for the disrepute into which intercollegiate football had fallen in America. I stood by my guns but explained that although I certainly felt something drastic needed to be done I nevertheless felt he should have done away with the evils that had developed around the game, not the sport itself. He agreed but pointed out the seeming impossibility of ever getting rid of the evils. Thus the door was opened to conversations and gradually I was able to acquaint him with what we were trying to do for the women students through physical education, and little by little I broke down his disinterest in physical education—at least enough to win him over to give my department the support we so very much needed.

After all it was not so difficult a task, for fundamentally he was personally interested in physical education even though he refused to-admit it to me at first. The information given out about him when he first arrived included the statement that he had been a distance runner in his youth and had once held the faculty tennis championship at the University of Texas and the faculty golf championship at the University of Chicago. So I made the most of knowledge of these interests to counterbalance the word that preceded his coming to the effect that he would gladly eliminate physical education in all colleges. I knew that the women's department at the University of Chicago, which had been one of the nation's best before the Great War, had sadly deteriorated of late years and perhaps he judged all departments by that one. Soon I was able to bring Patty Berg to demonstrate golf to the students and to be available for conferences for a couple of days. I invited him to meet her and see her play. In his enthusiasm for that sport, the chancellor came out and walked around the golf course with me and some of my staff and students while Miss Berg played an exhibition game at the Lincoln Country Club. Such maneuvering brought him to take a closer look at our department and to readjust his thinking about physical education in general—all to our benefit.

In an early interview with the editor of the student paper, *The Daily Nebraskan*, the new chancellor had said that he had "no panaceas, no cure-alls, no formulae for educational success." And the editor had concluded: "Whatever he does will come from the deliberation of a frank and open mind."[2] Shortly after his arrival, Chancellor Boucher set up an administrative council composed exclusively of deans. Shortly thereafter, he informed me that he was appointing me as a member of this council because he felt that there should be another woman besides the dean of women and I was the only other woman on the faculty directly responsible to him for my work. Not being a dean, I felt like an interloper, but the deans welcomed me cordially and later, on two separate occasions, both they and I were glad I was there. At first I was appalled at the new chancellor's autocratic handling of the council. At its first meeting he unabashedly laid down the law and left no misunderstanding as to some things he would not tolerate.

The first occasion when I was glad that I was present came when eight of the deans were presenting their recommendations for advancement in rank of their various faculty members for the coming year. At that time the two departments of physical education were under no college and so their recommendations had to be presented by the directors themselves. I had none to make that year, having acquired all the advancement ranks for my staff that I sensed the "traffic would bear" at the time and I did not wish to push too hard for too much too fast and thus lose important future support.

Dr. Clapp appeared alone before the group to offer his two recommendations for promotions, one for an advancement to an associate professorship and one to an assistant professorship. Immediately several deans spoke up against the recommendations, boldly declaring that physical education was unworthy of such recognitions. At the same time, they gallantly bowed to me, adding that they had no quarrel with the full professorship conferred on the two directors, but implying that such nonsense should stop there. From the expression on the faces of the chancellor and the other deans it was apparent that all concurred with this viewpoint. Their seeming assurance that physical educators were unworthy of such recognition angered me. Amazing myself as well as the others, I jumped to my feet and made a determined speech not only in behalf of my profession but also in behalf of the two young men concerned who, I declared, I personally knew to be dedicated, earnest, hard-working teachers. My little speech turned the tide and in the end Dr. Clapp's recommendations received a favorable vote. However much more than that had been at stake. When the meeting adjourned aging Dean LeRossignol[3] took me by the hand and said:

"My dear, thank you, for setting us straight. We were not being fair to your profession."

Dr. Clapp graciously thanked me for my support and a bit more of the high wall that had separated us for so many years came tumbling down.

Later I came to see that that little victory had meant another important thing—that I, a woman, heretofore trying to get the men's department off my back and so becoming classified as a man-hater, would fight for the interests of men in my profession when I felt the cause was worthy. This change in my classification greatly improved my standing among diehards critical of any woman who dared stand up against a man for her rights. When they saw I would fight for their rights, too, the last barriers were removed between me and a few previously disapproving men.

The second occasion came a few years later when a new, young, lesser officer came to the military department and deciding that the University of Nebraska was missing a great publicity opportunity not to have drum majorettes or twirlers such as other schools were showing off to the world, stirred up a few men students who presented to the athletic department a petition that such publicity be adopted for the football games. The athletic department passed the buck to the chancellor. I always felt that had the athletic department wished such a novelty, it would have gotten away with it by going ahead on its own. This passing of the buck meant to me a lack of interest. The chancellor turned the petition over to the Dean's Administrative Council but before the deans got into a discussion about it, the chancellor must have seen what must have been a look of dismay on my face at such a proposal, for immediately he said:

"How about letting Miss Lee settle this matter for us? This concerns the women students. Why shouldn't she decide whether to accept or deny this petition?"

There were immediate cries of "Yes! Yes!" from several deans at once and all turned to me for the decision. But I replied:

"I have a very decided opinion on such things but I think it only fair to know how you deans feed about it."

"No, no! It makes no difference. We are in no position as are you to know about such things," someone said. And the chancellor a bit impatiently exclaimed:

"Come now, your decision, Miss Lee! Shall we accept or refuse this petition?"

"Refuse it, by all means," and before I could say another word all broke into applause, and Dean LeRossignol seated next to me gave my hand an approving squeeze. And so the University of Nebraska maintained its dignity as an educational institution. I never objected to such performers on the vaudeville stage or in circus parades, but how could an institution of higher learning present its comely girls prancing about almost naked in the name of education? Thus, as long as I was an active faculty member, I kept these inanities off the campus. I was proud that the chancellor and deans let me make the decision for them because although it let them all off the hook, it was an acknowledgement that they would sometimes let me make a decision for them, which did me no harm.

By the close of the 1930s, women had made a huge jump from bloomers to shorts but not all of us were ready yet for the "Golden Girls" as a part of academe.

* * * *

The decade of the Depression thirties ended for my department with a grand Fortieth Anniversary celebration which came about in a most unexpected way. One day in the early fall of 1939, Chancellor Boucher informed me that the administrative offices were cleaning house of old records and that in the basement of the Administration Building were several boxes of materials that seemed to concern my departmental work. He asked if I would take a look at them and decide what should be preserved.

"What do you know of your department history?" he asked.

"Very little for sure but a whole lot that is very confusing," I replied.

"What do you mean by that?" he responded. And I explained that to my knowledge no official records had been preserved by the department before my coming into the directorship, and I had been trying to piece together the history from reminiscences of former staff members and graduates whom I had met in my 15 years at Nebraska. But frequently such encounters only added up to confusion since these memories gave much conflicting information which could not be conclusively settled by checking with college catalogs since these, too, often gave inconclusive evidence. I assured the chancellor that I welcomed the finding of any records that might possibly throw light on our history and that I would look into the boxes of old records.

The task proved to be such grimy work from years of gathering dust that I could not tackle it an hour here and there, throughout the workweek. I finally had to devote many Saturday afternoons to the task when with the chancellor's orders to the janitor to let me into the basement storage room, I, arrayed in old clothes and a huge kitchen apron, went at the work in all seriousness.

However, as I explained to the chancellor, we had previously made some headway in piecing together bits of our history and collecting important departmental records. For instance, from my very first year at Nebraska, I had started to establish a list of all current majors and graduates of the department before 1925. This proved an arduous and uncertain task since the registrar's office could not help me with the necessary data. In my third year I started to put out an annual department newsletter to all graduating majors and former staff members insofar as I had been able to procure names and addresses and asked these to inform us of names missing from the lists given by years. At that time no one who gave me information recalled when the first major had graduated. These newsletters proved valuable, but it was a slow process pulling together the department history.

In 1937 I heard Dr. Clapp say one day that Nebraska was the first state university in the United States to offer a major in physical education leading to an academic degree. This was the first I had heard of such a claim in my 13 years at Nebraska, and it caught my attention because for several years I had been told that Oberlin College graduates claimed their college to be the first of any school in this regard. I resolved to follow up Dr. Clapp's claim as soon as time allowed.

The next school year we had a break and were offered the services of a National Youth Administration student for research work. I was informed that much information I wished was available in old records in the registrar's office but that we would have to dig it out for ourselves. Now I received permission to send this student to look into these records for us, and from this work I learned for the first time that the University of Nebraska graduated its first student with a major in physical education, a woman by the way, in June 1900. All of a sudden I realized that 1940 would mark the 40th anniversary of the graduation of Nebraska's first physical education major and since, as far as I knew, no recognition of that event had been given in any of the preceding years, I felt strongly that we should whip up a celebration for the spring of 1940. The majors and staff were solidly for it. And due to a strange break just then in news from Oberlin College it turned out to be a greater celebration than at first dreamed of.

Shortly after this, Dr. Gertrude Moulton of Oberlin College informed me that in 1902 her college had graduated the first woman in the United States to receive an academic degree with physical education as her major. This date stuck in my mind. Although I had always accepted Oberlin's claim as fact, I had never known the date on which Oberlin based its claim. 1902! And I had discovered Nebraska's date of two years earlier. (Had Oberlin and Nebraska at that time been aware of the 1903 article by Dr. Delphine Hanna, then head of physical education at Oberlin College, which showed that both the University of California and the University of Nebraska had established majors ahead of Oberlin,[4] we could have spared ourselves all the red tape of a formal challenge.)

Wanting very much in 1939 to have the exact truth from official Oberlin records, I wrote to the registrar. The reply verified 1902 as the date. I withheld public announcement of my finding until I could notify the department of physical education for women at Oberlin. To my surprise, I learned from the outpouring of letters from Oberlin faculty and graduates (once some of them learned of Nebraska's claim) that Oberlin was not going to take this challenge lightly. Oberlin not first—ridiculous! Someone asked why Nebraska had kept silent all those years—an embarrassing question which could only be answered satisfactorily by Nebraska eating humble pie and acknowledging the many years of neglect of its own history.

The Oberlin partisans, unaware of Dr. Hanna's 1903 survey, demanded proof by way of full records from the registrar's office and early catalogs. These I gladly furnished but also asked for official proof to back their claim.

260

Lest it would seem that we were personally quarreling over this, I wish to report that Gertrude Moulton, Oberlin's director of physical education for women, was one of my closest friends, and this challenging back and forth took on the aspects of true historical research untinged by personal feelings, at least as far as we two were concerned. We could laugh together over the indignation of some of the more loyal Oberlin graduates who refused to accept the facts and cede their long-cherished claim. In fact, I am told that a few of the graduates, these many years later, have still not forgiven me for what they called the "unwarranted attack" on their school. I felt close ties to Oberlin College, but in search for the truth we had to let the chips fall where they would.

The entire school year of 1939–40 was taken up with this research and correspondence and demands for still more proof resulting in exchange of copies of the registrar's records of all courses taken with dates by the earliest departmental graduate of each school, showing exactly what was offered at each school to be claimed as a physical education major. Even then Oberlin did not capitulate until the eleventh hour of our Fortieth Anniversary celebration, but when they did the timing was perfect for us. Just before our celebration banquet, I received a telegram from the registrar of Oberlin College and one from Dr. Moulton:

CONGRATULATIONS TO NEBRASKA FOR HIGH STANDARDS
SET FORTY YEARS AGO. OBERLIN FOLLOWS AND REJOICES WITH YOU.

Almost 40 years since that banquet I still smile at these memories for ironically, it is now Nebraska's turn to eat humble pie on this claim. In 1972 I was researching material for the publication of Parts I and II of *Seventy-five Years of Professional Preparation in Physical Education for Women at the University of Nebraska-Lincoln: 1898-1973.*[5] A staff member at the University of California (Berkeley) suggested that I might find some interesting data in the archives of Stanford University. I began corresponding with that office in the summer of 1972 and soon received official information that Stanford conferred an academic degree on its first woman to fulfill a major in physical education in September 1899. Thus, September 1899 is the earliest known date as of now for an academic degree to a woman with a physical education major conferred by any college in the United States.

So much for the ups and downs of historical research. In a recently published article,[6] I corrected my earlier published claim of Nebraska being the first and acknowledged Stanford's claim, and have challenged any college or university to better Stanford's claim. Stanford was quite unaware of its being first in this respect until I pointed it out to them, 73 years after the event. What fun historical research can be!

We worked up quite a 40th anniversary celebration in June 1940. Although Nebraska's first graduate, Alberta Spurck (Mrs. Albert Robinson) could not be with us, she sent greetings from Seattle. However, several graduates from 1902 to 1924 (before my directorship) and many graduates from all classes 1925 through 1939 did return for our two-day program. We feted Mrs. Anne Barr Clapp who 48 years earlier had come to the university to teach Indian Club swinging to the young ladies and subsequently had opened many doors to women. By the close of the thirties, women had made a big jump from bloomers to shorts and leotards, and from Indian Clubs to modern dance!

* * * *

The thirties brought many new campus responsibilities my way beyond departmental work. Of the few women on the faculty, several complained that the men were keeping doors closed to them, but when asked to serve on faculty committees, they steadfastly refused. As a result, we few women who would work on committees drew more than our share of these assignments, many of which were time-consuming and thankless jobs that nevertheless had to be done.

Night after night for weeks on end I would be back on campus attending various faculty or student-faculty board or committee meetings of mixed groups, but usually I was the only woman present. After several years of serving as faculty head of women's Panhellenic Board and complaining bitterly to the chancellor who appointed me that it was a great time-waster over trivialities, I was freed of that but pushed instead into work on the Board of Associated Women Students, the Honors Convocation Committee, the Faculty Memorial Committee, the Dean's Advisory Council, and as the one woman faculty member on the Student Union Board, not to mention several other lesser committee appointments.

The Student Union Board assignment was very interesting because I worked directly with students. I always preferred working with them than with faculty because students, men as well as women, usually accepted us faculty women as equals with the faculty men, whereas many faculty men let us subtly know we were quite acceptable to do secretarial work on committees but should not attempt to offer ideas or

262

proposals for advancing committee work. To them, we were second-class citizens.

There was never a dull moment on the Student Union Board. In the earliest days there was no student union building and that board was established to see that such a building be erected and that all plans be laid for the running of it. On the board were, as I now recall, three faculty men and one faculty woman, an alumnus and an alumna representative, and several student representatives of important student organizations, some Barbs ("Barbarians," non-members of Greek-named organizations) and some Greeks.

It was an interesting group to work with and to observe, for there was always campus "politicking" going on in the background of many important decisions. It was fun secretly to watch from the sidelines as the fraternity men on the board maneuvered for good position against the Barbs or other Greeks, and particularly to watch two of the three faculty men maneuvering, as they thought unobserved, to do the bidding of the particular Greeks whose interests they were always eager to further. I was often disgusted with these two for I felt strongly that the faculty on the board should look after the best interests of all the students.

For a while as the site for a building was being decided upon, then as architects and contractors were selected, still later as building plans were submitted with important and many choices to be made, we met frequently of evenings. It was time-consuming yet quite interesting. Finally as the building was nearing completion, we were able to settle down to meetings less demanding of our time and for discussions and decisions, moving into the realm of care and maintenance of the building and organization and administration of the activities to be carried on there.

The building was completed in the spring of 1938, and the first banquet to be served there was for the Women's Physical Education Club of my department.

A few years later I had to take my turn at the chairmanship of the board. All in all I served on that Board seven or eight years. It took a lot of time but it gave me an interesting contact with students, faculty and alumni.

* * * *

In the thirties our department was helping the Women's Athletic

Association select a site for and building and maintaining an outing cabin financed by the profits from concessions at football games. In the spring of 1934, we started search for a site in the country within five miles of the city campus, no small task in the somewhat treeless Lincoln countryside. Weekend after weekend, we scoured the countryside, hunting first for a shaded spot off the beaten path, by some creek or brook, and second, for a farmer who would lease us such a spot. With no luck, we widened our area to 10 miles and spent almost every weekend in the search. It took until November to find a place along Stevens Creek, northeast of town off Adams Street, and until the next June to get a lease signed. That June the cabin was built, in July the keys were turned over to us, and by fall school opening we had it furnished and ready for use. Three years later, to reduce the worry over a fire from careless girls with kerosene lamps, we had it wired for electricity. The cabin was a joy for years even though it was difficult to get the general run of university women to take an interest in such outing activities. However the WAA girls, the physical education majors and the women's physical education staff used it constantly and enjoyed it tremendously.

The real joy of extra-curricular departmental work was our intramural sports programs put on by the Women's Athletic Association under the sponsorship of the staff and as an official departmental offering. What fun the girls had! How they made the rafters of Grant Memorial Hall ring of late fall, winter, and early spring late afternoons and Saturdays! The great lack of outdoor playing fields of our own hampered the late spring and early fall offerings, but we always had a good turnout.

By the late 1930s we were offering 10 sports in team tournaments and 7 in club activities, with bowling heading the list in popularity in the team sports, and riding heading the club activities. The second most popular team sport was volleyball, the second in club sports, swimming. In team sports there followed in this order of popularity: basketball, soccer, baseball, deck tennis, softball, ping pong, badminton, swimming and tennis. Of the club sports there followed in this order, swim club, Orchesis, Outing Club, with archery, golf and rifle marksmanship bringing up the rear together.

All 15 sororities on the campus and 11 independent groups entered teams in the tournaments, averaging seven sports per group. One sorority one year had 96 percent of its total membership entered for team tournaments.

When we started the intramural program in 1925 we were able to interest only 3 percent of the women, but the idea caught on and by

Corecreation at Nebraska during the Depression years.

the fifth year we had 31 percent out. The percentage went up to 36 percent shortly thereafter and throughout the thirties it varied from 20 to 36 percent, despite lack of proper facilities.

An interesting and highly-approved development arose in the thirties —co-recreation in the schools, in the YM and YWCAs, and in the community centers. Co-recreation had existed from time immemorial, developing spontaneously wherever and whenever boys and girls or men and women who liked to play games would get together, but this movement as a school- and organization-sponsored activity was new. This wholesome trend was clearly to the advantage of girls, even at this date long after doors were first opened to women to take their place at the side of men in the work-a-day-world. Girls on the whole still had much to learn even in the 1930s about living in what was (and still is in the 1970s although to a lesser degree) a man's world. They always have had much to learn from boys of the "give and take" that is so much a part of the man's world, and educators now came to see that engaging in sports with boys offered them an excellent educative situation for this learning. Of course, there was much for boys to learn, too, from engaging in sports with girls.

Chapter XIV
A Multiplicity of Concerns

A "late bloomer" throughout life, I had been unusually slow at throwing myself into professional concerns beyond my own little teaching job. But then my professional organizations had done little before the Great War to reach the local levels beyond the eastern seaboard, and we young teachers were awakened slowly to broader professional interests. I had been teaching eight years before I plunged my first two irons into the professional furnace (as discussed in my earlier book, *Memories of a Bloomer Girl*) when I discovered the Middle West Society of Physical Education and the Middle West College Women's Directors Society in 1918.

The 1920s presented still more irons for my professional fire when I discovered the Women's Athletics Committee of APEA and the American Physical Education Association, besides the Women's Division of the National Amateur Athletic Federation, the National Association of Physical Education for College Women, and the State Leagues for High School Girls' Athletic Associations. Throughout the 1930s these old irons glowed warmly as with each passing year I was drawn deeper into the inner workings of each. At the same time I added four more irons. In 1931, Earl Johnson of the Lincoln Public Schools and I founded the Nebraska State Association of Physical Education. This followed an unsuccessful attempt in 1926, which followed earlier attempts by others in 1897 and 1917 each with but brief success.[1]

* * * *

At the turn of the century, a group of 11 questioning men, most of them physicians and all working in physical education, led by Dr. Luther Halsey Gulick, banded together to foster research in the physical education profession and to think through together the philosophical basis for the professions's existence. Dr. Gulick was shortly to preside over the birth of the American Playground Association and the Camp Fire Girls of America. Dr. George Meylan of Columbia University, later to be one of the founders of the camping movement in America, had a summer camp on Sebago Lake in Maine close to the Gulick summer camp, and he offered it for the annual week-long September get-together of this small but dedicated group. Their young organization was named the American Academy of Physical Education.

Besides Dr. Gulick, then head of all physical education for the New York City public schools, and Dr. Meylan, the other nine members were Wilbur Bowen, founder of physical education at the University of Nebraska but by then of the State Normal School, Ypsilanti, Michigan; C. Ward Crampton of the New York City public schools; Clark W. Hetherington of the University of Missouri, to become one of the founders of the Boy Scouts of America and at the time on leave of absence from his Missouri directorship to do advanced research on biological psychology at the University of Zurich; Fred Leonard of Oberlin College, later the profession's first historian; Dr. James Huff McCurdy of Springfield YMCA Training School, for many years editor of the *American Physical Education Review*; Dr. R. Tait McKenzie of the University of Pennsylvania, later to become an internationally known sculptor; Dr. Paul Phillips of Amherst College; Dr. Dudley A. Sargent of Harvard University, at the time an anathema to many Harvard alumni for his efforts to clean house in American intercollegiate athletics, particularly football; and Dr. Thomas A. Storey of Leland Stanford University, later the first state director of physical education in America.

These men spanned the continent. The organization had no officers, no constitution, no dues. The members convened informally to discuss each other's research, and according to legendary tales that have persisted through the years, much good talk for the advancement of physical education took place.

When the Great War broke out, most of this group were almost immediately caught up in important war work both here and abroad, and the annual meetings had to be abandoned. In August 1918, the guiding spirit, Luther Gulick, died suddenly at his Lake Sebago camp where he had gone for a brief rest from his arduous war duties in Europe where he had been head of all YMCA work in behalf of the American Expeditionary Force. With his death, followed shortly by the death of Dudley Sargent and Fred Leonard, the organization died out.

In 1926 Clark Hetherington, then head of physical education at New York University, decided that the profession still seriously needed a small group of leaders banded together to advance knowledge within the profession. He presented the idea to two others who also had known the inspiration of membership in the original Academy—R. Tait McKenzie of the University of Pennsylvania and Thomas A. Storey who for the past several years had held the New York State Physical Directorship, but by 1926 had returned to Leland Stanford University. These three invited two others to join them as the founding group for a new Academy of Physical Education: Dr. William Burdick, Maryland State Physical Director, and a graduate of Oberlin College, Jay B. Nash, a younger man whom Hetherington had met in California and had brought to his staff at New York University. These five founders of a revived Academy met on December 26, 1926 at the Astor Hotel in New York City.

At this meeting, Clark Hetherington was declared organizing chairman and Jay B.Nash, secretary, and five more persons were invited to join these five to make up the organizing committee. They included Dr. James Huff McCurdy and Wilbur Bowen of the first Academy, Carl Schrader, Massachusetts State Director of Physical Education, and Dr. Dudley B. Reed of the University of Chicago. In choosing the fifth person, the original five gave recognition to the fact that the world had changed since the first Academy. The 78-year-old Woman's Suffrage Movement had ended in victory in 1920 and opened the doors to women in a man's world. Thus the Academy opened its doors to its first woman member, Jessie Bancroft who, for many years had been head of girls' physical education for the public schools of Greater New York City.

These 10 decided to follow the pattern of the American Academy of Arts and Letters in selecting, by unanimous ballot, five new members each year. Each member would be assigned a membership number. Mr. Hetherington was assigned the number one spot, Tait McKenzie, number two and the other founders numbers three through five. Those selected in the next group were assigned numbers six through ten. It was now agreed that when there were 20 members, a constitution would be adopted; at 30 members, the charter membership would be declared completed, and the American Academy of Physical Education would be officially born.

Before adjourning, these 10 members unanimously elected 5 more members, selecting Amy Morris Homans as the one woman in the group. By then Miss Homans had been retired several years from her position at Wellesley College but had maintained her interest and contacts with the profession.

268

In May 1928 (probably at the time and place of the APEA convention in Baltimore), the group, now grown to 15, elected another group of 5, this time all men.

Among the next group of new members chosen some time in 1929, was the third woman member, Dr. J. Anna Norris, one of Miss Homans' early graduates. She had earned a medical degree and had been associate physician of the School of Education, University of Chicago, for several years before going to the University of Minnesota as director of physical education for women, which position she held until her retirement. She was a strong leader not only in what we then called the Middle West (all states from the Alleghenies to the Rockies) but also nationally, having been the guiding force in the creation of the Middle West Society of Physical Education, the Middle West Society of Physical Education for College Women, plus the two recently established groups, National Association of Physical Education for College Women and the Women's Division of the National Amateur Athletic Federation.

At the fifth organizing meeting held during the Christmas holiday of 1929 in New York City the group elected Tait McKenzie its permanent president. A constitution was adopted and the group proceeded to elect the last of the charter members, adding 4 more to bring the total to 29 rather than the 30 originally decided upon. (Probably there was no unanimous decision on a fifth person, with 25 members voting.)

The last group included the fourth woman, Elizabeth Burchenal who at the time, after many years with the public schools of New York City, was director of the American Folk Arts Society. Elmer D. Mitchell, C. H. McCloy and Arthur Steinhaus were the other three chosen to complete the charter membership.

The predominantly men's group (25 out of the 29 members)[2] had thus far taken no chances upon accepting women into membership. The four women were in every way an excellent match for the men of the group.

With the charter group completed, all living members of the first Academy of pre-Great War years were now members of the new Academy except C. Ward Crampton, who had left the profession for private medical practice.

* * * *

Two finer yet more dissimilar personalities could scarcely be imagined than the persons who gave birth to the Academy—Clark W. Hetherington and R. Tait McKenzie. Hetherington, in his early years, did two years of graduate work in psychology under the great G. Stanley

R. Tait McKenzie, president of APEA four years, 1912 through 1915, and first president of the American Academy of Physical Education, 1930–1938.

Hall and also studied in Europe, but did not acquire advanced degrees since he preferred to do research rather than spend time at degree-requirement courses not related to his research. R. Tait McKenzie in his early career was house physician to the Marquis of Aberdeen, gov-

270

*Clark W. Hetherington, one of the founders of the American Play-
ground Association, 1906; Athletic Research Society and the Missouri
Valley Athletic Conference, 1907; Boy Scouts of America, 1910; Middle
West Society of Physical Education, 1912; the National Amateur
Athletic Federation, 1912; and the American Academy of Physical
Education, 1926.*

ernor general of Canada, and held a lectureship in anatomy at McGill
University and later at the University of Pennsylvania. He had held
exhibits of his sculpture in France, Scotland, Holland, England, and
Canada as well as in the United States.

Hetherington was contemplative and introspective, friendly but a bit formidable. He was a perfectionist whose masterpieces were denied the profession because he could not bring himself to write *fini* across his several manuscripts, long contemplated and worked upon and long awaited by an expectant profession, before death overtook him. McKenzie, on the other hand, was an outgoing, warmhearted personality, charming and creative. He, too, was a perfectionist, but a restrained one whose masterpieces of sculpturing made him internationally known; he was hailed as the first artist since the Greek Phidias to specialize in sculpture of athletes. Despite these differences, there were many similarities between the two men—both were ardent fighters for the correction of abuses in collegiate sports that were rampant in the early years of this century. Both were idealists with a great vision for our profession, Hetherington approaching it from the viewpoint of a psychologist and educator, McKenzie from that of a physician and artist.

* * * *

The newborn Academy held its first meeting on December 30 and 31, 1930, at Hotel Pennsylvania in New York City. At the meeting the group gave the president authority to invite 10 to 12 men prominent in physical education in foreign countries to become corresponding members. The first projects discussed were cooperation with the international Committee of Physical Education and Sport for the 1932 Olympics in Los Angeles, the offering of awards and scholarships for excellence in the profession, and the publication of lists of master's and doctor's research theses to date.

At the second official meeting, December 30, 1931, also in New York City, the charter members elected the first group of members to be taken in under the constitution which called for a 90 percent favorable vote of all members. The first such membership, number 30, fell to me, with four men elected at the same time as numbers 31 through 34.[3]

Things were done most casually in the early years, chiefly, I believe, because the president left all mundane tasks to the secretary who did not take readily to mundane tasks. My membership certificate was not received until over two years after my election and not until four months later was I notified by the secretary. Three years after that, in January 1935, I received the first notice from the secretary that there would be a meeting of the Academy in Pittsburgh in April in connection with the APEA convention.

At that meeting, I was the only woman with 11 men, but I was by no means a stranger in this gathering. Our president, Dr. McKenzie, I had first met 10 or so years ago and had been his guest just three years before, for an unforgettable afternoon at the University of Pennsylvania. He had shown me his unusual collection of photographs in his private office and some of his sculptured pieces in his studio in a quiet retreat in the gymnasium. Since then he had sent me a large autographed photograph of himself to start my personal collection of photographs of leaders in the profession.

Up to then I had seen only the graciousness and dignity of Dr. McKenzie. I had not yet discovered that he, like Old Jolyon in John Galsworthy's *Forsyte Saga,* had behind his courtly and gentle facade a great capacity for uncompromising sternness when an occasion demanded it. Such an occasion occurred the evening before our Academy meeting. When I entered the ballroom to attend the APEA banquet, Dr. McKenzie hastened to my side asking if he could escort me to a seat. He led me to a small table of 8 to 10 persons. Seated across the table from me was a man with whom I had had an unpleasant encounter a few years before. Ever since, he had nursed a grudge against me and never let pass an opportunity to be rude. This evening proved no exception. We were no sooner seated than he quickly seized upon some remark of mine and, twisting it to mean something other than what I had intended, hurled it back in a most insulting manner. I was stunned at this open hostility, but before I caught my breath from the surprise, Dr. McKenzie had partially risen from his seat and leaning over the table toward the offending one, held his eye with a stern look of disapproval. The doctor never uttered a word, but his reproachful, unrelenting gaze was sufficient reprimand. Suddenly in that tense silence the culprit pushed back his chair and hastily left the banquet room, not to return. With his departure, Dr. McKenzie, with a quick apologetic smile, glanced about the table, saying, "Pardon me for the interruption, now what were we talking about?" and broke into light and gay conversation. As others nervously picked up the conversation, I whispered to him "Thank you" and he reached over and patted my hand, whispering, "Do forget it. He isn't worthy of your concern."

Dr. McKenzie recently had autographed for me a gift copy of Christopher Hussey's biography of himself, published in London and containing illustrations of most of his pieces sculptured from 1900 through 1927—a cherished possession. I was quite overwhelmed that it was he who had been my defender in an unpleasant episode.

At the 1935 meeting of the Academy, C. H. McCloy of the University of Iowa was elected secretary and he immediately pumped new life into the infant organization.

273

For four years no new members had been elected, but by the 1936 meeting, Agnes Wayman of Barnard College, who was serving as the third woman president of American Physical Education Association, joined the group. She and I developed a strong friendship first forged in work together in the Women's Division and in APEA but now strengthened by our closer Academy fellowship.

When Dr. McCloy became president-elect of APEA in the spring of 1936, he asked to be relieved of the Academy secretaryship. He was replaced by Arthur H. Steinhaus of George Williams College, known internationally as a specialist in physiology of exercise and a lecturer here and abroad. This secretaryship he filled most effectively for many years.

I was very disappointed not to have a reunion with Dr. McKenzie at the 1936 spring convention. When he and Mrs. McKenzie invited me to be their guest that coming summer at their summer retreat, the Mill of Kintail[4] near Almonte, Ontario, Canada, his boyhood hometown, I was greatly disappointed that I could not accept the invitation. By then I had a commitment with a publisher for my first book and felt I had to bring that work to its conclusion. This decision was one of the great mistakes of my life. I was promised a rain check on the invitation, but fate decreed that it would never be claimed.

* * * *

In April 1937 the Academy met in New York City in connection with the APEA convention. I had waited impatiently for the first Academy meeting when our president might be presiding at a formal dinner meeting. This time there was no disappointment. Elizabeth Burchenal, Agnes Wayman and I were the only women present in the group of 19 male members, the largest turnout the Academy had enjoyed. The unusual charm of our president as he presided over the banquet table was well matched by the elegance of the members, all in formal evening attire to mark the Academy's first formal dinner. The evening before, Dr. McKenzie's statue, *The Column of Youth*, had been exhibited for the first time in the great ballroom of the Pennsylvania Hotel (today's Statler Hotel) at the APEA banquet. Frederick Maroney and I had been invited by Dr. McKenzie to unveil *The Column*.[5] This, however was not without a bit of embarrassment. As I attempted to lift the great blue chiffon veil from my side of the tall column topped by figures of heads of a young man and a young woman back to back, the veil caught on something and refused to slide off until Fritz came to my aid and loosened it. As I was returning to my seat, feeling chagrined at my faux pas, Dr. McKenzie said to me, "It is a good omen to have something go wrong at an unveiling."

At the Academy dinner the next evening, Dr. McKenzie explained how he had selected the models for *The Column* to represent the ideal type of American girlhood and boyhood and how he had first studied these types in early Egyptian and later English forms. From this statue, he later designed AAHPER's official seal. The statue became the property of AAHPER and, as of the writing, is housed at the entrance to an auditorium in the NEA building in Washington, D.C.

For many years the profession knew practically nothing of the existence of the Academy. Even we new members before election knew little more than the rank and file of the profession. But having once experienced the friendliness and charm of our leader and having felt the great earnestness of his ideals for our profession, one came away inspired to greater efforts.

It was a rare experience to see Tait McKenzie preside at a formal dinner. He was not only a scholar, a man of culture and refinement, but also a "gentleman of the old school" such as we like to recall in these days of the commonplace. Even in the 1930s he represented a type fast fading from the social scene, and to my great amazement and delight he had adopted me as if I were the daughter he never had.

At the formal dinner in New York City Dr. McKenzie presented his design for an Academy seal—a hand grasping a flaming torch and above it a second hand opened ready to receive the torch. He hoped the Academy would bring the sacred fire to the altar, increasing knowledge, raising standards and lifting our profession to the level of other learned professions. This was the second piece of his work we had received within two days.

The next year we met in Atlanta, Georgia, again in connection with the APEA national convention. (However, by then APEA had changed its name to American Association for Health and Physical Education.) Dr. McKenzie was his most charming self although quiet and pensive, seeming glad just to sit back and let the rest of us carry on, happy to be one of our little group of 12. Before I left home for the trip to Atlanta I had received a note from him asking me to have breakfast with him the morning of our first session. When we met, he said he was distressed that the nominating committee wished him to continue as president. He had served for over eight years and felt that the torch should be passed on to younger hands. The committee refused to listen to him and after thinking it over seriously he had decided to serve just one year more provided I would be his vice president. Amazed, I reminded him that I was one of the newest members and was not even one of the charter members. He said his mind was firmly made up. "I need you and want you at my side." With tears in my eyes I gave in to his wish. "There, there," he said as if consoling a little girl with a broken toy. "That is settled! Let us smile now and enjoy the rest of our breakfast."

When the Academy held its annual dinner meeting there were 12 of us present, including our newest member, Rosalind Cassidy, then of Mills College. Out of a total of 39 members, only 6 were women, one of whom was deceased and 2 retired, leaving Elizabeth Burchenal, Agnes Wayman and me to carry the torch for women, so we were particularly delighted to have Rosalind joining us. Dr. McKenzie set the tone for the gathering. In those days the Academy membership was small enough that all could be seated at one large table, and our president was past master at keeping interesting conversational balls rolling.

We were particularly merry that evening as if Tait McKenzie had willed it so. When Charles McCloy was telling a funny story, acting it out with queer facial expression, he threw us all into such a fit of laughter that after the spell had subsided, all of a sudden the laughter would break out again and again until we were dissolved into a group of seemingly small children with a bad spell of the giggles. Tait McKenzie looked on with the indulgent smile of a doting father. His quiet dignity and all-enveloping, kindly smile and friendly eyes created an atmosphere of comradeship that was irresistible.

As the climax of the evening, Dr. John Brown, the Academy's vice president, presented our president with an illuminated scroll signed in gold script by all the living members of the Academy—the first award of the Academy given to our first president in recognition of his many achievements in the fields of medicine, physical education, and art. He was deeply moved by the beautiful scroll—this man who expected no honors himself, but was usually the first to plan honors for others. At last a group was paying honor to Tait McKenzie.

The next day Elizabeth Burchenal and Dr. McKenzie had tried in vain to get in touch with me after lunch for a drive around the city. Not being able to locate me the two had gone on and then returned to check out. They had hoped to find me at least to say goodbye. I was deeply disappointed to have missed that drive and a leisurely afternoon with these two good companions. I had missed the visit at the Mill of Kintail two years before and now this. I wondered why I had let myself get tangled up in what now seem trivial professional affairs when, had I been free, I could have spent the afternoon with Elizabeth, blithe spirit that she was, and Tait McKenzie, that rare soul.

Five days later, April 28, 1938, Tait McKenzie died of a heart attack at the age of 70. Early that spring he had accepted the invitation of St. Andrews University in Scotland to come there in the fall to receive an honorary doctorate, LL.D. McGill University had so honored him in 1921, the University of Pennsylvania in 1928 with the degree D.FA. But for this third honorary degree, death intervened.

I never received the notice of Dr. McKenzie's death sent to each Academy Fellow. Strange as it may seem (although I was not in touch with Philadelphia papers which gave large space to news of his death) I, out in Nebraska, knew nothing of his death until May 6 (8 days later). I was attending the annual spring dinner of the department majors. The out-of-state guest speaker seated next to me, not even an Academy member, remarked most casually that she supposed that I, too, had been distressed over the news of Dr. McKenzie's death. I was shocked beyond words to get such news in this fashion. To conceal my sorrow I sat quite benumbed throughout the rest of the dinner.

Now I suddenly sensed the reason for his insistence that I be his vice president. Ever since 1931 when I had become APEA's first woman president he had teasingly called me "APEA's first lady." Now that insistence had made me the first woman president of the Academy, too. I was overwhelmed at the thought that this was in all probability his desire. Gradually we began hearing of bits in his last letters to old friends and in spoken words which reinterpreted after his death, let us know that he had indeed made the supreme effort to be with us for a last time in Atlanta doubting that he would ever be able to be with us again. On January 24 of that year he had written to William Stecher:

> I congratulate you on attaining your four-score. I have just passed the three-score and ten, and only hope I may be as vigorous as you are ten years from now; the betting is rather against it, however.

In his last remarks to us in Atlanta, he had advised us not to become oppressed with much machinery of organization, but instead to protect our leisure, to have time to appraise professional movements, to reflect upon serious pieces of work, and to have leisure to taste of comradeship.

Now wheels were set in motion by both the Academy and AAHPER (by fall of 1938, the Association had added Recreation to its title), for a memorial for this unusual man. The Academy established the R. Tait McKenzie Lecture given annually at the AAHPER Convention when an outstanding person from some field closely allied to physical education speaks to our profession from his point of view (such speakers as Dr. Paul Dudley White, a famous heart specialist). Preceding each lecture the current Academy president pays tribute to Tait McKenzie. AAHPER, which McKenzie had served as president for four years before World War I, devoted an entire issue of its *Journal* to his memory.[6]

Twenty-nine years after his death, AAHPER at its 1967 convention celebrated the 100th anniversary of his birth by establishing the R. Tait McKenzie award for "outstanding contributions to the welfare of man through service to the profession and participation in the wider education and community relationship." A year later to my overwhelming surprise I was chosen as the first recipient of this award—an honor which for me was charged with emotion which the younger leaders who selected me could scarcely appreciate. Little did they know that Tait McKenzie, old enough to be my father, had in years gone by offered me a rare friendship. It was a deeply stirring moment to me when I accepted the award from the stage of the St. Louis Opera House which was filled to capacity but probably with only a few who had had the privilege, as I had, to know this exceptional man. The words of Roman Rolland in *Jean Christophe* were with me that evening:

> Everything must pass ... but the contact of souls which have once met and hailed each other amid the throng of passing shapes, that never can be blotted out.[7]

Tait McKenzie, then 30 years deceased, I felt strongly in spirit by my side that evening. In the words of another, also writing of a lost friend, "My remembrance of him will be forever green, verdant with promise of eternal spring. I thank Fate that in Nature's ordering of things he passed my way."[8]

* * * *

Following Dr. McKenzie's death, I, as new vice president, had the responsibility of carrying on for the rest of the year in his place. Never have I felt more inadequate, but the other members rallied to my assistance. We were holding our next meeting in San Francisco with our organizing chairman, Clark Hetherington, recently retired from Stanford University, living in retirement nearby.[9] Since he had returned to California from New York he had been too frail to make the long

278

journeys back East to Academy meetings. The sudden death of our president brought home to us the need to honor our other great leader before too late.

In 1932 Tait McKenzie had first suggested that the Academy create an award for the founder of the organization[10] but the idea had become lost while getting the infant organization started. Dr. McKenzie's death woke us and one of our earliest decisions was to present the Creative Award for 1939 to Clark Hetherington. He was able to be with us at our annual dinner[11] and Jay B. Nash, his protégé of years gone by and his secretary in the organizing years of the Academy, made the presentation in a happy and just-right speech. As acting president, I handed him the Award Certificate and, suddenly touched by his frailty, his appealing kindliness, and his little-boy-like shyness of the moment, I impulsively kissed him on both cheeks. It had been an emotion-charged dinner with memory of Tait McKenzie's recent death heavy on our hearts and now this new honor to another fast-failing founder. In response, he told us of his efforts in the early 1900s to found a federal university—efforts that met such resistance that they had to be abandoned—then of his dreams that this new Academy of Physical Education might become a body of leaders within the profession who would correlate and integrate research and scholarship which might be of value. The following day he was the honor guest at a luncheon given by the California State Association for Health and Physical Education when I was the guest speaker for the occasion—once more doing him honor. Three years later he died at the age of 72.

* * * *

Before we parted after the 1939 meeting, the members insisted that since I had carried on all the year as acting president, I now accept the presidency in my own right, but I was still deeply mindful of my experiences in France and England a few years before. They led me to see so clearly that other countries were not prepared to accept a woman as their leader in our profession. We in America were being drawn ever closer into the conflict already embroiling Europe and, of all our profession, the Academy was the closest contact to our fellow workers across the seas. Already we were drawn into emergency correspondence with associate members from various parts of the world, all in a man's world. I felt strongly that we must keep the channels of communication open in times so troublesome to many of our European fellow workers and that those channels could not be kept open readily with a woman president. Two years later, with foreign contacts completely broken, I did accept the honor and became the Academy's first woman president.

* * * *

In the thirties, professional concerns seemed to multiply. Interesting things were on the move to claim attention. One, the American Youth Hostel Movement, had grown considerably in New England. Eager to learn about it first-hand, I persuaded Dr. Gertrude Moulton of Oberlin College to investigate it with me in the summer of 1935. We "did" several hostels and afterward I contacted the movement's national office in the hope of learning more to help me open this new door of recreation to my students. This resulted in several years of service in the AYH Association on the National Board of Directors for one year (1943–1944) and the National Council for four years (1944-1948).

In the 1920s I had started writing in my field. No short articles I wrote in later years received the recognition that my second offering did, "The Case For and Against Intercollegiate Athletics for Women," of 1923 and its revision in 1931. The latter was published wholly in two periodicals and one bulletin and in part in two textbooks, three bulletins, and several handbooks, and, reprinted in leaflets, was distributed by the hundreds all over the country by the Women's Division of NAAF. Twenty-five years after the first publication, a large part was reprinted verbatim in another periodical and to my astonishment, as the original work of another author.

Another article published in the 1920s was reprinted in three other publications and another reprinted in six other publications, so with the coming of the 1930s I was deeply into the professional writing business—all, as is true of writings in most professional fields, without pay but for the advancement of one's profession. However, I turned out 11 articles in the 1930s despite many professional commitments in other directions, fulfilled speaking engagements in 14 different states and produced my first book.

Besides the several experiences previously related, I had been appointed a delegate to President Hoover's 1930 White House Conference on Child Health and Protection, elected the first American woman associate member of the German Academy of Physical Education, made an honorary faculty member of Mortar Board by the University of Nebraska chapter, elected an alumna member of Phi Kappa Phi (honorary scientific fraternity) by the Coe Chapter, received the Honor Award of APEA, and, to top off the decade, had garnered an honorary LL.D. from my alma mater, Coe College, in recognition of leadership in my career. It had been a most challenging and busy decade!

Chapter XV
"A Pretty Kettle of Fish"[1]

In the thirties I was drawn into arguments with some leaders of the Athletic Federation of College Women (the Athletic Conference of American College Women of 1917, renamed in 1933) who were pushing toward intercollegiate athletics. Many young teachers were turning to me and to others of my age group for advice and support in holding back on such sports programs. This angered several leaders among their advisors. And as some of the new leaders in NSWA had backed the editors of *The Sportswoman* in attacks on me, I who had been in the front line of battle to get NSWA officially recognized by APEA in 1931 and 1932, now in 1936–1938 became persona non grata with that group too, so that I had a small group of leaders in both AFCW and NSWA at sword points with me. The AFCW displeasure had little strength back of it and was short-lived but the NSWA grudge grew from 1936 on.

Since NSWA had busied itself almost exclusively with rules-making and promoting women's sports, and the Women's Division with standards-setting for sports, their work was complementary. WD's reason for existence was purely to back up the work NSWA was doing and in its own endeavors to reach the lay world to give it an understanding of what correct athletics for girls and women in America should be. Its efforts were to supplement, not duplicate, NSWA.

Since NSWA was purely a professional endeavor not committed in any way to woo lay women into its membership, the Women's Division became the organized connecting link between the profession of physical education and lay women interested in correct sports for women.

The birth of the Women's Division of NAAF in the twenties had been timely. The forces generated for the promotion of sports for girls by men, who apparently had little understanding of the psychology of girls and women or of their physiological differences from men, were too great for physical education women alone to cope with. It took an organization of physical educators plus lay persons who believed in sports as a valuable part of life and desired to keep them free of commercialism and exploitation. NSWA needed help to reach the lay world. The Women's Division offered this help.

At the organization meeting, April 6-7, 1923, in Washington, D.C., over 200 delegates approved a set of 16 resolutions on the conduct of women's sports drawn up by a committee headed by Dr. J. Anna Norris. Out of these grew what came to be called the Women's Division platform which was adopted at the first annual meeting in 1924 in Chicago.[2]

At the April 1931 meeting in Detroit, the platform, revised in a few details under the chairmanship of Helen McKinstry and with a new plank calling for use of girls' official rules for girls' sports, was adopted. Subsequently 100,000 copies of this platform were distributed all over the United States to groups offering sports to women. It was also translated into German, French, Italian, Portuguese and Japanese and sent out to many foreign groups as well. At this meeting it was determined that the Women's Division's second function should be to serve as a clearing house for problems about girls' sports. This was greatly needed in the world of sports under lay promotion and control—a task untouched by workers in NSWA.

In April 1930 I was offered the position of field secretary then being created with a promise that Mrs. Hoover would personally guarantee the salary and travel expenses if I could procure a two-year leave of absence from my position at the University of Nebraska. The salary was better than my university one but I felt I could not accept it, most importantly because I knew I was not cut out for a traveling position or for a public relations job. My refusal turned out to be to the Women's Division's great advantage for fate led them to Anne Hodgkins, then recreation director of the Eaton Company of Toronto, Canada.

She loved the constant traveling all over the United States, meeting many people, making speeches, and conferring with many community groups, "preaching the gospel" wherever she could procure a hearing. Wherever she went, people were enthusiastic about her. When I arranged a series of meetings for her in Lincoln, I watched her in action and studied the reason for her instant successes. Outgoing, she met strangers head-on. I could never have matched her performance. I reveled in watching her in action and we became warm friends. As it turned out, at the end of two and a half years, we were deep in the worst of the Depression and the position had to be closed out. It was the first year since the Women's Division was founded that Mrs. Hoover's large check in support of the work was not forthcoming although she continued her financial support for all the remaining years of the organization, but on a smaller scale.

Two years after refusing the field secretary position, I refused a place on the executive committee simply because I was weary to the bone after the responsibility of two district spring conventions followed by two national ones, plus my full-time work at the university. I offered to do what I could in odds and ends of assignments to keep a finger in the pie, for the Women's Division work was close to my heart. Then with a year of rest (of sorts), I re-entered the arena as a member of the board of directors of the Women's Division, working on it for the remaining seven years of the organization's existence.

As the thirties wore on, the lower echelon of workers in NSWA began to be jealous of the Women's Division. Even as early as 1933, it began to show. At that time WD was celebrating its 10th birthday with a luncheon meeting in Louisville, Kentucky in connection with the APEA convention. I was shocked to learn that some lower echelon workers in NSWA (most assuredly not its leaders) were urging women to boycott the luncheon. Others attended but openly poked fun at the program, their bad manners annoying other guests considerably.

I wondered at the wisdom of WD holding its annual meetings in connection with APEA conventions (even though a large block of APEA members, especially its leaders, were physical educators) when the major objective of WD was to sell the principles of correct sports for women to the lay world, which would never be reached at APEA conventions. On the rare occasions when we met in New York City apart from APEA, nationally-known men and women from the lay world joined us. Then the Women's Division got much top rating in metropolitan papers with interesting headlines calling attention to its work. There were important lay people on the programs as well as physical educators, and we seemed to be fulfilling our mission. Meeting so much in connection with APEA, however, apparently did not bother the other WD members.

All this time the Women's Division was trying valiantly to bridge the gap between physical education and the lay world interested in sports for girls and women. This was its unique contribution, but the younger and newer NSWA leaders couldn't see this. Many of us felt that this was their blind spot.

The thing that in the end caused the Women's Division the most concern was the animosity toward it within NSWA which should have been its closest ally. They were allies until after the mid-1930s when a clash of personalities and jealousies between the leaders of the two groups developed, ultimately causing a great rift.

As early as 1930 a few whisperings were heard from the "not ins" that WD was controlled by a little clique and that too many of them were college teachers. The charge was somewhat true, but when Agnes Wayman stepped out of the chairmanship of the executive committee in 1933, the hold of the college group was broken. The chairmanship was taken over by Edith Gates, head of physical education of the National YWCA, followed by Anne Hodgkins from the recreation field, then director of the Girls' Service League of America, who was followed by Emma F. Waterman of the physical education department of the New York City public schools.

By 1934 whisperings came from NSWA that there was unnecessary overlapping of functions within the two organizations. Edith Gates, chairman of WD's executive committee, called for a joint conference of the leaders at the 1934 APEA convention in Cleveland to discuss and, if possible, define the function of each in relation to the other. Some lower echelon worker in NSWA raised the questions, "Why do the two groups not merge?" and "Do we need both groups?" But this conference clearly defined the functions of WD as standards setting for the conduct of girls and women's sports and establishing contacts with lay leaders on behalf of correct sports for American girls outside the schools. NSWA was described as the rules-making body for sports for girls and women and the contact group for the schools and colleges in the field of girls' sports. The leaders of both groups felt that both organizations were needed. Each had its own special function to perform in behalf of both.

By 1935, NSWA, then under the chairmanship of Eline von Borries, had grown tremendously in its working personnel. It supported an executive committee of eight members, a legislative board of 19 members with a representative from each APEA district, two representatives from the Women's Division (NSWA had reciprocal representation on the WD executive committee), five advisers, and six members-at-large. Of these 27 top echelon leaders, 22 were working in the college field so that NSWA was now also criticized by the "not-ins" as being too much in the control of college teachers. What could a group do when, as a rule, it was the college teacher rather than any other who was permitted to be off the job to attend professional meetings? On this point, critics of WD within NSWA were now silenced.

* * * *

In 1936-1937, NSWA started to put out a *News Service Bulletin* without APEA's authorization. It caused financial difficulties because subscriptions to the *Journal* were cancelled in favor of the less expensive *Bulletin*. As cancellations kept pouring in, Elmer Mitchell, the APEA editor, wrote me in dismay to ask if I could find out what was back of the movement and to suggest ways to stem the tide.

I put my finger at once on the new *Bulletin* as the troublemaker and informed him. He asked me to approach the ladies in his behalf. So I turned to the president of APEA, William Moorhead of Pennsylvania State Department of Education, calling his attention to this financial threat to APEA. He sent a copy of my letter to the chairman of NSWA, who, without any effort to learn the extent of damage her project was doing to the mother organization (APEA), wrote me an indignant letter accusing me of being a "traitor to NSWA." As she spread the word of my "perfidy," I received letters from some of her ardent followers, calling me a "busybody," "an obstructionist," "a troublemaker," and offering the suggestion that I "attend to my own business and leave NSWA alone."

This was a hard pill to swallow when so recently I had, in NSWA's behalf, fought a hard core of men determined that women were to be allowed no form of organization above the committee level, men whose belligerency I alone had calmed down in NSWA's behalf. Now when called upon to help protect APEA's larger interest from their unwise actions I was severely criticized. As one wrote me, "How do you have the temerity to raise a dissenting voice about NSWA?" Well, I had dared for I had been called upon for help and I felt NSWA must be informed that it could not enter upon projects that might endanger the larger interests of APEA without first presenting their plan to APEA, making adjustments if necessary and procuring APEA permission. This was a hard lesson to learn for the younger ones who had now taken over control from the more experienced members. In the end, the problem was solved and the News Service became a *Service Bulletin, a Supplement to the Journal of Health and Physical Education,*[3] under the editorship of Alice Frymer, a former physical education teacher, then with A.S. Barnes Publishing Company, and subject to control of APEA to protect its own interests.

With settlement of this problem, the NSWA chairman apparently had better thoughts about my "meddling," for she asked me for suggestions on how NSWA could better reach rural and small town schools. I suggested she work through the state directors of physical education and not try to go it alone. I frankly told her that NSWA was doing too much on its own and should use all cooperative agencies possible. She then asked how I felt NSWA and the Women's Division could work better together. I said I could not see how any difficulties should arise between them as long as neither duplicated the work of the other. They should supplement one another and keep in close touch.

When she asked what I thought was the function of each, I said that the Women's Division was the standard-setter and liaison with the lay world and NSWA was the sports rules-maker and liaison with the schools. It seemed strange that the new corps of younger workers hadn't been told this in their professional training years. Many of the older workers were impatient with their lack of knowledge and non-cooperation which had grown out of their ignorance.

There was one area which the leaders of both groups came to claim in the late thirties—promotion, and that caused trouble between them. I felt a bit impatient with both sets of leaders, not understanding why they couldn't both do promotional work. They were dealing primarily with different groups—WD with the out-of-school world which so naturally seemed its province with the woman head of physical education for the national YWCAs now chairman of the Women's Division, and NSWA with the schools which so naturally seemed its province. I couldn't understand why these fields didn't seem to be clear-cut and why neither group understood that there was work enough for both if the entire field were to be served. But it didn't work out that way and this area caused a serious rift between the two groups.

NSWA began urging that it was not necessary for both groups to have a representative from each state—one person in each state could serve both. When this idea was put into operation with WD's consent, it was invariably a school or college physical education teacher, not a recreation or YWCA director who was given the appointment—not on purpose but because the school people were more available in most states. Their chief interest lay with NSWA to the neglect of WD's problems and advancement. This gradually led to many school and college teachers dropping out of the WD which was hard hit anyway since the affluent lay persons who had financed the Women's Division in its early years had been forced to stop sending their annual contributions during the Depression. Now the Women's Division was having great financial difficulties.

No sooner were the 1936 storm clouds over ths NSWA *News Service Bulletin* dispersed than 1937 brought a new storm. The NSWA chairman of 1936-1938, backed by some committee or group within its own organization, put out a surprise set of NSWA standards and principles for women's sports disregarding not only the many years of the WD offerings but even the rank and file of its own workers. Many openly protested this venture and asked why it had been entered upon, especially when NSWA, at its 1936 annual Christmas holiday meeting of all officers and committee heads, reaffirmed its support of the Women's Division Platform and publicly announced this stand.

Concern immediately arose over the differences between the two sets of standards. The Women's Division's set was drawn up in explicit detail to give support to the non-professionals leading girls and women in sports by approved standards. The NSWA set was stated in broad generalizations and drawn up primarily for in-school workers, most of whom would be professionally trained and able to read correctly between the lines of the generalization. We older workers sensed the dangers of misinterpretation of the NSWA standards, by workers in small towns and rural areas lacking professionally-trained leaders to guide them or purposefully misinterpreted by others to suit their own wishes if a strict interpretation interfered with their personal desires not to conform.

By the NSWA standards it would have been permissible for my own University of Nebraska girls to engage in intercollegiate athletics if varsity teams arose from a wide base of intramural sports and if the intercollegiate practices and matches did not interfere with the sports program of the vast majority of other girls interested in sports participation.

Had a University of Nebraska varsity women's team played a varsity women's team from the University of Omaha at that time, the newspapers would have ballyhooed the event throughout the state. The high schools, very few of which had trained women in charge of physical education and sports for their girls, would have immediately jumped on the interschool bandwagon to emulate the university. Our actions would have been completely misunderstood. NSWA's five points of permissiveness would never have been recognized. The long, hard struggle of the twenties to eliminate the undesirable type of interschool sports for girls that had been rampant among many schools, would have flared up again in an even more virulent form with the seeming approval of the university, the example-setter for so many things within the state.

I felt quite strongly about this and fortunately my staff backed me 100 percent. We took seriously our opportunity for statewide leadership as good example-setters. So we stood by the so very explicit standards of the Women's Division knowing that by so doing we were also adhering to NSWA standards but not taking advantage of its permissiveness for the temporary pleasure of a handful of highly-skilled sportswomen. As example-setters we didn't want to cause "a younger sister" to stumble.

* * * *

Almost immediately after publication of NSWA's standards, the chairman of WD's executive committee wrote me of the financial plight of WD brought on by the Depression and asked what I thought of seeking a merger with NSWA. This letter was soon followed by another, telling of renewed hope. There had been a surprise financial windfall to tide them over a bit, and now they were planning to pump new life into the organization by holding a sort of pep rally at the time of APEA's convention which, fortunately, was to be in New York City. William Moorhead, Pennsylvania State Director of Physical Education, then president of APEA, gave WD his blessing, and he was still annoyed with NSWA leaders over troubles they had caused with the unauthorized *Woman's Service Bulletin* and with their standards ignoring those of the Women's Division.

Edith Gates, chairman of WD, wrote that they had secured the promises of John Findley, editor of *The New York Times*, Mark McCloskey, director of National Youth Administration in New York City, and John Tunis to speak at a rally luncheon the second day. She asked me to sit at the head table and be ready with a few remarks including some word of encouragement from mid-America. This of course I agreed to do.

Immediately upon my arrival in New York City that spring day of 1937, Agnes Wayman rushed me off to a luncheon meeting with Blanche Trilling, Alice Belding of Vassar College, Helen McKinstry and Ethel Perrin to discuss the problem of combatting this threat to WD's Platform from within our profession. We decided to stand up to the new NSWA leaders who seemed intent upon upsetting the professional apple cart. No sooner had the WD conference opened than it became apparent that the breech was widening between the two groups as personal clashes erupted now and then throughout the sessions as certain proponents of each side became equally unwilling to compromise in order to discover some common ground for even casual discussion of mutual problems.

* * * *

Within the next two years, certain uncompromising members of NSWA even went so far as to continue the start made in 1933 to try to dissuade women attending APEA conventions from attending Women's Division breakfasts and luncheons, ridiculously claiming such attendance as evidence of disloyalty to NSWA. Those of us within the profession who served on the WD's executive committee and board of directors were especially suspect of these highly emotional women who seemed to regard work in NSWA as the be-all and end-all of existence. Many men in the profession considered such women a great joke even though they had made trouble for them, too. We women who were deeply interested in the work of both groups and seeing a place of value within our national sports field for both saw nothing funny about these troublemakers, the worst of whom worked anonymously (at least so they thought) behind the scenes influencing the elected officers and appointed workers.

This was human nature at a bad level—a small vocal group ill-disposed toward anyone not seeing things from their own view. Since the WD executive committee was headed during these troublesome years by women trained in our field but working in the recreation, industrial, and YWCA fields rather than in the school and college worlds where the great majority of the NSWA workers were to be found, they were especially vulnerable to cantankerous workers in the NSWA groups.

In the spring of 1937 I was elected to another four-year term as a member of the WD board of directors as one of only three women actively working in physical education. The other two were Agnes Wayman and Germaine Guiot of the University of Southern California, the three of us representing the two coasts and mid-continent. Vera Barger of the Cleveland YWCA and Ethel Perrin, both former physical educators from the YWCA and public school fields, were also members of the new board. Also re-elected was Dr. Lillian Gilbreth, the famous industrial engineer who was a great friend of physical education.

Of this group, Agnes Wayman and I bore the brunt of NSWA's displeasure in the spring of 1938 as we were the only WD board members to attend that convention. Since neither of us expected any trouble, imagine my surprise to be waylaid at the convention by the NSWA chairman at the head of a long, wide stairway leading to the main entrance of the headquarters hotel. I was returning alone from a meeting and in a voice louder than necessary she said, "It would be a great favor, Miss Lee, to NSWA if you would attend to your own business."

Amazed, I stopped dead in my track (as did several of the passersby who were also taken by surprise at this rude encounter) and stared at my interlocuter in open-mouthed astonishment.

"You don't need to look so innocent. You know very well what I am talking about."

"I haven't the slightest idea," I replied.

"Well, think it over. It will come to you after while." Then haughtily tossing her head, she started down the stairs with a last barb, "We are fed up with your troublemaking." She ran down the stairs leaving me standing there alone with the little group of curious onlookers now melting away, embarrassed.

I dashed to my room, threw myself on my bed and burst into laughter as I sought release from the sudden tension. Almost at once there came a pounding on the opposite side of the wall by my bed. I knew it was Coley who chanced to be assigned a single room next to mine.
"Lee, are you weeping or laughing?"

"I am laughing. Come over."

And so Coley came over and reverting to her role of our student days demanded to know "What now?" I told her about the encounter, and at Coley's, "What caused that outburst?" there came to my mind the unpleasantness of two years before when Elmer Mitchell had begged me to come to his aid over the NSWA *Sports Bulletin* affair.

"That's probably it. Now ancient history. But that group is like elephants. They never forget," Coley said. "But Lee," she added, "don't let it bother you. You were acting for the best interests of our larger organization. These women are selfishly promoting their own lesser interests at the expense of the majority. Forget it. They are not worth worrying over."

"Well, Coley, I was only laughing, not weeping!"

"But I know you. The next thing you know you'll begin worrying over this. Now forget it!"

But this encounter proved to be only a prologue. Agnes, too, had received some snubbing and rude remarks although not quite so publicly delivered. We found it easier to laugh it off together.

Charles Harold McCloy of the University of Iowa had in the spring of 1937 become president of APEA as it changed its title to the American Association for Health and Physical Education. He received from NSWA a long report of its activities in the summer of 1937 and later a set of recommendations to present to the Legislative Council of AAHPE at the Atlanta convention of 1938. Puzzled over both of them, he sent me both sets of papers, asking if I thought these women had delusions of grandeur. For one thing they were asking for $5,000 to finance promotion work for girls' sports and paid assistance for the secretary.

I was critical of their request for money to promote sports when the country was full of local and state school departments of physical education, public and private, on all grade levels through college, besides many state leagues for girls sports and local GAAs, WAAs, YWCAs and many other like organizations promoting sports for girls and women. Why should NSWA become sports promoters as well as the official sports rules-making body? They were also trying to take over from the Women's Division its acknowledged function of setting standards for sports.

With a bit more time to think over my "sins" after that attack at the head of the hotel stairs in Atlanta, I realized that maybe the NSWA chairman had been informed of my correspondence about NSWA with both Presidents Moorhead and McCloy at their seeking and maybe had even seen some of my letters. That alone would explain the outburst!

Many NSWA grassroots workers as well as several of their subcommittee workers from various parts of the country had asked me for advice about what seemed unnecessary demands made on their time. I was also bombarded in person by several young girls in my profession who were "out of tune" with NSWA and what they called its "wild schemes." Later reports from close friends across the country disclosed that they, too, had similar experiences. These young protesters claimed that there was a constant drive by NSWA for them to do more and still more work at the local as well as state and national levels, and that much of it was just "make-work to look important" (as some of them spoke of it). Some men also expressed their annoyance with this group over their constant demand for large sums of money for what seemed to them unimportant projects or for duplication of the work of others, in particular, research work that was the province of the Research Section.

I discussed this problem frankly with those who came to me about it. No doubt I had been quoted by several and no telling how my remarks had been altered by the time they had reached Madame Chairman. She had advised me to think it over and on doing so and recalling all these seekers of advice, I began to understand a little the possible cause of her displeasure with me.

At this time the Women's Division still had over 700 individual members and 400 organization and institution members from colleges, public and private schools, industrial groups, recreational organizations, youth serving groups, and YWCAs. It had disbursed over $106,000 of donations from individuals, foundations, and trusts, in addition to generous sums from Mrs. Herbert Hoover.

Shortly after this, I later learned, a movement was underway within NSWA to eliminate WD as a no-longer-needed organization now that NSWA was setting its own standards for women's athletics. Unfortunately, the Women's Division was in no position to defend itself against any formidable onslaught since most of its financial sources were drying up because of the Depression. Also, WD was merely an organization affiliated with AAHPER, not a subdivision as was NSWA with subsequent support from the mother organization. But there was one vast difference between the two: NSWA came solely and directly out of the profession of physical education, and the Women's Division, mostly a lay group, stood completely alone.

With two conflicting sets of standards, the battle lines were drawn. These lines were not drawn between the young newcomers and the "old guard," but between the liberals and the conservatives. But these labels do not seem correct either. As I look at it another way, recalling the actual battle as it unfolded in 1939 in San Francisco when I unexpectedly found myself in the very "eye of the storm," I have come to the conclusion that it was the bullheaded of one group pitted against the hotheaded of the other group, with neither side willing to give an inch in the cause of peace and goodwill. I was caught in the middle trying to blow the whistle for moderation and compromise but getting nowhere, with mistrust and ill will seemingly at its worst—both sides guilty but one side (NSWA) decidedly the aggressor. I was not only sick at heart, I was disgusted.

* * * *

The behind-the-scenes story that follows of the demise of the Women's Division of the National Amateur Athletic Federation, as I experienced it from a front row seat, has never before been brought out from behind closed doors. Believing that it is part of our history, now almost 40 years old, I offer it here in part even though it is a sad commentary on women's difficulties at times to get along with each other. Nevertheless it is a true picture of human nature as we find it.

In 1938 the American Association for Health and Physical Education again changed its name, adding Recreation. It also affiliated with NEA as one of its departments, establishing executive offices in the NEA Building in Washington, D.C., and appointing a full-time executive secretary, Neils Neilson, formerly of Stanford University.

A feeling now developed within the Women's Division that it needed some affiliation that could give financial support. From that grew the idea that now that AAHPER had a home of its own and an executive secretary and a staff, perhaps it would consider taking WD under its wings. On February 13, 1939, Anne Hodgkins, then chairman of the WD executive committee, discussed this possibility with Dr. Neilson, who suggested that WD appoint a special committee to meet with him to pursue the subject. On February 18 a committee of the executive committee met and out of this meeting came a proposal from Dr. Neilson that WD draw up an operating code defining the exact work WD would hope to continue under a merger. On February 20 the code was drawn up.

On March 2, Anne wrote to me, and doubtless to many others, about the possibility of the merger and stating that representatives of both groups would meet on March 10 in New York City. She asked me to write to her at once with my idea of how best WD could merge and still preserve its work. But she gave me no clue as to what was the thinking of the group back East and did not mention that the WD committee had gone so far as to draw up a code. So in my ignorance I wrote that I felt WD should not merge with AAHPER but remain an affiliated organization and not bury itself in a teaching organization. I called her attention to the fact that when AAHPER the year before had merged with NEA as one of its departments, it clearly defined itself as a school organization. I was still unhappy over that merger and now here was talk of yet another non-public school merger. WD was reaching groups completely outside of our profession such as Girl Scouts, Camp Fire Girls, YWCAs and the like. I said to her in my letter of March 7, 1939:

> NSWA should be the technical body in reference to athletics for girls and women. As a body of experts trained in the profession, it is, of course, the logical thing that it should prepare the rules for girls' sports, and I am not so sure but what it really is, after all, the logical group that should set standards since it is the group of experts.... On the other hand, WD should be the interpreting group, the contact group for laymen who are interested in athletics for girls.... It should be a Federation and not have individual

memberships.... NSWA should furnish technical information and advice.... the Federation would disseminate this information and advice to its member organizations.

Thus I was placed on record with WD as one who felt that NSWA was after all the logical group to set up standards for women's sports, even though I disapproved of the standards set up by it so far. Pure logic dictated this stand. But it was difficult to discuss this calmly with the new young leaders in WD. They got so emotional about it and were shocked at what they felt was disloyalty to WD.

I deplored the fact that WD and NSWA were both now offering standards duplicating each other's efforts and confusing everyone since the two sets did not agree. I felt strongly that, unhappy as I was over some of NSWA's latest pronouncements, we needed to be logical and fight for what we wanted regarding standards within NSWA itself.

Agnes Wayman (another physical educator on the WD board of directors) shared my views on this matter. Of course, we both recognized that WD had initially undertaken the standard-setting projects because a set of standards was greatly needed as a guide to lay persons and no professional group, not even NSWA, had yet formulated a set. Since WD had at its inception the most outstanding women physical educators in its top echelon, it was understandable that they undertook the task in the name of WD.

It was widely noised about by NSWA members that the 1936-38 standard-setters of NSWA had functioned without official sanction and without even a vote of approval of the new standards by its own members. Such an uproar of disapproval of these standards arose from all parts of the country that a vote on this matter was called for at the convention in San Francisco in April 1939.

A meeting concerning a merger of WD and AAHPER was held March 10, 1939 in New York City by 13 representatives of AAHPER appointed by its president, Frederick Cozens of UCLA. It consisted of the executive secretary and three men and three women supposedly interested in NSWA in particular, and six representatives of the executive committee of the Women's Division and its executive secretary. This joint group drew up recommendations to be presented to the AAHPER Legislative Council for approval at its annual convention in San Francisco and to the Women's Division members for a mail vote. If approved by both groups, a merger would occur. WD would be absorbed into AAHPER as the standard-setter of sports for women, while NSWA would continue its work of rules-making and promotion of sports according to the standards.

When I heard of this, I was amazed that the AAHPER representatives would approve such an arrangement. Apparently the men at least were unaware of the feelings of NSWA's leaders regarding WD's standards or they would have sensed that these leaders would fight before they would accept WD as the standard-setters for girls' and women's sports in AAHPER. Obviously even NSWA's own representative in that group was not of their own choosing and was not aware of or not in sympathy with the NSWA standards which rejected WD's platform.

I received a letter shortly after from Agnes Wayman. She had been a member of the committee that had met in New York City on March 10 to consider the merger but had to leave before the final vote. She heartily disagreed with the committee's so-called unanimous decision. She told me she could not attend the San Francisco convention but wanted me to know what her proposals were for a solution of the problem in the hope that I would give them serious consideration in any way that I might be drawn into discussion at the San Francisco meeting.

One of her proposals was that the NSWA coordinate its published standards with the earlier platform of WD of NAAF, defining exactly what it meant by intercollegiate and interscholastic competition. The two groups needed to come to some agreement on this point as it was the greatest difference of opinion between them. I felt strongly that if we would recognize NSWA as the body to set standards and make sports rules and WD as the body to endorse and make known NSWA standards and rules to the lay world, there would be no difficulties between them once a set of standards could be drawn up that both could endorse. But there was the rub—how to reconcile these two opposing groups on the matter of interscholastic and intercollegiate athletics for girls and women?

Looking back on this problem over 30 years later, I can see it clearly now, as none of us apparently did then. This quarrel was not one of a generation gap nor of the laity versus the physical education profession. It was one group of women physical educators, mostly older ones plus a large following of young women, versus another group of women physical educators, mostly the middle age group and die-hard, outspoken ones. It was wholly an intra-professional argument with the lay members of WD clearly lined up with one side alone, taking their cue from it alone, that side being the defenders of non-recognition of interscholastic sports and their equivalent in the lay world outside of the schools.

Reconciliation of the two groups on this point would not solve the Women's Division's financial difficulties. I couldn't see any help for them by merging with AAHPER since that organization had no funds to spare to permit a presumably lay group to function in behalf of girls' sports alone. Really, as I told both Agnes and Ann, there seemed nothing for WD to do but quietly close up shop, pointing with pride to its many years of splendid undertakings on behalf of wholesome sports for all American girls and women. But I was saddened by the thought of its demise. As I saw it, it was still needed. I wasn't ready yet to call it quits.

* * * *

On March 29, 1939, Anne Hodgkins wrote me that the executive committee of the Women's Division, in spite of its four representatives voting for the AAHPER proposals, refused to go along with the joint WD—AAHPER committee on the plan for a merger and that acceptance of its plan was now out of consideration. She added that she now also felt that unless WD could come to an agreement with NSWA on standards, it should close doors and let its work of the past 16 years stand on its own merits. In a separate enclosure, Anne said the WD executive committee was asking me as a member of the board of directors who definitely intended to attend the San Francisco AAHPER convention, to be its official representative at AAHPER Legislative Council meetings and to hold its proxy. I was also to seek conferences with the AAHPER president and the NSWA chairman and in WD's behalf arrive at whatever decision would be in its best interest. She assured me that my advice would be honored, but added: "Do protect the vested interest of WD members in the standards for all women's sports which they have drawn up and promulgated for all these years." With a "best of luck but do hold your own," she concluded the letter.

That final "do hold your own" worried me. I realized that any final settlement about standards agreeable to both groups had to be a compromise, and knowing that some of the members of the WD executive committee would adamantly insist that their version of standards not be tampered with, any compromise I agreed to would be interpreted as not holding my own. I was not bound by any predetermined stand on WD's behalf so I accepted the assignment and prayed for guidance, for I knew there were hotheads and iron wills to deal with both sides. One ray of hope was the knowledge that the NSWA chairman who accosted me so rudely the year before in Atlanta no longer held that position. Her successor, no matter who she was could not possibly be a more difficult person to deal with. As a matter of fact, it turned out that she was a reasonable person although it soon became evident that she was under the thumb of older persons who were dictating to her behind the scenes.

Why me? Why pick on me for this task that most certainly would be difficult and probably unpleasant? I understood that whoever represented the Women's Division should be a professional rather than a lay member. On the WD board of directors at this time the 12 seats were divided evenly between lay women prominent in community life on the national level (the one most generally known, Mrs. Lillian Gilbreth) and physical educators. The latter six were Vera Barger, Germaine Guiot, Ethel Perrin, Agnes Wayman, Eva Whiting White and I. Most of the other women were wives of men prominent in national affairs and were women active in national women's movements who could wield considerable influence in many directions. Of the professional members the only person who could be counted to attend the AAHPER convention was the one who was a committee member by virtue of her being the chairman of NSWA. Naturally she would be that group's spokesman. So the task clearly fell to me.

Anne's letter arrived just a few days before I was leaving for San Francisco. It was followed by a long-distance call informing me that Mr. Hoover had been appraised of my appointment and approved it. There was nothing to do but accept.

Almost immediately I received a letter from AAHPER President Frederick Cozens, saying that he had been asked by WD to appoint a new committee to reconsider a merger of WD with AAHPER, a committee that would give the matter more careful study than did the first one and submit recommendations. WD also had informed him that I would serve as their official representative in any discussions that would take place at San Francisco between WD and AAHPER and/or NSWA. He added that he hoped I could arrive a day early so that as acting president of the American Academy of Physical Education I could accompany him to an interview with the mayor of San Francisco to receive the keys to the city before the opening of our two conventions.

When I asked permission of Chancellor Boucher to leave a day earlier than planned, telling him about Mayor Rossi, he was highly amused and declared it to be a refreshing alibi over the old excuse of a grandmother's funeral. All the way to California, I wondered just what was back of Fred Cozens getting me out there a day early. I knew him well enough to know Mayor Rossi alone would not have that big a pull.

I settled down and enjoyed the long cross-continent trip on the magnificent Union Pacific train. The famous "flyers" were the only means of fast transportation yet known to most of the traveling public. The

298

first-class facilities were excellent, the meals enjoyable, and for excitement one was sure to encounter at least one celebrity on every trip.

It was no surprise the next morning when I arrived to find that Fred had used the call on the mayor as an excuse to get me to town early so we could have a secret talk about WD and NSWA affairs alone before too many other things claimed his attention.

At Mayor Rossi's office we received a warm welcome. Fred was handed the keys of the city and I was presented an armful of gorgeous red roses. A photographer took pictures of the three of us. Then the mayor escorted us to a balcony from which we could see the beautiful formal gardens of City Hall, after which he called for a secretary to bring him the city budget he was working on. He pointed out some of the highlights of the city costs and inquired how politics were going in Nebraska. In fact he even teased me a bit about them, though I have long forgotten what politics were boiling just then in Nebraska. Then Fred and I dashed back to the hotel for our secret conference.

A letter from WD was awaiting each of us at the hotel—a last-minute communication to the president of AAHPER, with a copy to me, dated March 22. It offered new proposals for a merger to replace the earlier ones arrived at in New York City which WD in the end refused to go along with.

Apparently word that WD representatives had met with an AAHPER committee on March 10 to discuss a possible merger with WD to be recognized as the standards-setter for girls and women's sports had gotten around the country by some grapevine, for President Cozens had been bombarded with letters protesting such a move. He showed me a folder full of letters from NSWA members protesting any plan for AAHPER to take over the Women's Division. They wanted it to be absorbed by NSWA itself and placed completely under its jurisdiction. Some even went so far as to beg him not to allow representatives of WD to confer with him. He read to me many of the letters, unwarranted attacks on the good intentions and integrity of the leaders in the Women's Division.

I was distressed to see for myself how deep was the dislike of so many women for other women working in the same cause on behalf of girls' sports in America. These letters smacked of jealousy, unjustified rancor, and a meanness of spirit that sickened Fred Cozens and me.

"What a pass have we come to?" I asked Fred after he had read several of these letters to me.

"What is the matter with women, not just NSWA women?" he

replied. He reminded me that it had been at the request of the Women's Division itself that he had appointed a committee to meet with members of their executive committee, and the WD had asked the committee to approve a merger of WD with AAHPER. After plans had been drawn up and the committee had approved it and was ready to present the request to AAHPER for final decision, the WD's executive committee had decided it could not accept the plan after all—this after AAHPER had sent a representative from Washington to New York City to confer with them and had wasted much time and effort and some money on the meeting.

"They, too, seem to be a temperamental bunch, not sure of what they want," he added, and then he asked me to brief him about the work of the Women's Division and tell him what I knew of the conflict with NSWA.

"I fear the fate of the Women's Division is sealed," I said to Fred. "The handwriting is on the wall. We might as well face it. In light of the Women's Division's financial straits and our desire to hold onto its standards as long as possible, we have to do a lot of compromising with NSWA and it is being very difficult to deal with."

"There can be no other decision as I see it," he replied gloomily. "You are surely caught on the horns of a dilemma."

"But," I added, "maybe if the NSWA chairman and I could get together alone, we two just might be able to come to some mutually acceptable agreement. We might even between us think of an altogether different solution from anything considered thus far by either side."

So I asked him to go ahead and do what WD was now suggesting, namely, "appoint a new committee to give the matter careful study and submit their recommendations to the AAHPER Council for vote." This he consented to do at once.

"I'll tell the NSWA chairman that you and she are both to be on the committee and that I want the two of you to get together as quickly as possible for a conference to get discussions started while I am getting the complete committee organized and deciding who I want to serve as chairman," he added. But this was easier said than done.

The full story of Frederick Cozens' and my efforts to bring NSWA to the conference table, even to get the NSWA chairman to talk with me alone, is almost unbelievable. After a three-day merry-go-round, day and evening, she avoided a meeting with me, willing to talk only when I had speaking engagements which were listed on the convention program. Finally I pinned her down to a date when she said she would see me and would bring two advisers with her. I reminded her that President Cozens had asked that we meet alone, at which she gave in and came to my room alone.

When we did get down to discussing the problem, at every point she kept insisting she must return to her room "to think it over." I knew this meant her "advisers" were in her room to learn what we were talking about and to tell her what she should say, as if she had to be protected from me. Then when we finally did get together on a joint statement to present to the president's committee for consideration and when a date was set for that committee to meet—NSWA's maneuvering killing another two days—the NSWA representative sent word at the eleventh hour she couldn't meet with the committee. (We learned later that she and the other NSWA representatives, suggested by her and appointed to that committee by President Cozens, decided to go to some college nearby to play hockey.)

For six days I had been given the brush-off, but I managed to set another hour and held NSWA to a promise to honor it without fail.[4] Thus we did belatedly get in a meeting and decided upon a proposal to submit to the AAHPER board—later by mail since NSWA's delaying tactics had held up our meeting until the last board meeting was over.

I knew there were diehards in the WD group as well as in the NSWA group, and I dreaded having to persuade them that they must accept a compromise. Never before or since have I encountered people who said they would talk with me but constantly refused to do so. Along with all this, I had four speeches to deliver within those few days and to preside at meetings of the American Academy of Physical Education which were held in conjunction with the AAHPER convention.

* * * *

There were compensations for serving as WD's representative that far outweighed the worries, chief among them a wonderful afternoon with Mrs. Herbert Hoover in her home in Palo Alto which came about in this way. The Women's Division put on a lovely banquet in San Francisco during the AAHPER convention in honor of Mrs. Hoover, its founder. She had been informed by the New York City office that I was to be the official WD representative for merger negotiations at the AAHPER convention. I was also to be one of the speakers at the WD banquet in her honor.

Neils Neilson had been appointed her official escort to San Francisco that evening. Eager to learn first-hand what form negotiations between NSWA and WD might be taking by that date, Mrs. Hoover asked Neils to inform me that she wished to speak with me at the close of the banquet. At that time she had asked that someone bring me to her home for a full afternoon of talk. Neils offered to see that I got there. I thus had an opportunity to tell her fully what I hoped to accomplish in behalf of the Women's Division in its troubles, but I carefully avoided letting her know of the uncooperative behavior of the NSWA representatives or of the emotional attitudes of some of the WD people with whom I was trying to keep in contact. I was ashamed to have Mrs. Hoover know of the smallness of some of our physical education women who, immature adults, could not face difficulties objectively. So as we sat together on the floor of the family room and helped her grandchildren cut out paper dolls, I told Mrs. Hoover of proposals to be presented to AAHPER for consideration. I felt more than rewarded for all the worries and inconveniences of the previous few days when she told me she felt that in light of its difficulties, my task was well done in behalf of the Women's Division.

As it was now spring vacation at the University of Nebraska, an entire week lay before me without professional commitments. The time was my own until the convention of the Athletic Federation of College Women at the University of California, Berkeley the following week, when I was to serve as sponsor of the University of Nebraska delegation. So I visited Los Angeles for a happy reunion with friends of Centerville and Coe College years who were living there. It was a most welcome breather from the strenuous days just passed.

I did manage to get off a long detailed report of my labors in the Division's behalf as quickly as possible to the WD national office. I warned them to expect a compromise solution but that Mrs. Hoover had approved it, considering the circumstances. For three full months I was left on tenterhooks. Not even an acknowledgement that my letter had been received, let alone a "thank you for your efforts." Finally in late summer came a curt reply which said in conclusion:

> I am completely stunned over the final draft [of the Committee report] .... Our great mission has been to set standards not work with the community .... We haven't a leg left to stand upon ....
> I wish something worthwhile might have come from your labors.

I had worn myself out trying to save what I reasonably could from the wreckage for them! Mrs. Hoover had congratulated me on "a job well done," recognizing the circumstances that prevented WD from having its own wishes fulfilled. Logic and reason had been on the

NSWA side even though several of its leaders had been emotionally unreasonable about it.

True enough, the Woman's Division, a lay organization, had been the first in all the country to produce national standards for sports for girls and women, and it was lucky that the lay organization had recognized that this was a task for the professional physical educators and had entrusted it wholly to them, doubly lucky in that these members were the profession's most notable leaders of the 1920s when the Women's Division platform had been written. But 15 years later there was a group within our professional organization (NSWA) of a younger generation of leaders who pointed out the logic that the profession itself, not a lay organization, should set such standards and proceeded to do so. There would probably never have been a rift between these groups had the two sets of standards been in accord; had they been, WD would probably have gracefully withdrawn its standards and confined its work to promoting the standards among lay groups—community service, I had unfortunately labelled it. Upon this premise the AAHPER committee had built its plans for a merger. The WD executive committee wrote me over three months later: "Our great mission has been to set standards *not work with the community*." (Italics are mine.) So it had been utterly impossible to make the new leaders of WD see that golden opportunity for reaching out into the lay world. In the end, the Women's Division repudiated this second plan for a merger made in all good faith by AAHPER. All our efforts had been in vain! Never did I feel so futile!

* * * *

Neils Neilson, executive secretary of AAHPER, had been the soul of patience. With the blessing of Margaret Bell (the new AAHPER president since the 1939 convention), he began negotiations once more to try to save something from the wreckage since WD would certainly have to close its doors shortly or find a sheltering organization to take it in. Its executive committee, which apparently had power to act, was being most unreasonable, refusing to look reality in the face and making it difficult for anyone to help it.

By late September, the executive committee apparently was having second thoughts for Neils Neilson wrote me on September 27 that he was having renewed conferences with the new chairman of that group. By October, the executive committee was offering new suggestions of its own to AAHPER, and as of November 7, 1939, it submitted to AAHPER four proposals for a merger, proposing to turn over its group memberships to AAHPER. On May 1, 1940, the executive committee and board of directors of WD asked its members for approval of a merger with AAHPER with no mention of any tie with NSWA. The vote was favorable. Then WD turned over its records to AAHPER and quietly passed out of existence.

For 16 years the Women's Division had done a magnificent job of setting standards for girls and women's sports in America but its good angels, President and Mrs. Herbert Hoover, could finance it no longer; nor could AAHPER take on such a responsibility. The leadership of its early years had given way to a new and younger group of leaders who could not hold their own against the younger and militant leaders in NSWA who were jealous of WD's position and challenged its right to set standards.

As a dying gesture, Alice Sefton, one of the members of the last WD executive committee, wrote the history of the organization which was published by Stanford University Press and dedicated "With Deep Affection and Sincere Appreciation To Our Founder, First Chairman and Permanent Honorary Chairman, Lou Henry Hoover." This book stands as a fitting monument to an organization born of high ideals and lofty purposes in behalf of the very best for girls and women of America in their pursuit of sports—an organization that was in the end one of many victims of the Depression of the 1930s. It came to an end still clinging to its noble slogan: "A sport for every girl and every girl in a sport."

The details of this story are known today to only a few people still living. The real story of the demise of the Women's Division, aside from its financial difficulties, is a story of the willful, obstinate behavior of a small group of women on each side of the conflict. In the end there was a sad clash of personalities that made negotiations difficult—a far cry from the noble beginnings of both groups.

Twenty years later, the Women's Division and its splendid work was largely forgotten within the profession. Thirty years later, a few graduate students are trying to resurrect its story as a graduate thesis topic with little help other than Alice Sefton's book of the Women's Division's successful and fruitful years.[5] Would that it had been a happy-ending story—the story that picks up where Alice Sefton's book ends—the part of the story I knew first-hand as only a few others did.

In the end, WD did just what, to its dismay, Jay B. Nash had suggested in the first place and which many of us came to see was the only solution. Seeking no further affiliation, it closed shop, resting on the laurels of its early years. It had filled a real need of the twenties and thirties. Its records and its archival materials were presented to AAHPER and they now make up a collection in that organization's archives.

Bitterness toward me, engendered at this time by a few women working both in the NSWA and WD, followed me for several years, and no doubt followed others too. But my conscience was clear! I did the best I knew to do in a hopeless situation.

* * * *

The 1930s were difficult and tiring years yet full of rich experiences. I had devoted a great deal of my energies and time, beyond my work at Nebraska, to several professional organizations not only on the state and district levels but largely on the national level.

If the courtesies bestowed upon me by my national professional association and later by Chancellor Boucher by his appointment of me to his Dean's Administrative Council were silver linings to my clouds in the Depression years, there were two other never-to-be-forgotten experiences of those years which have clung to my memory as bright stars. One was the pleasure of standing at General Pershing's left with his sister, May, at his right, Governor Charles Bryan next to May and Chancellor Burnett next to me, one December evening as the general "reviewed the troops" at the University of Nebraska Military Ball, following which the Pershing Rifles did a breathtaking precision drill in the general's honor.

The second was the afternoon in April 1939 when, as a guest of Mrs. Hoover in her home, we discussed the protection of high standards for the future development of sports for girls and women of America. Such experiences were a crowning glory to a worrisome decade.

Chapter XVI

Another World War and
A Call for Physical Fitness

Ever since the Great War of 1914-1918, Germany had been trying to evade or revise the postwar peace terms imposed upon it. There had ensued crisis after crisis, resulting in German reoccupation of the Rhineland in March 1936, leading to Germany's attack on Poland of September 1, 1939. Two days later, England and France declared war on Germany and the Second World War was on.

As early as 1935 the American Council on Education, made up of national education associations and institutions, had created the American Youth Commission to study the needs of youth and to publicize and promote plans of action in their behalf. The commission was non-partisan, non-sectarian and non-governmental. At its beginning it had 15 members with Owen D. Young, one of America's leading citizens, serving as chairman. Serving under him were the presidents of the University of Wisconsin and Harvard University, the dean of Teachers College, Columbia University, the U.S. Commissioner of Education, the president of the American Council on Education, the executive secretary of the National Education Association, and other notables.

In October 1939 Owen Young called the American Youth Commission together "to consider the needs of youth in the light of the new situation resulting from the outbreak of war abroad." At that time he prepared a statement, "A Program of Action for American Youth." In June 1940, one month after the fall of France, the commissioner issued a bulletin, "Youth, Defense and the National Welfare," in which, acknowledging the need for conscription, the obligation of the state to youth was pointed out calling upon all citizens to serve in the common defense of the nation and to assume "full responsibility for the provision of adequate economic, educational, health and recreational conditions for youth."[1]

At this same time, Dr. Hiram Jones of the New York State Department of Public Instruction and president of AAHPER appointed a Committee on Legislation and Preparedness to draw up plans for action by AAHPER. The U.S. Office of Education, the National Education Association and other related groups joined forces with this committee and drafted a bill which was introduced in the House of Representatives,[2] calling for the "promotion of national preparedness and welfare through the appropriation of funds to assist the states in making adequate provision for health education, physical education and recreation in schools and school camps."

In January 1941, the American Youth Commission issued a long statement calling for immediate attention to the physical conditioning of all citizens in behalf of national defense and national welfare. It called for curtailment of interscholastic sports in favor of all-out intramural programs for all children. In May 1941 President Roosevelt, by Executive Order, set up the Office of Civilian Defense (OCD) with Mayor LaGuardia of New York City as its director. The OCD setup called for two divisions—the Board for Civilian Protection and a Voluntary Participation Committee. The first was under military control, and the second was divided into three subdivisions—Physical Fitness, Participation of Women, and Group Participation.

On my own campus, as everywhere else, tension mounted. Finally in May 1941, the University of Nebraska faculty drew up a Memorial to the President and Vice-President of the United States, the Speaker of the House, the Secretary of State, and the senators and representatives of Nebraska, begging that our government use every means at the disposal of our nation to aid the allied peoples and "not necessarily short of war."[3] I gladly signed this Memorial along with 186 other faculty members, although this action caused much consternation among many of the faculty, especially among the women.

* * * *

The Division of Physical Fitness of the OCD was to be headed by John P. Kelly, and the section on Participation of Women by Eleanor

Roosevelt. Mr. Kelly, a prominent Philadelphia citizen, was a self-made man who had achieved great financial success as a building contractor. A well-known amateur boxer in his youth, he had in 1924 won the Olympic championship for the U.S.A. in both single sculls and in double sculls. In the 1928 Olympics he won again in single sculls and with Paul Costello in double sculls. Since then he had retained a keen interest in physical fitness and became well-known nationally as a proponent of fitness.

Physical educators were not too happy over Mr. Kelly's appointment although we were glad that the President was recognizing the need for physical fitness of the citizenry. We were pleased at least that the appointment had not been political and felt that because Mr. Kelly was a physical fitness advocate and amateur sportsman, he would be wholeheartedly sold on the importance of getting our citizenry physically fit as quickly as possible.

Nine OCD regions of the country were recognized, one for each service command of the U.S. Army. The Division of Physical Fitness in each was under the person in charge of the OCD in its region. Mr. Kelly decided to establish under his direction two co-directors of physical fitness in each region, one for work with boys and men, one for girls and women. In his first bulletin he called for the use of professionally-trained persons at all top levels in the Division of Physical Fitness.

To my great surprise in late October of 1941, I received a letter from Mr. Kelly's executive assistant asking if I would be interested in an appointment as regional director of the Division of Physical Fitness in the Seventh Army Service Command, provided "Colonel Wilbur" approves. He wrote that this would be strictly volunteer service but necessary travel and related expenses would be provided through Col. Wilbur's Omaha office. I sensed at once that I was interested, so I wrote back asking for enlightenment of the questions that puzzled me. I soon learned that "Col. Wilbur" was Col. Edward LeRoy Wilbur, military head of the Office of Civilian Defense of the 7th Army Service Command covering nine central states with Omaha the headquarters.

My chancellor deprecated the idea of being able to accomplish anything "with that Kelly outfit," as he put it. Nevertheless, he was pleased to have them offer this assignment to a University of Nebraska faculty member and finally gave the appointment his begrudging blessing.

Apparently the national office had assumed that I would reply in the affirmative and had at once sent in my name to the proper authorities. Before I had even sent my acceptance, the director of the Division of Central Administrative Services of the Office for Emergency Management wrote me on October 31, stating: "At the request of Mayor Fiorello H. LaGuardia, Director of Civilian Defense, Office of Emergency Management, you are appointed as Consultant without compensation for an indefinite period, effective November 1, 1941." It was followed by information on reimbursement for necessary travel expense and asking that I return "the oath of office and personnel affidavit after proper certification by a notary public."

On November 5 I received a telegram from Mr. Kelly's office informing me that I would be co-director with Frank McCormick, director of athletics at the University of Minnesota, as physical fitness regional representative for women. I wired my acceptance of the offer and immediately word of our appointment was announced in the papers of the nine states in the Seventh Army Service Command. This gave me my first clue as to why I had been offered this appointment instead of one of the many other women of my profession of these nine states. Mr. Kelly could scarcely be expected to know who were the leading professionals in the midwest states, so I wondered who had suggested my name to him.

As soon as I learned that Frank McCormick was to be my co-worker, I suspected that I had him to thank for this appointment. The April before, he, then a stranger to me, had come to my rescue at a district convention in Fargo, North Dakota. He saved the day for me when I was speaking to an audience of men coaches and superintendents of schools on the subject of interscholastic sports for girls and was being unmercifully heckled by some of the coaches.

Mr. McCormick's selection was most understandable for besides being the director of athletics and men's physical education at the University of Minnesota and well-known in the Big Ten Conference, he had recently come into national prominence as chairman of the American Legion's Committee on Preparedness. For over a year, the Legion had been seriously at work on defense and Mr. McCormick's committee had been working ever since its first meeting in Washington in January 1941.

Even before the Division of Physical Fitness was established within the OCD, Governor Harold Stassen of Minnesota had set up a State Council of Defense and had appointed Mr. McCormick chairman of a recreation and physical education subcommittee under the Welfare and Advisory Committee of the State Council. By October 1941, this committee had already published its first bulletin, a guide to all local defense councils and groups of any kind concerned in the development of fitness and morale of the citizens.

It was not until quite some time afterward that I learned who my compatriots were in co-directorships of physical fitness in the other civilian defense areas. When I tried to get this information from the Philadelphia office so I could check with others on plans, I was informed that other women directors had not yet been appointed. So apparently Frank McCormick and I were the first regional directors of physical fitness to be appointed. We were off and running before we could get the names of any of our other co-workers at the regional level.

As I was trying desperately to get my work planned and organized and was feeling deeply frustrated by my inability to get necessary information and doors opened, I received a letter from the New York City physical fitness director of the Second Region. She asked about my plans and informed me that she had already been able to put across a performance of professional skaters in Madison Square Garden and had worked up a lot of publicity. She was planning to have a lot of parades of thousands of school children with the fire departments and other city groups involved to make them colorful. I was dumbfounded! This was far from my idea, and I was sure from Frank McCormick's and John Kelly's, too, of what a physical fitness program should be.

I sent her an outline of my first plans trying to stress tactfully that I was aiming everything at getting all American girls and women into gymnasiums, on playfields, into the byways on foot or bicycles—anything for *all* to be exercising vigorously daily instead of watching others exercise or putting on parades. I gave her a chart showing how I hoped to reach the girls and women in their homes, schools and business places through an organization that would reach from the regional level into every state and from the state level into every city, town, hamlet and farm. This must have impressed her, for I learned later that in a report to her Second Area Council she said she was interested in what a woman in Nebraska was trying to do for her defense area.

* * * *

Life was so frantically busy just then and continued so even into my retirement years that I never did hear the stories of the other women regional directors of physical fitness. If they had half the interesting experiences I did, they had plenty of rich memories for years to come. One of them later did tell me that as far as she knew (also as far as I knew), I was the only one of the group who was handed a government railroad travel order book by the OCD regional director and given a blanket permit to go ahead with my work as I saw fit to cover the states in my area as frequently as I felt necessary.

The next few months were one wild scramble. Up to then I was quite ignorant of the ways of politics and government bureaucracy, but I had a real baptism by fire. Fortunately I was assigned to a regional civilian defense director who was deeply interested in the division of physical fitness and supported Frank McCormick and me for all our plans. In fact, in the first few weeks I was on the job I worked under three regional civilian defense directors. The first, Col. Wilbur who served until a civilian replacement was named when he became liaison between the regional defense council and the Armed Services; the second, Bert Murphy, a prominent Omaha businessman, served only a few weeks in December 1941, then resigned because of pressure of personal business; the third, Joseph D. Scholtz, a former mayor of Louisville, Kentucky, was sent into the region by Mayor LaGuardia to step things up in this corps area. All were most friendly, cooperative and sincere about the need to promote a physical fitness program.

Mr. Murphy, sensing that I was a babe in the political world, warned me that as a regional director I was to work directly with state directors, not the local ones except on invitation or advance approval of the state director. Upon entering a state to do my physical fitness organizational work, I must first pay a courtesy call on the governor, then the state director of civilian defense, then the state director of physical fitness if appointed and if not, ask the governor with whom I could work.

This advice to approach no local group except through the state physical fitness director was a ticklish point, for immediately after my appointment was publicized, local groups in my region such as women's clubs, recreation groups and school groups from four states in particular, began inviting me to their communities to help set up physical fitness programs. All these had to be informed that they should work through their state directors of physical fitness, and if they did not have such an officer, to go to their state civilian defense council and ask that one be appointed. In the end, since the grassroots people were eager to get started, much of my time was spent in four states— Arkansas, Missouri, Kansas and Iowa—conferring with groups at the local level in the larger cities but in each instance only on invitation of the state physical fitness director and, in many instances, through state conferences on physical fitness which state civilian defense directors had convened.

The first meeting with Frank McCormick was on November 30 in Chicago instead of within our own region. As co-directors of physical fitness we wanted his plans for boys and men and mine for girls and women to be in complete accord and were delighted to find that we were in instant agreement on all levels.

We had our conference at the Chicago Executive Office of the Big Ten Commissioner of Athletics. Before we completed our work, Dr. Coleman Griffith of the University of Illinois, psychologist and director of research in athletics, and also commissioner of athletics for the Big Ten Conference, dropped in. We went over our plans with him for a first critical questioning. He approved and gave his blessing, making us feel as if our plans were officially launched. We now had to present them to our regional OCD director for approval. We had no worries about Mr. Kelly's go-ahead orders.

The following day, on the way home, I stopped off at Iowa City on the morning train to spend the afternoon at the University of Iowa conferring with Dr. C.H. McCloy, who as research specialist in the Child Welfare Department was recognized as one of the nation's leading experts on physical fitness. A professional friend of many years standing, he was glad to review the plans for our regional program. He too added his approval and blessing. Then the women's physical education department, having heard I was in town, rounded up its staff and majors for an informal talk and I had my first chance to go over the plans with college girls preparing to enter the profession of physical education. I also talked with a student committee on recreation which had been organized within the University's Women's Association as one project of their college program in National Defense. This last group had been in touch with me by mail. Now we were able to have an unexpected person-to-person chat about their plans to aid in defense through promotion of a recreation program.

Although we were not yet drawn into the war, these Iowa college girls were organized and on the move for national defense. Nebraska girls, as individuals, had immediately rushed to my office to ask what they could do to help, but as far as women's organizations were concerned, the Nebraska campus had not yet awakened to opportunities in national defense in any aspects.

Six days later (December 7, 1941), Japan made a surprise attack on Pearl Harbor. The day after that the United States declared war on

312

Japan, and the day after that Germany declared war on the United States. We were at last into it! Now with the western hemisphere at war as well as Asia and Europe, this new world conflict gave the Great War of 1914-1918 a new name—World War I, as we were now settling into World War II.

The day after Pearl Harbor, Lincoln's Mayor Johnson set up a local Civilian Defense Council, calling a public meeting for that evening at city hall. I attended and learned that there was already a State Civilian Defense Council organized with a Lincoln citizen, Wade Martin, serving as its executive vice-president. Spotted in the audience as one of the regional council members (the state and local papers had only the week before carried the news of my appointment), I was called upon for some remarks. I took the occasion to urge the local defense council to give the women of the community civilian opportunities to serve in this war effort.

It seemed that as far as Lincoln was concerned, every man's organization was eager to help and had sent representatives to this meeting, but the women and their organizations were conspicuously absent, perhaps from the age-old belief that war was exclusively man's concern. But I rejected this thought, feeling that the men of Nebraska, as men every place else, were not yet alert that we were living in a new day in which most women desired to stand side by side with men and do their share in the world's work if only doors were opened to them.

Following this, Mayor Johnson invited me to attend the Lincoln Defense Council meetings in the interest of physical fitness of the citizenry for the emergency, but since I was swamped with my university position plus the regional work, I urged him to name someone to head this work for women who would be a bona fide member of his defense council and who would represent Lincoln on a state group.

Mr. McCormick's and my joint report of plans for a physical fitness program for the Seventh Army Service Command was sent to Mr. Kelly at once. A few days later I received copies of letters sent from his office to the governors and heads of state defense councils in all nine states of our region, specifically introducing Mr. McCormick and me as his representatives for physical fitness work in this region. He also stated that he would be grateful for any assistance they might give us in setting up the physical fitness program in their state under their council of defense. We were at last ready to go to work.

* * * *

313

Almost immediately upon the creation of the OCD and its subdivisions, the Division of Physical Fitness became embroiled in a lot of unpleasantness involving Mrs. Roosevelt and her attempts to intrude in the women's physical fitness work. As head, under LaGuardia, of the Division of Participation of Women she evidently interpreted her duties as being in charge also of women who volunteered to work under Mr. Kelly in his Division of Physical Fitness. Accordingly, out of a clear sky and apparently unknown to Mr. Kelly, she announced to the public that she had appointed Miss Mayris Chaney as head of women's physical fitness work. Miss Chaney, a young woman who had a dance studio in Washington, D.C., was a personal friend of Mrs. Roosevelt.

Although Mr. Kelly did not claim her as a member of his staff, the entire nation was well aware of her; newspapers throughout the country, particularly those of Republican leanings, were having a heyday poking fun at the idea of a social dance teacher heading the physical fitness program for the girls and women of the nation. When it was ferreted out that Miss Chaney was drawing quite a nice salary for this work, the papers seized upon it with great gusto, for all OCD work was supposed to be volunteer (as indeed it was for everyone else in it). We women, in particular, working in the physical education field, were doubly incensed to learn that not only did we have foisted on us one who was totally inadequate for the task but also one who, despite her inadequacy, was to receive a good salary.

Perhaps it is doing Mrs. Roosevelt a disservice in intimating that she was using this important position to offer a nice financial plum to a friend. Be that as it may, Mrs. Roosevelt stands accused anyway of another mistake in thinking for one moment that a woman who had absolutely no training in physical education, sports or even dance other than ballroom, could know enough to head up such work on behalf of a country caught up in war emergencies.

The more the First Lady was attacked and ridiculed about this appointment the more it became difficult to learn anything about Miss Chaney's possible talents that might recommend her for such an important appointment. She was not even a wealthy socialite of the Democrat party as an excuse for such an appointment. Never was Miss Chaney listed as a member of Mr. Kelly's staff in any capacity—at least not in any material sent out to regional directors.

Finding no other haven for her after her resignation forced by the great hue and cry against her in newspapers all over the country, Mrs. Roosevelt once more forced Miss Chaney upon the OCD as director of children's activities, thus tossing her directly into Mayor LaGuardia's bailiwick. Ultimately he, too, got rid of her, but not without great embarrassment since it meant opposing the President's wife.

A bit of good came from this faux pas of Mrs. Roosevelt. After the flare-up, Mr. Kelly did create an official position under him of Director of Women's Physical Fitness and appointed Alice Marble, the international tennis champion. It was a volunteer position which Miss Marble filled as a splendid public relations person for the cause of physical fitness.

But if Mayor LaGuardia had grief with Miss Chaney, it was nothing compared to later difficulties over OCD affairs which multiplied and stirred up contention in so many directions that on February 10, 1942 he finally resigned the OCD post and was replaced by James L. Landis, dean of Harvard Law School and noted troubleshooter for FDR. On February 20 Mrs. Roosevelt also resigned her post in the OCD.

* * * *

The national program of physical fitness was supposed to function through the nine regional offices with a man and a woman appointed to serve as regional co-directors in each office. In the First Region, Daniel Kelly of Boston and Ruth Evans of the Springfield, Massachusetts Public Schools served for Maine, Massachusetts, New Hampshire, Rhode Island, Connecticut, and Vermont; in the Second Region, William Saunders and Mrs. Kenneth Ives of New York City, for Delaware, New Jersey and New York; in the Third Region, Louis Burnett of Baltimore Public Schools and Lillian Davis for Maryland, Pennsylvania and Virginia plus the District of Columbia; in the Fourth Region, O.K. Cornwell of the University of North Carolina and Fannie B. Shaw of the University of Florida for Alabama, Florida, Georgia, Louisiana, Mississippi, North Carolina, South Carolina and Tennessee; in the Fifth Region, Delbert Oberteuffer and Gladys Palmer, both of Ohio State University for Indiana, Kentucky, Ohio and West Virginia; in the Sixth Region, Carl Stockholm of Chicago and Margaret Bell, of the State University of Michigan for Illinois, Michigan and Wisconsin; in the Seventh Region, Frank McCormick of the University of Minnesota and I of the University of Nebraska for Arkansas, Iowa, Kansas, Minnesota, Missouri, Nebraska, North Dakota, South Dakota and Wyoming; in the Eighth Region, Harry Scott of Rice Institute and Gertrude Mooney of the University of Texas for Arizona, Colorado, New Mexico, Oklahoma and Texas, and in the Ninth Region, Charles

W. Davis of the San Francisco Public Schools and Louise Cobb of the University of California (Berkeley) for California, Idaho, Montana, Nevada, Oregon, Utah, and Washington, with Alaska as an extra.

Of these 18 physical fitness directors, 16 of us were from the field of physical education, and 10 of these in physical education were friends of mine. So John Kelly did see that the profession of physical education was drawn into his program on the regional level.

Later the majority of states that did get state physical fitness directors appointed drew heavily upon our profession. Outstanding among these were Dr. Prohaska of Connecticut, Mrs. Aldrich of Vermont, George Ayers of Delaware, Hiram Jones of New York, Elliot V. Graves of Virginia, Jessie Garrison of Alabama, Simon McNeely of Louisiana, Charles Spencer of North Carolina, Seward C. Staley of Illinois, Robert Nohr, Jr. of Wisconsin, Wilma Haynes of Missouri, C.S. Blackburn of Arkansas, D.K. Brace of Texas, Frank R. Williams of Arizona, Hal Orion of California, Bernice Moss of Utah, Dean Leighton of Oregon. Nearly all of them were friends of mine and most were from State Departments of Education.

On December 17, Alice Marble met with the Sixth Region group on her way to Omaha and San Francisco. On January 3, 1942, the head of publicity from the national office, and on January 13 John Da-Grossa, head of the Sports Board, met with them. With the aid of Arthur Steinhaus and his physical education staff at George Williams College, they had a course in physical conditioning under plans for publication. Never did anyone from the national office except Alice Marble visit our Seventh Region. However, we were at work by the time of our first conference November 30, 1941.

By December 9 the Third Region made its start to organize the physical fitness program; by December 19, the Second; by December 20, the Eighth; and by December 23, the Ninth with Alice Marble meeting with them. All regional programs were underway before New Year's Day of 1942 except the First, Fourth, and Fifth Areas where the regional directors were not confirmed until later. When the First region did get started in early January it got off to a well-publicized start with a banquet held in Boston with 600 in attendance including many sports celebrities.

In the Midwest we avoided the spectacular and instead tried to set up a program that would reach all school children, college age youth and adults—all aimed at participation, not "spectatoritis."

Almost at once after public announcement of my appointment in the Division of Physical Fitness, I was beseiged by many people hopeful that there were pay positions in the national or regional office. How little they knew that this was to be wholly a volunteer project. I also received several crank letters that the Regional Office of Civilian Defense advised me to turn over to the FBI, also, as probably happened to the other women directors of physical fitness, several proposals of marriage no doubt prompted by my publicity picture in the papers. These I hastily destroyed.

To be a member of the Regional OCD staff proved a most interesting experience, for whereas my professional work threw me almost exclusively with educators, I now was thrown with men of the armed services, politicians, a cross-section of business and professional men, and a few business and professional women.

Mr. Murphy shortly called all of us assigned to his OCD staff to his Omaha office. The military group explained plans for military defense of our nine states, particularly of highways, railroads and factories against possible sabotage. Other group heads reported on their plans for use of volunteers for defense. Frank McCormick and I presented our plans for organizing strenuous exercise and sports activities to reach people of all ages and walks of life. With gasoline rationing seriously under consideration, I made a plea for all present to take to bicycles to set an example of gas-saving, informing them that I had an order in for a wheel for myself. I also urged them to get and keep physically fit and to urge others to do the same. There was much enthusiasm for all plans presented.

Frank McCormick suggested that since his home state, Minnesota, was already well organized on both the men's and women's level, thanks to the head start through the American Legion project, it would be most agreeable with him if I would first organize both the men's and women's program in Nebraska, and then we could use the programs of our two home states as models. This I gladly consented to do.

Of all the nine regions, none had as many states assigned to it as the Seventh, which meant that Frank McCormick and I had nine state programs to set up, nine Governors and nine State Councils of Defense to deal with, to only three each for three regions, and four to eight for the other five. Nor had any other region as many lower schools, public colleges and universities (114). And, except for the Fourth Region with 199, no other region had as many private colleges and universities as our Seventh with 162. In all, there were 71,662 public and private elementary and high schools in the Seventh Region, serving over 3½ million pupils. These pupils comprised 13 percent of the nation's lower school population. Although this region had more schools, it ranked fifth of all the nine regions in total pupil population, meaning that it had more schools of small enrollment than did the other four ranked above it.

A brief glance at these figures, which I put together from statistics about the U.S. population and its schools sent to me from Mr. Kelly's office shortly after my appointment, quite took my breath away. How could we reach even a fraction of these children to get them physically fit, especially the high school boys and girls, and quickly? Beyond these were all the adults who would be needed in industry and all other war-related work and others to "keep the home fires burning," all of whom should be fit too. It seemed an impossible task. Where to begin? And then I recalled my mother's oft-repeated advice, "Divide and conquer." (When the war was over, the whole world came to see that it had been Hitler's motto, too.) I realized that this job, parcelled out region by region, could be tackled within each region, state by state. Then each state committee could break it down into local units, down to where the people were whom we needed to reach. Each local unit could then do the actual job piece by piece.

* * * *

With high hopes and much enthusiasm, encouraged by the enthusiasm of Lincoln's mayor and by my own desire to get things moving, I asked for a conference with Nebraska's governor, Dwight Griswold, only four days following Pearl Harbor. Mr. Kelly had sent the governor a telegram three days earlier, asking that he give "his cooperation in behalf of the Hale America program instituted through the physical fitness representatives working out of the regional defense headquarters" but not naming me specifically as one of the representatives. I felt that surely my word for it was sufficient that I was coming to see the governor not as a member of the state university faculty, but as Mr. Kelly's representative.

However, I was told firmly that the governor was too busy with important things to give me time, nor would he give me an appointment for a future date. Having made this gesture of courtesy, I decided that, although rebuffed, I was free then to seek a conference with the director of the state health department, Dr. A. L. Miller, whom the governor had appointed as head of the Health, Welfare and Consumer Section of the State Defense Council. Physical fitness and recreation were among his responsibilities. But here, too, although the door was not closed to me, the welcome was slightly chilly. Later, when the chart

318

for state defense organization was published, I found many organizations listed to aid Dr. Miller, such as county health offices, county medical societies, but no mention of physical education, sports or recreation groups. Apparently the state concern for physical fitness was limited to the medical aspects only.

At my first conference with a state-appointed head of physical fitness I was given only a few minutes and these mostly were filled with his denunciation of Mrs. Roosevelt and her dance friend. I told him that we physical educators also were dismayed and that Miss Chaney had been removed from the program, at which he countered: "What? With a young girl who plays a good game of tennis?" The news had just broken that Alice Marble had been appointed as Mr. Kelly's assistant director in charge of women's physical fitness.

I assured him that only professionally-trained persons were to be appointed as regional directors of physical fitness and that the actual physical fitness program was to be set up at the grassroots level, not the national level. The state director of health was unimpressed. To my dismay he told me he had no more time to talk and that I was wasting my time on this project. Didn't I realize that physical fitness is entirely the responsibility of the medical profession? With this I was politely but firmly dismissed.

Since Nebraska was one of the few states, despite repeated efforts of various state groups, without a directorship of health and physical education in its state department of education, which should now take over the work of wartime emphasis on fitness, I had hoped to make a start in getting a state director of physical fitness appointed under Dr. Miller. With these two rebuffs I recalled the rebuff I had suffered 10 years earlier from Governor Charles Bryan when I had led a statewide organization attempting to secure a state director of physical education. So the climate toward physical education hadn't changed in 10 years, even now under a Republican governor. I also recalled recent unfavorable reports in midwest papers of Mayor LaGuardia's attempt to stir up interest in civilian defense at a meeting of midwest governors. According to the newspaper reports, La Guardia had received a cool reception from the Middle West.

This high wall of resistance could be a real obstacle when it came from governors and medical doctors in high state positions. I called Frank McCormick to ask what he thought. As to the medics, he replied:

"Oh! I didn't think to warn you that you might encounter this very thing within medical circles, but don't let it bother you! We have the unqualified support of much of that profession."

319

After this opening experience in my own state, even my hometown where the welcome mat was decidedly not out, except in the mayor's office, I decided to try another state and give Nebraska time to cool off. Shortly, I learned that because of my appointment to this position I was immediately suspected of being a loyal Democrat and was therefore one to be rebuffed by loyal Republicans. This amused me for I had always voted Republican. I was dismayed that Americans would, in wartime, place politics above doing work in defense of our nation. As it turned out, Nebraska was the only state in my region where I was not given a warm welcome by everyone I needed to contact from the governor down—well, that is, by everyone else but the governor of Iowa, who finally did open doors for me once he learned I was a Republican.

* * * *

These rebuffs in Nebraska were soon forgotten when Mr. Murphy called a surprise meeting of his Regional Civilian Defense Council for December 19-20, 1941 in Omaha, when Alice Marble would visit the regional office and meet with Omaha welfare groups. I was informed that hotel accommodations were being held for me with the thought that I would wish to spend the night there for as much time as possible to confer with Miss Marble and Mr. McCormick on physical fitness work. This was welcome news for I was chafing at the bit over the delays of getting work underway. I drew up three whole pages of questions to ask Miss Marble on procedures for our work. I scheduled the weekend in Omaha with high hopes.

Miss Marble's visit turned the weekend into a gala event for not only was she a national sports figure but also a charming and attractive person. Everyone, it seemed, wished to see and entertain her. As her counterpart for fitness work at the regional level, I was included in the festivities. Sandwiched among a luncheon, an afternoon reception and a dinner party in her honor were the Council meeting and a visit to Boys Town.

It was a day so full that I had not a moment to talk with Miss Marble alone. I was thus glad when her official escort informed us that because of wartime pressures they had not been able to procure two single rooms for us and hoped we wouldn't mind sharing a double room. We assured him it was all right. As it turned out, it was a boon for both of us for by bedtime we were weary and this arrangement permitted us to go to bed at once when free from engagements and thus relaxed and together we talked far into the night. Almost at once Miss Marble called across to my bed:

"Oh, Miss Lee, I'm scared stiff of this job. Please, you must help me!"

"I help you? It is you who must tell me about Mr. Kelly's plans and what the national office desires of us at the regional level."

"Oh, that! Well I can tell you quickly all that I know, but I may as well confess to you right now that I know nothing at all about physical education except to play tennis."

She told me of her girlhood wish to go to college and major in physical education with the thought of teaching but that family circumstances and the Depression had upset those plans.

"You must help me!" she called out. "What should I say to all these people when they ask me what they should do to get physically fit?"

She laughingly said she had "gotten by" that day in Omaha as she had done in other places when her scheduled talks allowed only a few moments. At Boys Town she suddenly thought to give the boys a demonstration of rope jumping instead of a speech other than opening remarks. I assured her that her remarks at the various functions had been to the point and excellently done. We both laughed at the remembrance of the hit she made at Boys Town, as well as at the luncheon and dinner. Father Flanagan had given a most ingratiating introduction at Boys Town and as Alice Marble stepped out before that roomful of young boys, an attractive young woman of superb posture, clad in the beautifully tailored blue OCD uniform with the eye-catching OCD shield of stars and stripes on the breast pocket, those boys about raised the roof in their welcoming applause. Then she spoke a few words about the importance of being physically fit in this time when our nation was at war and with sudden inspiration asked, "Would you like to see what I do to keep fit for my tennis playing?"

The room rang with shouts of "Yes, yes!" Someone was sent to fetch a jump rope and she gave a breathtaking exhibition, even in street skirt and street shoes, of a great variety of rope jumping techniques. Then she asked if many of them jumped rope at which there was a great showing of hands and shouts of "Where's Joe?" At this, Miss Marble begged to see Joe do his tricks. Finally a bashful black boy was brought to the stage and put on a demonstration that more than held its own with Miss Marble's, whereupon she suggested that Boys Town would do well to have this boy instruct all the other boys in rope jumping as a part of their own physical fitness program.

"But," said Miss Marble, "I am going to have to know more than this when I get into groups that want to get down to business and begin to ask questions I can't answer, as might well be the case tomorrow for the Omaha Welfare Society meeting. You must help me!"

So we tried to think of all the questions that might possibly be asked and I told her how I would answer each.

"You do the answering," she said. "When the question is asked, I'll turn to you and say, 'Here is an expert in this line. Let us hear what she has to say.' "

"Oh, no you don't," I exclaimed. "To the lay world I am just a fuddy-duddy school ma'am and worse still just one of their own, a citizen of their own state. They don't care a whoop what I might have to say. But you are a national figure, sent out here from our national capital. They'll drink in every word you have to say."

I finally persuaded her to accept this thought. We planned replies for what surely would be a stock set of questions. I set her straight on the subject of dancing in a physical fitness program, determined that Mrs. Roosevelt was not to have the final word on this. Apparently, Mrs. Roosevelt, still trying to defend herself for the appointment of Miss Chaney, had primed Miss Marble for when someone at the luncheon that day had asked her if she agreed with Mrs. Roosevelt that dancing is an ideal conditioner, she had replied, "Dancing is as good for physical recreation as almost anything else." I knew that to the lay world dancing meant but one thing—ballroom or social dancing.

I felt strongly that we should drop all support of this form of dance as part of a specific program to get rid of the bad name thrust upon the movement by Mrs. Roosevelt's ill-advised appointment. But, for our purposes I recognized as very valuable such dances as folk dance, square dance and modern dance, all of which give vigorous exercise and are enjoyable. I felt it important that Miss Marble recognize these forms as different from ballroom or social dance and promote them as body conditioners.

Miss Marble brought with her a six-page plan from Mr. Kelly explaining the Hale America program. She had been studying it and had a copy for me. This was the first writing I had seen of the national office's basic thinking on the program which was to be set up. I could see that it was most useful to lay workers to acquaint them with the proposed program and was delighted to discover that Frank McCormick's and my thinking was in accord with it.

Many of my questions on details of work Miss Marble could not answer because she, too, was groping about. I explained to her Frank

McCormick's and my plans at the regional level and from her pleasure I gathered that this was her first briefing from any of the nine regions. I was beginning to suspect, and later learned, that this was her first "down to business" visit to any of the nine regions.

I warned her to avoid at all costs antagonizing the medical profession and to say at every opportunity that in speaking of physical fitness she was referring to that part of fitness that could be attained through big-muscle activity and under the advice of physicians. She got the point at once.

She gave me the names of women who had been appointed to serve as regional directors of physical fitness in a few other regions. To my joy, they were of my profession, all excellent choices, and I was able to allay her qualms about the work in those regions with them at the helm.

If I didn't get my questions answered by her (I realized that her task was almost purely public relations and that I shouldn't have expected her to know the answers on organizational matters), I at least learned an important lesson—people of public acclaim can be of great publicity value for any cause if only they are persons of integrity with a certain degree of charisma and enough interest to become informed about the cause for which they are a public front. Such persons can popularize a cause far more readily than so-called eggheads who might know the fundamentals but do not know how to catch public attention. I would never again protest the political appointment of a public figure to promote a cause *if* persons with the know-how are brought in under the public figure to do the behind-the-scenes real work for the cause.

This was my only encounter with Miss Marble. She did an excellent job in getting attention for our program from a public that had to be attracted first by some glamor. Fifteen years later through a newspaper clipping from California I learned that she was in Encino, California, where she was a nurse's assistant in a doctor's office. She had done some reminiscing to the reporter about her work under Mr. Kelly relating that she had given 13,441 talks on health and sportsmanship, talking to groups ranging from 8 to 10,000 people at a time. Earlier she was fighting to break the color line in tennis.[4] She was still, all those years after her national and international championships, playing tennis for pleasure and keeping fit—quite unlike a later American woman tennis champion who gave up the sport entirely once she had won top honors. That is the difference between one who plays for the love of playing and one who plays to win honors.

* * * *

At the meeting with Miss Marble, Frank McCormick and I decided to split the states between us. He would do all the organization work for both men and women in Minnesota, Iowa and the two Dakotas, and I in the five other states, Nebraska, Wyoming, Kansas, Missouri and Arkansas. After all states were organized, he would cover my five states to check on the work for men, and I, his four states to check on the work for women. I protested at first that the men would not be too pleased to have a woman advising them, but he said, "Nonsense! Utter nonsense!"

The day before Christmas, I received a telegram from Mr. Kelly:

MAYOR LA GUARDIA HAS ASKED YOUR DIVISION TO CONDUCT CLOSE MILITARY DRILLING AND CONDITIONING EXERCISES FOR AIR WARDENS, AUXILIARY POLICE AND FIREMEN AND ALL OTHER PROTECTIVE PERSONNEL. USE PARKS, STADIUM SCHOOL YARDS AND ROPED OFF STREETS.

This meant work at the local level and our work was supposed to be done exclusively through the state defense councils who in turn would organize the local groups who would be able to move the authorities to get streets roped off for military drill and conditioning exercises. They could put pressure on the local defense councils to get the air wardens, auxiliary police and firemen out for these drills for which the local physical fitness personnel would supply volunteer leaders. All any of us regional people could do was to urge this on the various state physical fitness people who would pass the order down to the local groups, and we were still begging the proper authorities to get these persons appointed.

Mr. Kelly's office couldn't help but be fully aware, from my many letters pushing to get appointments made, that I could not fulfill his request. It was very frustrating and a waste of taxpayers' money to send out such telegrams. As time wore on I learned how unrealistic that Philadelphia office, as well as Mayor La Guardia's, was about these things. Much "hoop, hoop, hooray" but little common sense!

At one time that office sent me a thousand large posters to distribute throughout the nine states. They depicted a comely maiden, arrayed in what my conservative part of the country would consider an indecorous costume, doing some eye-catching bit of exercise proclaiming her support for the Division of Physical Fitness in behalf of the war effort. At one glance I realized that this poster would indeed call attention to our program, but would at the same time bring down one more avalanche of ridicule upon our heads. So I hid the posters in my home and when the war was over, destroyed them. Would that I had saved at least one

324

for the archives! I wonder if that poster would seem as bold today as it did then.

These unusable posters were but a drop in the bucket compared to the mimeographed materials that the Philadelphia office sent for distribution. They sent so much that for weeks on end I had my dining-room table drawn out to its fullest length, plus at times a card table or two for the overflow. In my office at the university I set up a card table and cleared the tops of my filing cabinets for these materials. Some of it I distributed by mail with help from members of the university's Women's Physical Education Club. But some of these materials were so sensational or unpractical that I considered them unusable in this section of the country. The people back East seemed to understand so little the nature of midwesterners or their views on many educational matters. So I disregarded much of the material and prepared my own materials for Mississippi and Missouri Valley consumption, and with help from my students, sent them out instead to state directors.

As to stationery, postage, mimeographing supplies and the like, never in my several months of work for the Division of Physical Fitness was I given a penny for such expenses. When Mr. Murphy, director of our region, learned of my needs, he sent a few letterheads and some postage from his office. After hearing that I was digging into my own pocket, the Woman's Athletic Association of my university offered to finance these expenses as a war contribution. In some states, the American Legion, 4-H Club or other state organizations financially assisted the state physical fitness workers. Somehow we all scraped along, got a lot of work accomplished, and paid the bills, but with no help from the budget of many thousands of dollars allocated by Congress, albeit most begrudgingly, to the Division of Physical Fitness. Presumably this money was spent only for expenses of full-time workers at the national office.

When the Division of Physical Fitness was first established for the year 1941-42, Mr. Kelly was allotted a budget of $96,000. That figure represented 1/13th of one cent per year per citizen of the USA—mere peanuts. In April 1942 he asked $300,000 for the coming (fiscal) year— $5,000 to each state and $60,000 for the national office. At this the "Economy Bloc," the Congressional faction that opposed spending for anything the President advocated, raised a great howl insinuating that all workers in the movement were to be paid salaries. They labelled them leeches and parasites and called the program a project of nothing but useless frills and boondoggling. Supporters of the budget pointed out that the Axis nations were spending many times that amount to develop fitness in their youth, also that this amount was less than one-third the cost of a grade-B Hollywood film.[5] But Senator Harry Byrd, carrying the ball for the opposition, largely won his battle and the budget remained at the former figure, wrecking plans to redistribute funds to the states.

By June 1942 the public was awakening to the need to push physical fitness programs. Things were moving in that direction in many states and enthusiastic supporters were beginning to be heard. Even the newspapers began favoring the Division and many were upbraiding Congress for its niggardly budget. By then the Division had lost its baby teeth and was growing up and becoming less flamboyant and better organized, therefore, more acceptable to the citizenry.

But the bother over finances, the concern over the strange ways of help from the national office and the ridicule of our work from some segments of the public were nothing compared to the work itself— getting things moving at the local level where the program was to be put into effect.

The grassroots had to be reached through the state level and we regional directors could do nothing until the governor of each state appointed a state director of physical fitness. To me, this policy meant political appointments of friends for whatever political value might come to them without regard to qualifications for such a task. Yet in every one of my states I knew professionally-trained persons who would be excellent for such volunteer work. If only I could make recommendations. I could have had all appointed in no time and work long ago underway. What patience it took to be tied into a political setup. Several weeks already wasted and by then we were actually at war!

But if financial aid from the national office was scarce at the regional level and nonexistent at the state level, apparently this was not the case at the national level from tales that came out of Philadelphia where the national physical fitness office was located. One person who worked there later remarked about the seeming waste of money and the unrealistic things that went on there.[6] She told me she was appalled at much of the newspaper publicity sent out from that office which seemed to her most undesirable. The high-powered promotional schemes she felt warranted the accusations that the Division was indeed spending government money on boondoggling but accomplishing little. She found it strange to work with promoters rather than with educators. As she said in a report later, "They would get wildly enthusiastic at times, marching around the office exuberantly trying out new songs about fitness, and they also phoned all over the country at the slightest excuse. Their disregard of money took a little adjustment in my thinking after all the penny-stretching we had to do elsewhere."[7]

326

However, that office did set up a worthwhile project using the Philadelphia public schools as a model for a physical fitness program to reach all schoolchildren. With $100,000 at his disposal, this project was put on by Grover Mueller, director of physical education for the public schools. But the Division of Physical Fitness failed to follow up and make material on the project available to the regional directors to pass on to the state and local groups. There was lacking a sense of realism to get things down to earth.

In the end, the following was the form of organization mostly adhered to as far as I ever knew. There were five sections of personnel: (1) administrative personnel, (2) advisory board, (3) coordinators, (4) a sports board, and (5) regional directors. The administrative personnel consisted of Mr. Kelly as director of the Division directly responsible to the national head of the Office of Civilian Defense; Alice Marble, assistant director, head of women's work; Ellwood Geiges, a full-time employee, as I understood it, on leave from the public schools of Philadelphia, executive assistant in charge of the Philadelphia office; Raymond A. Hill, head of publicity; John DaGrossa, head of sports and recreation; Mary K. Browne, well-known sportswoman, deputy assistant in the Washington OCD office; and George Holstrom, liasion officer with the OCD Washington office.

The Advisory Board consisted of a secretary, William L. Hughes, director of physical education, Temple University, and 12 to 33 persons representing such national organizations as the American Association for Health, Physical Education and Recreation; American Legion; College Physical Education Association; Industry and Sports; Medical Board of OCD; National Association of State Directors of Physical Education; National Collegiate Athletic Association; National Council of Parents and Teachers Associations; National Council of Recreation Workers; National Council of Social Workers; National Education Association; United States Office of Education; and Veterans of Foreign Wars.

I have often wondered how much these groups were given an opportunity to advise Mr. Kelly and his staff. The setup looked fine on paper, but surely if they had been given a chance to make their collective voice heard, the Division would not have become so controversial or incurred so much unfavorable publicity which only held up the work and made it more difficult to put it across to the citizens. William Hughes, Glen Howard, then at Ohio State University, and Frank McCormick were members of that Advisory Board, all three physical educators and practical, commonsense people. I can't believe the others on that board were not the same. Apparently they were used only as figureheads.

There were eight coordinators, all working in the fields of physical education, recreation and sports, with William Hughes, the head of the group, designated as consultant. The others were Hiram Jones, director of health and physical education in the New York State Department of Public Instruction; August Pritzlaff, director of physical education in the Chicago Public Schools; Anne Schley Duggan, president of AAHPER and director of physical education, Texas State College for Women; F. S. Mathewson of the New Jersey Recreation Department; V. K. Brown of the Chicago Parks and Recreation Board; C. W. Brewer of the Detroit Recreation Department; and John DaGrossa, coordinator of programs in industry. How much this group actually served as coordinators I never knew. Although six of these eight persons were professional friends of mine, only once in the months I worked as a regional director in the program did I have contact with any of them about the work. It never was suggested by the national office that I might make use of their services in my regional work.

Just what they did to coordinate our regional programs, our various plans, I never knew. On the occasions when I saw several of the regional directors following the war, we were always too busy with current work to hear each other's stories of our war work. It is still a story to be told. Since all of them were dedicated people, they no doubt "coordinated" things well as far as they were given authority beyond being a setup on paper for an inquiring public to wonder about.

The Sports Board was made up of 63 people, one each for every imaginable sport to be put to use in a physical fitness program, plus, for publicity purposes, a few other persons, nationally known in their sports fields. This board became a great source of controversy and a whipping boy for people who had grudges against FDR, Mayor La-Guardia or Eleanor Roosevelt and were willing to settle on a chance to belittle the Physical Fitness Movement.

This board in particular was one instance of the Philadelphia office's complete lack of proper coordination and utter lack of common sense. These sports persons annoyed governors with constant and repeated requests when all such requests should have come instead to one office —the regional director of physical fitness who would have passed them on to proper persons.

Even Mr. Kelly at times ignored chains of command. He had appointed regional directors of physical fitness supposedly to be his representatives in a region for everything having to do with the physical fitness program and then in many instances ignored their existence. After every trip out in the field I sent Mr. Kelly a full report and kept him informed on what was going on in my region, state by state, but I often wondered if he ever read them. For instance, in February 1942, after several of our Seventh Region states were organized, he asked Mr. Scholtz (the new OCD Director for the 7th Region) to have each state in his region get local physical fitness directors appointed as quickly as possible. Mr. Scholtz, well aware of what had been going on in his region, for I was keeping him informed, was surprised at his being bothered with this directive. He sent the wire on to me in Lincoln, asking if I understood why this wasn't sent to me instead. Why was I appointed and then by-passed? I wrote Mr. Kelly at once that his message had been turned over to me as the proper person to receive it and that this work was already underway as I had reported to him earlier.

I now studied the population statistics state by state for the Seventh Region which Mr. Kelly's office had sent me and I found the largest problem as far as population went would be Missouri, then Minnesota, Iowa, Arkansas, Kansas, Nebraska, North Dakota, South Dakota, and Wyoming, in that order. Missouri had 21 percent of the entire region population to Wyoming's 1 percent. Unknowingly, Frank McCormick and I had divided our region evenly between us: his four states with 42 percent of the regional population and my five with the remaining 56 percent.

From the very start of our work together, Frank McCormick was called to Washington so frequently for conferences with a Naval Advisory Board that finally in January he asked me to take on Iowa along with my other five states. Then in February 1942, he wired that he was entering the army as a major and resigning his position in the Division of Physical Fitness. He asked that I carry on in the nine states alone since so many men were now joining the armed forces that it was hopeless to expect to find a man to take his place. He had been such an excellent co-worker. Now I was on my own.

Chapter XVII
Politics and Red Tape

Having been rebuffed in my own home state on my first attempt to set up a state organization of physical fitness, I decided that, for my own morale, I had better try another state as quickly as possible. So I asked Bert Murphy, the OCD 7th Region Director, to write to the governor of Kansas, introducing me as one of his Seventh Defense Area Council members in charge of physical fitness and informing him that I would call on him during the Christmas holidays.

From the very start I had realized that out of fairness to my university work I should make my out-of-state trips on the weekends and during vacations and, of course, take care of the desk work and planning and letters on evenings and Saturday afternoons and Sundays. For the office work I was fortunate in that my department secretary volunteered her services to get out my letters for this regional work during evenings. Three of her secretarial friends helped evening after evening for several weeks. One alone gave me 70 hours of secretarial work in a two-month period.

Several women students who were majoring under me volunteered to do their war-service bit by helping me during the weekends when I was in town. I couldn't have swung the job without those enthusiastic and capable volunteers, not one of whom asked for a volunteer badge to wear or that a record be kept of the many hours she put in in the hopes of recognition later as an aide in civilian defense. It was all work purely for work's sake and for love of country.

I was still trying to get information from the Philadelphia office on how to handle travel expenses. I was also begging for some sort of identification card from Mr. Kelly which I could present as an introduction while on official division business, but as yet I had no response to either request. However, I did later receive two felt shields of the OCD, Division of Physical Fitness, one 4 x 3½ inches and one 3 x 2½ inches. Each had three white stars on a navy blue background across the top and the red letters HEALTH on a white background filling the lower part of the shield. It was suggested that the larger shield be worn on the breast pocket of my uniform and the smaller one on my cap. Since I never purchased a uniform I had no use for the shields except that on my first trip after their receipt I did wear the smaller shield on my tailored coat lapel to stand in lieu of an official calling card. It attracted such stares and curiosity in the hotel lobby on my first public appearance that I dashed to my room and removed it before calling on the governor. Nothing else was issued for identification but as I always preceded all calls by a letter of intent to call, I got by without a card, even though I was a woman.

As I was going to be in Lawrence, Kansas for Christmas with my family, I decided I could drive over to Topeka from there and cover that trip at little expense to myself (travel permits were still not issued) so I decided to go ahead and try to get Kansas organized.

From the tone of the letter Mr. Murphy sent from the Omaha OCD office to the Kansas governor, with a copy to me, I gathered that he and the Kansas governor were on most friendly terms and I departed for Topeka the day after Christmas feeling assured of a welcome. And how right I was! Governor Payne Ratner was most friendly and interested in my plans and quickly had all necessary doors opened for me. He urged me to stay over for a second day so there would be time for him to arrange a conference with state leaders of various groups that could help the fitness program. He called in a group of newspaper reporters at once so the evening papers could announce the meeting.

I spent two days there with the head of the State Department of Health, the publicity director, and others of the State Council of Defense. They arranged conferences for me with many heads of important state organizations such as welfare, recreation, and schools, and also women's clubs and men's service clubs who could reach down to the local levels. The governor decided immediately to place the Division of Physical Fitness under Dr. F.C. Beelman, state director of health, saying that Dr. Beelman would take under advisement the appointment of a state physical fitness director and would name this person soon.

* * * *

The rest of the Christmas vacation I spent working all day and some evenings on OCD work. The year ended with announcement that Mr. Murphy, a $1-a-year man in OCD work, had resigned as civilian defense head of the 7th Region and would be replaced by Joseph D. Scholtz, a former mayor of Louisville, Kentucky, with whom LaGuardia had become acquainted earlier in the Conference of City Mayors. Mr. Scholtz had been drawn into the OCD plans from their beginnings and when they were put into effect LaGuardia appointed him inspector general of the OCD. He happened to be in Omaha at the time Mr. Murphy resigned and LaGuardia had him stay on as acting director for the Seventh Region. He was in that position for the remainder of time that the Division of Physical Fitness was in OCD.

I found him a joy to work with because he listened to my plans for my work and let me know that he considered the Division of Physical Fitness an important part of his organization. When he saw that I was a comparative newcomer in the man's world of political strife and jealousies, of political diplomacy and government red tape, he advised me and in many ways made my path easier. When I was held up in getting my work underway because I was still waiting for telephone and telegraph charge accounts and travel forms to be issued, he provided me with the necessary accounts and a government railroad travel order book and told me to use my own judgment without bothering him to procure a permit to travel for each journey. This saved much time and energy for me, functioning as I was from Lincoln instead of Omaha where the regional office was located.

I had his constant enthusiastic support. He even took enough interest to ask me what I was doing for my own physical fitness with a full-time position at the university and this volunteer work claiming most of my evenings and all of every weekend. When I told him that this problem had bothered me to the extent that I had a bicycle on order so I could at least get in a six-mile ride each day between my home and university office, he clapped his hands and called out, "Good, good!"

Mr. Scholtz's interest extended to turning me over to Harry Wertz, director of public relations for the Seventh Regional OCD Area, for educating me in the art of using untrained persons for our program. He took time to educate me about the "flag wavers" for causes and how to make use of their desire to be helpful.

Mr. Scholtz became so interested in our physical fitness program plans for the Seventh Region that he took early opportunity on a trip back East to meet with the new OCD director, Dean Landis, to tell him about our program plans with the result that the Dean sent back a message to me, "Keep up the good work, Miss Lee." This did a lot for my own morale working as I was against limitations of time and a shortage of enthusiastic supporters.

* * * *

If my own state proved a hard nut to crack, it was a different and more pleasant story organizing the other states of my region. I met with some "stiff-arming" at first in Iowa, but in Kansas, Missouri and Arkansas, nothing but warm cordiality from the very first. For several weeks at the opening of 1942, each Friday night found me in a berth on a Pullman train headed for the capital city of Arkansas, Iowa, Kansas or Missouri. I arrived early Saturday morning, worked with state groups all day and on Sunday, and Sunday night I was once again on another Pullman train, arriving in Lincoln early Monday morning and dashing to the campus to look after my university work until the next Friday evening. It was a hectic but rewarding time for, away from my own home state, I was no longer "a prophet without honor" and I found I could get things moving quickly and successfully.

Arkansas was an unknown state to me and I made only one trip there. However that seemed to be sufficient to get the state physical fitness organization set up and going, for I found all with whom I came in contact enthusiastic, self-winding, full of practical ideas, and ready to go. My first call was at the office of the governor, Homer M. Adkins. Mr. Scholtz had alerted him about my visit and he had alerted Ben H. Wooten, head of the State Defense Council, the director of the State Department of Health, and the state superintendent of education about my visit and asked that they give me hearty cooperation.

When the governor noted my interest in the many oil portraits in his suite of offices and learned that this was my first visit to his state, he took me on a brief tour of the main parts of the Capitol, pointing out chief items of historical significance and briefing me on the state history. It was a most gracious gesture. Then he turned me over to Mr. Henry, executive secretary of the State Council for Civilian Defense who wished to have plans for a State Division of Physical Fitness explained so that he could enlighten his entire council. He was meeting his council that very afternoon and invited me to sit in on the meeting and explain the Division of Physical Fitness. I found it most interesting. How forward-looking these Arkansans of early 1940s were! As early as April 8, 1941, a month before the National Office of Civilian

Defense had been proclaimed, eight months before Pearl Harbor, they had organized to defend the industries, the railroads and other strategic parts against possible sabotage. At that meeting I sat on the edge of my chair enthralled at the reports of citizen groups on how they were organized to guard strategic railroad bridges in particular. All such talk was new and strange to me.

The director of the State Department of Health and the state superintendent of education quickly agreed that Clifford S. Blackburn, former football and basketball star at the University of Arkansas, former director of athletics at North Little Rock High School and presently supervisor of health, safety and physical education in the State Department of Education should head up the fitness program for the OCD. It took but a brief chat with Mr. Blackburn for me to realize that he had been an excellent choice. My first impression remained my permanent one for he was not only most personable, but also splendid to work with and, what was of the greatest importance, deeply interested in the need for a physically fit citizenry and the place physical education and sports could play in meeting that need.

My two days there were filled with conferences and meetings. State leaders of both women's and men's clubs, the American Legion, PTA, and recreation groups were called together for me to talk with and to answer questions. Not once did any of these people berate me about Mrs. FDR and her friend, Mayris Chaney. They seemed to sense that that episode was beside the point and that there was too much important work to be done to waste time on trivialities.

A second group meeting was arranged for public school teachers alone. We got down to brass tacks about the school's responsibility for developing physical fitness in all school pupils with emphasis on high school boys who might soon be drafted for the armed services. Amy Mason Little, a physical education teacher of Jonesboro, was appointed head of the women's state physical fitness program, and the state university physical education and athletics departments swung into line. Quickly a state program to reach every county and every town and city was under way. Many groups had already been at work.

The American Legion started a statewide campaign to educate the school boards to put a physical education program into all schools to reach all boys and girls, not just the few boys who went out for interscholastic sports. The State Selective Service, the American Legion and the men's department of physical education and athletics of the state university had set up a test program in Washington County for all men of draft age. The Selective Service was to give to the committee the names of all men selected to come up before the Draft Board. Each of these would be personally contacted by the American Legion Committee and urged to attend a mass meeting for all men of draft age to explain the program. When the program got under way, each session was to offer a period of physical exercise followed by briefing in first aid and a discussion period. All who wished to attend but had no way to come in to the county seat for the class sessions were to be transported by an American Legion Transportation Committee. The idea was to be tried out first in Washington County and then if successful carried out in every county in the state. The plan was put into effect by the first of March and according to the Little Rock papers, it did click, as reported by a Little Rock paper:

ARKANSAS CARRIES ON WITH PHYSICAL FITNESS PROGRAM
WHILE MOST U.S. CITIZENS BICKERED ABOUT OCD'S
CO-ORDINATORS DEFENSE LEADERS HERE DIDN'T
LOSE SIGHT OF WORTHY OBJECTIVE OF BODY-BUILDING

by Bill Shirley

The national physical fitness program may have been knocked out by congressional and public tacklers, but Arkansas' adaptation of that national program is still headed toward the goal.

Chief Ball-Carrier, C.S. Blackburn, is convinced that a physical development program is necessary and is determined that Arkansas shall have such a program....

The article also told about the American Legion-University of Arkansas program for men subject to the draft as follows:

Mr. Blackburn's office encountered opposition right off the bat on this idea from the draft boards, who finally consented but limited the department to one county, Washington, in which to experiment. Just to make a long story interesting, the idea clicked.

Fifty-two draft eligibles responded voluntarily to the department's call in Washington County and just to prove he was serious about the whole thing one youngster footed it 15 miles to Fayetteville for the training program.[1]

Later news informed me that 15 other counties had installed the program and "that when these selectees were selected they were not only physically fit but they also owned a pretty good idea of what goes on in the army."

This Arkansas State Committee on Physical Fitness didn't stop with the school and draftee programs. They went out at once after the men and women employed in war production industries, in railroad shops

335

and the like and asked all colleges to train a "small army" of prospective instructors to supply the needs throughout the state.

The problem of drawing blacks into our plans was encountered here as well as in Missouri. In February I received a letter from the assistant co-ordinator for Negro activities of the Division of Physical Fitness, asking what I was doing to draw Negroes into my program in the Seventh Civilian Defense Region. I was glad to be able to reply that I had held a special conference with Negro leaders of recreation and physical education in both Arkansas and Missouri in an attempt to search out black workers to be assigned to our state and community councils. As yet I had found but few who could take on such special volunteer work in addition to their regular paying jobs and other duties.

* * * *

Missouri was another state where it was a joy to work. I had been informed as early as January 7, 1942, that an old hometown friend, Wilma Haynes, had been appointed by Governor Forrest C. Donnell to be state physical fitness director in the OCD, to work under Hugh Stephens who had been appointed director of the Missouri Council of Civilian Defense. Mr. Stephens had for many years been the chairman of the board of trustees of Stephens College in Columbia, Missouri, and no doubt knew firsthand of Wilma's fine work at Stephens College as director of physical education and had recommended her appointment to the governor. I was delighted to get the news for I had known Wilma since first grade; we had even gone to college together and were both graduates of the professional training course in physical education of Wellesley College. I was well aware of her excellence in public relations work as well as in the routine professional job.

I was able to work in my first trip to Jefferson City on my way to Little Rock and there I received as warm a welcome from Governor Donnell of Missouri as I was later to receive at the governor's office in Arkansas. I spent an entire day there with morning conferences with heads of the state departments related to fitness work. For the afternoon, Wilma and her co-director of physical fitness, Dr. Darwin Hindman of the University of Missouri (later succeeded by Dr. Jack Mathews, also of the university) had arranged a meeting open to the public to discuss the physical fitness program and how to meet Missouri's needs.

This was one meeting during the dozens of meetings of those hectic months which I can never forget because of one incident in particular. The large auditorium in Jefferson City was packed, for the Division of Physical Fitness had by then been so attacked, so ballyhooed, so praised, so blamed by so many segments of society all over the country that people had become very curious about it. They were also eager to see one of those queer persons of the OCD even if she was only a lesser one working at the regional level but nevertheless one of those supposed-to-be high paid officials wasting the taxpayers' money.

All sorts of people turned out for the meeting—a good cross-section, I should say, of any state's citizenry. No sooner was the meeting open, introductions made, the program from the national level explained and questions called for, than a man arose to demand an explanation of the large salary I was drawing when the OCD was supposed to be built entirely around volunteer service. I had a difficult time to get him to accept my word that I had a full-time paid job at the University of Nebraska from which I was free on weekends and school vacations to do my volunteer bit for my country and that I drew no salary from the fitness work. He finally grunted disbelievingly and sat down to be followed by a woman who arose belligerently and informed me that she considered me personally responsible for the death of her son. The audience gasped and I, struggling to keep calm, asked her to explain just what she meant. She burst into tears and informed us that only a few days before she had learned that her son had been lost at sea. His ship had been sunk and, although help was near at hand, he had never been taught to swim so he was unable to get to this help. And, she concluded, he went to a school where there was a pool and other boys had been taught to swim but not her boy.

"Why didn't your physical education teachers make every boy and girl in school learn how to swim?" she cried. "That's the reason it is your fault that my boy is dead!"

It was a dramatic moment. Sure enough, why hadn't physical educators insisted that every boy and girl learn to swim, especially in every school with a pool? But the educators of that day were shouting that such things should not be compulsory; let the boys and girls make their own choices—that was democracy!

After the war was over, figures were released informing America that up to June 6, 1944, the date of the invasion of Europe, more American servicemen lost their lives from drowning than in battle. To think that many of those lives might have been saved had those men been able to swim to whatever aid was at hand or been physically fit enough to hang on longer to the rafts and debris until rescuers could reach them! All who followed the news of those early war months will recall the frequent reports of ships sunk and men lost at sea. That woman's accusation led to a determination to stress swimming in the state physical fitness program. After the meeting, the stricken woman came to the platform to apologize to me and thus gave me an opportunity to offer her my deep sympathy in her loss and to assure her she had aroused us to a real need.

Late that afternoon I went on to St. Louis where all the next day I worked at the State Physical Fitness Committee's invitation with a bevy of St. Louis organizations which had been alerted about my coming. Then I took the night train to Little Rock. All this was at the between-semesters interlude at the university so I could cover a lot of ground in the one trip.

By the time I returned to St. Louis from Arkansas, the St. Louis Welfare Council had arranged a meeting with all physical education teachers and recreation workers to set up the city physical fitness program, the real grassroots one. Wilma Haynes came from Columbia to join me. I had my first experience of speaking over the radio when the woman commentator of KMOX-CBS and we two had a three-way conversation about physical fitness.

The next day was spent in Columbia, Missouri, with meetings of townspeople, university people, and groups from the two local women's colleges, Stephens College and Christian College. Late that afternoon in Kansas City, Missouri, I met at City Hall with local agencies and a group of 80 civic leaders from Warrensburg and St. Joseph. Later at a dinner meeting I tried to calm down several disgruntled women from the Kansas City Chamber of Commerce. It had been nine busy days, filled every moment it seemed, taking me to Kansas, Missouri and Arkansas. I was glad when I could settle down that last day for a night's sleep on a Pullman, bound for Lincoln and my university work that seemed now like child's play after these nine days of constant meetings.

A month later the Missouri State Council of Defense arranged a statewide conference on physical fitness in Jefferson City. The call came jointly from Governor Donnell and State OCD Director Stephens and both were interested enough to attend the conference and take part in the proceedings. As regional director, I was urged to attend, which I did. It was an inspiring meeting and there were interesting reports from delegates from all parts of the state about what the schools and out-of-school groups were doing in their fitness programs. Mr. Stephens told the delegates:

> Regardless of what may be the verdict elsewhere on civilian activities for physical fitness, Missouri has no idea of side-tracking

338

an activity of such importance to human values in these days of war emergency.

One of the largest and most thoroughly organized groups which has assembled in the state capital in weeks met February 28, in the interest of physical fitness. The lengths to which the group had gone in its organization was a surprise. *The committee members also are one of the most determined in their objective, which is building war-time stamina among Missourians.*

This committee is allotted no money. They are planning no "frills and furbelows." They are made up for the most part of men and women, who for years have been responsible for character-building and health programs in our schools, in the 4-H groups on farms, Camp Fire Girls, Girl Scouts, Boy Scouts, YMCA and scores of others.

In these days when we are calling for gigantic production, it would seem strangely inconsistent to me for us to demand supreme effort on one hand and on the other hand turn down the voluntary services of those who offer to build people up so they can be capable of such production. *The physical condition of the people, ninety-five per cent of whom will be out of the line of military service, should be a prime requisite for victory.*[2]

At this conference it was reported that 750 physical educators had volunteered their services to put on out-of-school hours programs of physical fitness in 275 schools throughout the state, also that in St. Louis alone 50,000 people had registered with the OCD for volunteer work of all descriptions.

The next day I moved on to Kansas City to see how I could help a local group calm down a very large group of women in Kansas City who were deeply offended at criticism from school and college groups of their program sponsored by the Women's Chamber of Commerce. A movement had been started in November 1941 as a cooperative venture of the Kansas City Chamber and the Kansas City Welfare Department, using the Municipal Auditorium with the WPA band furnishing music for calisthenics. By January 20, 500 business and professional women were coming to the class once a week and having a most interesting time getting physically fit. Wilma and I thought it splendid and we couldn't understand the criticism of some physical educators who thought this class was ridiculous. "The idea," one prominent woman physical educator exclaimed, "of doing calisthenics to music when they should be playing basketball, tennis and golf or even swimming!"

How could you bring 500 women together one night a week on one large drill floor and give them all a real workout in a sports situation? Frankly I was disgusted with the unrealistic thinking of some of my professional co-workers, but I felt it wise to hold my tongue and not get embroiled in local jealousies. There was one valid criticism of the Kansas City program in that it did not accept school teachers into the program. When I later talked with the State Works Progress Administration (WPA) recreation people in Kansas City they told me that the school people "high-hatted" them because many of the leaders were poorly trained but as unemployed people they were used in this program which WPA sponsored. Their main complaint was that they were being severely criticized for using mass calisthenics instead of sports and recreational activities.

As soon as I got a chance I called these WPA and Women's Chamber of Commerce leaders into a meeting with the heads of physical education in the schools of Kansas City. I said to them:

> The people in our profession who for the past 15 to 20 years have been preaching a philosophy of softness in physical education have betrayed our profession as effectively as the pacifists and isolationists of the past 15 to 20 years have betrayed our democracy.

I said that we are at war and the Army is telling us that although physical education is not to blame for the disabilities of most rejectees, it is to blame for the softness of the boys who have been selected to serve. It is up to us now to make fit as rapidly as possible not only the young men who may soon be called up by the draft, but also all citizens who may serve in the war effort in any way, volunteers as well as paid personnel. I added that when space, leaders and time are limited, strenuous mass calisthenics are most worthwhile for our programs. And I called attention to the fact that giving 500 young women strenuous calisthenics in one huge drill hall in one hour of time was preferable in this emergency to trying to give the same 500 women basketball or volleyball or some other sport, which to reach all would take many more leaders, much more in facilities and equipment, and many more hours of time. I begged the various groups to pull together rather than war over differing philosophies of what activities serve people best.

I thought I had cleared the atmosphere and had made peace in Kansas City but a week later, when the Missouri State Physical Education Association held its annual state convention in Maryville, a prominent physical education leader in the public schools of Kansas City arose before all the delegates and asked if the workers in the Division of Physical Fitness were to be allowed to wreck the physical education profession in Missouri. She went on to say that she had recently, to her amazement, heard the regional director of physical fitness say that sports, swimming, dance and recreational activities were to be dropped, keeping only mass calisthenics as our entire physical education program. This called forth a great note of disapproval. Unfortunately I was not present to defend myself and let the delegates know how my remarks had been twisted to suit the pleasure of a jealous and ambitious co-worker who hoped to discredit me. She probably wanted to get even for my taking the side of the ladies of the Kansas City Chamber of Commerce and the WPA workers who were trying so hard in the only way they knew to be helpful in the war effort. Many Missourians, indignant at this snide attack on me when I was not present to set straight exactly what I had said, wrote begging me to refute this statement at an early date. My opportunity came a few weeks later when the Central District Association for Health, Physical Education and Recreation met in convention in Des Moines, and from the platform at a general session I did get a chance to set the record straight.

Later the St. Louis Social Planning Council invited me to come, at their expense, as one of four guest speakers to a physical fitness conference they were sponsoring. Several months later I was again guest speaker when the St. Louis Physical Fitness Council put on a "commencement" for its 800 volunteers who were graduating from a course it had been giving for several weeks in recreational leadership. The course had been taught by the St. Louis public school physical educators who gave their time. Now 800 persons were ready to go throughout the city to help put on recreation programs for all the citizens, a huge undertaking.

This visit turned into a circle trip to Jefferson City for conferences with state leaders, to Columbia for meetings with college students, to Warrensburg to speak at a women's convocation at the State Teachers College, then to Kansas City, and finally to Lawrence, Kansas, for a brief vacation at Christmas with some of my family. What a trip it was at that time of year with mobs of travellers for every train, missing connections because of delayed trains, and in the final leg of it, along with a group of soldiers, standing outside in bitter cold from midnight to 1 a.m. on the platform of a day coach from Kansas City to Lawrence because there wasn't even standing room left inside the coach filled with men in uniform, young mothers with little children, and, to my great astonishment, numerous pregnant young girls. (This latter I became accustomed to before the war was over as wives moved back and forth across the land trying to keep up with their in-service husbands.) Believe me, the conductor's call, "Lawrence—Lawrence" was a welcome call on that cold morning.

* * * *

341

Iowa was another state where, as in Nebraska, civilian defense activities were held up at first by the foot-dragging of the Republican governor who was playing politics, unwilling to follow President Roosevelt's leadership and accept John Kelly and his Division of Physical Fitness, seizing upon the nationwide outcry against Mrs. Roosevelt and her dance protege as an excuse to decry the work of all of us. It was easy to vent the full force of one's spleen upon that movement. And that is just what Iowa's Governor Wilson started out to do. But finally under pressure from Mr. Kelly's office, the governor had in late December appointed the state superintendent of public instruction as head of the Division of Physical Fitness under the state council of defense.

I had been invited by the Iowa Farm and Home Organization some time earlier to be one of the speakers at its statewide convention which was being held just about that time at the State Agricultural College at Ames. I decided to use this occasion to tackle the Iowa situation since I would be in the Des Moines region. Mr. Scholtz, the regional director of OCD, had informed the governor of my plans to call on him, but he could not see me when I first arrived. I had been tipped off that he was not at all friendly toward the physical fitness movement and I interpreted the "could not" to mean "would not." I refused to be put off thus and asked his secretary for an appointment the following day which she said was out of the question. But I persisted until I was given a definite date for two days hence, and the secretary informed me that it would be quite correct for me to go ahead with my plans.

Finally on my last day there I had a belated and, at first, a most obviously begrudged appointment with the governor. My earlier rebuffs from the governor of Nebraska had taught me a lesson. Sensing his reluctance to give me an appointment in the first place and feeling a decided chill in the air when I first entered his office, I hastened to inform him that I was a native Iowan, brought up in an old Republican stronghold, at which he took on an immediate look of interest.

"Where is that town?" he asked.

"Centerville," I replied.

"Then you must have known former Governor Drake whose home was there."

"Yes, indeed. As a little girl I saw him frequently. My father knew him."

With that, Governor Wilson waxed eloquent for apparently he had admired Governor Drake and he spoke of the university in Des Moines that bears his name. This broke the ice. I was no longer persona non grata in his office, suspect appointee of LaGuardia and John Kelly—

342

those Democrats—but a native Iowan and a Republican, who as a little girl had frequently seen former Governor Drake. All doors were opened to me now and it was time to return home, all interviews concluded except for an appointment with the mayor of Des Moines and a conference that afternoon with the State Recreation Association, to be followed by an appointment with George Walker, State WPA Recreation head.

Kathryn Kreig, city superintendent of recreation, had told me the mayor was interested in the physical fitness movement but was awaiting some nod from the State Council of Defense before he set up a city program. Sensing that such might not be forthcoming I told Kathryn, who was one of my own University of Nebraska graduates, that there was no need to wait any longer. I urged her to come with me to see the mayor, saying we could bypass the state organization if it refused to function. There I received a friendly reception and our conference ended with his appointment of Kathryn as head of physical fitness on his City Council of Defense. Now one piece of Iowa was in the bag for us. I knew I also had the group at Ames, both the physical educators and the extension people, and also the physical education people at Drake University and the University of Iowa pulling for our program. At last surely the Iowa program would get going.

Evidently after my call on him, the governor sent word to the superintendent of public instruction that he was ready to recognize the Division of Physical Fitness. No doubt he prodded her to action for she now sent me word that she would be happy to have suggestions and advice on the work.

* * * *

By then I had Arkansas, Missouri, Kansas and Iowa organized at the state level and Frank McCormick had Minnesota well organized. Wyoming was still to be organized, Nebraska was still balking, and the two Dakotas were Frank McCormick's territory. We were so busy I never did hear from him how they were moving.

However, I doubt if any other regional director met with such intransigence from the "politicos" as did I in my attempts to get my own home state organized. For my second attempt to see Nebraska's governor I decided to play some politics myself. I went to a prominent businessman in the city who was known to have access to the governor and was a good friend of mine, one to whom I could talk confidentially and who knew that I was a staunch Republican. He was amazed when

I told him the governor had refused to receive me as a representative of John Kelly and also refused to give me an appointment for a future day. I told him what we hoped to accomplish by pushing for a good physical fitness program in this state where there were so few schools offering good physical education programs, even sports programs for all pupils, but our hands were tied by a governor prejudiced against us because of his dislike for Franklin Delano Roosevelt, his wife and Mr. Kelly. My friend said, "Leave it to me. I think I can get his door opened to you. Just sit tight for a while. I think he will come around."

So I sat tight for almost three weeks and then early in January I was tipped off that I might find the climate at the State House a bit warmer if I once more asked for an appointment. Apparently someone had been at work, for this time the governor was friendly but warned me that he had little sympathy for the Division of Physical Fitness.

"Why can't the schools do this job through their physical education departments?" he asked, giving me a long desired opportunity to tell him how backward Nebraska was in this branch of education. So many schools offered no physical education other than interscholastic sports for a few boys, and many of the few schools that were offering physical education had mostly inadequate and untrained teachers. I also pointed out that in this war emergency we must reach not only all high school pupils to toughen them up quickly for possible military needs, but also out-of-school citizens who will be helping in the war effort on the home front. I hastened to point out that since Nebraska had no state director of physical education in the State Department of Public Instruction, as did so many states, it would mean much to the physical fitness movement if the person appointed for this volunteer work were trained in the field and could quickly organize the workers at the local level throughout the state. At this he suggested I talk with Dr. Miller of the State Health Department again.

So Dr. Miller had been softened up, too. Maybe now we could get on with the work. As I was leaving, the governor said, as if seized by a sudden thought, "You might find it helpful to talk with Walter Roberts, the executive secretary and state coordinator of civilian defense. Why not go see him right now?"

It proved a good idea, for I found Mr. Roberts most friendly, eager to hear of my plans for a state program in physical fitness, a bit bemused by the anger of others at Mrs. Roosevelt and her dance friend appointee and at Mayor LaGuardia and John Kelly. He was inclined to overlook the ruckus over them stirred up by the news media. He said I could count on him to back up the fitness program and to come and talk with him whenever I wished.

344

A few days later I was able to get an appointment with Dr. Miller who this time received me cordially and informed me that he was appointing Charles Moon, state athletic commissioner, to be state director of physical fitness. At this news I tried to keep a poker face although his appointment seemed as ridiculous as Mrs. Roosevelt's. Although I knew little about the qualifications of Mr. Moon and was no better informed as to just what the position of state athletic commissioner meant, I had instant premonition that any real hopes for a state physical fitness program were dashed. I felt at once that his had been a trick to block the program. But I kept my first thoughts to myself, smiled as gamely as I could, and said I would look forward to meeting Mr. Moon and working with him.

I made a beeline to my businessman friend downtown to tell him what had happened and ask him what he thought it meant. He was as dumbfounded as I, but consoled me by saying that the appointee was a dyed-in-the-wool Republican and therefore would follow the Republican line and have Republican backing. He added that I would find the appointee pleasant, cooperative and, incidentally, open to suggestions. Then he briefed me on his background. As athletic commissioner under Dr. Miller, he was in charge of boxing and wrestling permits. So I had, after all, met the gentleman recently even if only indirectly. Several other women and I had led a protest over his granting a permit for "lady" wrestlers to put on a match in the state, which had resulted in a decision to cancel Lincoln matches but to permit them in Omaha. Perhaps he would be holding a grudge against me for this. I also learned that before taking on the athletic commissioner's job, Charles Moon had run a pool hall in Lincoln and been manager of a professional welterweight champion and a baseball team (Green's Nebraska Indians) and the Lincoln Western League Club. At least he knew something of a few sports if only from a managerial viewpoint.

I asked for another conference with Dr. Miller as early as possible when Mr. Moon would be present so we could get down to work. It was two weeks before this request was granted and then the conference was very brief—we were introduced, then dismissed. But in a brief chat in the hallway of the State House I sensed that Mr. Moon was friendly and willing to work, also, was taking the appointment seriously even if his superior officers were not.

Recalling Mr. Roberts' cordiality, I asked him if Mr. Moon and I could have a conference with him to get the state physical fitness program under way. The following day we met with Wade Martin, state chairman of the Civilian Defense Council, joining us. Both these gentlemen were interested in the problem at hand. When Mr. Moon, as Miss Marble had done ahead of him, protested that he knew nothing of or-

345

ganizing and promoting a physical fitness program and frankly told me he would lean heavily on my advice and suggestions, I felt free to plunge in and advise and suggest. As I hoped, he asked me, with the approving nods of the other two, to name people throughout the state who would be good persons to invite to be on an advisory committee for him. I suggested Ruth Diamond of Omaha University as a specialist in work with women, James Morrison of Wayne State Teachers College, W. A. Rosene of the State Department of Public Instruction, and James Lewis of the Lincoln City Recreation Department. The three men said this sounded like a good state committee and to make it official as a state OCD appointment, Mr. Roberts offered to write to each officially inviting them to be members of this committee.

No sooner were the acceptances in than Mr. Roberts sent for me to say that when the governor learned of these advisory committee appointments, he sent for Mr. Roberts and told him he had no intention for such a committee to be set up. It was to be disbanded at once and Mr. Moon would carry on alone or not at all. I could scarcely believe my ears!

The Lincoln and Omaha Councils of Civilian Defense had been urging me to meet with them, which technically I should not do except on invitation from the state physical fitness director and no one was taking Mr. Moon's appointment seriously. However, Mr. Roberts gave me his blanket permission from the State OCD to confer with any group anywhere in the state in the name of a state physical fitness setup.

I had already accepted speaking engagements with the Lincoln Welfare Council and for the big Victory Luncheon which the Lincoln Council of Defense had recently put on at the Cornhusker Hotel. It had brought out the city's leading citizens who gave me a most encouraging round of applause at the conclusion of my brief speech telling them what we hoped to accomplish in Nebraska whenever we could get the state program rolling. So with Mr. Roberts' blessing I went that very afternoon to a meeting of the Lincoln Defense Council and at their invitation helped to organize a local physical fitness committee. Mr. Roberts assured me the governor would have no objection to organize locally. A day or so later upon invitation from the Omaha Council of Defense, I went over there and finally got its Committee on Physical Fitness organized.

In the meantime I tried to see the governor again to see if I could persuade him to reverse his decision about an advisory committee but once more I found his door closed to me. All this took place before Frank McCormick resigned. I told him of the Nebraska situation and

346

tipped him off that the governor would be attending the State American Legion convention at Grand Island where the national commander, who was pushing for a national physical fitness program, would be speaking. Could he see that Commander Stinbaugh talked with the governor in behalf of a Nebraska program? Evidently he did see to it, for a week or so later the governor asked Mr. Moon to bring me to his office for a conference. We had a good, friendly talk, and the governor relieved himself of a lot of pent-up feelings against the many so-called sports coordinators of the Division of Physical Fitness who had become a great annoyance to him.

I was amazed at what he had to tell me. I knew that Mr. Kelly had set up a Sports Board with a coordinator for each of the great variety of sports, but it was my understanding that all of these would be functioning within the states only through the regional directors of physical fitness. I had not heard one word from a single sports coordinator and was beginning to wonder when they would be ready to get to work. Now it developed that telegrams and letters from a great variety of sports persons had been pouring into the governor's and Dr. Miller's offices, urging immediate appointment of a state chairman of whatever sport the particular person was pushing.

When the governor learned of my amazement at this and of my disapproval, as strong as his own, he lost much of his belligerency toward me. I assured him I would take the matter up with Mr. Kelly's office at once and would see that he had no further annoyances of that sort.

By this time the State Department of Public Instruction had set up a State Health Education Committee to advance physical fitness within the schools of the state, insisting that I be a member of the committee which would proceed at once to develop a State Bulletin for War Emergency on Health and Physical Education. We did spend several Saturdays, all day long, at this task, stretching into the fall of 1942. I have wondered all these years if the governor hadn't suggested this as a way to make amends for his refusing to recognize a physical fitness setup in the State OCD.

* * * *

Ever since Frank McCormick's resignation I was on my own to cover our entire region. It was entirely too much for one volunteer to cover nine states, so I gave no thought to Minnesota which had been so thoroughly organized even before Mr. Kelly's Division of Physical Fitness was created, thanks to Frank McCormick and his American

Legion national fitness work. I also gave no thought to the two Dakotas since neither asked for help. I did get calls for help from Wyoming which had been on my original list. But with the insistent calls from the other four states, all heavily populated and with needs for intensive programs, it was easy to neglect Wyoming, which was so sparsely populated and with only a few persons trained in the field of physical education.

Those few and I corresponded and by late March, Wyoming did have a state program organized with H. J. McCormick of the University of Wyoming appointed by the governor as state director of physical fitness. Fortunately, this group was self-winding. It persuaded the governor and the state director of the Civilian Defense Council to serve on the executive committee of the Division of Physical Fitness ex officio. It also managed things no other state group of the 7th Region accomplished—to have its own letterheads as a Division of Physical Fitness of the Wyoming State Council of Defense and funds for office supplies and postage furnished by the council and travel expenses from the state adjutant general's office for the state physical fitness chairman. Regional representatives were appointed, the chairman of each county defense council was contacted, and finally a program was under way with much enthusiastic backing from the citizens of the sparsely populated areas.

* * * *

The year 1942 marked the zenith of John Kelly's dream of a Division of Physical Fitness for America. Within the early months of the year all his regional directors, both men and women, and most of the state and some local directors were at last appointed. On the national level his greatly touted Sports Board was organized with its numerous coordinators. Besides these, there were coordinators in general and coordinators of coordinators, and consultants and an advisory board, besides assistants, office executives, an office manager, and a publicity director.

There was a constant stream of letters and telegrams going out from Mr. Kelly's top assistants in his Philadelphia office, many ignoring the chains of command Mr. Kelly himself had set up. I sometimes wondered if the right hand knew what the left hand was doing. It was most obvious he was receiving much poor advice. I wished he would come to see what we were doing and what we were like out in the Midwest. He obviously little sensed the temper of this part of the country, the hotbed of isolationism, and had no understanding of the political discord between Republicans and Democrats in these parts.

348

I had urged him early in our work to visit us but receiving no reply had forgotten about it. Then when in early March he informed the St. Louis people—not telling either the regional or state director ahead of time—that he would drop in on them, they descended upon me via telephone and post dispatch from several quarters begging me to have him cancel his plans. By then he had been held up to so much scorn (including undeserved criticism because of FDR and his New Deal) that the St. Louis people felt he would not receive a warm welcome. It was an unpleasant task but I got the plans cancelled.

Later, again bypassing me, Mr. Kelly's office alerted the Missouri state chairman of OCD that Mr. Kelly might visit Jefferson City. Immediately a long-distance call from there asked me to get this trip also cancelled. The state OCD director felt such a visit would be inadvisable because of the bad feeling on the part of many citizens towards the Division of Physical Fitness at the national level. As Mr. Hugh Stevens, state director of OCD, said, "Just let us go about our physical fitness work without him making a personal appearance until people have forgotten all this hoopla." So again I wired that the date would be inconvenient for the state group and, as tactfully as I could, suggested that he let me arrange the dates and places for visits in the Seventh Region for him.

In early March I received a letter from the president of a national woman's educational group informing me that she had been told by a seemingly well-informed man that the Division of Physical Fitness was to be transferred to Paul McNutt's Federal Security Agency (FSA) under the President's Defense and Welfare Division with Mark McCloskey as head of the Division of Physical Fitness and Recreation of industrial workers. This woman hoped we would be allowed to continue under Dean Landis in the OCD. Four days later when I chanced to be in Kansas City, Missouri, I sounded out one of Mr. McCloskey's recreation leaders. He told me that Mr. McNutt had said that the Division of Physical Fitness was to be placed under him, but Mr. Landis, head of OCD, said the Division was to remain in the OCD. A week later I heard in a roundabout way that President Roosevelt had signed papers for transfer, but there had been as yet no official word from Mr. Kelly's office or from the regional OCD office in Omaha.

About this same time, both Mr. Scholtz and I were informed that Carl Nordly of the University of Minnesota had been appointed to take Frank McCormick's place and the Division of Physical Fitness was to carry on just as it had since its establishment.

After carrying on alone for several weeks I once more had a co-worker, but there was a subtle change in the national office in regard to our relationship. In the first weeks when Frank McCormick and I were working together, all communications about our work as regional directors of physical fitness were addressed to us jointly. Then when I carried on alone for several weeks, all letters were addressed to me alone. From now on, I never received a word from that office except indirectly from copies they sent me of their letters to Mr. Nordly. At least Mr. Kelly's office wished me to know what they had to say to my co-worker. Also, I never had any communication directly with my supposed-to-be co-worker. We were strangers at the time although later years threw us together and we became good friends. But for reasons I never understood, the friendly working together that had existed between Mr. McCormick and me was not carried over into the new setup. And strange as it may seem, despite many years of work together, Carl and I never found time to reminisce about the physical fitness work. Since all communications from the national office of Physical Fitness were addressed to him alone, it was understandable that he did not regard me as a co-worker.

It was late March before Mr. Nordly received travel authorization and at that time Mr. Scholtz informed me that he had asked that my travel authorization be extended through June. Since it was the regional civilian defense office that procured these authorizations, these expenses evidently were paid out of the general OCD budget, not out of Mr. Kelly's Physical Fitness budget. Thus we were spared having these items dragged up for ridicule in Congress by Senator Byrd.

At this same time I received a letter from the Philadelphia office saying that the work in that office had been frozen pending a decision about transferring the Division out of OCD into the FSA under Paul McNutt. Therefore, no more materials would be coming out to the regional offices until further notice. I went ahead and sent out to my state directors my third monthly bulletin in which I urged them to stress much walking for all civilians as an excellent conditioner requiring no facilities, no special equipment, other than correct shoes, and for high school boys and college men, much swimming, tumbling, and wall-scaling. I continued to send Mr. Kelly long monthly reports of what I was doing in the various states and the regional office, with copies to my state directors and interested workers.

No sooner were my February reports in the mail in late March, than I received a letter from Mr. Kelly informing me that the Division of Physical Fitness was being dropped from the OCD and transferred to the FSA on Presidential orders of February 28, 1942. He had been asked to appear the following week before a Senate Committee when he would at last have a chance to challenge Senator Byrd on his criticism of his work. Evidently Mr. Scholtz got the word of our transfer at the same time for in the next mail I received a note from him saying that I was no longer a member of his regional civilian defense council. He said he regretted it very much and expressed appreciation for the work I had done. In the end the transfer was not completed until April 14 and the work was carried under the OCD until then.

A day or so later I received a copy of a letter sent from Mr. Kelly's office to Carl Nordly informing him that he was to remain in the Division of Physical Fitness as regional representative of the FSA region with Minneapolis as the headquarters. A check at the State House in Lincoln gave me the information that the FSA region including Minnesota covered five states—Minnesota, Iowa, Nebraska and the two Dakotas. So Carl Nordly and I still belonged in the same region but not one word as to my own status in the new grouping. I had not been told my position had been eliminated although Carl had been definitely informed that he was to stay on. Some time later I received a letter from the Philadelphia office informing me that the Division organization was to be kept intact as in the OCD and that there would still be a man and a woman head of physical fitness in each region. Carl Nordly and I would work together in the five states of the Minneapolis area.

Finally in June 1942, the Division of Physical Fitness was transferred to the Federal Security Agency when Mr. Kelly made the public statement that "Our regional representatives and consultants include some of the best-known people in the field of physical education. Senator Byrd and his 'hatchet men' are afraid to attack them and the programs in the schools." From then on, Mr. Kelly purposely kept the Division of Physical Fitness out of the schools, leaving it to each state to step up its own fitness work in the schools on its own.[3]

The ongoing story of the Division of Physical Fitness, as it unfolded under the Federal Security Agency, is told in the chapter that follows.

As said earlier to have been a member of the regional staff of the OCD proved a most interesting experience. Almost all of the people with whom I had to work I found to be quite different types of persons from the general run of educators. And to be quite honest about it, I found most of the people from outside the ivory towers quite interesting with their fund of common sense and ability to get things done and with dispatch.

Chapter XVIII

A Victory Corps, a Women's Commission, and a Women's Army Corps

In January 1942 a War Emergency National Conference of College and University Presidents was held in Baltimore where the delegates endorsed the promotion of a physical fitness program but urged that it be conducted along approved scientific and educational lines. Paul McNutt, head of the Federal Security Agency (FSA), asked John W. Studebaker, U.S. Commissioner of Education, whose office was under the FSA, to establish within his office a Wartime Commission to study special services that could be given in wartime by the nation's schools. Out of this grew a commission of 59 leaders in education (college and university presidents and school superintendents) and representatives of a great variety of national organizations interested in education. From this Commission developed the realization that a permanent government agency was the one to be concerned about physical fitness of the nation and that the FSA with the U.S. Office of Education under it was the logical organization to promote this. The recommendation of this Commission was accepted by the President and the move from the OCD was ordered.

The reorganization of the Division of Physical Fitness under the FSA, authorized February 24, 1942, called for three groups aimed at keeping the citizenry fit: the U.S. Office of Education, concerned mainly with developing fitness in the schools; the Recreation Division, under Mark McCloskey, a New York City social worker, to promote recreational activities in industry; and the former Division of Physical Fitness under John Kelly concerned with fitness of all other citizens.

What happened to the other pairs of regional directors in the other OCD areas I never knew, but we two of the Seventh Area happened to belong to states that were in the same FSA area. Carl Nordly and I were informed that we were to carry on as FSA regional directors of physical fitness, but now for a different set of states, Minnesota, Iowa, Nebraska, North and South Dakota. Under the FSA, I received great quantities of mail and information about the promotion of physical fitness; but, although I was told I was to stay on under the FSA, my actual position seemed in limbo. I never had been in touch with Carl Nordly so I did not know how things were with him.

Needless to say, this letdown and uncertainty was a period of relief, a rest from weeks of rush, rush, rush! I was glad Frank McCormick and I had set up as many state physical fitness organizations as we had before the transfer came. I had "about knocked myself out" as the saying went, weekend after weekend for weeks for the OCD. Gradually I realized that work on the regional level had died out in favor of all-out attention of the FSA directly to the states. However, no official announcement ever reached me.

* * * *

We of the earlier physical fitness organization had been working under a handicap of misunderstanding of our purposes by people outside the organization. But now we had to cooperate with someone in the overall group who was as unfriendly to the Division of Physical Fitness as most outside critics, Mark McCloskey. All I knew about him had come from professional acquaintances who had heard his snide remarks aimed at the Division of Physical Fitness under the OCD and all its workers. I was just learning of this man's antagonism toward us when I was due in Des Moines to attend the annual spring convention of my district professional association. This gave me not only an excellent opportunity to have a first face-to-face conference with our new regional director but also a chance to meet Mr. McCloskey. The program had been arranged a few months previously and I was assigned to explain the Division of Physical Fitness of the OCD to the delegates and introduce the various state and local directors in our district. But after this program had been arranged, the transfer to FSA was made and, not wishing to seem to ignore the newcomer, Mr. Nordly, I hastened to invite him to share all these meetings with me and at the general session to preside with me as a co-chairman.

Mark McCloskey, head of the Recreation Division for industrial workers of FSA, was also booked for a speech at the convention and I asked Mr. Nordly to introduce us. Imagine my surprise when that gentleman refused to acknowledge the introduction, but instead gave me a cold look, let out a rude "Hump" of disapproval and, turning his back on the two of us, walked away. I was thunderstruck and to this day I still wonder what had called forth such rudeness. Later I did meet one of Mr. McCloskey's staff, and had a most pleasant and profitable chat about how our work could be coordinated.

Mr. McCloskey's dislike of John Kelly's Division of Physical Fitness must have been deep-seated for in his speech at a general session of the convention he ridiculed the Division, declaring that it had nothing to offer for the fitness of our nation but "jerks" (referring to calisthenics, no doubt) and all that was needed was a program of recreational activities. Highly indignant, a large number of us in the audience jumped to our feet to challenge him the minute he concluded his speech but he hastened from the platform and disappeared through a back door. If we were foiled in an attempt to dispute points with him, we did have the last word after all, even if in a sort of closed-door situation. Charles H. McCloy, research professor of the University of Iowa, went straight to Paul McNutt with a protest of Mr. McCloskey's speech and said that since that gentleman disappeared immediately after his speech he (Dr. McCloy) hoped to discuss with Mr. McNutt the mistaken idea that recreational activities alone would get industrial workers and draftees physically fit in a hurry and keep them fit for the war effort. Mr. McNutt responded with interest and later had lengthy discussions with Dr. McCloy on the subject.

In addition to physical education groups, the movement was at last backed by many important national organizations, such as the American Medical Association, the American Association of University Women, the General Federation of Women's Clubs, national health organizations and the like. But we now had to reckon with Mr. McCloskey's animosity. His rudeness to me in Des Moines was soon to be repeated.

Preceding the war he had been working in the New York section of the National Youth Administration and was director of community education for the New York City Board of Education. But these facts

354

gave me no clue as to what might have aroused in him such antipathy towards the cause of physical fitness and its workers.

About a month after the Des Moines meeting I was in St. Louis as one of four guest speakers at a conference of the City Social Planning Council. The other three speakers were Floyd Eastwood, a friend of several years from Purdue University, Tom Deering of the National Recreation Association with whom I was on most friendly terms, and Mark McCloskey who refused to be drawn into any conversation with me and completely ignored my presence. The four of us had radio and press interviews and endless conferences and I, like the other three, was scheduled for three speeches, mine all on the physical fitness program as set up by Mr. Kelly.

In Mr. McCloskey's first speech he made derogatory remarks about the Division of Physical Fitness which I wished to challenge but again, as in Des Moines, I was given no opportunity. As I wrote to Mr.Kelly's office, later:

> I resolved, therefore, to make the opportunity for myself (to challenge Mr. McCloskey) from the platform when I was to speak the following morning—remarks that were to be made directly to him, but again I was foiled due to the fact that although he was booked for two speeches that morning, he failed to put in an appearance and the committee was unable to locate him any place. He simply walked out on them without one word of explanation.

Shortly after this, Mr. McCloskey left the FSA to become director of the Office of War Community Services, and we physical fitness people were no longer subjected to his rudeness.

* * * *

The new form of organization for the Division of Physical Fitness under the FSA functioned for over a year on a trial basis. On April 29, 1943, by Administrative Order No. 42, a special national committee on physical fitness was created within the Division of Physical Fitness, and it held its first meeting in Washington on June 16, 1943. At that time it declared its functions to be fourfold: (1) to "define and study problems relating to the promotion of physical fitness, in cooperation with national agencies and organizations, and encourage the development of cooperative programs for their solution," (2) to "serve as a center for stimulation of state, district, and local programs for the promotion of physical fitness," (3) to "make available to states, localities and organizations and agencies, upon request, the services of specialists in physical fitness," and (4) to "prepare materials and serve as a clearing-house on informational matters, pertaining to the development of a national program of physical fitness." It also stated that the peculiar responsibility of the Committee on Physical Fitness was "with the development of strength, agility, stamina, and endurance in the civilian population."[1]

This new committee of 1943 included only three physical educators (15 percent of the committee membership) and one of these, C. Ward Crampton, had long since left the profession for private medical practice. The other two were Hiram A. Jones, New York State Physical Director and former president of AAHPER, and August H. Pritzlaff, supervisor of physical education of Chicago public schools and incoming president of AAHPER. Not one woman physical educator was on the committee, but also there was no wealthy socialite or sports figure, either man or woman, for publicity value!

The other committee members represented United States Selective Service, Athletic Institute, intercollegiate athletics, Special Services of Armed Services, United States Public Health Service, Bureau of Naval Personnel, Training Department of United States Navy, Community War Services, National Federation of High School Athletic Associations, Physical Training Department of Army Air Forces, U.S. Commissioner of Education, one sports editor (Arch Ward of the *Chicago Tribune*), one professional sports association (baseball) and the assistant to the head of the FSA. Such a membership meant that experts would have to be called in to get the actual work done, and that is what happened. Physical educators were called into the U.S. Office of Education and other government agencies within the FSA to work full-time.

Women's physical education was represented by Dorothy M. LaSalle, for many years head of physical education of East Orange, New Jersey public schools. She was on the administrative staff as senior specialist heading up the work for girls and women. She was also listed as specialist in Physical Fitness in the U.S. Office of Education, with Jackson Sharman, former Alabama State Director of Physical Education, listed as Principal Specialist on Physical Fitness for the U.S. Office of Education. Frank Lloyd, on leave from New York University, was later executive officer of this new National Committee on Physical Fitness.

Under this committee several subcommittees were set up such as one on state and local organizations, one on schools and colleges, one on national organizations, and one on promotion. George R. Holstrom was named head of the first one, and, as the acknowledged but unofficial Nebraska State Chairman of Physical Fitness, it was under him that I continued my somewhat hopeless task with our still unyielding governor. He was informing people that I was the state chairman but refused to give that chairmanship official sanction. However, the new Physical Fitness Committee blinked at this queer informality and Mr. Holstrom placed my name on his official list of state chairmen. Thus we in Nebraska could move forward somewhat.

From now on, much of the printed matter sent to us workers acknowledged indebtedness to the Athletic Institute (headquarters, Chicago) for financing the printing. Apparently even the FSA was given a scant budget by Congress for the Division of Physical Fitness as had been the case with the OCD before it.

A National Council of Physical Fitness was established shortly as an advisory group for the new National Committee on Physical Fitness. It consisted of 78 persons, 27 of whom were physical educators, 13 men and 14 women (I was one of them). The makeup of the Council represented such national groups as AAU, American Legion, American Red Cross, American Medical Association, American Federation of Labor, American Camping Association, Broadcasting Corporation, CIO, Federated Women's Clubs, Four-H Clubs, Girl Scouts, NYAA, PTA, U.S. Junior Chamber of Commerce, Veterans of Foreign Wars, War Production Board, Motion Picture Industry, AAHPER, and NAPECW.

The hectic pace of the Physical Fitness Movement was now slackening for us volunteers since under the FSA full-time professionals on salary entered the scene. They were advancing the cause quietly, effectively and without political fanfare or ballyhoo.

* * * *

One of Mr. Kelly's first moves, after the transfer, had been to ask regional directors to use their influence with state departments of education to provide school facilities for citizen use at hours not in use by the schools. As early as December 1941, Mr. Kelly had made this plea but few states were as yet organized for fitness programs. On his second appeal, the heads of 33 (out of 48) state departments of education ordered their school facilities to be made available to non-school groups.[2]

Now with the United States Office of Education entering the picture to take over the fitness work in the schools, the movement was pretty much taken out of Mr. Kelly's hands. Heralded as the outgrowth of the deliberations of the War Manpower Commission and the Wartime

Commission of the U.S. Office of Education, fitness was given a great push. Immediately William Hughes of physical education and Ruth Grout of health education (both professionally trained for their work) were added to the staff of the U.S. Office of Education to push fitness. All lower schools and colleges were urged to (1) require physical education daily of all pupils, (2) use all facilities for the adult population to get physically fit, and (3) use the schools as community recreation centers for all.

Under the Wartime Commission a subcommittee was appointed to determine how effectively college students could be brought to a high level of physical fitness quickly. N. P. Neilson, formerly of the California State Department of Education, but then executive secretary of AAHPER, was assigned by Mr. Studebaker to organize this subcommittee. Dr. Neilson, aware that the regional directorships of the Division of Physical Fitness as set up within the OCD were being abandoned, enlisted several of us former regional directors to join this committee. So in May I picked up another assignment.

At this same time the College Physical Education Association made a survey which revealed that 92 percent of all colleges had made physical education compulsory for all students. Of these, 49 percent required daily participation, 97 percent required medical examinations, 87 percent attempted to correct remedial defects, 68 percent added new activities to the program, and 80 percent granted college credit for the work. As a result of this survey, the U. S. Wartime Commission strongly recommended that in this emergency all colleges require physical education daily for all students for all four years.[3]

Although the National Association of Physical Education for College Women did not make a survey of physical education requirements for college women, it immediately began a study of the programs and what could be done to step up physical activity for all women college students. President Elizabeth Kelley of Pomona College and a small group of us women college directors from seven states met in June 1942 at a retreat cabin on the Mississippi River at McGregor, Iowa.[4] We drew up resolutions and suggestions which, in the name of NAPECW, were sent to colleges throughout the country, urging them to stress the development of agility, muscular strength, physical courage, flexibility and relaxation, and the correction of remedial defects—all this physical activity coupled with knowledge of weight control.

From now on it began to look as if we needed to stress activities such as walking, running and general conditioning exercises which do not require special facilities and equipment. Such a program I had all my professional career held as valuable, so that I fell in with it at once.

I was greatly amused at many of my professional friends who lamented that we would accomplish nothing without gyms, playing fields, pools, and lots of balls, bats and everything else. I had been raised in circumstances where we had no physical education facilities, no equipment, even no leadership to speak of, yet we who had an inner drive for it enjoyed a rich life of physical activity. The moaning ones could not be consoled by the fact that our program could go ahead and use facilities and equipment to further enrich the program wherever and whenever we could find them.

As the new form of organization for a Division of Physical Fitness was shaping up, Jay B. Nash, president of AAHPER, set up several committees to help the movement. Rationing of many supplies was threatening setbacks in some parts of physical education and sports projects which were essential to a fitness program. Particularly we women were being handicapped by a ruling that sneakers were to be purchased only through shoe-rationing coupons. Older girls, especially, refused to use such coupons to purchase sneakers which they would wear only in physical education programs. Therefore, women's departments were pushing for sneakers to be taken off the ration lists. Through a committee headed by August Pritzlaff, AAHPER did get sneakers and other sports items removed from such lists.

Finally with the issuance of Administrative Order #42 creating the Commission on Physical Fitness under the FSA, Mr. Kelly sent out letters which were the death knell of the regional directors of physical fitness under him. In his letter to me of dismissal from the regional directorship under the OCD setup, he expressed thanks and hoped I would continue to serve unofficially as a consultant whenever called upon. Of course I replied in the affirmative. Although I no longer had funds for travel and telephone calls and had to refuse all long-distance calls, the Women's Athletic Association at my university continued its financial support to meet my stationery, postage and mimeographing expenses. The volunteer secretaries stayed with me, so I responded to all continuing calls for help as I could meet them through correspondence. Thus I was able to turn out a lot more work unofficially for the war effort.

* * * *

When it was official that the Division of Physical Fitness was to be dropped from the OCD I had a final conference at the Nebraska State House in early April 1943 with Dr. Miller and Mr. Moon. I informed them officially that the Division was being reorganized and transferred to the Federal Security Agency. I fear that it was with tongue in cheek that I thanked them for their services to the cause but I was determined to make the correct gestures. Mr. Moon had been willing to help but his superiors never gave him a go-ahead signal.

It now became a source of great but secret amusement to me that when upper echelon workers in the FSA physical fitness program asked for reports from Nebraska, the governor always referred them to me as the Nebraska Chairman of Physical Fitness although he never officially appointed me as such. This was not the only area in which Nebraska was dragging its feet. It was also slow (I was told by workers in the OCD regional office) in lining up volunteers for civilian defense, in organizing local defense councils in all countries and towns of over 5,000 population, and in getting the American Legion organized for aircraft warning service. We were still strongly isolationist even after the country was drawn into the war.

Despite my repeated announcements to him that the governor was still adamant that there would be no Nebraska State Physical Fitness organization, Mr. Kelly doggedly continued to recognize me as the state's physical fitness director under him for he retained his old state setups of OCD to reach out-of-school groups. So materials for Nebraska kept coming to me from Mr. Kelly's office and I did what I could about them, sub rosa as it were. The Nebraska State Physical Education Association backed me in this and we had an unofficial state committee which helped both school and non-school groups in many ways behind the scenes. Finally, after four months of working in this round-about way, the State Superintendent of Public Instruction took our committee under his wing and by October 1943, we were officially recognized as a State Committee on Physical Fitness of the Nebraska AAHPER, sponsored by the state superintendent.

When the first published report of state programs of physical fitness came out in June 1942,[5] I, still feeling keenly the inability to get my home state organized, turned to the report eagerly to see what other states might also not be in the physical fitness fold. There I discovered to my relief and concern, that only half of the states were organized. Mr. McCormick and I had six states in our region that were organized, more than any other region. This was followed by three states organized for four regions each, two states each for two other regions and one state for one region, and none for one.

While pushing for action in the remaining 24 states through the summer, Mr. Kelly asked me for permission to reproduce the bulletins I had issued for my state chairmen. I was pleased to grant it. In July alone I had prepared 18 pamphlets and leaflets to send out to 10 state directors asking for help.

* * * *

The promotion of a High School Victory Corps was one of the developments of the Wartime Commission of the U.S. Office of Education under the FSA which was presented to public attention through a pamphlet published in August 1942.[6] In its foreword, the U.S. Commissioner of Education called attention to the fact that the National Policy Committee, representing the War Department, the Navy Department, the Civil Aeronautics Administration of the Department of Commerce, the Wartime Commission of the U.S. Office of Education, and civilian aviation interests, had given its hearty endorsement of the Victory Corps and offered to help develop the program. The Secretaries of War, Navy and Commerce (Henry Stimson, Frank Knox and Jesse H. Jones) as well as Paul McNutt of the FSA and President Roosevelt contributed opening statements for the bulletin. In his opening words, Commissioner Studebaker said:

> We are engaged in a war for survival. This is a total war—a war of armies and navies, a war of factories and farms, a war of homes and schools. Education has an indispensable part to play in total war. Schools must help to teach individuals the issues at stake; to train them for their vital parts in the total war effort; to guide them into conscious personal relationship to the struggle.

> Students in the Nation's 28,000 secondary schools are eager to do their part for victory. To utilize more fully this eagerness to serve, to organize it into effective action, to channel it into areas of increasingly critical need, the National Policy Committee recommends the organization of a Victory Corps in every American high school, large or small, public or private.[7]

Physical fitness was included as a major part of the high school Victory Corps program and was tied into a program encompassing guidance in critical services and occupations, wartime citizenship, competence in science and mathematics, preflight training in aeromechanics, and community services. It took on an aura of respectability that assured success.

The U.S. Office of Education published *A Victory Corps Physical Fitness Manual* which was produced by the joint efforts of the armed forces, the Public Health Service and physical educators.[8] The program for boys was developed particularly to stress aggressiveness, strength, endurance and muscular coordination. The total program was to include calisthenics, body-building exercises, running, jumping, climbing, tumbling, wrestling, team sports, marching, hiking, swimming and rhythmic dancing, to be accompanied by health examinations, correction of remedial defects, nutrition schedules, safety education, first aid, and knowledge of hygiene.

This was to be a voluntary program offering a choice of specialization within five service divisions—air, land, sea, production and community, with all divisions participating in the physical fitness program. There were insignia for the various divisions of service to be worn on the Victory Corps cap. The Division of Physical Fitness of the Victory Corps set up regional three-day institutes to cover all parts of the country to train leaders who in turn would set up a series of state physical fitness institutes to train local leaders for the program. Dr. Jackson Sharman headed this project. Working under him was an 18-man committee on Wartime Physical Education for High Schools. Assisted by representatives of the United States Army and Navy, the Health Education Department of the U.S. Office of Education and AAHPER, Jackson Sharman and his group, calling themselves a travelling circus, toured the country putting on these institutes, all patterned after the program planned in Washington.

Since Lincoln, Nebraska was a state capital, centrally located within the nine states to be covered by one institute, to cover two FSA areas the planning group in Washington chose it for the site. No doubt because Jackson Sharman knew me better than any of the other leaders in these states, he asked me to serve as local chairman for the three-day institute. The skeletal program was already made out. The Physical Fitness Program of the Victory Corps would be explained by the specialist, and the Army and Navy representatives from Washington, were scheduled to put on several sessions each for boys in combatives, aquatics and gymnastics, leaving it to me and any local committees I wished to set up to arrange demonstrations in gymnastics, aquatics and rhythms for girls. Some foundation in Chicago would send out a speaker on mental attitudes in relation to wartime fitness and the consultant in health education of the U.S. Office of Education would handle health topics. All announcements would be sent out from Washington to the schools, communities and newspapers of the nine states. My local committee and I were to fill in the rest of the program as we thought best.

I immediately set up a local committee, including Mr. W.A. Rosene of the State Department of Public Instruction, the Nebraska University Health Services, the president of the Nebraska AAHPER (Jimmy Lewis of Lincoln), and the state directors of physical education and/or state physical fitness directors in the nine states. We filled in the gaps with talks and demonstrations by leaders in physical education from Minnesota, Missouri, Kansas and Iowa. We called on the Nebraska State Department of Health, the Nebraska Agricultural Extension Department and the Nebraska State Nutrition Organizations to help us.

When the institute opened on November 19, 1942, we were delighted to have 260 registered delegates. The meetings were held on the university campus. One evening we put on an all-conference dinner at the Student Union, the cost per plate, 65 cents.

On the opening day I hosted an afternoon tea at my home in honor of the "travelling circus" or "barnstormers," inviting the state directors of physical education and of physical fitness of the old OCD program, all who were to participate in the program, and my local committee. That "travelling circus" was a jolly bunch consisting of Major Birch Bayh of the U.S. Army, formerly head of physical education of the Washington, D.C. schools (father of today's Senator Birch Bayh); Lt. John Miller, USNR, one of Tom Hamilton's Navy Air Force Staff on loan to the U.S. Office of Education; Lt. Commander Charles Forsythe of the U.S. Navy, formerly Michigan State Director of Physical Education; Neils Neilson, executive secretary of AAHPER; Jackson Sharman, that delightful and gallant southern gentleman from Alabama; and Ruth Grout, the last two with the U.S. Office of Education. When I asked Birch and Neils if they would "pour" at my tea they consented to do so only if I would supply them with fancy hats to wear as they had noted was the accepted headdress for those who "pour" at teas. So I outfitted them with flower-bedecked hats, and the get-acquainted tea party immediately turned into a rollicking, hilarious affair. It quieted down after a while for instructions to local committees and those who were to put on the program so that we were ready for a fast start once the institute was formally underway that evening.

The one stranger in the group was young Lt. Miller but he was a stranger for a brief time only. After the institute was over, he wrote me a delightful letter of thanks for my hospitality and shortly after that a goodbye note saying he was leaving for active service overseas. That was the last I heard of him. I have often wondered what became of that charming young lieutenant. I hope he came home safely.

The exercises presented by the Victory Corps were most strenuous— so much so that several women delegates complained about them as entirely too strenuous for girls. But the women offering the girls' part of the exercise program stood their ground, insisting that in the past decade with gymnastics eliminated from school programs our girls had grown soft and now needed some toughening up. What the Victory Corps was offering would do the job. I had carefully chosen the women to put on the girls' exercises from among the few I knew in the nine states who believed as I did in the values of strenuous disciplined exercise for girls as well as for boys and had kept in touch with gymnastics teaching. In 1942 such teachers were a rarity but luckily we still had a few of them at hand.

With the institute over, the delegates were urged to set up a series of district institutes in their own states to carry the program down to the grassroots.

The year 1943 brought increased activity throughout schools in the promotion of physical fitness as a result of these regional institutes. In Nebraska, we put on 31 district institutes on two Saturdays in January covering the entire state in such a way that no one needed to travel more than 50 miles. These institutes were sponsored by the State Departments of Instruction and Health, State Medical and Dental Societies, the State PTA, and the State Association for Health, Physical Education and Recreation, with the programs planned by the still-unofficial Nebraska State Committee of Physical Fitness. These institutes, put on (presumably) in all 48 states and supported by the U.S. Army and Navy and the U.S. Office of Education, had a far better chance to reach the nation's 28,000 secondary schools than did John Kelly trying to go it practically alone under the OCD.

* * * *

At the annual convention of the Central Association for HPER, held in Kansas City, Missouri April, 1943, I was scheduled to speak at two general sessions—two more chances to promote physical fitness in our area. John Kelly had consented to be the banquet speaker to explain the new set-up to our region. At last we in this part of the country had a chance to meet him. We found him interesting, sincere and a splendid exponent of physical fitness himself. Seated next to him at the banquet I was treated to a showing of pocket photographs of his very pretty young daughter, Grace (today's Princess of Monaco) and his still younger son (recently president of today's AAU).

Military rejection figures were now out. General Lewis B. Hershey, director of Selective Service, was with us at our national convention in Cincinnati in April 1943. He told us that over 40 percent of the draftees were unqualified for military service by wartime standards. In the 18 to 20-year-old group, 20 percent were rejected, and in the 35 to

364

38-year-old group, 60 percent were rejected. Later we learned that as of March 1, 1944, 3½ million had been rejected with mental disease, topping all causes for disqualifications. June 1 figures raised that to more than 4 million for men 18 to 37 years old. By June 1, over a million men inducted into the armed forces had been discharged, mostly for physical and mental reasons.

* * * *

In August 1943 I was called to Washington by the United States Office of Education to work on a committee to study how to manage in the face of the terrific shortage of teachers confronting all schools. This small committee was specifically concerned with the problem as it was affecting physical education in the schools. Early in my work in the OCD I had, with the help of my physical education majors at the University of Nebraska, made a nationwide survey of women trained in physical education who had left teaching and could be sought out as possible volunteers for the physical fitness movement in this war emergency. This survey, as related in Chapter XIX, resulted in a list of several hundred names of women with their current addresses. I sent a copy of the list to Mr. Kelly and to the U.S. Office of Education for whatever help it might be there.

My invitation to serve on this committee on teacher shortage no doubt stemmed from this survey. This trip was my first to Washington in many years and I found it thrilling to be caught up in the excitement of war emergencies. The Germans had, a few months before, surrendered at Stalingrad, the Axis Army had been captured recently in Tunisia, Hitler had started another Russian offensive, and Allied troops were on the verge of landing in Italy from North Africa. This last was of course a secret but close to the surface, and tension was building. In Washington you felt in the air that important things were brewing.

The lobby and promenades of the recently built Statler Hotel were filled with men and women dressed in all manner of military uniforms, American and foreign, including some in costumes of the Far and Middle East. Of course we were used to seeing military uniforms in Lincoln since there was an air base nearby, and I had recently visited the Women's Army Corps at Fort Des Moines, but Lincoln and Des Moines offered nothing as exciting as Washington.

Would that I still had a copy of the final report of that committee's recommendations to the U.S. Office of Education to give the highlights of our planning. My diary and memories alone are not sufficient. Whether any good at all came from our efforts, I never knew.

* * * *

Immediately following D Day in June, the American Medical Association, which had been taking a new look at the Physical Fitness Movement since the Selective Service report on military service rejections, accepted the invitation of the Committee on Physical Fitness of the FSA to put on a special emphasis year for further development of better fitness for the general population. A joint committee of AMA and the National Council of Physical Fitness of FSA was formed, headed by a ruling committee made up of five members from each of these organizations. Among the physicians of the AMA were Morris Fishbein, editor of the *Journal* of the AMA, C. Ward Crampton, well-known physician of New York City, and Colonel Leonard Rowntree of the Surgeon General's Office, formerly of Johns Hopkins University. Two physical education members from the National Committee of Physical Fitness of FSA were Hiram Jones and August Pritzlaff. Colonel Rowntree was named chairman of the committee and our own Frank Lloyd of New York University, its secretary. The committee established coordinators, two each in six areas of concern, to help plan and conduct the year's program.

Although I was a member of the larger FSA Council on Physical Fitness, I was not a member of the smaller FSA Committee on Physical Fitness, which had no women members. However, Colonel Rowntree invited me to accept an appointment as one of two coordinators for programming, representing the National Council of Physical Fitness, to work with a similar coordinator appointed from the AMA. This was contingent upon my ability to come to Washington July 27-28, 1944, for a meeting of the joint AMA and FSA committees. This invitation came as a great surprise to me for I had earlier received a revised four-page poster-type bulletin of the FSA Committee on Physical Fitness explaining to the public the committee's functions and latest plan of operation. On the back page were listed the names and professional affiliations of the members of both the National Committee and the Committee of Physical Fitness. On this, my name, along with those of 10 other women and 5 men physical educators who had been named as members on an earlier bulletin, was omitted.

Since I had been immersed quite steadily for three years in the physical fitness work, plus my full-time position, I had accepted an invitation to join a small group of close professional friends for a canoe trip over the Canadian border for a complete change in pace. The date coincided with the date for this meeting. It had been so long since I had relaxed that I was loathe to give up the canoe trip, but I couldn't say no to this one more call to duty. So I accepted this work invitation. Here at last seemed to be hope of getting something quite worthwhile under way.

Frank Lloyd sent a letter of instruction on travel arrangements which were to cover railroad and Pullman fare plus $10 per day for expenses as a consultant while in travel status. He had proclaimed, "This is perhaps the most outstanding opportunity for service in the area of physical fitness that has confronted any of us."

As the conference opened I was surprised to find that of the 90 or so delegates, only 6 were women, representing the Federated Women's Clubs of America; the National YWCA; the Parent-Teacher Association; the nursing profession; and two of us representing physical education, Dorothy LaSalle and I. The men included all the officers of the American Medical Association, the president of the American Dental Association, leading physicians and sports writers, many men physical educators, manufacturers of sporting goods, and top male officers of the U.S. Army and Navy. It was indeed a man's world.

The one person of all that group who interested me the most was C. Ward Crampton, M.D., of New York City, whom I had heard of ever since my earliest teaching years but had never met. When he saw my name in the list of delegates as director of Physical Education for Women, University of Nebraska, he searched me out. He had been out of touch with our profession for many years and was eager to be brought up-to-date about it. He was accompanied by an attractive young woman, a representative of the nursing profession, with whom he had worked on joint AMA projects wishing support from her organization. He insisted that the two of us have dinner with him the first evening. We had a merry time for Dr. Crampton, whom I had known of merely as the author of folk dance books which I had used for many years, was an entertaining dinner companion. He had graduated from medical school in 1900 at the age of 23 and immediately went into private practice in New York City until he was appointed to succeed Luther Gulick as head of physical training for the Greater New York City Public Schools which position he held from 1907 to 1919. During this period he had been active in the work of the American Physical Education Association. After a two-year stint as dean of the Battle Creek Normal School of Physical Education in Michigan, he had returned to his medical practice in New York City. It was in this latter period that he had developed an interest in physical fitness. When he had introduced himself to me, I exclaimed:

"C. Ward Crampton! Could you be the C. Ward Crampton who wrote the folk dance books I used for many years as a young teacher?"

"Imagine meeting someone these many years later who recalls those books!" he replied, seemingly greatly amused. By then he was known across the country for his many years of writing on physical fitness and as the originator of the first national broadcast series on preventive medicine, and for his Columbia Woman's Health Radio Series. Now as a physician who was a long-time writer and radio personality in the field of physical fitness, he was drawn into the work of this joint endeavor of the AMA and the FSA Committee on Physical Fitness.

At dinner that evening Dr. Crampton was amused over the memories of his youthful enthusiasm for folk dancing. (He had done his books on the subject in his twenties.) He insisted that we do a folk dance or two right there in the hotel dining room. I finally persuaded him that I had long since forgotten the dances and challenged his memory, too. Dissuaded from public display, he exclaimed merrily:

"But wait till I get back home and tell the medics of New York City of my youthful indiscretion—my early fling at dancing!"

What keen delight he took in reminiscing about the turn of the century when folk dancing was of great interest to him. Inspired by Luther Gulick, both he and Elizabeth Burchenal put out their first folk dance books in the same year. It was a special bonus for the uncomfortable trip to Washington to have had this brief encounter with Dr. Crampton. Sixteen years later we were to meet again.

I also had an opportunity to chat with Colonel Rowntree. When I pointed out that there were no women physicians on his AMA-FSA committee, he said that two leading women physicians had been invited but had declined. Later I called to Frank Lloyd's attention that there were no women, not even a woman physical educator, on the new FSA Committee on Physical Fitness or in the Sports Group sub-section meeting of this planning conference, and that I had been the only woman at that group's meeting and then only as a last-minute guest. I insisted that there were many competent women in the physical education profession deeply interested in promoting sports for women and that they should be given an equal chance with the men to work in these groups. He agreed to correct this error.

* * * *

368

When this joint AMA-FSA conference was over, six of us physical educators stayed for an extra day at the invitation of J. W. Studebaker, U.S. Commissioner of Education. We drew up proposals for adequate staff physical education specialists to serve the country in health instruction, physical education, athletics, and recreation. The Commissioner could use these suggestions to strengthen his demands for improved services and increased budget.[9] It was an interesting assignment. The six were Dorothy LaSalle of the U.S. Office of Education staff, Ben Miller, the new executive secretary of AAHPER, Edwin Henderson, head of physical education for all black schools of the District of Columbia (all three living in the Washington area) plus Carl Nordly, Margaret Bell, one of the few women physicians in our profession, and I.

I cancelled my railroad reservations to stay over and was rewarded by a strange but interesting experience resulting from the coincidence that Frank Sinatra had a hotel room next to mine. In order to get out of my room to leave the hotel that morning I had to be rescued by police from the yelling and screaming mob of teenage girls who filled the hallway. When I arrived at the U.S. Office of Education a bit belatedly and asked in all innocence, "Who is Frank Sinatra?" the group was thrown into a bit of hysterics of their own to think there was a woman anywhere in the United States who had not heard of him.

"Where have you been living?" was all the reply I could get.

My memories of that extra day in Washington take on a special note as I realize that this was the first time I was ever involved in a professional meeting with a Negro in top level deliberations. Edwin Henderson proved a splendid addition to the group. This belated recognition from our national association workers bespoke our profession's slowness in opening its door to blacks, even up to the World War II period when Mr. Henderson's qualifications had been recognized by the Federal Security Administration to the extent that he was the one black person on the FSA Physical Fitness Committee. He was pushing a vigorous physical fitness program for the schools of Washington, D.C. He had been teaching there in the Negro schools since 1904 and at that early date he had established intramural sports, many years ahead of most white schools.

It was 27 years before we met again. I often wondered what had become of him. Then in March 1971, when I was one of five guest speakers at the Big Ten Symposium on the History of Physical Education and Sport sponsored by Ohio State University, I discovered him once more. He, too, was a guest speaker. He was 88 and I, 85. We had a great time reminiscing of the 1890s and the turn of the century, but how different had been our childhood experiences. Yet how similar in a way had been our professional experiences, he battling in his quiet way for a place in education for blacks; I, battling in my way for women's fair place in physical education.

We enjoyed for those two or three days, three meals a day together with whoever else of the conference would join us. Following that, we exchanged friendly letters and I followed his career until his death in 1976 at the age of 93. In 1974 he was belatedly inducted into the Black Sports Hall of Fame along with Jesse Owens, Henry Aaron, Willie Mays, Althea Gibson, Wilma Rudolph and several others. He had years before organized the first black athletic league in America, was the first black person to write of Negroes in sport. He had done much for blacks in sports and was most belatedly being recognized. Through great adversities he retained his kindly spirit, refusing to become embittered or belligerent over the racial difficulties he encountered.

* * * *

After my return home from the joint AMA-FSA conference, Colonel Rowntree sent out a letter to those of us who had worked on the Physical Fitness Planning Conference asking us to continue in the same capacity for the coming year. This, of course, I agreed to. With the fall opening of a new school year, the Committee on Physical Fitness renewed its efforts to get all the state physical fitness committees on the move again. George Holstrom, chief of State and Local Organizations for the new Committee working out of the FSA office in Washington, renewed efforts to get Nebraska's Governor Griswold to set up an official state physical fitness committee. The governor was still adamant that there was to be no such organization in his state. Mr. Holstrom was still sending me literature that I was supposed to send out over the state, suggesting various plans of action, and I was still protesting to him that I had no official status for carrying out his suggestions. So now a new approach to the governor was tried. The new Joint Committee on Physical Fitness with the AMA in partnership with the FSA Committee on Physical Fitness made an appeal to the citizenry of the nation heretofore not done by the Committee on Physical Fitness alone. Through its influence, Major General Hershey of the Selective Service wrote Governor Griswold soliciting his interest in the work of the Joint Committee. The governor pledged his cooperation but did nothing.[10] Following that, Colonel Rowntree, himself, wrote the governor asking his help to bring Nebraska into the physical fitness movement. He suggested that the governor establish a state physical fitness committee, bringing into it the state organizations and agencies he deemed advisable and asking that he be informed of the person or persons with whom he could communicate if he wished to delegate this responsibility.[11]

As of late November the governor had not answered the letter. In a gesture to excuse the governor, I replied that he had undoubtedly been too busy getting himself reelected to office to take care of such extras. Mr. Holstrom informed me that if an answer were received he would let me know, but the word never came, so Colonel Rowntree must have been compelled to write off Nebraska. At home, things still drifted on the state level.

In early December, Dorothy LaSalle, then senior physical fitness representative of the Committee on Physical Fitness of the FSA, wrote to see if I could influence the Nebraska state organization of the American Association of University Women to recognize the need for better health education, physical education and recreation in their legislative platform. She also asked that I contact Bessie O. Randolph, president of Hollins College and chairman of the AAUW Legislation Program Committee. Since I had found it difficult to assume all the extra professional work I had undertaken in recent years besides my full-time position, I had some time before dropped out of the Lincoln chapter of AAUW. I discovered how displeased the local chapter was over my frequent absences from their Saturday meetings. So I wrote Dorothy:

> In view of the fact that I have dropped out of AAUW I am wondering if a letter from a non-member would mean anything. With all the important things going on in the world that need the attention now of college women, our branch is this year discussing "Old Glass." I have been entirely too busy the past few years to spend my Saturday afternoons on such topics even though they are interesting.[12]

* * * *

In February 1945 I received an invitation from Paul McNutt, administrator of the FSA, to become a member of a Women's Commission being established to study the fitness problems of girls and women in relation to their changing role in society. Accompanying literature indicated there would be 30 members drawn from a great variety of fields and organizations. If we felt any field of particular concern had been omitted we were to alert the secretary of the Commission. I suggested

371

that the physical training departments of the women's branches of the military services be included. (By then, WAVES, Spars and similar groups had joined the WACs in military service.) Apparently others also made suggestions because the final list included, besides the women's military units, editors of women's magazines, consultants of women in industry, and the like.

The Commission ended up with 115 persons listed, 46 of whom finally came to Washington for the meeting of March 21-23, 1945. Seven were physical educators; Dorothy LaSalle, FSA executive officer of the Commission, Laurentine Collins of the Detroit public schools as chairman, Ruth Atwell of George Washington University, Dr. Margaret Bell of the University of Michigan, Rosalind Cassidy of Mills College, Elizabeth Halsey of the University of Iowa representing NAPECW, and I. It was an interesting group—several women editors, top-ranking women in government work, heads of important national women's organizations, as well as general educators and a handful of women physical educators.

The opening morning session was chaired by John Kelly who introduced Dr. Lawrence Frank, well-known consultant on child development, who gave the keynote address. At the afternoon session, Margaret Mead, a noted anthropologist, was the opening speaker, and after her Dr. Frank spoke again.

At this second session Dr. Frank got down to practical talk of "Basic Biological Concepts Relevant to the Fitness of Girls and Women." Officers of the WAC and Spars and the Women's Medical Corps reported to the delegates on the fitness programs of women in the armed forces. Dr. Frank felt that the movement for physical fitness would be better served if we would use the term *physical conservation* since the word *fitness*, whether warranted or not, was in disfavor among many people and hindered the movement. But we were too habituated to the phrase to change readily. (Over a quarter of a century later some people are still asking for better phraseology but none seems to serve as well as the time-worn term.)

The next two days we divided into four small groups for discussions of fitness problems of women—(1) in lay groups, (2) in schools and colleges, (3) in business, industry and labor, and (4) in youth-serving organizations. Each group produced a set of recommendations later released to the press.

My group tackled the problem of how to meet the fear of so many high school and college girls that taking physical education would build bulging muscles. The truth was that it was a rare course offered in any physical education department anywhere that gave exercise strenuous or long enough to produce bulging muscles, with the rare exception of intensive ballet dancing which overdevelops the muscles of the gluteal region and the calves of the legs. Such intensive exercise, we all acknowledged, is rarely encountered except in schools preparing students for the stage.

Talk of the physiological "overload" principle occupied much of the group's time. This principle, although never spoken of as such, had been drilled into me in my professional training days and throughout all my teaching years I had felt that any physical education class hour for my students was largely time wasted if every girl had not left for the dressing room after a thorough workout of all the large muscles within her own physical capacity, be it a gymnastics, dance or sports class.

To my dismay I had become aware through the 1920s and 1930s that the new much-heralded educational philosophies, calling for life-adjustment and psychosomatic training, had been eroding our principles of the physiological whys and wherefores of our programs. The battle of the humanities versus science had affected physical education until it was difficult to find staff members who had been trained to respect the tenets of physiology of exercise. They were giving their pupils exercise periods so mild there was little need for donning a gymnastic or sports costume.

Class work had come to such a pass that I felt many times, even in my own department, that the girls had a real complaint about the demand to change costumes or the suggestion for a shower following class when they hadn't exercised enough to require either. As I had looked about me at my own departmental program as well as many others across the country, I became somewhat cynical about our current physical education professional training courses. As I became more and more disturbed over the demise of gymnastics—victim of theories in the name of progressive education—I became more and more interested in modern dance, the one activity common to all college courses of that day that was really worthy of the designation, "course for physical fitness."

Now I was delighted to sit in on a meeting where important lay women were questioning our physical education activity classes as offering too little strenuous exercise. We even drew up resolutions urging that schools and colleges in their physical education classes offer class work that would actually build physical strength and endurance.

At these meetings I became acquainted with Judge Anna Kross of New York City, spoken of as "the poor man's judge." On my next trip to New York City I spent a day as her guest at her court in Harlem—a never-to-be-forgotten experience.

Of all the many meetings of top level workers I attended throughout the war years in behalf of physical fitness, none was so down-to-earth and to the point as this conference of the Women's Commission of the FSA.

* * * *

Throughout 1945 the Committee on Physical Fitness, supported by our profession and many other groups, was trying to get through the 79th Congress a bill known as the United States Physical Fitness Act, sponsored by Samuel Weiss, Democrat of Pennsylvania and Fred A. Hartley, Republican of New Jersey. The bill (H.R. 2044) called for a commission to advise and aid the states and territories to set up programs of physical fitness to serve everyone. This commission was to consist of nine persons appointed for two-year terms—two senators appointed by the President of the Senate, two representatives appointed by the Speaker of the House, and five persons appointed by the President of the United States. Of the five presidential appointees, there was to be one man and one woman "expertly qualified in physical training" and one other person qualified in the conduct of athletic competition. This commission was to appoint an administrator to be known as the U.S. Commissioner of Physical Fitness. The bill called for an appropriation of $25 million annually to start July 1, 1945, with each state and territory matching its allotment by 50 percent, the money allocated according to the population of each state. The commissioner's salary was set up at $10,000 per annum, the members of the commission were to receive $25 per diem allowance plus travel expenses when on commission work. The bill did not pass, but it was a good try.

On June 30, 1945, Mr. Kelly wrote me, as he did the many others who had worked with him, as follows:

> On April 29, 1943, the Committee on Physical Fitness was established by President Roosevelt and was given a budget of $80,000 per year from Presidential funds. You were appointed as a member of the Council under authority of this order.
>
> Because of the size of our budget we have not been able to meet very often but we feel that the money has been well spent and we have laid the groundwork for a real physical fitness movement.
>
> Funds for the Committee beyond June 30, 1945, have not been appropriated. Therefore the Committee on Physical Fitness will cease its functions as of that day. The reason for this is that the

Director of the Federal budget feels that physical fitness has grown to such proportions that it should be put on a permanent basis by Act of Congress.

We regret that we have not been able to accomplish more but we are quite encouraged by the impetus given to physical fitness in schools and in industry and by the great interest shown in Living War Memorials which is promoted by a commission appointed by your Committee.

I wish to thank you for the service you have rendered to the cause and I feel certain that one day you will see this great nation aroused to the need that we have seen for many years.

So the great venture was over. I was glad to have had a part in it, starting with the work under the OCD in the fall of 1941 and terminating with the work under the FSA in July 1945. It had been an interesting four years of time-consuming but worthwhile work.

* * * *

With the war intensifying, an American Women's Auxiliary Army Corps was established on May 14, 1942. In the British Isles, thousands of conscripted women were already at work in the uniform of the Auxiliary Territorial Services (ATS), not only on jobs common to women but also as truck drivers, electricians, radio mechanics, gunners, and the like. On May 16, Mrs. Oveta Culp Hobby was named director of the WAAC with the rank of colonel, and the old Army Post at Fort Des Moines was made a training center for officer candidates. Catherine Van Rensselaer, a pupil of the Central School of Physical Education in New York City and of Nils Bukh School of Gymnastics of Denmark, was appointed physical director of the Corps.

Since a howl of protest went up at once from women physical educators over this appointment, I decided to withhold judgment (also my tongue) until I learned about her work firsthand. I wrote the Commandant and asked if visitors were permitted at Fort Des Moines and explained my interest. Receiving a prompt reply of welcome, I dashed over in August. To my surprise, I found in Miss Van Rensselaer's place as head of physical training, a pupil of my good friend, Marjorie Bouvé, Brenda Boynton, who had resigned her physical education position at Boston University to "join up." The following spring I met her again at the AAHPER convention in Cincinnati along with Capt. Donna Niles, a graduate of St. Olaf College who had majored in physical education under my good friend, Mabel Shirley. She was assigned to the Surgeon General's Office in Washington, D.C. as head of Health and Welfare of the WAAC.

The following month I was able to bring Lt. Boynton to the University of Nebraska to talk with our women students, the great majority of whom were cynical about the WAAC and war work for women in general. She was a sensation, even among the men student Army trainees who by then had taken over several university buildings for their quarters. Practically none of them or the regular students, faculty or townspeople had as yet seen a woman in military uniform. In the meantime, as president of the American Academy of Physical Education, I had written Colonel Hobby offering the services of the Academy and of myself, as one trained and experienced in the field of physical education, in whatever way we might assist in the civilian capacity.

By July 1943 the WAAC had ceased to be an auxiliary organization and had become a regular part of the U.S. Army—the WAC. The following May, to my amazement, I received a letter from General George C. Marshall, chief of staff of the U.S. Army, inviting me to become a member of a National Civilian Advisory Committee of the Women's Army Corps. He was setting it up to advise him on matters of recreation, health, nutrition, housing and the like in the military's first venture of accepting women into service. Chancellor Boucher was delighted with the news and I accepted the invitation.

My experiences on that committee, which extended over a four-year period, serving under Generals Marshall, Eisenhower and Bradley, proved most interesting. The full story is enough for a whole book in itself. Suffice it here to touch on it lightly and only on the aspects relating to physical training and sports for the WAC.

In my four years on this committee, we were called to Washington for one meeting under each of the three generals and once at Fort Des Moines when all Lt. Colonel WACs were called from posts all around the world to meet with us. Other meetings were in small subcommittee groups sent to posts for specific investigations. I made one trip to Fort Des Moines, one to New York City to meet "off the record" with military representatives from Washington, D.C. on future plans for the WAC, and one two-week inspection trip to Army hospitals on the West Coast in the summer of 1945 to check on the first WAC medical technicians and physical therapists being used after a crash training course to help with the 40,000 or more wounded or sick soldiers arriving per month from overseas.

This committee of 22 women was the Chief of Staff's own personal committee. Thus our reports, records, queries and recommendations did not go through military channels but through Colonel Hobby directly to him. Of the 21 other members, I knew Dr. Lillian Gilbreth, the famous industrial engineer with whom I had become adquainted in the 1930s. I was delighted to have this new contact with her. Twelve of the members were professional women representing diverse fields. One member represented Negroes, and one each the interests of three religions, Protestant, Catholic and Judaism. The remaining members represented the nine Army Service Commands and the District of Columbia.

I soon discovered that the top echelon of WAC officers under Colonel Hobby were most unhappy with the WAC physical training program, particularly with the fitness tests to which officers were to be subjected at regular intervals. But I found it difficult to get the problem on the agenda for discussion in either the main committee or in the subcommittee on health and welfare. Even these many years later, I still do not understand why this PT program situation existed. I soon saw that my value, if any, on that committee was in giving moral support from the civilian approach to the young WAC officers at the head of the PT program who were 100 percent committed to a stiff physical development regime for all WACs—a program many young lieutenant colonels were obviously unhappy about.

The statistics for rejection of women desiring to enlist was as poor as for the drafted men. Among those accepted for training, the percentages of women who were overweight, underweight or in poor physical condition were also bad. The need, as I saw it, was for strenuous physical conditioning. I was all for it, and Dr. Gilbreth supported me. The young lieutenant colonels who had hoped for my support to ease up on the PT program were disappointed with me, once they learned that I was no follower of the progressive education movement to make all facets of education as soft as possible for everyone.

As to the WAC sports program, as early as July 1944, the War Department released its circular #282 which called for all commanding officers to ensure that WAC activities be conducted according to the rules approved by the National Section on Women's Athletics of AAHPER. But this directive was ignored in many situations where Army men rather than WACs were in charge of WAC sports. Anna Espenschade of the University of California, Berkeley, was at that time chairman of NSWA, and we worked together on this problem.

An interesting outgrowth of this committee work developed as the war closed and thousands of young women were pouring through military separation centers. Many wondered how to return to their former fields of work. I decided that here was something down-to-earth and useful I could do on that committee—establish a setup whereby physical educators could help physical education trained women find positions quickly. Through NAPECW we set up a special placement committee. The University of Nebraska physical education majors came to my assistance, and from my home in Lincoln we ran a placement aid bureau, establishing contacts through the military services separation centers throughout the United States. As a result we helped over a hundred girls find positions quickly, as related later.

This WAC National Civilian Advisory Committee was a worthwhile and interesting assignment. Out of it came my first experience with flying. A few years before the war I was scheduled for a speaking engagement in Fargo, North Dakota and was having difficulty finding trains that went there from Lincoln that were not too time-consuming or impossible for hours and connections. Just then Jay B. Nash came to town from New York University and hearing me "fuss and fume" over this, said "for Heaven's sake, why don't you fly?" I had never been on a plane and at that time the only flight to Fargo from Lincoln meant two or three hops each in a little two-engine plane.

"Oh, no!" I exclaimed, "when I have my first ride on an airplane, I want it to be something glamorous!"

At this Jay B. laughed and said, "When you do have your first ride, promise me you will let me know what it turns out to be!"

I promised, and in September 1945, safely back home from my first meeting in Washington of the National Civilian Advisory Committee of WAC, I sent Jay B. Nash a special letter:

I have just had my first trip on an airplane, flying one day from Washington to Des Moines, the next from Des Moines to Chicago to catch a night train back to Lincoln, both flights on—guess what! It was glamorous! General Marshall's own army plane!

Chapter XIX

A War-Time Campus

As soon as the United States entered the war, the military services commandeered for training purposes facilities in many colleges and universities, including the University of Nebraska.

By December 1942, the entire university was in an upheaval because of the war. The army had taken over the just completed, handsome Love Library and the new Field House for barracks for the military unit assigned to our campus. It also commandeered the kitchens and dining rooms of the rather new Student Union for mess facilities but under the Union management. On the Ag Campus, three miles east of the main city campus, it had also taken over the new Foods and Nutrition Building for barracks and headquarters for a STAR unit, the Specialist Training Assignment Reclassification School. By spring the old ROTC unit had vanished from campus and the boys of the Army Air Corps had moved into the new Love Library with signs posted: "No Trespassing—Government Property." At the time there were around 2,500 civilian students on campus, with 2,500-2,800 men trainees in uniform, marching to and from classes and mess and usually singing as they marched. On weekdays the men in uniform had scarcely a free moment. Campus life as usual was out of the question. The women students outnumbered the civilian men students by 3 to 1—a most unusual situation at Nebraska and men students in uniform counted practically not at all in the extracurricular or social life of the campus.

As for my own departmental work, I immediately set about trying to strengthen our offerings to the women students to embody the resolutions and suggestions of NAPECW and the Wartime Commission of the U.S. Office of Education for the physical education of college women. My staff fell into line 100 percent behind me as did our majors and many other women students. But we struck an immediate snag not only with the faculty but also with many women leaders on campus who could sway campus thinking.

Under the OCD, a National Youth Activities Organization had been set up and under it a College Volunteer Services Section to interest college students to organize their own local war emergency committees which would push for all students to get physically fit and to work on war projects during their free hours. My work as director of physical fitness for girls and women of the OCD of the Seventh Army Corps Area gave me an opportunity to watch developments elsewhere and to compare the Nebraska student war-consciousness with that of other universities. The impressions of these experiences confirmed my belief that Nebraska students were dragging their feet. In April 1942 I had attended a national conference in New Orleans, where I had an opportunity to check the experiences of physical education departments from the two coasts and the south, where great war-consciousness existed even at that time. This still further confirmed my belief that Nebraska women students were not ready even then for the emergency changes that were fast becoming necessary. Two months later I attended a conference of several Directors of Physical Education for College Women from across the country, called by the United States Office of Education for the revision of our college programs to meet war needs. Exchange of experiences there once again showed that our Nebraska women students were slow in acquiring an appreciation of the war situation as it might affect them personally.

Two months later, realizing that it was the college woman who was being called upon for officer material for both the WAVEs and the WAACs, I spent a day with the WAACs in charge of the physical training program at Fort Des Moines discussing the physical fitness needs of women who may be drawn into that type of war work.

As a result of these experiences, I resolved to sound out students early in the fall to see if they had awakened on their own to the need of a vigorous conditioning program, fully determined that if not, the staff would assume active and vigorous leadership to make our young women understand that every young woman must do everything she could to make herself as physically fit as possible so she could contribute her utmost to the war effort.

Our effort soon paid off. A number of upperclass women elected to join our body-conditioning classes offered for the lower-class girls. Some of the older girls were backing a movement to require all women students to take physical education all four years as the U.S. Office of Education was recommending to all colleges. Still others, somewhat unrealistically, inquired about the possibility of sending our instructors to the organized houses to give the girls setting-up drills at bed time or early in the morning. Many women were awakening to the emergency at last.

But what foot-dragging there was by most women students, not only lack of interest in getting physically fit but also in committing themselves to the war effort in any way. Even *The Daily Nebraskan* carried indignant letters to the editor deploring this apathy.

Besides the letter writers, the student leaders of the Women's Athletic Association as well as the women physical education majors were impatient to get into war work of some kind, such as women students were doing at other colleges and universities all across the country. I waited patiently, but in vain for the Associated Women Students (AWS) or Mortar Board—both Greek controlled at Nebraska—to take the lead, and finally the WAA put on a rally luncheon to which were invited the heads of all women's organizations on campus.

This started the ball rolling. Within a week the heretofore ineffective Student Defense Committee changed its name to Student War Council. It stirred up a rally and convocation for all faculty and students, getting out the university band, the Innocents (men's senior honorary) and Mortar Boards (women's senior honorary), the chancellor and deans, the commandant of the campus military, even U.S. Senator George Norris, and others, including about 3,000 students. But even this awakening with promises of support of the war effort did not deter the editor of *The Daily Nebraskan* from having a blast at the many feet-dragging coeds the very day of the rally (March 12, 1942). He said, among other things:

> This editorial also has a point: that university women, University of Nebraska women in particular, still have not figured out what they should be doing now that the nation is at war. They have just found out that there was a war; a lot of their boy-friends are leaving, so they have reason to fret. . . .

This isn't to suggest that every woman immediately drop out of school to join the WAACs, WAVEs, WAAFs, SPARs or the "Marionettes," altho that wouldn't be such a bad idea for more than a few of them.

But it's about time they stop sneering every time they learn that a girl is joining one of the service organizations. They seem to look down upon these organizations. Coed snobbery?

And, more important, it is about time they stopped griping about phys ed and go about the business of getting themselves into the best physical condition, for absurd or not, that is what the government wants them to do.

At that time I was just swinging into intensive work in the Division of Physical Fitness under the OCD and was very conscious of the need to awaken the women of my university to their need to get physically fit. To arouse the women students to the realities of the emergency, I had worked long hours to organize a movement for physical fitness on campus. The Women's Physical Education Club and WAA were behind the movement but found it tough going against campus complacency, student inertia, and still existent pre-war student politics, particularly among certain sororities. With these difficulties in mind, we adopted a policy of watchful waiting, sounding out student opinion as the months passed and seizing every opportunity to discuss the problem with student leaders.

While pursuing this policy toward the upperclass and graduate women not enrolled in our classes, we revised our freshman course in the direction of more vigorous body mechanics and strengthened our offerings in other directions.

Despite our lack of adequate facilities, my staff put on such a program of class credit work that we managed to have our work approved by the students to a degree that surprises me as I look back on it after 30 and more years. It is easy to recall the girls who loudly proclaimed they "hated" gym and to forget the others, the big majority. In my last years before retirement 83 percent of the junior girls who had completed the two-year physical education requirement elected to take more work in the department for their junior year and 81 percent of them in their senior year decided to take a fourth year of work with us.

After much prodding, women students finally began to give serious thought to their own need to be physically fit resulting in criticism of class work that did not give them a strenuous physical workout. Now students began dropping into my office complaining that this or that teacher did not work them hard enough and that there was too much talking by the teacher and too little strenuous exercising. I had suspected this to be the case in some of our classes but no amount of prodding seemed to convince those particular teachers, so with the backing of my dedicated teachers I created a student board to let student voices be heard by all in the hopes of stirring up one or two foot-draggers on the staff. We called it a Planning Board and asked each class section to elect a representative.

To my surprise and pleasure, the girls took this board very seriously and looked upon election to it as a privilege and honor. In the end, the board meeting once a month became so valuable to the department in creating interest in our class work that I kept it in existence all the remaining years of my directorship. It took up departmental rules concerning cuts, absences, make-up work, costumes and the like. The student members made many valuable suggestions and as an important sideline, each representative interpreted the department administration to her class, establishing for us a bond with the great run of students.

To our surprise, some of these students called for stricter rules than we teachers set up, as for example, compulsory shower-taking after each class with a system of checking on it—a ruling most departments of physical education for women had long since dropped. This request the staff was not willing to grant. The students asked for a new style of costume. This we gladly granted and permitted them to help select the new one. They asked that we have lots of jump ropes at hand in both the gymnasiums so that the girls could use them the minute they arrived on the floor instead of standing around lazily waiting for roll call. This we gladly did, feeling a bit foolish that we hadn't thought of this ourselves after one enterprising teacher with a small class had asked for ropes for her class. She motivated the girls to use them; they enjoyed this informal pre-class rope jumping so much that many made it a point to arrive early for this bit of warming-up and the word about it had spread to other classes. Now we ordered 100 more ropes and hung them conspicuously all along the gymnasium walls and they were used happily and continuously after that, one more thing the girls themselves asked for once they got the idea.

Although a small minority who disliked physical education work were very vocal about it, many students suggested through this board that physical education should be a daily requirement and that the teachers should make the exercising a greater part of the class period and more strenuous. We were constantly amazed at the interest expressed by so many students after we established the Planning Board and communication between us had thus been established.

As a result of Planning Board discussions, we revamped parts of our freshman fundamentals course year by year, and, unrealized by the girls and with no thought on my part to procure such information, I got a good idea of which teachers were doing a fine job and which were not. Unfortunately one or two were not, having become physically lazy themselves and therefore, not committed to pushing their students to serious hard work.

* * * *

When I reflect that in the 1940s women students at the University of Nebraska had no athletic field (previous fields having been taken over for building sites and not replaced), so that we had to use borrowed space wherever we could get a toehold and without rights for permanent markings, and that indoor sports were limited to no more space than we had at our disposal a quarter of a century earlier, I marvel that we interested more than a mere handful of the women students.

Some way though we managed a big sports program. The intramural program alone called out over half of all women enrolled in the university. In post-war years even a larger percentage turned out, thanks to the skillful management and promotion of our staff member, Mary Jean Mulvaney, who did her undergraduate work at Nebraska, her graduate work at Wellesley College, and is today head of both physical education and all athletics for both men and women at the University of Chicago.

In my last year before retirement, 81 percent of all women registered in the university came out for some sport in our intramural program; 23 percent of all women entered the volleyball tournament alone.

During the post-war years the athletic department bargained with the Women's Athletic Association to give up the concessions contract they had held for around 30 years. It was becoming increasingly difficult to get girls to come out and sell, at football games in particular where the big money was, and the men felt they could work it into a bonanza for their grants-in-aid fund if only they could have it back into their hands. The WAA president and I had several conferences with Assistant Coach Klein of the athletic department and Edward Schwartzkopf, the student assistant business manager for the Athletic Board. We finally settled on an Athletic Department contract to pay WAA $1,500 plus up to an extra $500 each year as needed for the WAA cabin.

This contract was honored for over 25 years when finally Robert Devaney, then head of the athletic department, in light of grants-in-aid demanded by women athletes, which because of Title IX interpretations had to be paid out of athletic department funds, refused to honor it any longer. By then the old WAA had died out—victim of a new day. (Today Edward Schwartzkopf, member of the university board of regents, just having completed two years as chairman of that group, and I have a laugh together over the excitement that $1,500-$2,000 annual payment to WAA caused—in light of the vast sums of money taken in on concessions in these days of "Go Big Red!" football. But as Ed says, the percentage profit is about the same today as it was then.)

In these war years, conditions on the whole were far from favorable for interscholastic sports for high school girls, even for intercollegiate sports, except in a few unusual cases. Of the sum total of lower schools and colleges in the country only a few could boast of girls and women's physical education departments directed by women professionally trained or of facilities and staffs even adequate for good intramural programs let alone interschool programs. The wise thing still seemed to be to take a stand against interschool and intercollegiate sports for women in the best interests of the total physical education program for the great majority of girls and women. This stand was applauded and supported by the great majority of men physical educators and school administrators, the loudest voice against it coming from men sports promoters whose motives in wishing to advance their own programs for girls were far from altruistic.

Some men were still trying to lure high school girls into the interschool sports field, patterned after boys' sports programs. Professionally-trained women were few, and these few were deeply committed to looking after the interests of the great majority of girls, not just the highly skilled. But with most men caught up in the war effort, there was a let-up of men's attempts to promote girls' sports. We had few complaints against AAU compared with the many confrontations in the 1930s.

In Iowa, the Girls' High School Athletic Union was still going strong, with high school girls as a rule not drawn into the war effort and the older men who promoted their Union also free. However there was a let-down in travel even for them with gasoline rationing cutting deeply into "plans as usual." During the war years I was cut off the air twice on radio stations in Iowa when I was asked what I thought of the Iowa State High School Girls Athletic Union and started to tell the truth as I saw it. Both times before I had finished the "give away" sentence as to my honest feelings about it, I was off the air facing an indignant interviewer.

In my first year at Nebraska with an intramural program well underway opened to all women in the university, 3 percent of the women enrolled turned out for it, in my last year 81 percent. The number of sports offered increased from 5 to 20. In the forties it shot up to 51 percent, varying from 24 to 51 percent and averaging 32 percent. This happened under the enthusiasm and expert management of Mary Jean Mulvaney as related earlier.

* * * *

Shortly after the war we were drawn into the fight against the American Bowling Congress because of its ruling against black players. Bowling was a very popular sport with the University of Nebraska girls and we had heavy enrollments in several sections of bowling classes besides large numbers out for our WAA bowling tournaments. With no alleys on campus we rented commercial bowling alleys. As we used the alleys at hours and days when they were not in popular use, this was a great boon to the alley management and they were eager for our trade. But when the day came that the first black girl registered for a bowling class and was refused admittance, the war was on. The poor manager was caught between the American Bowling Congress that would withdraw his charter and the university that would close down our use of the alleys. Even before this, our department had year after year refused ABC's plea that we join their organization. We informed ABC officials we would never join as long as they had a clause discriminating against blacks, even though a black had not registered for bowling.

At this time the Recreation Department of United Auto Workers-Congress of Industrial Organizations from its national offices in Detroit was waging great battle over this and our Women's Athletic Association joined forces with it and urged other WAAs in colleges across the country to join also. Finally, ABC capitulated and the bowling alleys of America were opened to blacks. We were proud to have taken active part in that crusade.

* * * *

With the end of the war, much attention diverted for the past several years into the war effort could be re-directed to "normal" pursuits. Women's acceptance into the armed services and many positions heretofore closed had brought an awakening to women's rights, to equal consideration with men, and this became an undercurrent felt in education as well as in other realms. In my own work at Nebraska, I began an intensive study of salaries of my staff, all women, compared to those for men physical education teachers.

I no longer accepted the dictum from the finance office of earlier years that there was no salary scale to go by in making out budgets, that each teacher's salary was a law unto itself according to his or her merits and not defined within maximum or minimum scales according to academic rank. A new finance director faced up to the truth with me and other women heads of departments (what few of us there were). We learned that there were indeed salary scales which had been known to men heads of departments for many years.

Only a few members of my staff were being paid even the minimum for their rank. Even I, at the time of my retirement after holding the rank of full professor for 28 years and head of a department in addition, was getting only 5 percent above the minimum to be paid a full professor without administrative responsibility. However, I waged battle first to bring all other salaries on my staff up to the minimum ranks. This was not an easy fight considering that women had been so underpaid all the years previously. It was a pattern hard to break. It was a task for my successor to bring those salaries up toward even the average. In the few years left to me, I could only do what I could to break that pattern of discrimination against women in my corner of the educational world. We did not as yet have federal laws to back us in this struggle.

Salaries were not the only target for battle in this women's war now emerging. Another form of discrimination against women which I had to fight at the University of Nebraska (and no doubt my friends at other colleges and universities were waging the same battle) was to procure a staff large enough to keep a favorable ratio of teachers to pupils. Men athletic coaches and physical education teachers had much lighter schedules than the women. Some of them, I had noted, had plenty of free time to play chess and checkers during school hours and to visit together, a great deal. They also had time to moonlight, selling insurance or managing service stations, while my staff of women carried average schedules of 25–30 hours of classes a week. Also I discovered that my staff were for the most part carrying heavier schedules than most women physical education teachers in other schools.

Unable to break the pattern without facts I undertook a study of the situation for women at other schools. I found Smith College at the top of the list for favorable teaching loads with one woman physical education teacher to every 81 women students—a woman's school with no pressures to favor men's departments. Of the state universities, the University of Michigan headed the list with one physical education teacher to every 122 women students. In our department, almost at the bottom of the list of 14 colleges and universities of my survey, we had one teacher to every 157 women students. These figures did impress the chancellor and procured for me one extra staff member.

As Grant Memorial Hall deteriorated more and more, year by year, every strong wind made us fearful of using the main entrance for fear of swaying overhead structures. On more than one occasion faculty members in neighboring buildings, seeing the possibility of imminent danger, telephoned us to put up danger signs. In the early forties the administration finally alerted us to prepare new building plans at once. Still remembering our disappointment with our first plans under Chancellor Burnett, we persuaded Chancellor Boucher to list the women's gymnasium as the top priority on the university building agenda.

The entire staff labored many a Saturday and Sunday afternoon on that assignment. I worked many nights at home alone until 2 and 3 a.m. to have all our wishes and dreams transformed into definite statements against the day the regents would give our building the go-ahead signal. But to our dismay we had to give up these second plans in preference for a new library. We, too, felt deeply the need of a new library. After that our gymnasium was back at the top of the list and we were seriously beginning to wonder if Grant Memorial Hall would be able to stand up to any more heavy wind storms from without and deterioration from within. Hoping for a new building for us soon, the chancellor would no longer permit large sums of money to be spent for the upkeep and repairs for the old building.

When at last we were to have our new building, the home economics department opened a campaign for a new building. It was a difficult defeat to accept having a home economics building crowd our gymnasium out of its preferred place on that building priority list. As it turned out we were glad it happened, for World War II engulfed us as this building went into construction and desired materials were no longer available. They had to accept all manner of second choices in materials and cut here and there on size until the finished building was a great disappointment to that department. Today that unfortunate building has already given way to something bigger and better. So we lost our building plans a second time, but again kept our dreams.

In the late 1940s and early 1950s, under Chancellor Gustavson, we were again alerted. By then our ideas had changed, new materials were on the market, and a more favorable site for our building was available, permitting more ambitious plans. Also new staff members were offering new ideas. So for the third time we went to work, once more burning much midnight oil and foregoing weekend freedoms, and, with a third set of staff committee members, produced plans and detailed specifications for a women's gymnasium. This time, knowing exactly where the site would be—a lovely large tract of land affording a large athletic field on a lower terrace adjacent to the building and stretching to the north and east—we planned the building on the upper terrace at street level. Its facade would be a companion to its neighbors, the coliseum and Morrill Hall. Our building was to be at the northeast corner of the plaza with a semi-circular portico main entrance at the corner of Vine and 14th, with white columns to match those at the entry way of the coliseum and with wings stretching to the east on Vine Street and to the north on 14th Street, and a central wing extending out toward the playing fields from the central portico. We were enthralled with the vision of the plaza with a new building adding its beauty to the enclosure, with the stadium and its main entrance enclosing the west end; the coliseum and its fields, the north side; Morrill Hall and Bessey Hall and the Mueller Tower of carillon bells, on the south side; the open street on the east side; and the women's gymnasium on the northeast corner.

The building was promised to us before I retired which would be early in the 1950s. But again fate intervened, our building was shunted aside for first this, then that, for other departments until I finally retired without the dream of 28 years yet to come true. My successor in her turn was promised a new building but she was on the job 16 years before it became a reality.

In the spring of 1945, both the head of the Health Service and Dr. Clapp (then 70 years old) retired, and Chancellor Boucher did some reorganizing of those two departments. He brought in a new person to head up both departments and for good measure threw in the department of physical education for women to make it a division of three departments. Before this the Health Service had been under Dr. Rufus Lyman, the dean of Pharmacy College, a physician. Now a specialist in physical education was brought in as head of a new Division of Health and Physical Education and under him a young medical doctor was appointed as head of the Health Service.

After 21 years of being directly responsible to the chancellor, I was now under the direction of a man who was not only head of physical education for men but also the head of the three-section division.

The chancellor gave me every assurance that I was still absolute head of all physical education for women, that the department was not to be absorbed into the department for men. But that proved to be easier said than done. In no time I had to begin fighting to protect our budget from the budget for the men. It soon became apparent that the women's budget was to be cut to cover raises in salaries, equipment and additions in staff for the men.

The women's outing cabin which the women had financed and built and maintained for exclusive use was now to become the property of both the men and women. I no longer had direct access to the chancellor in behalf of women's interests and needs. Fortunately, just then John Selleck, business manager of the Men's Athletic Department, was advanced to the position of university finance secretary. We had worked together for many years amicably in relation to WAA concessions for the Athletic Department. Now I turned to him for help with these troubles threatening the total welfare of my department and he was able to rescue us from these onslaughts.

It soon became apparent that the Health Service was faring no better than my department under this new division organization. In a way unknown to me, it was able to summon enough help and influence by the end of the first year of the new arrangement that it was able to gain its freedom. We were reduced to merely a two-section department of physical education, headed by a man whose direction proved to be a most unhappy experience. We were relieved from it only when at the end of the second year the chancellor separated the two departments, leaving him only head of men's physical education, and moved both departments into Teachers College. This move, however, proved to be "jumping from the frying pan into the fire."

The next five years before I retired proved to be the most frustrating and unhappy years of my entire career. I found it utterly impossible to adjust to the unpredictable whims of an educator who was a dictator of the first water. He brooked no divergence of views from his own and loved to crack the whip over the heads of those in a position below him, especially women. Since his philosophy of education was at great odds with mine, and I stubbornly clung to my ideals and beliefs, we were in constant conflict and from his position he had the last word—well almost always. On more than one occasion he threatened to fire me and each time I gritted my teeth, looked him straight in the eye and dared him. Each time he backed down and the conflicts between us went on. This made the thought of retirement seem a pleasure indeed.

Never before had I experienced working under a tyrant. Strange to say that although an autocrat, he was in great demand as a high school commencement speaker. He was spoken of as being particularly good on the topic, "democracy." He ordered me about, shouted commands at me, pounded his desk and told me "what was what" and constantly refused to listen to my explanation or opinion about anything. He even gave me orders one day as to how I was to conduct my own staff meetings. How he loved to "lay down the law" to women placed in positions under him!

The four chancellors under whom I served at Nebraska all treated me as an equal in the educational work we were pursuing. All were "gentlemen of the old school" in their attitude toward me as a woman. They held to the idea that accepting a woman as an equal was in no way incompatible with treating her with courtesy.

* * * *

The 1940s were an exceptionally busy time for everyone. As for myself, the extra volunteer work in the Division of Physical Fitness in particular and on the Civilian Advisory Committee of the Women's Army Corps to a lesser extent claimed much of my extra time as related earlier. Special assignments with the United States Office of Education and the committee of NAPECW to find positions for returning servicewomen and the Sub-Committee for Physical Education of the Fulbright Committee for International Exchange of Persons under the State Department claimed time. In addition, there were many university claims on my spare time, such as work on the Honors Convocation Committee, Faculty Memorial Services Committee, and on the Board of the Student Union as the faculty women's representative, including a stint in the forties as president of that Board, a great time-consuming, thankless, yet interesting job.

As if all this were not enough, I was concerned about young people on the faculty who seemed to be somewhat at a loss to find satisfying recreation during the tense war years. So, just as I had earlier in the tense years of the Depression, I started square dancing for them Friday evenings at the gymnasium with a few equally-concerned staff members helping me out. We found an old fiddler and his wife who came to help us and liven things up. Out of these efforts and the earlier ones grew much of the leadership that later developed into the Lincoln Folk Festival, a tradition still surviving today although in a greatly changed format.

With so much activity beyond my university work in the forties, my writing projects suffered. I turned out only a few magazine articles but I did produce my second book (sparked by the sudden interest in physical fitness aroused by World War II), *Fundamentals of Body Mechanics and Conditioning*, written with one of my former staff members as co-author. We got the book together during a few summer vacations and had it off press by 1949. It had a brief popularity and surprising foreign sales, chiefly in South America and Japan, but as memories of the last war faded into the distance and interest in body conditioning died out, it was soon no longer in demand. But producing it had been a good experience and it did meet some need of the moment.

In these years tragedy struck my family. My mother lost her memory. These were years before private nursing homes and care-of-elderly homes abounded on all sides as today. My three sisters and I searched diligently for a proper home in our four states, Illinois, Iowa, Nebraska and Kansas. Finally we found one in Missouri, and still later, unhappy with her care there, we found a splendid home in Kansas, where although she no longer knew us, the four of us visited her frequently. It was heartbreaking, and I was glad to have all my many projects to keep my thoughts from fruitless worry over her.

I was drawn into a controversial matter that for a period drove all other concerns out of my mind and I was glad when one of my graduates who had become a North Woods guide insisted that I needed to "get away from it all" and should go on a canoe trip with her. Ten days in the wilderness of canoe country in northern Minnesota, doing a bit of the trail of the French voyageurs, was an experience never to be forgotten with Ruth Schellberg as guide. Today she is active in Camp Fire Girls work on the national level and has for years taken not only her parents but her brothers, their wives and children, on family canoeing trips and dozens upon dozens of college boys and girls.

My two trips with her in the forties were old-maid canoe trips and what glorious life-renewing and energy-restoring canoe trips they were. The first venture into the wilderness of Quetico Forest was with Gertrude Moulton and Ann Hughitt (an old BNSG classmate), both of Oberlin College, and Mabel Shirley of St. Olaf College. What a quintet we were ranging from the 30s to the 60s in age!

* * * *

About this time Mrs. William E. Barkley, wife of one of Lincoln's leading businessmen (who before her marriage had been the University's first dean of women) was seriously losing her hearing. She became interested in a method of body mechanics which was being taught privately in Lincoln. Feeling that it was helping her in her hearing and speech difficulties, she decided that this method should be taught at the university to help all such handicapped persons as well as others needing correction of poor body mechanics. With that in mind she approached Chancellor Boucher, offering to finance the establishment of this work in the university. Since it seemed to him that it was related more to physical education than any other department, he sounded me out on the subject. He said that if I approved he would accept this offer and I would set up the work as a feature of my department's curriculum.

"What do you know about this method of body mechanics?" the chancellor asked me.

"Not as much as I should in light of this offer, but I do know a little about it," I replied.

"Enough to be interested in bringing it here?" he asked.

"Well, I am afraid not," I hedged and, seizing any straw, quickly added, "anyway I have no one on my staff who would be prepared or licensed to teach it."

"That need not be a worry. If we accept this gift it is with the understanding that this special work will be taught by a person who has been licensed to teach it by the person who has created this method. Mrs. Barkley is prepared to pay the salary of this teacher and finance the work."

Then I confessed to the chancellor that I was deeply troubled for I couldn't see how the university could afford to become involved in teaching a theory which could be taught only by a person licensed by the creator of the theory.

"And that is not all about this that is bothering me," I added. I took the occasion to tell him how, in the late thirties as a Student Union Board member, I had been placed in the position of seeming to be the one who influenced the Union to refuse a mural planned in honor of Mrs. Barkley and financed by a committee of influential alumnae. The students and faculty members on the board objected strenuously to having a mural in the main lounge. As the only woman faculty member on the board at the time, I was assigned to inform the ladies of the decision. Unable to change the board's decision I did manage with help of the alumna representative to change the decision from total rejection to acceptance for the mural to be placed in the women's lounge on the main floor. Although this offer was accepted, this compromise pleased no one. But it was I who bore that brunt of the ladies' displeasure. (As long as most of these ladies lived I was from then on persona non grata with them.)

"Now this!" I added, "Caught up in another controversy in which I will probably be placed once more in the position of seeming to be against Mrs. Barkley."

This Student Union affair the chancellor had not been aware of and he said he was glad to get the story from me, who knew about the controversy first hand. He sympathized with me over the possibility of still further offending Mrs. Barkley, and also seemed to be most understanding about my lack of enthusiasm over the new offer of a gift, this one from the lady herself.

I told the chancellor that as early as January 1938, a woman in the community, a stranger to me, had tried to interest me in this method of body mechanics, hoping that I might wish to use it in our university classes. She was taking the course from the person licensed to teach it in Lincoln. I had invited her to meet with my staff one evening in my home to explain this system to them. She had left some pamphlets for us to read, and three days later the staff met again at my home to discuss our reactions. They were unanimously of the opinion that this method smacked too much of being an "ism" and they were against following up on it.

The chancellor and I discussed the matter from several angles and finally, I said, "Why should I, alone, decide this? Why let my lack of enthusiasm stand in the way of giving this method a thorough investigation? Why don't you appoint a committee to look into this?"

"Splendid," the chancellor replied, seizing upon the suggestion at once. "Who should make up such a committee? I think first of all of Dr. Lyman as the chairman since he is head of our Health Service. Who else?"

So I suggested the dean of the Medical College, the head of the educational psychology department, the head of the speech department (since this seemed to involve speech correction also), some woman from the home economics department of Agriculture College and myself for the women's department. He appointed the committee and informed Mrs. Barkley's secretary, asking that all members of this committee be supplied at once with copies of literature about the method. At this Mrs. Barkley asked to meet with the committee in person to discuss the matter.

The committee came together in Dr. Lyman's office, and Mrs.

Barkley and a companion arrived with several copies of one book and various pamphlets to be parcelled out among us for study. In his opening remarks, the chairman chanced to say that the committee would study these materials and make an appraisal of them and then make recommendations to the chancellor.

At this, Mrs. Barkley became highly indignant, saying, "This method does not need to be appraised by you. It has already been thoroughly appraised by people in Europe. I do not approve any further appraising. All I need to know from you is whether you approve it as a course to be offered by the university."

After Mrs. Barkley and her companion left, the committee decided that in spite of her disapproval of any appraising and testing by the committee, it could not give consideration to any method of teaching that could not stand up to investigation. Therefore two members agreed to work together to plan some sort of appraisal and testing procedure to be undertaken that would be acceptable to Mrs. Barkley.[1]

All agreed that although this method of body mechanics might have certain good features, it was nevertheless, as they saw it, placed in the class of a cult by the sort of secrecy surrounding it and dependence upon its creator who would keep close hold on the teaching by his "disciples," by the seeming unwillingness to have the beliefs questioned and the almost fanatical loyalty of its followers. This matched my own feelings about it.

In the end, the heads of the departments of educational psychology and speech, along with me, carried the brunt of the task of getting evidence and studying the course work as offered by the local teacher. Each of the other two had personal conferences with Mrs. Barkley, summoning up all the tact possible, I am sure, to appease her for she was offended that her offer had not been snapped up at once without this "to-do." They explained to her fully the proposed research project to which she begrudgingly finally gave her assent.

It was decided to organize a class of university students, some from each of the three departments, to take the proposed course. From my department I sent a staff member, Aileene Lockhart, a Ph.D. who was teaching our courses in physiology of exercise and kinesiology and was in charge of departmental research work, a senior major who was taking Dr. Lockhart's courses, and a freshman major who had not, as yet, taken the requirement courses in human anatomy and who also was seriously in need of special posture training. Nine students from the educational psychology department volunteered to take this course, also several students from the speech department.

The class meetings progressed in the Temple building under the care of the speech department (we wanted to keep it away from the department of physical education for women during this appraisal period).

The committee appointed by the chancellor, having had a chance to look into the literature, met for lengthy discussion and finally in one voice declared the method to be a cult and that it was ridiculous for the group to waste any more time discussing it. In the end with appraisal in from the experimental class the committee reported to the chancellor that in its opinion the university should not engage in the teaching of this method of body training as a part of its educational program. This let me and my department off the hook! Or did it?

In no time the chancellor was called upon by a group of women graduates of the university, all highly indignant that Mrs. Barkley's offer of a gift to the university had been rejected, demanding an explanation. He referred them to the chairman of the committee that had advised the rejection of the offer. When the irate ladies descended upon him, that gentleman, apparently completely cowed by them, got himself out of the difficulty by informing them that "You'll have to talk with Miss Lee. It was her decision."

As chance would have it, one or two of these ladies had served on the Student Union mural committee and were still angry with me as the supposed villain in that drama. Now this seemed a second insult to Mrs. Barkley from me! If I had been relegated to the dog house by the first episode, I was now pushed far back into its darkest recesses by this second episode.

The word now got around by some mysterious woman's grapevine that the Barkley millions would not after all come to the university because of its bad treatment of Mrs. Barkley, this due completely to Miss Lee's intransigence. In a way it was falsely flattering to think that I wielded such power, in another way it was ridiculous to jump at such conclusions, and in yet another way it was most unfair to me that I, dragged into both episodes most innocently, had to bear the brunt of the displeasure of Mrs. Barkley and her loyal friends. Needless to say, the rumor upset me very much. As the rumor went, $4,000,000 had been at stake. It was all very disturbing, to say the least. I felt very guilty—yet quite innocent!

Before these rumors of my unwarranted attacks on Mrs. Barkley (as some put it) reached me, a mutual friend of the two of us asked me one day if she could take me to call on Mrs. Barkley. I replied I would be happy to meet her. But when my friend asked for an appointment, Mrs. Barkley hastily informed her that I would not be welcome in her

396

home. Amazed, my friend reported this to me and I then told her about the latest incident, which was yet a bit hush-hush.

In 1944, the year before this unhappy incident, Mr. Barkley died and in 1956 Mrs. Barkley passed away. By then I had retired. Several years after that, unknown to me, a group of young women who had majored at the university under my direction were pushing for a special honor for me. When this became known to some of the women who had been so indignant with me over the Barkley incidents they organized to see that this honor would not come to me. So imagine my surprise and delight to pick up the local evening paper one day several years later to read this headline:

Barkley Estate Settled! Four Million To The University!

I could scarcely believe my eyes! I hadn't kept the university from getting the four million after all! Yet all these years I had been so accused! What a load off my shoulders! Yet I knew if I had those two incidents to live over again I would still make the same decisions, come what may!

On September 24, 1976, the William E. Barkley Memorial Center was dedicated on the East campus of the University of Nebraska—to be devoted to the preparation of teachers of special education for the deaf and hard of hearing, to speech pathology, and to educational needs of other handicapped persons. Thus Mrs. Barkley's desire to help those suffering from a handicap similar to her own is at last being met and on a scientifically sound basis which an educational institution can be proud to offer.

* * * *

The most satisfying part of my work at the university was the preparation of women teachers of physical education. Athough I thus touched the lives of but a small minority of the total university enrollment, I reached these few in a very close personal relationship which meant much to them and to me. Their letters of appreciation through the years attest to this.

Our majors were my joy. Frequently frustrated by the mediocrity of some staff members and tempted by offers to go elsewhere at considerably better salary, I almost gave up and resigned, but each time I could not bring myself to abandon these wonderfully fine girls majoring under my direction at Nebraska. They were so appreciative of help, so fine in every way, so starry-eyed and eager about the future, so unsophisticated, trusting, and full of enthusiasm and fun that I couldn't

397

leave them. They were Nebraska to me—and I felt a great loyalty toward them.

They were worthy of my loyalty, even the few "late bloomers" whom we nursed along assiduously because we saw in them fine potential for the future. Some of them I saved from dismissal for low grades by begging the dean of student affairs to give them yet another chance, promising that my entire staff had faith in them if only they could once get on their collegiate feet and "get going." One of these late bloomers was later the first physical education major to earn the Ph.D. degree at one of our large state universities. Another went on to achieve high rank in the Army Medical Corps in physical therapy; another was later spoken of as the "distinguished" professor of one of our most prestigious women's colleges. Early bloomer, normal bloomer, or late bloomer—all were important to us and the placement records of these young women have been a source of great pride to me.

In college during the war years they helped me unstintingly in my various war-related projects. On Saturdays, when help was impossible to find, they gave me a lift at my home chores under their organization of Union Local Number 13 of the Amalgamated Storm Window Taker-Downers and Screen Putter-Uppers. This same group of girls inveigled the staff to take over the Omaha YWCA for an unofficial course in camping (when the faculty refused to honor our request for such a course) to be given on out-of-school dates on a voluntary staff basis. This we did and the camp, a week-long venture, was in existence for several years. When we were in residence it took on the temporary name of Camp Loy-a-Lee, in my honor, at the insistence of the irrepressible majors.

The good sportsmanship of students showed up on another occasion when I was waging a war with them against gum-chewing. We were going through an epidemic of this bad habit on our campus and with our majors in particular when suddenly the problem was solved for us nicely by a government decree that diverted practically all chewing gum supplies to the Armed Forces thus drying up supplies to civilians.

Shortly after this, my physician decided I needed drastic throat treatment for an old difficulty. The thickening of my vocal chords, resulting from an attack of laryngitis several years before and subsequent abuse of vocal chords, had to be burned off by acid. The doctor ordered me to keep complete silence (which turned out to be a nine-week ordeal) and also to keep my throat constantly moist. This last called for chewing gum—an embarrassing situation—and at a time when gum was on the market in very short supply and only at infrequent intervals.

398

Those wonderful majors passed the word about the campus, in the dormitories and sorority houses, that Miss Lee must have chewing gum because of a throat operation. Once the word got out students began dropping into my office, sometimes with a packet, sometimes with only one stick of gum, leaving it for me without leaving their name. Apparently the girls had passed on the word to their boyfriends for now and then a man dropped by with a donation. Thanks to these students, many of whom I had been scolding for gum-chewing, my supply held out for the necessary nine weeks. Teacher's gum-chewing had made it impossible for her to do any more scolding on the subject to the great glee of the students.

The Local #13 girls and the Camp Loy-a-Lee girls were especially irrepressible. It was this group who for three years went about lustily singing at every opportunity the song they prepared for the Physical Education Club spring banquet their freshman year, with due apologies to the Yale Whiffenpoof Song.

First Verse
To the P.E. room at Grant
To the place where majors dwell
To the memory of that room we love so well
We must serenade the freshmen, the sophomores, juniors, too
Till we pass (we hope) and exit like the rest.

Chorus: (as in the Whiffenpoof Song)

Second Verse
To the head of our department
To our dear instructors too
To Ruth, Herr Kahler and the rest,
We will serenade the freshmen, the sophomores, juniors, too
Till we pass (we hope) and exit like the rest.

"Ruth, Herr Kahler and the rest" in that second verse referred to the WAA office girl, the janitor, and the office help and matrons. No one was overlooked. The version above was as they sang it in their senior year.

Yes, these fine young girls at the University of Nebraska, of all the years of my teaching there, left me filled with fond memories. Their songs, their pranks, their loyalty to each other and to us the staff, their ups and downs, their constant eagerness, their joy of life, all contrived to make working with them such fun and so worthwhile!

*   *   *   *

Never can I forget the difficult task I had to face one day to teach a group of war-years majors a lesson in professional ethics. They made an innocent mistake but neverthless I could not overlook it as a golden opportunity to drive home a lesson about the rights of authors and publishers. A group of majors had, in great exuberance and at great expense of time and some money, prepared a booklet on camp counseling to be named *Camp Loy-a-Lee Notebook* in my honor. One of the younger staff members was sponsor for this project. It was to be mimeographed, bound and financed by the Physical Education Club to be sold to the majors and any other interested persons.

When the book was ready they asked me to sign the Foreword, which I gladly did, although I had not read their material but had unbounded faith in their sponsor. When it was "off press" they eagerly ran to my office to present me with the first copy. How proud they were of their 80-some pages of original offering. It boasted nine authors, each "doing" a chapter. Very busy at the time, I put the booklet aside and rejoiced with them as they reported their good sales campaign—even graduates had heard of the booklet and ordered copies by mail.

Before I got around to it, various staff members began complaining that this and that in the booklet was strangely familiar. Finally I called the authors in and put the question to them, "Are parts of the booklet copied from published sources?"

"Oh, yes," the girls replied unhesitatingly, and each pointed out what she had copied, and from what sources. To my amazement it developed that much of it was copied material. They added that they had listed their references at the end of the chapter (as if that were sufficient.)

"But where are your quotation marks showing what parts are copied material? And did you ask permission of copyright holders to use their materials? And where are your acknowledgments of sources?" My questions amazed them!

Never was I confronted by a group more innocent of knowingly doing wrong. My amazement was still further confounded when I learned from the young sponsor of this project (a graduate of one of the most prestigious departments of physical education in the country) that never in her entire course had the subject of rights of authors and publishers been called to her attention. As for our Nebraska majors, not one of them had as yet taken my course in principles of physical education, in which I always discussed professional ethics, including the rights of authors and publishers. How could they be so unaware that one does not quote from others without using quotation marks and naming author and publisher? I pointed out that it is not only unethical just to do it but then to sell the material is illegal, and these booklets were being sold. I told them I only hoped that none of the authors or publishers would ever learn of it before we could undo the harm.

After a long talk they themselves decided all books should be recalled and all money from sales refunded. To set up a situation to impress upon their minds indelibly the rights of authors and publishers, they decided that they would undo every vestige of wrong-doing by having one big bonfire and burning the entire edition and by some project earn the money to cover the cost of their error. I was proud of their decision. We urged the entire Physical Education Club membership to attend the burning ceremony. It was not a bonfire of jubilation or anticipation as are most college campus bonfires, but one of contrition. As the last copy went up in smoke there were tears in most eyes. Later when these student authors were in my course in principles, and this topic came up, I was greeted by hilarious laughter in which I could join wholeheartedly. The girls were such good sports. They had taken discipline in a splendid, wholesome way, without bearing a grudge. They had lost the money on their venture, too, but without one word of complaint as far as I ever knew. And they learned the hard way that authors and publishers have rights, moral as well as legal, which should be observed.

Shortly before this I, myself, had been the victim of a serious breech of ethics and it was still on my mind. As related earlier a young writer had published an article in a professional periodical which carried two entire pages of an over 20-year-old publication of mine. It was copied verbatim without even quotation marks or reference to my earlier work in any way, and palmed off on an unsuspecting editor as her own original work. It was flattering that the young author had considered my old material adequate for her day but, nevertheless, for the good of the author I confronted both the editor and the author with my charge of plagiarism. I was promised an acknowledgment of this use of my material in an early issue of the periodical—a promise that, to my knowledge, was never kept.

*   *   *   *

The spring of 1945, a captain of the British Auxiliary Territorial Services came out from Washington to Lincoln to discuss with me the physical fitness program of the OCD and FSA and the physical training program of the Women's Army Corps. She told me of the great need for women's clothing for nurses and aides in hospitals in France and England. I suggested that she talk to our women students directly about this as well as about volunteer services for women in general. This she gladly consented to do and the Women's Athletic Association called a mass meeting of all women students to hear her speak.

The girls toured all the sorority houses as well as the women's dormitories announcing the mass meeting, hoping to get out a crowd. Only a handful of girls responded beyond the WAA girls and the physical education majors; the sororities still dragged their feet. But with enthusiasm thus kindled in a small group of students for British and French relief, the two groups started a project that was to last through three and a half years and finally embraced Germany as well. In short order we established a shipping center in the basement of my home. The university physical education majors and the WAA girls collected clothing and delivered it to my office and on Saturdays it was transferred to my house for shipping preparation.

* * * *

During the war, our department graduates served in the American Red Cross, the American Medical Corps, and the WAC in many foreign countries as well as at home. Abroad they served in Australia, England, France, Germany, India, Iran, Italy, Japan, Korea, Luxembourg, Panama, Scotland, South America, and the South Pacific. Others served at home in the Marines, Coast Guard Reserves (SPARs), WAC, WASPs (flying bombers for the U.S. Air Force from factories to air bases), and WAVEs. Still others served in civilian jobs with the armed forces, in defense jobs in factories, in USO as directors of recreation, and in YWCA war assignments.

Our physical education majors and WAA leaders still in college gave unstintingly of their late afternoon free hours and Saturdays and Sundays to help me with Division of Physical Fitness tasks. The first of three large projects the majors helped me with was procuring names and current addresses of graduates from professional training schools and physical education major departments of colleges all over the country who had left the profession but perhaps could be called upon to volunteer their services in their home towns to help in the physical fitness work.

Women's PE Major Clubs of the state universities of the Seventh Army Service Command helped with the project, each doing the schools of one of the other areas and sending the returns to us. From this we collected the names and addresses of over 2,500 women which we made into a master list, town by town, state by state according to current addresses. Copies of this master list we sent to John Kelly to distribute to his regional directors and to the U.S. Office of Education for help in their problem of shortage of teachers.

Later our Nebraska majors helped me in my emergency "placement bureau" hunting for positions for physical education trained girls returning to civilian life from war services, and also in foreign aid work. The Women's Athletic Association gave generously of its treasury to finance this war work, and many of the members, non-physical education majors, gave freely of their time.

By September 1945, the war was ended in the Pacific as well as in Europe. A year later when I was in New York City attending a meeting of the National Civilian Advisory Committee of the Women's Army Corps, under General Eisenhower, I had an opportunity for a visit with Elizabeth Burchenal. I told her of my students' project of sending clothing to England and France.

"Why don't you interest them in sending some boxes to the Lehmann family in Germany?" she exclaimed. "At last after many tries I have been able to get in touch with that family. They still are in their old home in Hamburg. Dr. Lehmann's two granddaughters, both now college age, are almost destitute for clothing."

I was instantly concerned for I had for several years heard Elizabeth talk of her dear friend, Herr Doctor Otto Lehmann (a leading citizen of Hamburg, Germany, founder and head of the Hamburg Museum, until Hitler ousted him, and president of the German Folk Arts Society and president of the International Folk Arts Society—Commisseur Internationale des Arts Populaire) and of his interesting family.

It had been several years since she had heard a word of their situation, nothing in fact since the outbreak of war. Now with the war over she had established contact once more and learned that Doctor Lehmann, then in his 80s, his wife, his daughter, Frau Gertrude Thorning, and her two daughters had lived in their home in Hamburg throughout the war but their lovely home had been taken over for 21 evacuees with the Lehmann family permitted to remain in two of the rooms. When the Russian troops that had commandeered their house left, they took with them almost all of the warm bedding and warm clothing, with no possibility of replacing it with their bank assets frozen. This meant that in the long winters they were confined to their home since all their warm outer garments were gone. The two granddaughters were so destitute for clothing that they could not go on to school.

Dr. Lehmann's three sons were being held captive in Russia. The two who were physicians had been there since 1942 with assurance that they would be held there as long as any German prisoners were still in Russia. (They were finally released in 1950.) The daughter's husband who was a successful businessman in Hamburg before the war was presumably away someplace. At any rate, he was still living, perhaps a prisoner in Russia. He was soon reunited with his family, for in March of 1947, Frau Thorning wrote me that her husband joined her in sending greetings and thanks for our kindness.

From the spring of 1947 through 1948 we turned our entire clothing project to the Hamburg family sending many boxes each spring and fall, and including clothing for the grownups. As they wrote us, they divided it all with relatives and friends and other needy families. In one shipment we sent what was left of the WAA concessions jerseys, and the granddaughters wrote that they and their friends were dashing about the streets of Hamburg explaining that the letters WAA on their jerseys meant Women's Athletic Association of the University of Nebraska, U.S.A. After the last shipment in the fall of 1948, they wrote us that their situation was greatly improved and that we should now turn our attention to others but to remember always that we had their everlasting gratitude for our help in time of dire need.

It had been a project we all loved for we knew that we were doing something most useful. And incidentally we had lots of fun in those twice-a-year bouts of sorting and boxing and wrapping and then parcelling out the cartons to the post office, one per week until all were on their way. As we posted each carton I wrote a letter to Frau Thorning listing the contents of the package and in all those three and one-half years not one carton was lost. Our Physical Education Club and the Women's Athletic Association paid all the shipping costs. Those girls more than made up for their many foot-dragging sisters on the campus.

In the summer of 1947 Elizabeth Burchenal, representing the United States, attended the first post-war meeting of the International Commission on Folk Arts in Paris when Dr. Lehmann was in absentia elected honorary life president of the group. He was unable to make the trip because of failing health and Elizabeth was unable to get permission at that time to go into the British Section of Germany where Hamburg was located. In the years before the war she had frequently been a guest in the Lehmann home.

In 1949 Dr. Lehmann wrote me as follows:

Prof. Dr. Otto Lehmann   Hamburg 39, den Febr. 14./1949

My dear Miss Mabel Lee!

You will allow me to send a few lines of gratitude for the kindness you render and have rendered to my daughter and granddaughters. This, on account of your friendship to Miss Dr. Elizabeth Burchenal, my dear good friend, who has so amiably arranged that connection. By my daughter and the granddaughters I learned somewhat about your work. The lectures and practice of your students, and that with great interest. I have some knowledge about the education of the females in most countries of Europe. The worst as I think, is in Spain, where the education lies almost-especially of the upper classes, in the hands of the clergy. The women are so their instrument without a will of their own, stupid, knowing nothing but pray. When, in 1933 on a voyage in Spain, I sat in a compartment with an earl and his wife,—on the whole way from Madrid till the end she did nothing but turning her rosary, trimmed with precious stones, and murmuring prayers— but did not participate in our conversation. Also in France and Belgium the girls are mostly educated in cloisters and when married, they live their own life. Far better it is in London, where boys and girls are coeducated. For Germany we esteem too much the intellectual culture—it must be always a good balance between the intellectual and physical sector—according the old word: *mens sana in corpore sano*. I think, you are on the right way—a reasonable education of the girls is the best check for the future of the nation.

Excuse my detailed letter—and allow my request, to maintain your friendship to my daughter and the two granddaughters.

I am, my dear Miss Mabel Lee—

sincerely yours   Dr. Lehmann

A few months later one of the granddaughters, Armgard, wrote to the university girls as follows:

· We thank you very, very much for every gift. You have helped us and our friends and relatives through hard times which are over now, thanks God. We are searching now for something nice for your Clubroom, that you also may have some pleasure in return for your kindness and troubles about us here in Germany.

In the package from Germany was a family heirloom, a tile trivet from Friesland, a gift from the grandmother for me, a tea cozy hand-embroidered by the two granddaughters for me, and an etching for the girls' club room, the work of an artist friend of the family. It was a lovely gesture of gratitude.

In 1951 came the black-banded notice of the death of Professor Dr. Otto Lehmann on June 27 at the age of 86. Would that I had personally known this kindly internationally known defender of the folk arts as my friend, Elizabeth Burchenal, had known this man. Three years later while travelling in Germany after my retirement, I and my three travelling companions—my sister, Madge, Gertrude Moulton and Ann Hughitt, both retired from Oberlin College—planned our trip to include Hamburg. We wrote ahead to Frau Thorning to reserve rooms for us at some hotel convenient to her home and when we arrived she and her husband met us at the rail station. When we entered our hotel rooms there were beautiful flowers from the family to welcome us to Hamburg.

Needless to say the two days in Hamburg were the high spot of seven months in Europe. We met Frau Lehmann (a charming but frail grandmother), Herr Thorning and his wife and one daughter. The other daughter was at school at the University of Tubingen. They had long since been free of the 21 evacuees, and their lovely home was once more their own. The first thing we did upon return to New York City was to have tea with Elizabeth Burchenal in her home in Brooklyn to take to her greetings from the Lehmanns and Thornings. It was a happy occasion, but as Fate would have it, it was the last time I ever saw Elizabeth whose friendship had meant so much to me. She shortly became an invalid and before I could see her again, passed away. What a joyous spirit she had been!

* * * *

It was quite some time after the war ended before the campus came back to some semblance of a peace-time setting, before old collegiate activities abandoned during the war picked up again, longer still before the student body itself came back to some approach to days of yore. Although male students returned in large numbers, in a large percentage they were older than usual, many of them married and with families, so that housing for married students became a new and serious problem.

College life was never to be the same again!

406

Chapter XX

Post-War Awakenings
and Some Final Thorns

What a frantically busy time the 1940s were, as I have declared before! Beyond the demands of miscellaneous local war-related work, the Division of Physical Fitness covering three and a half years of rather heavy work, and interests concerning the physical training and sports of the Women's Army Corps, there were concerns of several professional organizations, each claiming much of my time beyond the local full-time appointment at the university.

In the Academy of Physical Education, Dr. John Brown carried on as president between 1939 and 1941. By then almost all the men of the Academy were on leave and scattered throughout the Armed Services. Now it was imperative for us few women members to carry on. The holocaust in Europe had wiped out all opportunities to be in touch with our foreign associate members. There was no longer valid reason why I should refuse the presidency of the Academy, so I permitted my name to be put up for election.

Within a month after the United States had declared war, I received a long letter from our founding patron, Clark W. Hetherington, who despite serious illness, was pushing himself to complete some scientific studies he had been engaged in since his retirement seven years before. He had returned from New York University to his alma mater, Stanford University, where he had been a classmate of Herbert Hoover and, under Thomas D. Wood, had been introduced to the profession of physical education. There with special endowments for his research he was still at work for the profession. He wrote me as follows:

January 12, 1942

My dear Lee:[1]

The Academy of Physical Education should right at this moment be dominating the problem in the nation's war effort of the physical education, health and recreation of soldiers as well as the citizens in civilian defense. When our national war effort is so poor that ex-pugilists can be put into the head of the administration of physical education and recreation of our soldiers, it is time for action by the Academy. Here is the most scientific task of any phase of the war effort except the applied physical sciences in the machines and materials of war and the strategy directed by generals and admirals, and the doctors who control the care of the wounded. No one in physical education or health or recreation is properly trained for the functions of these fields of work, but there is a whole list of men and women who have the best training and experience available, and the ghastly horror of seeing mere expugs and mere athletic trainers put into jobs that should strain the resources of the best trained among us—well the situation should rouse us to fighting action.

And then there are the examinations and tests to determine fitness and human quality for all these war functions. Just as surely as the night follows day, a great number of the men inducted into the Army and Navy will come back as mental cases. I was delighted to hear that Doctor McCloy was mixed up in this latter test problem. A young man here, by the name of Craig Taylor, is doing work on organic tests, and it is very encouraging to me after forty years of promotional effort to get something done about that problem that Taylor has money from the government to carry forward his work. Craig Taylor and Elizabeth Kelley have really gone after that problem. It requires a deeper training in physiology and chemistry than that required for the medical profession.

We will win the war whatever it costs, but I am not so certain about winning the peace. Personally I am convinced that we will not win the peace unless we have an organization of the intelligence and character of this nation and other nations of the world that will use science and apply science to see that civilization gets a chance to progress.

I hope you reign as a queen in the Academy and show the men what they should do, as women have shown up the men in most of the everyday aspects of human life.

Very sincerely yours,

Clark W. Hetherington

Eleven and a half months later (December 27, 1942), at the age of 72, Clark Hetherington died, his work, to our great loss, unfinished. In the death of this man our profession lost another great leader.

As the Academy had established the McKenzie Lectures in honor of its first president, it now established the Clark W. Hetherington Award to be conferred upon its retired members in recognition of their leadership in the profession. [2]

It was at the University of Missouri at the turn of the century that Clark Hetherington (at a starting salary of $1,000) perhaps met his greatest challenge—it developed into one in which he met much opposition and suffered much personal vituperation but he clung tenaciously to his ideals. This battle, no doubt, laid for his later professional years the foundation on which he adamantly stood against all comers who questioned his standards. This battle was his crusade to clean up the unfavorable situation in intercollegiate athletics of that day—a crusade also being bitterly waged back East by Dudley Sargent at Harvard. Out of the struggle, Hetherington had fathered the Missouri Valley Athletic Conference. [3]

He was the first in our profession to do intensive research on individual differences of pupils including psychological as well as physical tests. Fighting physical frailty all his life, at times even having to give up his work altogether to regain his health, he was handicapped in his attempts to write his philosophy of physical education which the profession eagerly awaited. Before his masterpiece was completed, he was claimed by death.

The two men, R. Tait McKenzie and Clark W. Hetherington, were giants of our profession: McKenzie strengthening the ties between physical education and medicine, and through his sculptured work of athletes uniting physical education and the world of art; Hetherington serving as physical education's link with the world of psychology and philosophy.

Again as happened after Dr. McKenzie's death four years before, fate withheld the sad news from me for several days. It was 10 days after Dr. Hetherington's death before I received word of it and could offer his family condolences as president of the Academy.

Since our 1939 meeting when, as acting president following Dr. McKenzie's death, I presented Dr. Hetherington with the Academy's Creative Award, I had had an opportunity to become better acquainted with him through what a group of six of us called "conversation by mail" in the interest of advancement of the Academy. The sextet also included John Brown, Jr., Frederick Cozens, C.H. McCloy and Arthur Steinhaus. This six-way "conversation," which lasted until Dr. Hetherington's death, was most interesting. It proved that the nineteenth century art of conversation by mail was still alive in the twentieth century. We added a modern touch through the use of typewriter carbons. This "conversation" became so interesting that our exchange of ideas and frank criticism and discussion of what the others had last "said" usually ran three to five single-spaced pages. It was a stimulating experience among six persons whose remarks and criticism of each other's ideas were given freely and with friendly warmth—a fellowship not too frequently enjoyed by busy twentieth century folk. Of this congenial, harmonious group, I, the one woman, still live.

* * * *

In April 1944 the Academy of Physical Education and AAHPER were granted permission by the government to hold conventions in New York City since important military personnel had what the War Department considered messages to bring to both groups. Major General Hershey, head of the Draft Board, and Joseph Raycroft, long retired from Princeton, were our special guests at the Academy dinner.

Following that dinner, we learned that Jessie Bancroft was in the city driven back to America by the war after many years of retirement as a resident in Paris. She was the first woman member of the Academy. I had long admired her pioneering work in physical education and had hoped someday to meet her. One evening as I entered the lobby of the Pennsylvania Hotel with my old Philadelphia friend, I glanced up the great stairway and saw a couple descending the stairs who instantly caught my attention—John Brown and a handsome woman of beautiful carriage and magnificent poise. She had snow-white hair and over her black dinner dress she wore an ermine stole. What a picture she was! Seeing me, John Brown motioned me to wait and when he and his companion reached the lobby I was presented to Jessie Bancroft. I have never forgotten that moment at the foot of that great stairway—the very spot where a few years before R. Tait McKenzie had introduced me to Joseph Lee of Boston, the grand old man of the American Playground Association. I never saw Jessie Bancroft or Joseph Lee again.

A year later the government granted the Academy permission to hold its convention again in the spring in New York City, but AAHPER was denied a permit. The State Department had approved our petition because we were sponsoring visits to New York and Washington of several foreigners whose missions had asked for appointments to meet physical education leaders. Seven of these from India, China and South America were to be our guests. Our American "brothers" were surprised at the amazement of these foreigners at the presence of three women as members of such an organization. Now I knew that at last they understood why I had so determinedly refused to allow myself to be nominated for Academy president in the spring of 1939 to succeed Tait McKenzie when the war clouds were blackening over Europe and we were deeply concerned over how best the Academy could serve our foreign colleagues.

One of these guests was a high-ranking South American Army officer—a dashing fellow who spoke no English. He had indicated a great desire to see the play *Oklahoma* which was having a great run in New York City. The State Department wished him to be given special attention so the Academy decided to treat him to dinner and an evening at the theater, with me for his companion. Although I would be delighted to attend, I protested vehemently for I did not speak Spanish. But the Academy president, Arthur Steinhaus, would not take a refusal. He arranged for Charles McCloy, who spoke fluent Spanish, to dine with the two of us and then, since Dr. McCloy could not attend the play, for an interpreter to accompany us to the theater. The interpreter, an attractive graduate student at Columbia University, was glad to see the play and receive a fee for her services. It was quite an experience, easier than at first imagined since after "Mac" left, most of the evening was spent watching the play. Between acts, the interpreter proved quite capable, and the three of us enjoyed the action and music of the play, even if our guest missed the dialogue.

At the last Academy meeting I attended before I retired, which was held in Los Angeles in April 1952, I had a reunion with Amos Alonzo Stagg. I hadn't seen him for several years and because he was 90 years old I doubted if he would remember me. But (just) as I began to say "I am Mabel Lee," he interrupted me with a pat on the hand,

"Oh, yes! Miss Nebraska! You were my dinner partner at a banquet 25 or so years ago. Remember?"

Yes, indeed, I remembered. It was that evening in Chicago (as told in *Memories of a Bloomer Girl*) when, because I chanced to be wearing an evening gown, I was suddenly summoned to the head table to be seated next to him when Mrs. Hoover's wired regrets had left a vacant place at the Women's Division banquet. That had been my introduction to Coach Stagg. I was flattered that he remembered.

At this meeting Dr. Ernst Jokl, a corresponding fellow from South Africa (for many years now of the University of Kentucky) and Mr. Stagg had an interesting discussion of the physiology of aging. Mr. Stagg attended all of the sessions for two days.

He lived another 13 years but I never saw him again. However, I did receive a note from him on his 100th birthday in response to my special greetings on that occasion.

* * * *

Having become interested in the American Youth Hostel Movement in the thirties, I continued my interest into the forties as best I could with all the war work disruptions. Having kept in touch with the national office by mail I soon found myself a member of the National Board for one year just in time to attend a board meeting in New York City while there for the Academy and AAHPER meetings in April 1944. For the next four years I served on the AYH national council and again chanced to be in New York City on Women's Army Corps business in the fall of 1946 when the AYH Council was meeting just before a few of us civilians on the WAC Advisory Committee were to meet in Mrs. Oswald Lord's Park Avenue home with a small group of Army personnel.

Ambassador John Gilbert Winant, deeply interested in the Youth Hostel Movement, having recently resigned from his position at the Court of St. James, had accepted the presidency of the AYH Board, replacing John D. Rockefeller, Jr. who had held the position for several years. Ambassador Winant expected to attend the AYH Council meeting and I went with great expectation of meeting him but was disappointed when illness prevented him from being with us. (He died shortly thereafter.)

The AYH movement had needed help seriously. John D. Rockefeller had tried to shift it to some semblance of a business-like organization from its earlier "floating about in the clouds," at which I had been so shocked when I attended the board meeting in 1944. Now John Winant was taking an interest in the organization. In 1948 our own physical educator, Ben Miller, resigned as executive secretary of AAHPER to assume the AYH executive secretaryship, but shortly gave it up to resume work in our profession at UCLA.

This organization had wonderful potential and I regretted its seeming inability to function successfully on the national level. I also regretted that the idea which Chancellor Boucher and I had talked of together in the late 1930s of wagon caravan trips along the Oregon Trail as Nebraska's offering to the American Youth Hostel Movement died aborning because of the war.

* * * *

In 1948, AAHPER conferred its Gulick Award upon me. The history of this award is interesting but little known. It was conceived by the Physical Education Society of New York City and Vicinity which in the early 1920s was one of the largest units in the American Physical Education Association. After Dr. Gulick's death in 1918, this society, which Gulick had founded, decided to honor his memory by conferring a medal annually upon one leader for outstanding service to the profession. Gulick's friend, Tait McKenzie, was commissioned to design the medal. By 1923, the medallion was ready for presentation.

Jesse F. Williams, who was then president of the Society, presided at the dinner meeting at the Waldorf-Astoria on May 2, 1923 when the Gulick Award was first conferred. The first ceremony was a memorial to Luther Gulick and the award was conferred upon him posthumously. The spring of 1924 the next awardee was Jessie H. Bancroft; 1925, Thomas D. Wood; 1926, Thomas A. Storey; 1927, no one; 1928, Clark W. Hetherington; and 1929, George J. Fisher.[4]

Following this, the Society died out and the Gulick Award was in limbo for 10 years until AAHPER took it over as a national award. As such, it was first awarded in 1939 to Jesse Williams. In 1946 Ethel Perrin became the second woman to receive the award; in 1947, Blanche Trilling became the third; and I the fourth, in 1948—three years straight to a woman. Before I retired, Elizabeth Burchenal became the fifth woman. Recognition of women for high honors was picking up.

413

During the years when the award was the property of the New York City group alone, the ceremony took place at a dinner meeting when the members took an evening off in honor of Gulick. Surrounded by friends, the honoree received tributes. Then, having been extolled and feted, the recipient was given an opportunity to say what may have been in his heart.

After AAHPER assumed this award and made it into a national honor, it lost this personal touch. There was no longer the intimate gathering of friends since it now belonged to a large nationwide group. In the new ceremony, a tribute was paid to the man in whose honor the award is named followed by a tribute to the honoree of the year, the presentation of the medal, and a handshake from the president. The honoree had no opportunity to say anything more than "thank you," and the ceremony was over. Gradually as more events became included in the opening General Session, the tribute to Luther Gulick was dropped and the ceremony became briefer.

Because of the strange circumstances surrounding the ceremony, I can never forget the evening I received this honor! At the eleventh hour the chairman of the Gulick Award Committee was called out of the city on what no doubt seemed important business to him. Not willing to give up his duty of paying the tribute to Gulick and of presenting the honoree to Vaughn Blanchard, our president, he, without consulting even the president, hastily arranged for the ceremony to be transferred from the General Assembly to the only opening he could find in the convention program—a meeting of the exhibitors one day at 4 p.m. in a small conference room. The exhibitors had obligingly offered to give up a part of their time to the AAHPER Council to make the presentation to me in a private ceremony for the Council alone.

After he had left town late that afternoon, messages were delivered to President Blanchard and me that the Gulick Award ceremony would not be held that evening but two days later in a private ceremony in a conference room. President Blanchard was as amazed as I. He immediately declared that plans to make the award that evening at the General Session were not to be interfered with. But Mr. Chairman had left town without leaving a copy of his tribute to Gulick or the tribute to the honoree the president was to read. By then it was the dinner hour with the opening ceremony following shortly after that. In great embarrassment, President Blanchard phoned and asked if I could suggest someone who could prepare at this late hour a tribute to Dr. Gulick and reported that he had asked a member of the Executive Committee to prepare a tribute to me. As fate would have it, Arthur

Steinhaus was conferring with me that very moment, having stumbled on a rumor of strange "goings-on." He gladly offered to forego dinner to help me prepare the tribute to Dr. Gulick. It had to be done hastily and without a chance to check for data, but having long been a great admirer of Dr. Gulick I had read all I could find about him and was glad to prepare the tribute with Arthur Steinhaus to help. Somehow, we prepared the tribute and Arthur delivered it to President Blanchard. Then I kept a belated dinner engagement, put on my new evening dress and presented myself on time to go on stage at the proper moment.

Since this convention was in Kansas City, not far from Lincoln, a large group of Nebraska physical education staff and majors was in the audience. In those days, it was a deep dark secret as to who would receive the various awards, the darkest secret of all, the Gulick Award. When I saw so many of my students in the audience, I thought what a pity if the award had been conferred in a private ceremony. As it turned out, when I was called to receive it my students, taken completely by surprise, leaped to their feet, screaming and yelling at the top of their lungs.

If I had been Frank Sinatra or a football hero I could have understood all this shrieking and yelling, but me! The whole convention crowd was convulsed with laughter at the girls' antics while I stood there wondering if the audience was wondering what else we might be teaching those girls besides yelling. Finally they calmed down and the ceremony proceeded.

When the session was over, the girls mobbed me. I was totally unprepared for their reaction. Then they dashed for a telephone and called the chancellor of the university and shouted to him that I had just received the Gulick Award. Later that bemused gentleman called me from Lincoln, laughingly reporting to me the call from the excited schoolgirls and offered his congratulations. The convention delegates teased me about the "yelling Nebraska girls" for several years after that. How could I ever, for a multiplicity of reasons, forget the evening I received the Gulick Award!

As for the chairman of the Award Committee, he must have been bewildered to return to the convention city two days later to learn that the ceremony went off as first scheduled. Although we were good friends for many years after that, he never offered a word of explanation for that peculiar incident. To round out the story, his letter informing me in the first place that I had been chosen to receive the

Gulick Award was dated April 1. As a child I understood that one should never take seriously any message written on April Fool's Day!

* * * *

During the war years I had an interesting assignment from the NAPECW. On April 9, 1946, in connection with the AAHPER convention in St. Louis, it gave a special luncheon in honor of eight members who had recently retired or were just then retiring, all women who had in the opening years of the century established our profession in many parts of the country and opened new doors to women. I was invited to be toastmistress (with Anna Hiss of the University of Texas chairman of the program arrangements). The eight honorees were Florence Alden, of the University of Oregon who had worked for many years in the Pacific Northwest; Alice Belding of Vassar College; Violet Marshall of the University of California (Berkeley); Gertrude Moulton of Oberlin College; Helen McKinstry, president of Russell Sage College; Ethel Perrin, whose latest venture was as executive secretary of the American Child Health Association; Blanche Trilling of the University of Wisconsin; and Agnes Wayman of Barnard College. An active member had been selected to pay the tribute to each and for Ethel Perrin I had asked Mary Channing Coleman to do the honors. It was a gala affair. The organization had never before (nor since) paid such special honor to its retired and retiring members. The honorees were seated at a long head table on a dais in the great ballroom of the Hotel Jefferson in St. Louis and those who were to pay the tributes were scattered about at the many tables below.

Coley had sent word that she would arrive early morning after a night flight from Greensboro, North Carolina, with two or three changes of planes and one long wait and would see no one until luncheon time. This was the first I had known of a personal friend flying to a convention. So I thought nothing of it when she did not appear for the luncheon, but when it came time to start the program and she had not yet appeared, I sent a page to call her room and was informed no such person was registered at the hotel.

As I introduced the speakers and resumed my seat, I studied the audience frantically to see if she could have come in unnoticed. Not finding her, I sent pages to watch every possible entrance and finally began searching for someone to pay the tribute to Ethel Perrin extemporaneously. Two persons refused. I was beginning to feel desperate and decided that I would have to pay the tribute myself. As the last

416

tribute to the others was being given (I had put off Ethel Perrin to last), I saw Coley being ushered to a seat. Almost immediately it was time to call on her. I was almost a nervous wreck but not Coley. In her nonchalant manner, she arose calmly and quietly asked us to excuse her dishevelled appearance for she had been up all night, her plane several hours late, and her baggage, including the copy of her tribute to Ethel, lost. Then she launched into a beautiful tribute to Ethel Perrin as only Coley could.

Following that, we had a joyous reunion for we had not been together for a few years. It was our last meeting. One and a half years later she died of a heart attack. What a rare soul she was!

* * * *

With the close of World War II it soon became evident, as following all preceding wars, that there was no such thing as returning to normal. The lack of discipline in the schools and in the home, even in life in general, which had been increasing since World War I, intensified with the new war. This resulted in a revolt of many parents and educators. It included attacks on the easy-to-master subject matter of much of the school curriculum and the stress on humanistic subjects at the expense of the sciences. The great failure of the schools of the nineteenth and early twentieth centuries had been their failure to recognize humanistic needs, but now the corrective pendulum had swung too far in favor of previous neglect.

Both the permissiveness and subject matter failures were blamed on the progressive education movement which had flourished from the late nineteenth century through the 1930s. Now strong reaction against it revived an interest in William James and his emphasis on hard work, clear thinking and disciplined education. There arose a revival of interest in his *Talks to Teachers* (1892), and his writings on *Habit* and *The Stream of Consciousness*. His books were in print once more, especially *Principles of Psychology* (1890), which he spent 12 years writing. He put out this work in a two-volume version for graduate students and a few years later in a one-volume version for undergraduates. According to legend, the Harvard students nicknamed them "James" and "Jimmie," respectively. The Jimmie version had been recently off press when I had used it as an undergraduate at Coe College. Now in the 1940s, some 50 years after its publication, it was being rediscovered.

Following the war, citizens, disturbed by postwar evidence that much was wrong with the education of our youth, held meetings throughout the country, asking, "What is it that is wrong?" "What can we do about it?" Periodicals carried articles by college professors critical of teachers colleges and schools of education, and by parents urging a revision of school and college curricula, particularly for those in the teachers colleges training teachers for the lower schools; these letters and articles urged a return to previously high standards. When I joined in an effort to retain the history requirement in the teachers college in my university, I was roundly squelched by one of the top authorities there. That experience came quickly back to mind when, a decade later, I ran across the following remark of the noted University of Illinois historian, Arthur Bestor, as reported in one of our leading news weeklies:

> A citizen who stands up and says he wants more science, more history and more foreign languages in his child's school is likely to have his ears pinned back by the school authorities. I know from personal experience.[5]

I, too, knew from personal experience. As the cold war between Russia and her former allies began to develop almost immediately after World War II, there was much talk that Russia, with its disciplined form of education, was developing more scientists, engineers and medical doctors, even far more women in the professions, than the United States. By mid-1950s figures were out to prove the claim.

The discussion of incompetence of public school teachers took on large proportions in the late 1940s, finally superseding the arguments that more Russian young people specialized in serious subjects than did American youth. So-called "professional educationists" now came in for much criticism. Who of us does not recall the attacks upon American schools by Admiral Hyman G. Rickover, the famous atomic-submarine expert? He voiced his criticisms in a book, *American Education, A National Failure*[6] in which he speaks of American education as the vapidity of the "progressive" system. He advocated lengthening the school day and year, eliminating all extracurricular activities during school hours, having textbooks prepared by "scholarly experts," upgrading teacher education, and above all, finding some way to "prevent the educationist bureaucracy from acting without a public mandate."[7]

There was such outspoken opposition to the progressive education movement by the early 1940s that membership in the Progressive Education Association was greatly reduced. But it managed to hold on until 1955 when it ceased to exist, although its journal, *Progressive Education*, was published for two more years. This movement had, from a feeble start in the 1870s, developed into a real force by World War I. It had influenced education profoundly for over 30 years, but in the end John Dewey, its proclaimed philosopher and guiding spirit, disclaimed it, asserting that his ideas, out of which the movement had grown, had been incredibly distorted by its later followers.

My own feelings about progressivism were well expressed by Professor Lawrence A. Cremin of Ohio State University, who said: "I'll never forgive my teachers for letting me flounder without help to which I was entitled."[8] Here was one critic who did not bow to William Heard Kilpatrick of Teachers College, Columbia University, who, departing from Dewey's theories, became the new fountainhead of progressive education.

At its best, progressive education never supplied a sufficient body of teachers skilled in teaching according to its precepts. Its precepts (teaching the whole child; recognizing individual differences; developing the child's personality; giving the child opportunities for social and emotional growth and creative self-expression, adjusting the school to the child's needs; teaching children not subject matter; and adjusting the teaching to life situations) excellent as they seemed, required teachers of superior teaching skill and great understanding of children. Such teachers the movement failed to produce in any but a mere trickle and teaching by these precepts, when done by mediocre and poor teachers, turned into a sorry waste. Poor teaching was as rife in physical education as in other sectors of education, playing false to the wisdom of our leader, Thomas D. Wood, through misinterpreting his philosophy or through inability to implement it at the teaching level.

However, the progressive education movement improved American schools in many ways. In my own journey through life both as a schoolgirl and as a teacher, I had in the 1890s witnessed the use of the birch rod on unruly boys by a man principal or superintendent or maybe even a janitor called in to punish the boy if perchance the room teacher was a woman, as most usually was the case. As a schoolchild, I experienced severe regimentation in marching in and out of the school building at opening and closing sessions and at recess periods but I never minded it for I did not have to fight for a place in line. I also experienced, along with the other little girls and the timid boys, the abuse by bullies who took frequent advantage because there was no supervision or leadership of our play at recess. These things largely vanished with the coming of the progressive education movement.

*   *   *   *

As told in an earlier chapter, I had been trying since the late 1930s to put together our department history, and now I forged ahead with my research on it. By the late 1940s, having the record more accurate and more complete, our department decided that since we had in 1940 celebrated the 40th anniversary of the graduation of our first professional training student, we should now celebrate the graduation of the 50th class and the 55th anniversary of the founding of the women's department. It was in the fall of 1894 that physical education classes for women were officially recognized by the faculty and regents and prescribed courses offered and a woman employed to teach the courses.

For our celebration, the first Nebraska graduate of the academic major in physical education, Alberta Spurck Robinson, came from Anchorage, Alaska. A handsome and vivacious woman, she looked exactly as we like to think a physical education trained person should look 50 years after graduation. In my research I had already unearthed the fact that one of Nebraska's early graduates had established the department of physical education for women at Ohio State University and now I learned from our first graduate of her part in helping to establish the department at the University of Washington. At the turn of the century the University of Nebraska played a big part in opening doors for women for our profession at both of these universities.

Our three-day celebration brought back to campus many graduates and several nationally-known professional friends as speakers. In addition to luncheons, teas and exhibits, there was a demonstration drill of the 1870s (thanks to Dorothy Ainsworth of Smith College for the historical research on that), an Indian club drill of the 1890s, an esthetic dance of the 1900s, a sports review, and modern dance of the 1940s. It was a great satisfaction to me as I was due to retire shortly and I felt it a fine climax to my career.

* * * *

The last few years of my teaching career were a strange mixture of joys and woes, the woes almost completely confined to the Nebraska scene, the joys, except for loyal staff members and majors, largely from contacts with the rest of the world established in years of giving fully of my time and energies to several organizations and to many people.

Speaking engagements at state teachers conventions in states as far as Tennessee and serving as consultant at career-day conferences at neighboring colleges and universities and as guest speaker at a preschool opening faculty conference at Cornell College one fall where I shared honors with the head of the physics department of the University of Iowa and the head of the sociology department of the University of Chicago, kept life stimulating in the postwar years. In a large way these appearances counterbalanced the unhappiness and unpleasantnesses that at times overwhelmed me on campus in the last years of my teaching career.

The year 1947 in particular held special personal sorrows for me. February 5 brought the death of my mother (after seven years of worry and unhappiness as my sisters and I watched helplessly as her memory slowly left her). Mother had been such a wonderful and understanding person and, in the 15 years before her health broke, had created a wonderful home life for this daughter who was having a career such as she, a generation earlier, had no doubt often dreamed of. Shortly following Mother's death came that of Dr. Carl Oscar Louis Collin, my Swedish gymnastics teacher, in March, which saddened me deeply. Fifteen years after his death, I, then 76 years old and unable to get help, could still climb a stepladder and swing a 12-foot porch awning into place and secure it by myself, yet I was never the "powerful Katrinka" type. I am sure Louis Collin could take much credit for my fitness for it was he who, in my early twenties, had faith that I could make good in my chosen career. He drove me relentlessly to become physically fit and gave me an interest in fitness which through all the years has kept me alert to this need.

On October 1 of that year, Mary Channing Coleman was talking in her office at North Carolina College for Women with some of her staff members about her retirement coming up the following spring. She asked that there be no special concern over it.

"I just wish to walk quietly out of my office without any fuss," she said. With that she walked quietly out of the office and got into her car to drive to the president's office for a conference. On returning to her office, she suffered a heart attack in the car and, with her foot pressing down on the feed pedal, the car careened wildly along the driveway, running over a curb, knocking down a student caught in its path, and finally stopping when it rammed a gatepost. When bystanders reached her car, she was dead. So I had lost another dear friend—Coley whose bravado had acted as a shield between sensitive me and stern Miss Homans when the going got too rough for me as it frequently did at the Boston Normal School of Gymnastics. She helped me safely through professional training which, had it not been for her, I might have given up.

Coley, who had carved out for herself a most successful career in physical education, had left behind a great following of personal and professional friends and former students who were deeply grieved over her death.

The year before this Chancellor Boucher had resigned amidst much unpleasantness between him and some of the faculty. It had been causing tensions that permeated the entire campus, making relaxation in work almost impossible. By then I had become the unwitting victim of a faction of women in the city that I came to recognize as a well organized hate group aimed at making things as uncomfortable for me as possible. It was not a current campus situation although the one faculty woman who had resented my presence on campus throughout my tenure there because of my philosophy on women's sports, was quick to enlist these women, all university alumnae, in whatever crusade she was leading against me at any given time. She was a leader against me in search of followers; they, crusaders against me in search of a cause.

As Chancellors Avery and Burnett had at some provocation over this woman's attacks on them as well as on me exclaimed in my presence, "That woman is a thorn in my flesh!" so, on more than one occasion, had Chancellor Boucher made the same remark to me. In a way we had been drawn somewhat together in our struggles to hold our own against this outspoken and vindictive woman. So I was sorry to see Chancellor Boucher depart, leaving me to stand up to her alone. Although she had retired at age 73 during Dr. Boucher's chancellorship, she was keeping the irons of her crusading weapons fired and both of us were now and then made aware of the heat.

As far as I have ever known, Dr. Reuben Gustavson, who succeeded Dr. Boucher in the chancellorship, escaped these experiences. But by then I no longer enjoyed the privilege of being able to go to the chancellor directly with my troubles, so there had been no occasion to discuss this woman with him.

Whatever the cause or causes of accelerated hate actions aimed at me, unpleasantnesses that had to my great relief died down during the war, accelerated in the postwar years. These were my last few years before retirement. They accelerated to such an extent that these last four years became a veritable nightmare to me and from the distance of 25 years later I look back upon this period as the low tide of my career. As the tide went out, it left uncovered a series of misadventures that even I, who suffered from them, am inclined to believe I must have dreamed all that—it just couldn't be true. But records at hand and my diaries prove that they were.

As troubles multiplied, I found myself quite alone. There was no one in authority upon whom I felt I could impose my troubles in my need for a safety valve and for help. Chancellors Avery, Burnett and Boucher were all gone. They would have listened to my story. Chancellor Gustavson's door was closed to me and the dean under whom I worked did not have one iota of sympathetic understanding toward anything I ever needed to discuss with him. So I kept to myself my worries and the tales of the unpleasant unexplainable things that were constantly happening to me.

I became the victim of harassment by telephone. Then annoyances whenever I worked at my office alone at nights as I frequently did all through the years began to multiply until even I became aware that I was under some sort of police surveillance.

Then I began receiving anonymous letters which did not bother me too much until they took a queer turn. They were strange letters sent to me by acquaintances to whom they had been sent, written on my departmental letterhead. To each of these my name had been forged. No two letters passed on to me were the same. Each was astonishing for it either didn't make sense or was of such a nature that the receiver found it hard to believe I was in my right senses when I had written it. All were typed with only the signature in longhand. A few receivers of these letters, quite familiar with my handwriting, questioned the signature. Others evidently didn't suspect forgery but were puzzled that I would send out such a letter and for some reason wanted me to see it again.

In the last weeks of my last year troubles increased and Chancellor Gustavson sent word to me one day to come to his office. When I reported to him, I found him deeply concerned for a citizen had informed him that I was in danger because he had overheard threats made against me. The chancellor asked if I had any enemies and when I told him I had several and it was a long story, he suggested that I come to his home the following morning for breakfast and tell him all I cared to of whatever I had on my mind that might possibly have any bearing on this rumor. Thus the door was open and at last I could pour out to him all that had been bothering me for quite some time— the hate group and all.

The upshot of this was that I was sent to a psychiatrist on a university appointment to tell these same tales and ask for advice on handling them. Evidently the chancellor sought advice, also, for shortly he sent for me again and informed me that I was from then on to be on special secret protection on campus. He turned me over to a plainclothesman who advised me and made plans for my arrival on campus each morning and departure late each afternoon, and also for leaving for lunch and returning. I was never to be caught anyplace alone. When alone in my office, the door was to be kept locked. Two staff members were let in on the secret, not only to help me but to help cover up the secret. It was important that no one sensed anything amiss. I never went into other parts of our building alone, and on the rare occasions I went back on evenings or Saturday afternoons or Sundays, I went only with a companion.

It was a tedious assignment. At home I was on my own, but under advice, I alerted two neighbors to be on the lookout for anyone hanging about and if so to call the police.

Shortly the forged letters became a larger problem and the chancellor and I had several sessions together about them. Handwriting experts were called in; it became a big undertaking still unsettled when I finally turned in my keys and ended my teaching career at the University of Nebraska. I never have known what happened after my departure but before I left these forged letters came back to me from questioning acquaintances from all parts of the country, leaving me wondering how many people not familiar enough with my handwriting to suspect forgery received peculiar letters and if so, what did the letters say and what did they think of my sending them a queer letter.

One that I heard of in a most roundabout way several years later was sent to a former student telling her that I was doing research on the subject of homosexuality (a word which no respectable woman at that time would utter in the presence of either man or woman) and that I suspected a friend of hers of being homosexual and would she spy on her and report to me what she learned about her. Unfortunately the girl who received this letter had no suspicion that my name was forged and was so shocked that she would never speak to me again, as she put it to another student several years later when telling her of the awful letter I had written her. Ever after that whenever I felt that a person might be snubbing me or a bit lacking in cordiality, I would ask myself, "I wonder if she (or he) got one of those queer letters with my signature forged! If so, what could it have said?" The fact that all were typed on my departmental letterheads made them seem authentic.

* * * *

There was one final thing to do before I retired—get that so long-talked-of new gymnasium a bit closer to reality. I had already made plans twice for a new building, only to have hopes dashed. Now we had a third set of plans ready. But not until 16 years later did a new building materialize—a building far surpassing the dreams of earlier years. By that time my third set of plans were 20 years old calling for an altogether different set of plans for a new day and a new site. By then the site on the corner of Fourteenth Street and Vine had been ruined for us by a small building of Teachers College.

* * * *

I was delighted the spring before my retirement when I received a long-distance call one day from the State Department in Washington, D.C., saying that they had learned through AAHPER that I would be retiring in June. They asked if I would be interested in a foreign assignment for the coming year in either India, Burma or Iraq. Indeed I was! I finally accepted a Fulbright Professorship in Iraq with headquarters in Baghdad—a most interesting experience and a story for another day.

Before I had heard of the possibility of such an assignment I had accepted a position as visiting professor for the following summer at the University of Southern California, so that in the end I had as a climax to my 42 years career, a summer session of teaching at the University of Southern California and a school year in Baghdad serving as a consultant on physical education in the Iraq Ministry of Education.

As a climax to my years of teaching, the staff, the WAA, the majors and the department alumnae united to give me a farewell banquet that was beautifully planned, organized, and carried out. My three sisters and two brothers-in-law came from Illinois, Iowa and Kansas, also friends from Coe College, one of whom had helped initiate me into my first year of teaching 42 years earlier. Many graduates and professional friends came from distant parts. The committee in charge planned a fun-filled program and with Ruth Diamond Levinson as toastmistress, all went splendidly. It was a wonderful send-off into retirement. It made up in a large way for many recent frustrations.

As I retired, I proudly left behind a department that had been built on an excellent foundation but which had sadly deteriorated from early 1900s on until in the late twenties when my staff and I had brought it back to its original excellence. Beyond that, we had given it an enviable reputation throughout the nation for excellent undergraduate preparation of women teachers of physical education.

During my 28 years as Director of Physical Education for Women at the University of Nebraska, 136 different colleges and universities asked for teachers trained under my direction. Calls came for graduates of our department from every state in the union but two; also from China and Japan (before World War II) and from Canada, Australia, India, Chile, Uruguay, Panama, Mexico and the Philippines. The colleges and universities that have taken my graduates on their faculties make a long, proud list, ranging from the Atlantic to the Pacific, from the Canadian border to the Gulf. Many who went into high schools, YWCAs, Camp Fire Girls, Girl Scouts, recreation, and physical therapy work, as well as in colleges, have filled top positions in those fields.

It was always a source of regret that we didn't have more girls to place for we offered so little help to the lower schools of the country because the other openings offered better inducements to the few graduates available. At the conclusion of the war an English couple from South Africa came to Lincoln to talk with me about sending their daughter to major under my direction, having heard of the work of our department from a government agency. When they learned I would be retiring before she would graduate, they chose another school.

I also proudly left behind me an interesting list of young women teaching in our profession. Graduates of other professional training departments, they came to my staff "fresh off the assembly line" as I liked to speak of them and "cut their eye teeth" under my direction. I was never afraid of inexperience as were many of my co-workers, and I liked to have youth at the helm when it came to teaching activity courses. Several of our own graduates I was happy also to retain for our own staff. Most of these, both Nebraska and non-Nebraska graduates, who stayed on in the profession after acquiring their early teaching experience under my tutelage, went on to graduate work and to splendid positions in other colleges and universities, where salary budgets were more favorable. I looked upon all of them as "my girls." Others did their graduate work and then came to my staff while still quite young to garner early experience under my direction. Several of these went on to important top positions, and a few are now retired themselves. Others still at work are in some of today's top positions in our field.

The summers after I went to Nebraska—28 of them—although never on a summer payroll, whenever in town I was on constant call from administrative offices, students and prospective students, and at the office some part of a few days each week. Without office help and with staff scattered for the summer, I made departmental preparations for

426

the coming new school year. This usually totalled up to the equivalent of three to four weeks of full-time work at the office each summer, and this summer work alone for all those years added up to the equivalent of at least two full nine-month school years of work for the University of Nebraska without one penny of pay. I am sure there were other department heads who were not employed on an 11- or 12-month basis who could tell the same sort of story throughout those years.

For those of us who retired before the University of Nebraska accepted the Social Security plan (and at that time it had but a sorry pension plan), retirement proved a difficult time financially if one had not seen the handwriting on the wall and built up other protective plans. In all my more than 25 years of retirement not one penny has been added to this meager pension in recognition of the constant rise in cost of living. Despite repeated university requests to the legislature Social Security and pre-decent pension years, the legislature year after year lets the bill die in committee.

Recalling the year several years ago when the university faculty women came to the financial rescue of one woman retiree of that pre-Social Security period, I realize that had she lived longer her need for financial help would have increased materially. We women felt that because she was a woman the responsibility was ours. Perhaps, faculty men came to the financial aid of needy male retirees, also.

* * * *

In the 42 years of my teaching career, (the year 1919–1920 out for illness) all on the college level, life was much simpler than today with its many strata of administrative staffs. A lowly head of a department today has many echelons of higher-ups to stand between him and final authority. In my first 35 years I was directly responsible to the president or chancellor. Then for one year I was under a man who was directly responsible to the chancellor as head of a Division of Health and Physical Education of which my department was one of three divisions. Then for a second year and a half of a third, I was under this same man but with health removed from his division. Then the department of physical education for women was removed from the Division and the two departments were placed in Teachers College under the Dean of that college. Thus I served the last four and a half years of my career. Those seven years under these two men were miserable, yet with most men I got along splendidly.

Both of these men were unable to accept a woman under their command as an equal in the educational game. It was a humiliating experience after 35 years of independence. My dean became increasingly difficult to work with, treating me as if he considered me utterly incompetent in every way, not to be trusted to make any decisions, therefore to be ordered about and dictated to in every aspect of my departmental work. The four and one-half years finally turned into a nightmare, especially for the last two years until Chancellor Gustavson, sensing that things were wrong, called me in, let me pour out my frustrations to him, and for the short time remaining, left his door open to me.

How I regretted that I had refused the splendid offer of 1946 to go to another position. But I was so near retirement and also did not forsee the miserable changes so shortly to come at Nebraska. Also family considerations made it impossible to give a change of position serious thought. So caught in this unhappy web there was nothing to do but suffer it out. I at least had some wonderful loyal staff members to stand firmly back of me and a wonderful group of majors, knowing nothing of my frustrations yet sensing my distress over something, offering me their youthful loyalty and concern.

It would have been difficult upon retirement to say goodbye to my loyal staff members and majors had I not been committed to teach a summer course at the University of Southern California in Los Angeles which forced me to pack up and leave shortly. In 42 years my third summer teaching engagement! This one proved so interesting that I had no desire to mark out the days on the calendar one by one; they raced along too speedily. Immediately with that over, I had to rush home to get ready to leave for the Fulbright professorship I had accepted for the year 1952–1953 in Iraq.

It was not as if, after I turned in my keys at Nebraska, I was going home to sit on my porch with nothing to do. I was free and I was heading straight into high adventure!

The American Export Line's *S.S. Constitution* pulled out of New York Harbor at noon on a beautiful late September day, with the orchestra playing and flags flying, with me aboard. As it glided past the Statue of Liberty, I stood on one of the upper decks alone watching the skyline of New York City fade into the distance. There were tears in my eyes but a smile on my lips. I inwardly saluted the "old girl," as Coley, my school-days roommate, would have spoken of the statue—the tears for the many happy years gone by that transcended the hurts of the past few years, and the smile for the inner assurance I strongly felt that the years ahead were to be free of harassments, happy ones. And indeed they have been just that—far beyond any expectations!

Except for the thorns I had found much satisfaction in my career. Now I welcomed retirement!

Epilogue

Retirement! My teaching career over! There was much I wanted to do yet and fortunately I was in excellent health. For the immediate present I was committed to a Fulbright professorship for the school year of 1952–1953 to help Iraq establish teacher-training work in physical education for women. I wouldn't have missed this undertaking for anything in the world. It was a year of strange new lands, new friends, to me strange peoples, and new kinds of experiences. I discovered for myself much of the Near East with headquarters in Baghdad and travels in Iraq, Lebanon, Syria, Jordan, Palestine, Egypt, Turkey and a wee taste of Greece. Never could life be the same again after 10 months of living in such history-filled surroundings.

The following year my sister Madge, Gertrude Moulton, Ann Hughitt, my old Boston Normal School of Gymnastics and Wellesley College classmate, both now retired from Oberlin, and I spent seven months running about Europe. My sister Madge's husband, Earl Vincent, the Iowa district judge with whom I had done so much summer mountain hiking, had died of a sudden heart attack while I was in Baghdad. Just a few weeks before that, my sister Ferne had also passed away most unexpectedly. The two deaths in the family so close together were devastating. Madge was having difficulties adjusting to living alone in her home in Iowa. I was planning what to do next, for Ferne, too, had retired and we had planned to make a home together for the years ahead. Now my plans had to be revised. We decided the thing for the moment, for both Madge and me, was to close both our homes and take off for several months in Europe. With two such good companions, we had a splendid seven months of travel in Europe and came home ready to face the task of adjusting to life without the dear ones with whom we had expected to spend retirement years.

Life seemed to be pushing me into the very things I enjoyed doing. There were invitations to speak here and there throughout the country. A publishing company asked me to revise an old physical education textbook whose author had died. At the same time, I was cleaning out the enormous stack of professional records and correspondence that filled my study and overflowed into the attic. I came upon a large carton filled with the diaries I had kept from my grade school days on. I had not given them a thought for years. While pondering what to do with them, I received an announcement from Wellesley College that they were closing out the funds left from the Mary Hemingway Endowment that had financed both the Boston Normal School of Gymnastics and its successor, the professional training section of the department of hygiene and physical education at Wellesley College. With that department by then closed out, they planned to parcel out the last of the funds in fellowship awards to graduates for research and writing projects relative to advancement of physical education.

I realized that these diaries could mean something to my profession and I applied for one of the Amy Morris Homans Fellowship Awards to write my professional memoirs. The request was granted and what developed into years of research and writing followed—interrupted for long periods by other professional writings of a historical nature, and for other projects that had an uncanny way of intruding upon my attention now and then.

Hence this one project has spread over a 20-year period bearing final fruit in the publication, March 1977, of a first volume, *Memories Of A Bloomer Girl*, and this book, its sequel. The third book of professional memoirs entitled *From Bloomers to Bikinis*, is, as of this writing, complete in its third draft. I hope to put it into final draft in 1978. After that there is enough non-professional material left in my diaries for three other books for lay readers, which should keep me happily busy for another few years. After that my Fulbright year diary calls for attention. The years dash away too quickly for all I have yet to do.

The many things that caused me to put my memoirs aside have been interesting. In the late fifties and sixties I discovered Florida and spent many winters there with my sister Jean, and her husband, Theodore Aszman who upon his retirement the same year as mine went to Miami to live.

In the months of the late fifties when I was back in my home in Nebraska, I rewrote entirely the America part of the old Rice book on *A Brief History of Physical Education* and in the late sixties, revised the revision. Between these two works, I researched and wrote the

431

histories of both the old Middle West Society of Physical Education and the Central Association of Health, Physical Education and Recreation, and with Bruce L. Bennett of Ohio State University wrote the 75-Year History of the American Association for Health, Physical Education and Recreation for the Association's 75th Anniversary in 1960.

* * * *

As the AAHPER was approaching its 75th year in 1960, having heard nothing of special plans underway to celebrate this special anniversary, I wrote President Arthur Esslinger, asking what was brewing, just as I had to the president 25 years before. He and his officers were taken by surprise about this bit of our Association history just as the officers had been in 1935. Again it was history-conscious I who sounded the alarm, this time well in advance of the important event. Caught up in a time-consuming emergency matter, the president begged me, since as he put it "you are retired and have time free," to whip up a 75th anniversary celebration "if we give you a whole block of convention program time for it." Anticipating that it would be a most interesting and exciting assignment I accepted the challenge and started plans at once. This led to a request that I write the 75-year-history to be published in convention month which I consented to do for the first 40 years with Bruce Bennett, a recognized historian in our profession, to cover the last 35 years.

For the one general session allowed our anniversary committee for a program, Laura Huelster of the University of Illinois whipped together a group of young teachers in the profession for a program long to be remembered. Costumed in attire of the late 1880s this dedicated group of young men and women staged a convention program of that period, giving portions of the actual speeches the early leaders had given at the early conventions. It was a smash hit but I doubt if the memory of that evening is one whit brighter in the minds of the actors than the memory of the day before when at the close of the dress rehearsal all were caught in a cloudburst of rain arriving at their various destinations looking more like almost drowned creatures than amateur thespians out on a lark. By some hook or crook the actors and their costumes got dried out and presentable before the next evening's "curtain."

At the 75th anniversary convention luncheon on another day, at President Esslinger's insistence, I served as toastmistress. To keep it on the historical theme, we rounded up early leaders, still living, as special guests, with C. Ward Crampton and John Brown, Jr., both in their eighties and living in Miami, as the stars of the occasion. A message from Amos Alonzo Stagg, then 98 years old, opened the program. To honor the occasion as toastmistress I wore the long, all-over eyelet embroidery gown I had worn for my college graduation 52 years earlier, along with my huge willow-plumed Merry Widow hat which had been in the family attic. The hat in particular delighted Dr. Crampton. The minute he spied it he called out joyously, "My wife was wearing a hat just like that, the first time I ever saw her." Shortly after that encounter, C. Ward Crampton went to his reward, and not long after that, John Brown, too.

For the occasion the quartet that had made itself famous at APEA conventions since my own presidency 28 years earlier staged a revival. Sporting old-time handlebar moustaches, Bill Streit led his group though a series of oldtime songs. Unexpectedly a flood light was thrown on me at the head table and the quartet burst into *Let Me Call You Sweetheart.* I jumped to my feet and beckoned Minnie Lynn, the new incoming president seated nearby, to join me. The two of us, the first woman president and the next woman president, took the tribute together with that huge crowd in the Miami Beach auditorium joining in the singing. That moment clings to memory!

Other groups equally dedicated put on special programs on various aspects of our history, held special "do you remember" get-togethers for retired members, and for one meeting had as a special guest, Margaret Hitchcock Emerson, the granddaughter of our first president, Edward Hitchcock. She came from Amherst to talk with us informally about her recollections of her grandfather.

Having been greatly frustrated the summer of '59 in trying to research our Association's history when we had not yet established our archives and brought together our records, I began a campaign to educate the officers of that day to a need for establishing our archives at once. In fact I made quite a nuisance of myself about it. Finally the executive secretary hailed me at the close of that 1960 convention saying:

"You'll be glad to learn that we have decided to establish our archives at once and to appoint an archivist to undertake and advance the project."

"Wonderful," I exclaimed. "Who is the archivist to be?"

"You!" was the reply.

"I? Why me? I know nothing of being an archivist."

433

AAHPER's 75th Anniversary Luncheon Quartette and Toastmistress, Miami Beach, April 1960. From left, Harlan Metcalfe, Clifford Brownell, Mabel Lee, Louis Roth and William Streit.

"Who of us does? We've all decided that since you are so deeply interested and are retired with your time free and since we can't now afford a paid person who is professionally trained as an archivist, we will offer to pay necessary expenses for secretarial help and office supplies if you will volunteer your services to make a beginning of this work."

So I asked for time to think it over. Later I accepted the appointment if the Association would also pay my membership dues to join the Society of American Archivists as its representative and my expenses to attend the annual convention of that organization so that I might learn as quickly as possible something about archives work, also expenses to visit the national office now and then to look after archival collections. This request was granted and I entered upon what turned out to be a 9½ year appointment from July 1960 through December 31, 1969, an utterly fascinating assignment although very time-consuming. At this same time Dr. Bruce Bennett was appointed the first historian and a year or so later, Dr. Paul Washke of Oregon State University at Corvallis, was appointed chairman of a centennial commission to set wheels turning for that eventful year (1985) in the life of our profession.

In 1962, a temporary archives depository was established at Ohio State University; in 1968, our Association employed a full-time assistant to the archivist, and the young National Foundation for HPER rented space for a depository for our archives in Washington, D.C., near our national Association offices. When I "passed the torch" on to Dr. Elwood Craig Davis, retired from the University of Southern California, I felt that I could drop my self-appointed role of watch dog over our historical milestones. Today Dr. Ruth Schellberg, retired from the University of Minnesota-Mankato, carries on.

The 75th anniversary celebration itself plus the drive to establish our archives sparked a great interest in our Association's history. There quickly arose to the surface a heart-warming group of young people deeply concerned about history and archives who evidently had only been awaiting some signal to take up the challenge. As for myself what a new world was opened to me and after I was past 74 years old.

In pursuit of these duties I visited one fall the archives of the New England colleges which were the fountainhead of our profession—Amherst, Harvard, Springfield, Smith, Wellesley, the Sargent School of Physical Education at Boston University. While I was on this trip I also met and talked with students at Springfield and Smith Colleges, Bouvé-Boston School, and the University of Massachusetts. On other trips in connection with SAA conventions I visited the state archives of North Carolina, Georgia, Texas, New Mexico, and the archives of several cities. Today our Alliance is looking forward to greatly enlarged archival quarters in a new building. It was pure pleasure to have been the one to spark the beginning of all of this.

* * * *

Suddenly in the summer of 1965 the state fire marshall condemned Grant Memorial Hall at the University of Nebraska and it was razed almost immediately, leaving my successor and her staff to carry on here and there all over the campus. The splendid new building of $2¼ million was finally completed in 1968, 44 years after that first promise to me. As the fire marshall had reported, "This 1887 structure, the oldest building now left on the campus, is a hazard to life," adding

> there is no mortar left between wall bricks, window frames are sagging and apparently so rotten they could fall out, coping stones over the doorway are dangerous, walls and roof leaking, downspouts need replacing, east and west arches need repair, floors and ceilings are in hazardous condition.

When the local paper announced that demolition would begin the following day, I drove to the campus alone that evening and in the twilight walked all about the huge, old building, reading for a last time the plaques at the two entrances, the one at the west dedicating that wing to the memory of the soldiers of the University of Nebraska who had given their lives to their country in the Spanish-American War, reading slowly all the names, each name representing a young man struck down in the prime of life. Now this old building commemorating their sacrifice was to die too, but it, unlike these young men, had lived a long life—the east wing 78 years, the west, 66.

In another 24 hours, its great walls would be levelled, the fleet of trucks would begin hauling away the last vestiges of its former grandeur. And as I walked sadly back to my car alone, I brushed aside a tear for the east wing of the old building that had known General Pershing also Wilbur Bowen, Robert Clark, and W.W. Hastings, pioneers in physical education. Would the University's fallen heroes of the Spanish-American War still be remembered after the west wing, Memorial Hall, erected to their memory was gone? In the waning twilight as I paid a last lone homage to these soldiers I thought of the lines of Rupert Brooke that begin "These laid the world away," written of other soldiers of a later war, lines I had long remembered from World War I.

In no time at all the old turreted building disappeared and as if to wipe out all memory of it, quickly the ground where the building stood was levelled and returned to greensward, as if the building had never existed. Of that trio, which the college textbook and gym suit salesmen liked to pun about when they went to Lincoln to see Lee in Grant, Lee, the teacher, has long been retired, Grant, the building is now vanished, but Lincoln, the city, is bigger than ever. However the name Lee is now on the 1968 building that replaces Grant Hall.

* * * *

At the christening of Mabel Lee Hall at University of Nebraska-Lincoln, May 7, 1977. (Courtesy of Ruth Schellberg and Arbor Print Shop, Lincoln, Nebraska).

The 1960s brought more sorrows when my sister Madge developed a brain tumor. I put aside my writing projects, closed my home and moved into her home in Iowa to be at her side for almost a year and a half as she slowly slipped away into death. A few years later Jean's husband also died in Florida and I spent much time there with my sister. Only Jean and I survive of our immediate family.

In the meantime more and more of my old friends passed away or gave up for the role of invalid in some nursing home, until I find myself almost alone in my own age group. Fortunately, I have been able to build up new friendships of the two generations following mine. These younger people offer rare friendship that enriches life immeasurably.

I have continued to attend our professional organization conventions and thus keep the coals of both new and old (what remains) friendships alive. I keep up my home and enjoy living alone but among all ages old, young, middle-aged—a resident of the normal world. And life is exciting.

In the mid-sixties I met Carl Diem of Germany, the world-wide acknowledged spiritual successor of Baron de Coubertin, in the home of Arthur Steinhaus in Chicago. Meeting him was a high spot of memories!

The seventies which have catapulted me into my nineties have outdone themselves in thrills. Early in 1976 a long-distance telephone conversation was arranged between one of the classes of professional training students at the Metropolitan State College in Denver and me at my home in Lincoln. We had a half hour's chat with questions and answers and much merriment for a unique experience. Then in April I had the pleasure of presenting to the president the first awardees for the Mabel Lee Award at the AAHPER convention—this award having been established the year before in recognition of International Woman's Year. The first two recipients were two charming young women, Sharon Ann Plowman and MG Sholtis, who according to the terms of the Award, were not yet 36 years of age and showed unusual promise in the field of physical education. Then in May a return to my *alma mater* and the scene of my first teaching position, Coe College, to be crowned Queen of the May—this in celebration of the college's 125th anniversary and of the 65th year since I started pageantry and the May Queen tradition at Coe. A May Queen very close to her 90th birthday! The occasion was celebrated with TV appearances and news interviews following the crowning ceremony. Again I recovered from storage the eyelet embroidered dress of my college graduation in 1908 which I also wore at my first pageant as director in 1911, again at my 50th year class reunion in 1958, all at Coe College, and at AAHPER's 75th Anniversary celebration at Miami Beach in 1960. That gown has been worn in the 1960s and 1970s in many colleges around the country much more as an historic relic than when it was new and still in style.

In July 1976, as an 89-year old Queen of May, I was "cover girl" on Coe's July issue of its *Courier* that goes out to all graduates. Again I was the "cover girl" in the December issue of the *Nebraska Journal of Health and Physical Education and Recreation*, with an article about my retirement activities.

The year 1977 kept up the pace of 1976—in January 1977 a feature article about my activities in retirement in the *Journal of National Retired Teachers Association*, in March my *Memories of a Bloomer Girl* off press with an author's autograph party at the AAHPER convention in Seattle, in April a trip to Wisconsin for an honorary Doctor of Humanities degree from Beloit College where I spent four happy years in the early twenties, in May a ceremony at the University of Nebraska-Lincoln naming the Women's Physical Education Building Mabel Lee Hall, now that it is a coeducational building. Then there were Nebraska Education Television interviews at home, indoors and in

438

my garden, the television showing in late June including scenes at the building-naming ceremony. In October I returned to Coe for more TV and radio interviews and for induction in Coe's Sports Hall of Fame, not as a sportswoman but as one who has spent a full career in organizing and promoting sports for women.

As Edna St. Vincent Millay, I fear I, too, at times have burned my candle at both ends. I pray that of mine, as of hers, it also can be said, "It gives a lovely light."

I started my schooling in the gay nineties, did my high school and college years at the turn of the century, started my teaching career in pre-World War I years, pursued it through the terrible twenties, the depression thirties, and fighting forties, retired in the frustrating fifties, took a new volunteer career in the sick sixties (the Age of Rubbish as Richard Hofstadter, DeWitt Clinton professor of American history at Columbia University calls it),[1] and am still "going strong" for my years—somewhat slowed down but in my nineties loving an active life in the world's seventies.

So in the words of Browning:

Grow old with me!
The best is yet to be,
The last of life, for which
  the first was made
Our times are in his hand.[2]

Author in her ninetieth year. (Courtesy of Nebraska State Commission on Aging).

439

Chronology

1886	Born in Clearfield, Iowa (August 18)
1893	Moved with family to Centerville, Iowa
1900–1904	Centerville High School
1904–1908	Coe College, Cedar Rapids, Iowa, B.S. Magna Cum Laude.
1908–1909	Boston Normal School of Gymnastics
1909–1910	Wellesley College, Massachusetts, Certificate of Physical Education
1910–1918	Director of Physical Education for Women, Coe College
1914	Student, Chalif School of Dance, New York City (Summer)
1917	Student, Vestoff-Serova School of Dance, New York City (Summer)
1918–1919	Director of Physical Education for Women, Oregon Agriculture College, Corvallis
1919–1920	Disabled by influenza epidemic
1920–1924	Director of Physical Education for Women, Beloit College, Beloit, Wisconsin
1922	Summer Physical Education Teacher, New York State Teachers College, Oneonta
1924–1952	Professor and Director of Physical Education for Women, University of Nebraska-Lincoln
1925–1927	President, Middle West Association of Physical Education for College Women
1926	Co-founder, Nebraska State PE Society
1926–1927	President, National Association of Physical Education for College Women (NAPECW)
1929	Acting President, Middle West Society of Physical Education (Feb–April) upon death of President
1929–1930	President, Middle West Society of Physical Education

1930	Vice-President, American Physical Education Association (APEA)
1931	President, APEA (first woman)
1932	President, APEA (January–April) in transition period
1932	Elected into American Academy of Physical Education
1933	Recipient of APEA Honor Award
1935–1940	Member, Board of Directors, Women's Division, National Amateur Athletic Federation
1938–1939	Acting President, American Academy of Physical Education, upon death of president
1937	Author, *Conduct of Physical Education,* A. S. Barnes & Co.
1939	Recipient of honorary Doctor of Laws, Coe College
1939	Summer Visiting Professor, University of Texas, Austin
1940–1942	President (first woman), American Academy of Physical Education
1941–1943	Director of Physical Fitness, Seventh Army Service Command under the Office of Civilian Defense
1943–1944	Member, Board of Directors, American Youth Hostels
1943–1945	Member, National Council on Physical Fitness, Federal Security Agency
1943–1945	Member, Women's Commission on Physical Fitness, FSA
1944–1945	Member, U.S. Office of Education Committee on Physical Education Policies in Colleges and Universities
1944–1948	Member National Council of American Youth Hostels
1944–1948	Member, Chief of Staff's National Civilian Advisory Committee, Women's Army Corps
1945–1949	Member, Board of Directors of American Folk Arts Society
1948	Recipient of AAHPER Gulick Award
1949	Co-author with Wagner, *Fundamentals of Body Mechanics and Conditioning,* W. B. Saunders Co.
1952	Retired, Professor and Director Emeritus, University of Nebraska-Lincoln
1952	Summer Visiting Professor, University of Southern California, Los Angeles
1952–1953	Consultant, Iraq Ministry of Education as Fulbright Professor, Baghdad
1955	Honorary member, Central Association of Physical Education for College Women
1956	Honorary member, NAPECW
1956	Recipient, honorary Doctor of Physical Education, George Williams College, Chicago
1957	Recipient Hetherington Award, American Academy of Physical Education

1958	Co-author with Rice and Hutchinson, *Brief History of Physical Education* 4th ed., Ronald Press.
1958-1959	Chairman, AAHPER International Relations Section
1960	Co-author with Bennett, *75-Year History of AAHPER,* "This Is Our Heritage" *JOHPER,* April 1960
1960-1970	AAHPER's First Archivist (July 1960-Jan. 1, 1970)
1963	Author, *History of Middle West Society of Physical Education—1912-1960.*
1966	Author, *History of Central AHPER—1933-1963.*
1967	Recipient, Honor Award of New Mexico AHPER
1968	Recipient, R. Tait McKenzie Award of AAHPER
1969	Author with Rice and Hutchinson, *Brief History of Physical Education,* 5th ed., Ronald Press.
1969	Recipient, Honor Award of Nebraska AHPER
1974	Recipient, Presidential Service Award as first woman president and first archivist of AAHPER
1975	AAHPER Mabel Lee Award established
1976	Recipient, Honor Award, North American Society for Sport History
1977	Subject of article, "Doctor Phys Ed" in *Journal of National Retired Teachers Association,* Jan. issue
1977	Author, *Memories Of A Bloomer Girl,* AAHPER publisher.
1977	Recipient, honorary Doctor of Humanities, Beloit College
1977	Former Women's Physical Education Building renamed Mabel Lee Hall, University of Nebraska-Lincoln
1977	Inducted in Sports Hall of Fame, Coe College
1978	Author, *Memories Beyond Bloomers,* sequel to *Memories Of A Bloomer Girl,* AAHPER publisher

Notes

CHAPTER II. THE TORCH IS HANDED ON

1. On file in University Archives.
2. As told to the author by May Pershing.
3. According to records in Archives of Michigan State College, Ypsilanti.
4. As told to author by Adelloyd Williams, assistant to Anne Barr.
5. Springfield College Archives.
5a. As reported in APEA *Proceedings* of 1894 convention.
6. "Anne Barr Clapp—A Pioneer in Physical Education," *Research Quarterly Supplement* 12, Oct. 1941: 679-681.
7. As told to author by Alice Towne Deweese, who audited courses there in 1905-1906.
8. Walter Kroll and Guy Lewis, The First Academic Degree in Physical Education," *Journal of Health, Physical Education, Recreation* 40: June 1969, 73-74.
8a. Ibid.
9. Letter to author, Sept. 14, 1972 from Mrs. Susan R. Rosenberg, assistant archivist, Stanford University.
10. As told to the author in June 1940 by Alberta Spurck.
11. The first published story of the beginnings of physical education at the University of Nebraska was written by the author as Part I of *Seventy-five Years of Professional Preparation in Physical Education for Women at the University of Nebraska-Lincoln,* published by the University Printing Office, April 1973. Much that was prepared for Part I had to be deleted, but the entire manuscript is preserved in the "long version" in the Department Archives and contains much material not included in this book.

12. Williams College Archives.
13. In news item in *Journal of Health, Physical Education, Recreation* 37: Feb. 1966.
14. *Journal of Health, Physical Education, Recreation* 44: April 1973, 89.
15. Springfield College Archives.
16. 1975 correspondence with the librarian of the Keokuk, Iowa Public Library which contains records of the old Keokuk Medical School.
17. In University of Nebraska Archives. Published with permission.
18. Published in *American Physical Education Review* 28: 1923, 143.
19. As told to the author by many graduates and staff members of those days.
20. According to listings in University catalogs year by year.
21. Letter from Fred Luehring, April 1920, in University Archives.
22. Letter in University Archives.
23. As told in *Memories Of A Bloomer Girl* (Washington, DC: American Alliance for Health, Physical Education, and Recreation, 1977).
24. M. M. Ready, "Professional Courses in Physical Education for Teachers," *Bulletin of U.S. Bureau of Education,* April 15, 1926.
25. A. C. Benson, *At Large* (New York: G. P. Putnam's Sons, 1908), p. 18.
26. At Department Celebration in May 1940, in recognition of graduation of the university's first student from the physical education academic major.

CHAPTER III. DIVERTISSEMENTS AND DILEMMAS

1. *Pound's Rules* (some spoke of them as "Pond's Rules").
2. *My Life With History* (Lincoln, NE: University of Nebraska Press, 1968).
3. Published in 1929.
4. *American Physical Education Review* 5: 1900.
5. *Journal of Education,* 1826, pp. 69–89.
6. As reported by Dean Macheckne in published paper given at AAHPER convention, April 1960.
7. New York: Macmillan, 1924, pp. 288–289.

CHAPTER IV. THE TURBULENT TWENTIES AND PROFESSIONAL CONCERNS

1. As related in author's book, *Memories Of A Bloomer Girl* (Washington, DC: American Alliance for Health, Physical Education, and Recreation, 1977).

446

2. Helen Barr et al., "History of The Middle West Association of Physical Education for College Women, 1917-1957," mimeographed.
3. As related in *Memories Of A Bloomer Girl* (Washington, DC: American Alliance for Health, Physical Education, and Recreation, 1977).
4. *American Physical Education Review* 28: March 1923, 22.
5. *American Physical Education Review* 28: Sept. 1923, 314-315.
6. Ibid., pp. 318-319.
7. Ibid., p. 315.
8. Thomas Gray, *In A Country Church Yard,* Stanza 17.
9. *Chicago Tribune,* April 25, 1929.
10. Ethel Perrin, J. Anna Norris and Magaret McKee.
11. Walter B. Pitkin, *Life Begins at Forty* (New York: McGraw-Hill, 1932).
12. *WAA Yearbook* (Lincoln, NE: University of Nebraska, 1926).

CHAPTER V. A DEPRESSION AND OTHER ANNOYANCES
1. As reported in *Journal of Health and Physical Education* 4: March 1933, 4.
2. "Shall We Abolish School Frills? No!" *School Life,* May 1933. p. 49.
3. As reported in J. E. Rogers, *News Letter* #66 (published by National Recreation Association in New York), Jan. 1, 1934, pp. 3-4.

CHAPTER VI. PROGRESSIVE EDUCATION MOVEMENT TAKES ITS TOLL OF PHYSICAL EDUCATION
1. Edward Hitchcock, *The Power of Christian Benevolence in the Life and Labors of Mary Lyon,* 5th ed. (Northampton, MA: Hopkins Bridgeman, 1852).
2. In *Harvard Monthly,* March 1903, as reported by Gay Wilson Allen, in William James (New York: Viking Press, 1969).
3. G. Stanley Hall, *Adolescence* (New York: Arno Press, 1969), pp. 206-207. Reprint of 1905 edition.
4. Canto V, Stanza 10.
5. In "A Half-Century Of Physical Education," *Physical Educator* 17, no. 3: Oct. 1960, 61.
6. David Hulburd, *This Happened In Pasadena* (New York: Macmillan, 1951); Arthur Bestor, *Educational Wastelands* (Urbana, IL: University of Illinois, 1953) and *Restoration of Learning* (New York: Knopf, 1955); and Lyman Bryson, *The Next America* (New York: Harper, 1952).

CHAPTER VII. PETTICOAT RULE COMES TO ONE NATIONAL PROFESSIONAL ORGANIZATION

1. Events referred to throughout this chapter as occurring earlier are related in the author's earlier book, *Memories Of A Bloomer Girl* (Washington, DC: American Alliance for Health, Physical Education, and Recreation, 1977).
2. As recorded in a news item in *American Physical Education Review* 5: 1899.
3. Letter from Grace Stafford.
4. *Journal of Society of American Archivists,* Jan. 1973, p. 7.

CHAPTER VIII. PRESIDENTIAL CONCERNS

1. Early information on thoughts on the National Education Association affiliation gleaned from reports in various issues of the *American Physical Education Review* of the 1890s and early 1900s.
2. Alice Oakes Bronson, *Clark W. Hetherington—Scientist and Philosopher,* multilithed (Salt Lake City: University of Utah Press, 1958), p. 88.
3. *American Physical Education Review* 15: Nov. 1920, 364.

CHAPTER IX. WOMEN'S LIB—1930s STYLE

1. From minutes of Council meetings and author's diaries and files.
2. Florence Somers, tape recording, 1966, in AAHPER Archives.

CHAPTER XI. THE 1932 OLYMPICS AND RELATED EXCITEMENTS

1. Published by John Day Co., 1928.
2. John Tunis, "The Great God Football," *Harper's Magazine* 157: Nov. 1928, 742-752.

CHAPTER XII. SHORTS AND LEOTARDS

1. Letter to Editor, Dec. 10, 1931.
2. Letter of Oct. 15, 1931 from the Superintendent of Schools, Louisville, Kentucky.
3. "A Survey of Athletic and Gymnastic Costumes Used by American Girls and Women," *Research Quarterly* 3: March 1932, 5-47.
4. Arranged from New York State Department of Education, "Recommendations for Schools In Which Interschool Competition in Basketball Exists," NRA *Newsletter*: Nov. 1, 1930.
5. Women's Division of the National Amateur Athletic Federation (WD of the NAAF) *Newsletter*: Jan. 1933.

6. Written from memory by the author immediately after a conference with R. Tait McKenzie—all spoken in such intense earnestness that it clung to memory.
7. New York: John Day Co., 1926.
8. Letter of Jan. 12, 1933 by Strong Hinman to New York City Office of WD of NAAF.

CHAPTER XIII. THE LOCAL SCENE OF THE DEPRESSION YEARS
1. Later to become acting chancellor.
2. September 11, 1938.
3. Founder and dean of the Business College, 1913-1941.
4. Delphine Hanna, "Present Status of Physical Training in Normal Schools," *American Physical Education Review* 3: March 1903, 293-297.
5. Lee, Ashton and Phillips. Published by University of Nebraska Printing Shop, 1973.
6. "Further Discussion of the First Academic Degree in Physical Education," *Journal of Health, Physical Education, Recreation* 44: April 1973, 89.

CHAPTER XIV. A MULTIPLICITY OF CONCERNS
1. As reported in news items in *American Physical Education Review* of 1897 and 1917.
2. Listed in Rice, Hutchinson and Lee, *A Brief History of Physical Education*, 5th ed. (New York: Ronald Press, 1969), pp. 391-392.
3. Emil Rath, Frederick Cozens, Neils Neilson and Frank Lloyd.
4. According to Andrew J. Kozar (*R. Tait McKenzie—Sculptor of Athletes*, Knoxville: University of Tennessee Press, 1975, p. 30), the Mill of Kintail is named after the mill of same name at the home of the head of the McKenzie clan in the western highlands of Scotland.
5. Later in an article by John Brown, Jr., in an issue of the *Journal of Health, Physical Education, Recreation* was the erroneous statement that *The Column* was unveiled by Agnes Wayman and Frederick Maroney.
6. *Journal of Health and Physical Education* 15: Feb. 1944.
7. Vol. 2 (New York: Henry Holt & Co., 1911), p. 271.
8. Isadore Perlman, "In Memoriam—Everett O. Alldredge, 1912-1973," *The American Archivist* 36, no. 4: Oct. 1973, 635-640.
9. The University of Southern California had conferred the honorary Doctor of Pedagogy degree upon him in 1935.
10. Minutes of Academy, Dec. 27, 1932.
11. Hotel Whitcomb, April 5, 1939.

CHAPTER XV. "A PRETTY KETTLE OF FISH"

1. William S. Gilbert, *Iolanthe*, Act 2, Peers' Chorus.
2. Original 16 resolutions in Alice Allene Sefton, *The Women's Division—NAAF* (Stanford, CA: Stanford University Press, 1941), pp. 43, 77-79. Translated into French, German, Italian, Japanese, Portuguese and Spanish.
3. Started early winter 1937.
4. This story in full detail is preserved in the Mabel Lee Collection of Papers under the heading, Women's Division—NAAF, which will not be available until after the author's death. Unless others deeply involved in the circumstances surrounding the death of the Women's Division also kept diaries of day-by-day happenings regarding the negotiations involved in trying to save WD and those diaries are preserved for the profession, the author's account is probably all that remains of the full story about this episode in San Francisco. Correspondence in WD files in the AAHPER Archives tell some of the tale but nothing of behind-the-scene actions.
5. Sefton, op. cit.

CHAPTER XVI. ANOTHER WORLD WAR AND A CALL FOR PHYSICAL FITNESS

1. As reported by Floyd W. Reeves, *Next Step In National Policy For Youth—Recommendations of American Youth Commission of the American Council on Education*, 1941, Foreword, p. 2.
2. Congressman Pius L. Schwert of New York, Oct. 3, 1941.
3. *Daily Nebraskan*, May 18, 1941.
4. As reported in "A Vital Issue," *American Lawn Tennis*, July 1, 1930, p. 14.
5. As reported in *P.M.'s Daily Picture Magazine*, June 16, 1940, p. 6.
6. As revealed in a tape recording by Ruth Atwell in AAHPER Archives.
7. Ibid.

CHAPTER XVII. POLITICS AND RED TAPE

1. Clipping sent to author without identification of the specific newspaper or date.
2. Missouri State Council of Defense, *Progress Bulletin*, No. 20, March 3, 1942, p. 3.
3. John B. Kelly, "School Plants Strong For U.S. Fitness Project," *P.M.'s Daily Picture Magazine*, June 16, 1942, p. 10.

CHAPTER XVIII. A VICTORY CORPS, A WOMEN'S COMMISSION AND A
WOMEN'S ARMY CORPS

1. As announced in a large four-page folder issued by the Federal Security Agency (FSA) displaying a shield with the word "Fitness" filling the lower part of the shield.
2. John Kelly, *Report of Division of Physical Fitness of FSA*, June 1942.
3. U.S. Office of Education, *Service Bulletin on Physical Fitness and State Programs*, June 1942.
4. Including Dorothy Ainsworth, Mabel Shirley, Elizabeth Halsey, Elizabeth Kelley, and Mabel Lee.
5. U.S. Office of Education, op. cit., June 12, 1942.
6. Victory Corps Series, *Pamphlet #1*, U.S. Government Printing Office, Aug. 1942.
7. Ibid.
8. U.S. Office of Education, *Pamphlet #2, Physical Fitness Through Physical Education*.
9. Members of the committee were William Hughes, AAHPER president; Carl Nordly, vice-president of Recreation, AAHPER; Margaret Bell, M.D., former AAHPER president; Ben Miller, executive secretary, AAHPER; and Mabel Lee.
10. As reported by Colonel Rowntree to author in a letter, Oct. 21, 1944.
11. Copy of letter by Colonel Rowntree to governor sent in Nov. 1944 to author by George R. Holstrom of FSA.
12. Letter to Dorothy LaSalle, Dec. 18, 1944.

CHAPTER XIX. A WARTIME CAMPUS

1. Confirmed by correspondence in author's files between Doctors Lyman, Worster and Laase, and author.

CHAPTER XX. POSTWAR AWAKENINGS AND SOME FINAL THORNS

1. Using my last name as though my first, a habit he had acquired from my BNSG schoolmates, many of whom he knew well.
2. The first to Jay B. Nash.
3. Alice Oakes Bronson, *Clark W. Hetherington—Scientist and Philosopher*, multilithed (Salt Lake City: University of Utah Press, 1958).
4. The story of this award is told in news items of various issues of *American Physical Education Review* between 1923 and 1929.
5. *U.S. News and World Report*, Jan. 24, 1958, p. 77.

6. Hyman G. Rickover, *American Education, A National Failure* (New York: Dutton, 1963.
7. Hyman G. Rickover, "The Trouble With United States Schools," *U.S. News and World Report,* Nov. 25, 1963, pp. 69-70.
8. Lawrence A. Cremin, *The Transformation of the Schools,* 2nd ed. (New York: Knopf, 1961), p. 222.

EPILOGUE
1. *Newsweek,* July 6, 1970, p. 23.
2. Robert Browning, *Rabbi Ben Ezra,* Stanza 1.

Name Index

Aaron, Henry 3, 370
Addams, Jane 105
Adkins, Homer 333
Ainsworth, Dorothy 218, 420
Alden, Florence 182, 229, 416
Aldrich, Alice 316
Anderson, William G. 152, 154, 155, 215
Andrews, Margaret 222
Applebee, Constance 225-226
Arnold, Earnest H. 183, 200, 211
Aszman, Mrs. T. H. (Jean, sister) 244, 431, 437
Aszman, Theodore Heinrich (brother-in-law) 243, 431
Atwell, Ruth D. 372
Avery, Samuel 3-5, 6-10, 41-42, 43, 45, 46, 58, 59, 62, 422, 423
Ayers, George 316

Babcock, Mrs. Wayne (Marion Watters) 152, 165-166, 206
Baldwin, Bird 77
Baldwin, Dorothy 35
Bancroft, Jessie H. 154, 155, 184, 268, 410, 411, 413
Barger, Vera 4, 290, 298
Barkley, William E. 397
Barkley, Mrs. William E. 392, 393-397
Barr, Anne (Mrs. R. G. Clapp) 17, *18*, 19-21, 23-28, 33, 261
Bates, Elizabeth 182
Bayh, Birch, Major 363

Bayh, Birch, Senator 363
Beelman, F. C. 331
Belding, Alice 75, 77, 87, 289, 416
Bell, Margaret 212, 303, 315, 369, 372
Bennet, Bruce L. 432, 435
Berenson, Senda 181-182, 187, 190
Berg, Ernest 248
Berg, Patty 256
Berry, Elmer 25
Bestor, Arthur 418
Bible, Dana Xenophen 110-111, 248, 249, 250, 251
Biggs, Elmore 195
Bingham, J. Lyman 220, 231, 233
Bjorksen, Eli 239
Blackburn, C. S. 316, 334, 335
Blanchard, Vaughn S. 156, 157, 164, 414, 415
Bok, Curtis 207
Bok, Mrs. Curtis. *See* Nellie Lee Holt
Bolin, Jacob 17
Borries, Eline von 183, 194, 201, 230, 231, 285
Boucher, Chauncy Samuel 125, 252-256, 258, 298, 305, 376, 388, 389, 393, 413, 422, 423
Bouvé, Marjorie 86, 87, 143, 148, 150, 196, 226, 376
Bower, Wilbur P. 17, 85, 267, 268, 436
Bowers, Ethel 87, 194
Boynton, Brenda 376
Brace, David K. 316
Bradley, Omar 376

Italicized numbers indicate pages on which subjects appear in photographs.